ISBN 978-1-5278-5604-2
PIBN 10018341

1 MONTH OF
FREE
READING

at

www.ForgottenBooks.com

By purchasing this book you are eligible for one month membership to ForgottenBooks.com, giving you unlimited access to our entire collection of over 1,000,000 titles via our web site and mobile apps.

To claim your free month visit:

www.forgottenbooks.com/free18341

English
Français
Deutsche
Italiano
Español
Português

www.forgottenbooks.com

Mythology Photography **Fiction**
Fishing Christianity **Art** Cooking
Essays Buddhism Freemasonry
Medicine **Biology** Music **Ancient**
Egypt Evolution Carpentry Physics
Dance Geology **Mathematics** Fitness
Shakespeare **Folklore** Yoga Marketing
Confidence Immortality Biographies
Poetry **Psychology** Witchcraft
Electronics Chemistry History **Law**
Accounting **Philosophy** Anthropology
Alchemy Drama Quantum Mechanics
Atheism Sexual Health **Ancient History**
Entrepreneurship Languages Sport
Paleontology Needlework Islam
Metaphysics Investment Archaeology
Parenting Statistics Criminology
Motivational

BOARD OF EDUCATION.

SPECIAL REPORTS

ON

EDUCATIONAL SUBJECTS.

VOLUME 15. *[handwritten: 3576]*

SCHOOL TRAINING FOR THE HOME DUTIES OF WOMEN.

PART I.

THE TEACHING OF "DOMESTIC SCIENCE" IN THE UNITED STATES OF AMERICA.

Presented to both Houses of Parliament by Command of His Majesty.

LONDON:
PRINTED FOR HIS MAJESTY'S STATIONERY OFFICE,
BY WYMAN & SONS, LIMITED, FETTER LANE, E.C.

And to be purchased, either directly or through any Bookseller, from
WYMAN AND SONS, LTD., FETTER LANE, E.C.; and
32, ABINGDON STREET, WESTMINSTER, S.W.; or
OLIVER AND BOYD, EDINBURGH: or
E. PONSONBY, 116, GRAFTON STREET, DUBLIN.
EYRE & SPOTTISWOODE, LTD., EAST HARDING STREET, E.C.

1905.

[Cd. 2498.]   *Price 1s. 9d.*

SALE OF GOVERNMENT PUBLICATIONS.

The under-mentioned Firms have been appointed sole Agents for the sale of Governmen Publications, including Parliamentary Reports and Papers, Acts of Parliament, Recor Office Publications, &c., &c., and all such works can be purchased from them either directl or through retail booksellers, who are entitled to a discount of 25 per cent. from the sellin prices :—
IN ENGLAND :—
  For all publications *excepting* Ordnance and Geological Maps, the Hydrographica Works of the Admiralty, and Patent Office Publications :—Messrs. WYMAN ANI SONS, LTD., Fetter Lane, E.C.
  For Hydrographical Works of the Admiralty :—Mr. J. D. POTTER, 145, Minories, E.C Patent Office Publications are sold at the Patent Office.

  For all Publications *excepting* the Hydrographical Works of the Admiralty, Paten Office Publications, and Ordnance and Geological Maps :—
IN SCOTLAND :—Messrs. OLIVER AND BOYD, Edinburgh.
IN IRELAND :—Mr. E. PONSONBY, 116, Grafton Street, Dublin.

  The Publications of the ORDNANCE SURVEY and of the GEOLOGICAL SURVEY can be purchased from Agents in most of the chief towns in the United Kingdom, through any Bookseller, or from the Director General of the Ordnance Survey, Southampton, or in the case of Ireland, from the Officer in Charge, Ordnance Survey, Dublin. In addition, Ordnance Survey Publications can be obtained through Head Post Offices in towns where there are no accredited Agents.

  The following is a list of some of the more important Parliamentary and Official Publications recently issued :—

Parliamentary :
Statutes—

Public General, Session 1904. With Index, Tables, &c. Cloth.	Price 3s.
Education Acts, 1870-1904.	Price 1s. 6d.
Local and Personal Acts, Session 1904. Are now ready, and may be purchased separately.	
Index to Local and Personal Acts, 1801-1899.	Price 10s.
Index to Local and Personal Acts, 1900-1904. Each year may be purchased separately.	
Second Revised Edition. A.D. 1235-1713 to A.D. 1884-1886. XVI. Vols.	Price 7s. 6d.
Revised Editions. Tables showing subsequent Repeals, effected by Acts of Session 2 Edward VII. 1902.	Price 6d.
Statutes in Force. Index to. 20th Edition. To the end of the Session 4 Edward VII. (1904). 2 Vols.	Price 10s. 6d.
The Statutory Rules and Orders revised. Statutory Rules and Orders, other than those of a Local, Personal, or Temporary Character, in force on December 31 1903. Vols. I. to XIII.	Price 10s. each.
Statutory Rules and Orders other than those of a Local, Personal, or Temporary Character. With a list of the more important Statutory Orders of a Local Character, arranged in classes ; and an Index. Roy. 8vo. Boards. Issued in 1890 to 1904.	Price 10s.
Statutory Rules and Orders in force on 31st December 1903. Index to.	Price 10s.

HISTORICAL MANUSCRIPTS. Reports of the Royal Commissioners. In course of issue.
[Cd. 2175, 2186, 2210.] PHYSICAL DETERIORATION COMMITTEE. 3 Vols. Report. Appendix, Evidence, &c. Price 6s. 9d.
[Cd. 2258, 2259.] SHEEP DIPPING AND TREATMENT COMMITTEE. Report, with Evidence. &c. Price 2s. 7d.
[Cd. 2304.] UNEMPLOYED IN FOREIGN COUNTRIES. Report on Agencies and Methods for dealing with. Price 1s.
[Cd. 2372, 2386.] FERTILIZERS AND FEEDING STUFFS. Report of Committee, with Evidence, &c. Price 2s. 4½d.
[Cd. 2376.] EARNINGS OF AGRICULTURAL LABOURERS IN THE UNITED KINGDOM. Second Report. Price 2s. 9d.
[Cd. 2377, 2378, 2379.] SPECIAL REPORTS ON EDUCATIONAL SUBJECTS—CHIEF CROWN COLONIES. Price 5s. 4d.
[Cd. 2407.] COTTON GROWING IN EAST AFRICA PROTECTORATE. 1904. Price 2½d.
H.C. No. 1. LIFE ASSURANCE COMPANIES. Statement of Accounts, 1904. Price 3s.
H.C. No. 16. POSTMASTER GENERAL AND NATIONAL TELEPHONE COMPANY AGREEMENT Price 3d.
ENDOWED CHARITIES, ENGLAND AND WALES. SEPARATE PARISHES. Reports thereon in course of issue.
CENSUS, England and Wales, 1901. Population Tables, &c., in separate Counties, with Report thereon. Price £3 10s. 9½d.
CENSUS, Scotland, 1901. Population Tables, &c. Price 14s. 7d.
CENSUS, Ireland, 1901. Population Tables, &c., in separate Counties, with Report thereon Price £3 2s. 1½d.
CENSUS, Islands in the British Seas, 1901. Price 6d.
MINES. Reports of H.M. Inspectors for 1903, with Summaries of the Statistical portion under the provisions of the Coal Mines Regulation Act, 1887 ; Metalliferous Mine Regulation Acts, 1872-1875 ; Slate Mines (Gunpowder) Act, 1882, Districts Nos. 1 to 1 Complete Price 7s. 10.
MINES in the United Kingdom and the Isle of Man. List of, for 1903. Price 3s. 5
QUARRIES Ditto ditto ditto 1903. Price 4s. 6
MINES ABANDONED. Plans of, List of the. Corrected to 31st December, 1903. Price 1

BOARD OF EDUCATION.

SPECIAL REPORTS

ON

EDUCATIONAL SUBJECTS.

VOLUME 15.

SCHOOL TRAINING FOR THE HOME DUTIES OF WOMEN.

PART I.

THE TEACHING OF "DOMESTIC SCIENCE" IN THE UNITED STATES
OF AMERICA.

Presented to both Houses of Parliament by Command of His Majesty.

LONDON:
PRINTED FOR HIS MAJESTY'S STATIONERY OFFICE,
BY WYMAN & SONS, LIMITED, FETTER LANE, E.C.

And to be purchased, either directly or through any Bookseller, from
WYMAN AND SONS, LTD., FETTER LANE, E.C. ; and
32, ABINGDON STREET, WESTMINSTER, S.W. ; or
OLIVER AND BOYD, EDINBURGH : or
E. PONSONBY, 116, GRAFTON STREET, DUBLIN.
EYRE & SPOTTISWOODE, LTD. EAST HARDING STREET, E.C.

1905.

[Cd. 2498.]   Price 1s. 9d.

Billings
May 12. 1911

Prefatory Note to Volume 15

OF

Special Reports on Educational Subjects.

———

The following Report was prepared by Miss Ravenhill as the result of an investigation made by her at the joint request of the Board of Education, the West Riding County Council and the Royal Sanitary Institute. Reports upon certain aspects of her inquiries have already been presented to the West Riding County Council and the Royal Sanitary Institute, whilst the present volume contains the Report prepared by her for the Board of Education. Miss Ravenhill's paper was, with the exception of the Index, to all intents and purposes ready for publication in June, 1903, but in the autumn of that year, when the plans for the issue of a series of papers dealing with School Training for the Home Duties of Women, which had been laid by Mr. Sadler, came to be considered in detail, it was found necessary for various reasons to delay the preparation and publication of reports dealing with the work being done in this country. The results of investigation showed that, until the new Local Education Authorities had found more opportunity to organise this part of their work by the introduction of more systematised methods than have hitherto been possible, it would be wise to postpone any review in published form. On the other hand the absence of any material relating to certain European countries which devote special attention to the teaching of Domestic Economy rendered delay in the publication of a volume dealing with foreign countries inevitable. The intention was, therefore, to await the completion of reports from these countries before issuing any of the material which had been collected, but the increasing attention drawn to all matters affecting the health and well-being of the individual and the family, which has resulted from the Report of the Inter-departmental Committee on Physical Deterioration and the action of influential organisations which represented educational opinion of various kinds, have made it seem desirable to publish as much of the information as possible immediately. The lines of development in the United States of America have been national and little affected by the continental conditions of the Old

World, so that there was less reason here for grouping Miss
Ravenhill's Report with the other foreign material. Hence its
issue as Part I. of the Series.

It must be understood that, as in the case of previous Special
Reports issued by the Board of Education, the Board do not
make themselves responsible for the terms employed nor for the
opinions expressed in the Report—such responsibility resting
entirely with the Author.

The Board desire to take this opportunity of expressing their
thanks to the many officials and teachers who, by their willing
courtesy, aided Miss Ravenhill in collecting the materials for
this Report; they also wish to place on record their indebtedness
for the loan of the blocks from which the various plans inserted
in this volume have been printed.

Office of Special Inquiries and Reports.
May, 1905.

THE TEACHING OF "DOMESTIC SCIENCE"

IN THE

UNITED STATES OF AMERICA.

TABLE OF CONTENTS.

INTRODUCTION.

PART III.—SOCIAL AGENCIES FOR THE PROMOTION OF
DOMESTIC SCIENCE TEACHING.

LIST OF ILLUSTRATIONS.

THE TEACHING OF "DOMESTIC SCIENCE" IN THE UNITED STATES OF AMERICA.

INTRODUCTION.

A.—SCHEME OF PUBLIC EDUCATION.

One essential to the acquirement of an intelligent knowledge of the scope, methods and ultimate value of any special course of study carried on in the schools of a country is a clear comprehension of its educational system. In the case of the United States this process is considerably facilitated by the general adoption of one broad, basic principle, *viz.*, the provision throughout the country, from public funds, of a system of free education in all grades, from Kindergarten to University; merely nominal fees being exacted for text-books and laboratory equipment. President Draper, of the State University of Illinois, refers in one of his luminous and suggestive addresses to the public school system of the United States as the "one institution more completely representative of the American plan, spirit and purpose than any other in existence." Limits of space permit only of a very brief *résumé* of this comprehensive system, but some of its most salient features have been selected for presentation. The whole may be grouped under six divisions:—

1. Kindergartens, open to children from 3 to 7 years of age, where attendance is voluntary.

2. and 3. Primary and Grammar Schools, the curricula of which cover the ages of compulsory school attendance (variable in the different States), usually from 7 or 8 to 12 or 14 years of age.

4. High, or Secondary, Schools, offering a four-years' course, for pupils from 14 to 18. (Provision for evening classes is usually made in all city Grammar and High Schools.)

5. Colleges (State, Agricultural, Normal, etc.), attended by students from 18 to 22.

6. Universities, for post graduate courses.

That part of the system usually described as PUBLIC consists of three or four grades of schools, known as Primary, Grammar and High, or as Primary, Intermediate, Grammar and High. These grades of schools are distinguished from one another by the topics and methods introduced into their courses of study, and by the kind of mental activity required in pursuing them. In Primary, Intermediate, and Grammar Schools (which are very generally grouped under the denomination "Grade Schools"), the curriculum usually includes reading, writing, arithmetic, geography, history, physiology and hygiene, drawing, nature study and physical culture. In the more advanced educational institutions the "elective" system in force permits selection from a wider range of subjects, while actually reducing the number included in the particular course selected by the individual student. The majority of High Schools provide six or seven alternative courses; these include a good "all round" general

A

course, a classical, a scientific, a commercial course, and so
forth. High Schools especially for "manual training" (mechanics, engineering, the domestic sciences, etc.) are provided
in most cities, and take equal rank with those whose special aim
is the preparation of pupils for college. The manual training
courses include modern languages, literature, history and geography, in addition to the study of chemistry, physics, drawing,
etc., with the direct object of developing breadth of view and
well-balanced minds in their students. The High School movement is growing with enormous rapidity at the present time.

Private Schools.

In addition to this general provision for the education of the
people, in which the nation believes enthusiastically, a certain
number of private schools (kindergarten, grammar, high, commercial, art, industrial, professional, denominational) are to be
found in large cities, such as New York, Boston, Chicago and
Detroit. In these the courses are practically identical with
those in the public schools, but the demands of social caste are
considered and secured by the exaction of fees.

State Agricultural Colleges.

State Agricultural Colleges are the outcome of a general
intellectual and industrial advance which widely affected public
sentiment in the United States about half a century ago, from
which arose a demand for a new class of institution to be
entirely devoted to scientific and technical education. Some
efforts were made to supply this demand by private enterprise,
but the people soon grasped the advantage which would result
from the organisation and maintenance of these new institutions under State or national patronage; consequently the Bill,
introduced into the House of Representatives in 1857 by
Mr. Morrill, for the purpose of donating public lands to the
several states and territories, received sufficient support to be
passed in 1862. This Act secured "the endowment, support,
and maintenance of at least one college in each State, where
the leading objects shall be, without including other scientific
and classical studies, to teach such branches of learning as are
related to agriculture and the mechanic arts, in such manner
as the legislature of the States may respectively prescribe, in
order to promote the liberal and practical education of the
industrial classes in the several pursuits and professions in
life." This great work has given free tuition to thousands
of students, who have by this means been enabled to bring
trained minds to the development of industries, and to utilise
scientific facts and principles for their advancement. Under
the provisions of the Morrill Acts, 64 State Colleges are now
in operation in the several states and territories. They may
be divided into three classes:—Colleges which have courses
in agriculture only; Colleges which have courses in agriculture,
together with others in a variety of subjects, including specially,
mechanic arts; and, thirdly, Colleges, or Schools, or Departments of Agriculture which form a part of universities. Their
organisations are so wisely varied to meet the needs of local
environment, that no one institution will serve as a type for
all, but a representative university of this kind briefly describes

itself in its publications as "simply the 13th, 14th, 15th, and 16th Grades of the State System of Public Free Education"; it considers itself to be related to the High schools just as they, in turn, are related to the Grades, and sets forth that it should be as natural for a pupil to look forward from the High school to the University as from the 8th Grade to the High school. The prevalent aim in these colleges is to give to the young people of both sexes the largest possible opportunity for both general and special training to prepare them for life; and to touch, in a practical and helpful way, every interest in the State. Admission to them has been hitherto on very easy terms; candidates are required to be 16 years of age, and can frequently matriculate on the strength of a High school certificate; but the whole standard of entrance requirements is likely to be considerably influenced in future, and undoubtedly will be raised, by the action of the recently formed College Entrance Examination Board.

The first Normal schools in the United States were founded in 1839. They, too, were an outgrowth of the national interest in popular education, particularly after German influence began to be felt; at first they were the joint product of private and public liberality; very soon, however, a considerable number became incorporated into the State system of public instruction. State or Municipal Governments now support upwards of 160, but this by no means represents the sources of supply for teachers in the States, as there are in addition, at least 178 private Normal schools; only about one-fourth as many students, however, graduate annually from these as from the institutions supported by public funds. *Normal Schools.*

The generosity of wealthy citizens is the source from which have sprung the magnificent, richly-endowed, Technical Institutes, which exert a perceptible influence to-day upon the social and industrial life of the United States. The Pratt Institute at Brooklyn, N.Y., the Drexel Institute at Philadelphia, the Eastman Institute at Rochester, the Lewis and Armour Institutes at Chicago, and many more, are affording opportunities to the ambitious, stimulating the laggard, and raising the tone and standard of student and professor throughout the country. The activity of these great independent educational centres "sets the pace" for institutions subject to state and municipal control; indeed, each derives benefit from the somewhat diverse methods adopted by its compeers to attain a common end. *Technical Institutes.*

To private munificence also is due, wholly or in part, the existence and endowment of some of the leading Universities, such as Columbia University, New York City, the University of Chicago, the Leland Stanford Junior University, California, and others. It is, perhaps, superfluous to draw attention to the adaptation to national needs of these as of all other parts of the educational system; but it is allowable to recall what Dr. W. T. Harris brings out in his monograph on "Elementary Education," prepared for the United States Educational Exhibit *Universities.*

at the Paris Exhibition, 1900, that "American universities exhibit only a portion of what, in Europe, is thought necessary to the constitution of a complete university, *viz.*, the traditional four Faculties of Theology, Law, Medicine, and Philosophy," because, "although all four may be in existence, they are not all organised and demonstrated on the same plane; but, on the other hand, they include elements which, in Europe, are strongly marked off from universities, *viz.*, technical schools and undergraduate schools." On this account the formation of new colleges and departments is effected with facility, and their curriculum is extended to include subjects unrecognised in such connections in Europe.

Co-education.

Co-education is the general practice throughout the whole educational system. though a few cities report separation of the sexes in High schools; and a very small minority report separate classes for boys and girls in some Grade schools. From the statistics published in 1900–1 by the National Commissioner of Education, it would appear that in about two-thirds of the total number of private schools reporting to the National Bureau at Washington, and in 65 per cent. of the colleges and universities, co-education is the policy; the advantages of the method preponderate so conclusively that reference to occasionally recorded disadvantages is rarely made.

Sources of Financial Support.

The national school system is supported wholly by taxation, imposed by each State or city, an appropriation for purposes of education being made from the general fund. The Federal Government has never exercised any official control over the public educational work of the country, but it has always shown its intimate interest by generous gifts to education in the form of land rights from the public domain; and its moral influence is wide reaching through the Bureau of Education at Washington.

National Bureau of Education.

This Government Department was organised for the purpose of gathering the fullest information from the whole educational world, at home and abroad, and for its gratuitous dissemination to all interested therein; when the Bureau is under the direction of such a master mind as that of the present National Commissioner of Education, Dr. W. T. Harris, the extent of this influence for good is wellnigh incalculable.

Compulsory Attendance.

Attendance is compulsory, either at a public or approved private school, in thirty States, one Territory, and the District of Columbia; the most general obligatory period is from 8 to 14 years of age. Though the length of the nominal school year is about 200 days, statistics show that the average is considerably lower, amounting to not much more than 140. This is accounted for by the fact that, in rural districts, in order to facilitate agricultural operations, it is still a common practice to open the schools during the winter only, when, owing to difficulties of transit and bad weather, the regular attendance is much interfered with; thus the "average" length of the school year for the whole school population is very materially diminished. Laws which absolutely prohibit the employment

of children under a specified limit of age, in mercantile or manufacturing establishments, are in force and enforced in several
States.

The Local Boards which have the management of the schools
are generally termed " Boards of Education," and form departments of the State or city government. (In townships and
districts the designations most generally used are School
Directors or School Trustees. A township usually signifies six
square miles of land, quite irrespective of the population, which
may be numerous or nil; so many townships constitute a county,
so many counties form a State.) These Boards are corporate
bodies, and are empowered to make contracts; to acquire, hold,
and dispose of property; to employ teachers and fix their
salaries; to make the rules and regulations for schools, and to
fix the course of study and the list of text-books to be used. Boards of Education.

The following notes on the typical organisation of a city
school system will serve to explain allusions in the text of this
Report. Each Board of Education, created by law, is, in the
majority of instances, elected by the people, though some important cities constitute exceptions to this rule of popular
control; in these cases the members of the Board are nominated
by the Mayor, or by the City Council, or even by the city judges,
as at Philadelphia. The members serve gratuitously, and have
full powers to establish, maintain, and control free public
schools for all children of school age within the limits of the
city, township, county, or State. In most cities the teachers are
appointed by a committee of the Board; to an increasing
extent they are required to be graduates of the city or county
Normal School, or of an institution of equal or higher grade,
i.e., they must have received definite training in the art of teaching. Annual estimates of the disbursements anticipated during
the coming year must be made and submitted to the City
Council. That body appropriates such varying sums of money
for the purposes named in the estimates as they think proper,
in view of all the other claims on the city's funds. Once
appropriated, all such money is controlled by the Board of
Education. Each Board has two principal executive officers,
a secretary and a superintendent. The latter is expected to be
an experienced educator, well versed in school management and
a student of pedagogy on its philosophical side, he should also
possess good administrative ability; the course of study adopted
is, to a great extent, framed by the superintendent, and usually
embodies his ideas. There are county superintendents of rural
or township schools in about thirty-five States. In thirteen of
these they are elected by the people, in the remainder they are
appointed by certain state or county officers, or are chosen by
the combined vote of the School Board. In addition, each State
has a Superintendent of Public Instruction; he is variously
described as Superintendent of Common Schools, of Public
Schools, of Education, or as Commissioner of Public Schools. Organi sation of City School Systems.

It must be always borne in mind that the central Government
of the United States exercises remote authority over the public Functions of Central Government.

schools, and has never attempted any control over education in the several States, though it has aided them by donations of land, and, in some cases, of money.

Development of Grade School Curriculum in Massachusetts.

A sketch of the progressive development of the Grade school programme in one State will best indicate the gradual expansion of the nation's educational ideals, and the influence exerted on public bodies by private initiative, when based on sound principles. The statutes of the State of Massachusetts require that in all the "common" schools, instruction be given in orthography, reading, writing, English language and grammar, geography, arithmetic, drawing, history of the United States, physiology and hygiene, and manual training. In cities and towns which have a population of more than 20,000, the same statutes *authorise* instruction, at the discretion of the school committees, in the following additional subjects : book-keeping, algebra, geometry, one or more of the foreign languages, the elements of natural science, kindergarten training, agriculture, sewing, cooking, vocal music, physical training, civil government and ethics. Thus to the reading and writing of the original colonial schools of Massachusetts have been added, in the following order : English grammar, spelling and arithmetic, in 1789; geography in 1826; history of the United States in 1857; music (optional) in 1860; drawing in 1870; sewing (optional) in 1876; physiology and hygiene in 1885; manual training in 1898. Several of these subjects were at first *allowed* and later *required*. Physiology, for instance, was *allowed* in 1850, *required* in 1885; drawing was *allowed* in 1860, *required* in 1870; manual training was *allowed* in 1884, *required* in 1898. The causes and the forces behind all this enlargement have been largely sociological, to a much less degree pedagogical. It is most significant that the original petition to the legislature in 1869 for compulsory instruction in industrial drawing was signed exclusively by business men, leaders in the great industries of the Commonwealth. They declared that for the United States to maintain its standard as a manufacturing nation drawing was an "essential" in elementary education. For similar utilitarian reasons manual training was introduced. Of the authorised subjects, several have been forced into the front rank of "essentials" by modern social conditions; this is specially true of sewing, cooking, physical training and elementary science ; the last under the modern title "Nature Study" has very strong claims, and is now often utilised as an introduction to the science of home life as well as to physiology.

Education as a Social Institution.

This outline, necessarily incomplete, endorses the assertion that "the present elementary school course in the United States is not a miscellaneous collection of subjects brought together by the chance efforts of enthusiasts, but a conscious and intelligent effort of the people to frame a scheme of elementary instruction and training adapted to the changing conditions of social life. It is wisely recognised that when the Legislature decrees a certain subject shall be taught in all the schools, it does not by that Act say that it shall be taught to each pupil; the principle of universal opportunity is the educational watchword." Dr. Murray Butler recently expressed this spirit in terms so suitable and explicit that their quotation from the "Educational Review" for May 1900 will best enforce the point. "Education, conceived as a social institution, is now being studied in the United States more widely and more energetically than ever before. The Chairs of education in the great universities are the natural leaders in this movement. It is carried on also in normal schools, in teachers' training classes, and in countless voluntary associations and clubs in every part of the country. Problems of organisation and administration, of educational theory, of practical procedure in teaching, of child nature, of hygiene and sanitation, are engaging attention everywhere. Herein lies the promise of great advances in the future. Enthusiasm, earnestness, and scientific method are all applied to the study of education in a way which makes it certain that the results will be fruitful. The future of democracy is bound up with the future of education."

Of the moulding influences at work on the great State system none is more powerful for good than the National Educational Association, which numbers its members by thousands, and is guided by some of the most gifted as well as most experienced educational leaders in the States. The bulky records of its annual meetings contain a mass of experience and suggestion combined with full recognition of the dignity and responsibility of teachers, and constitute a useful record of the worth of teaching ideals and of improved practice. Of the numerous organisations employed in the education of public opinion few can compete with this potent, wisely regulated force; though to University Extension lectures, Summer Schools and other culture agencies may be attributed a part of the prevalent public sympathy with, and respect for, the profession of teaching which prevails over a large part of the United States. *Influence of National Educational Association.*

Under such circumstances it is conceivable that rational and universal education is looked upon by the American people as an element of national as well as of social strength; and that the public mind is set upon utilising a well-balanced school curriculum as a factor in the attainment of that high standard of prosperous life to which the nation aspires.

In the United States, as in Great Britain, detailed conceptions of the best methods to follow in the scheming of a school programme are almost as numerous as the individuals who concern themselves with the question in any of its aspects; but, emerging from this sea of opinions, are a few prominent personalities, whose freedom from prejudices or party spirit, scientific bases for their convictions, and courageous perseverance in face of obstacles and apparent failure, secure a fair trial for their systems, and influence gradually the educational spirit and practice of their country. Of these one of the most notable is Dr. John Dewey of Chicago University, who has drawn public attention to two "tragic" weaknesses in the old school system where, in his opinion, social spirit was wanting, being replaced *The School and the Home.*

by "that mediæval misconception which limited learning to books." By precept and undaunted practice, Dr. Dewey impresses on those who have ears to hear and eyes to see that "the ideal school should reproduce systematically, and in a large, intelligent, and competent way, what in most households is done only in a comparatively meagre and haphazard manner;" while he maintains that "the root question of education is that of taking hold of a child's activities, of giving them direction, and of so training them as to produce valuable results."

B.—History and Development of Domestic Science Teaching.

Educational versus utilitarian value of Domestic Science Teaching.

It seemed to me that these two broad generalisations constitute to-day the chief motive forces at work in the organisation of the best Domestic Science teaching in the United States. The original purely utilitarian spirit which led to its introduction is now somewhat adversely criticised and often strongly resisted; while the undoubted pedagogical and sociological value of the subject is emphasised and evidenced under the auspices of its ablest exponents. But though the end is not yet (for the finest courses are admittedly tentative, and those responsible for them are only "feeling their way," and buying their experience often at a high price) encouragement is not absent; men and women of many interests and of diverse callings are giving in their adherence to the belief that on pedagogical and sociological as well as on utilitarian and economical grounds, Domestic Science, under one or other of its designations, deserves, and must eventually find, a place in the well-balanced curriculum of all grades of educational institutions. For a small proportion of the population, or even of its responsible directing units, to reach this conclusion has demanded time, as is demonstrated by the following brief sketch of the growth of the movement.

On both sides of the Atlantic the term Domestic Science is still limited by a surprising number of people to the two subjects of cooking and sewing. The scope is nevertheless usually extended sufficiently to include an introduction to the elements of personal hygiene and house sanitation; and, in England, laundry work frequently comes under the same head. In the greater number of the States, this latter subject is very rarely included in any elementary school Domestic Economy curriculum, though it is being gradually introduced into Household Science courses in the High schools and colleges. In the first instance, the utilitarian aspect of Domestic Science alone was that considered in America; those who pressed its introduction into the schools were stimulated by a realisation of the deficiencies apparent in home management and experienced a sense of dismay at the evils to the community which result from this ignorance. A quarter of a century ago education was still defined as "the preparation for life," instead of being recognised, as it is now, as co-extensive with life; so, as this period of preparation was limited for a large proportion of the population, the desirability of including a practical knowledge of the Domestic

Arts in the Grade school programme seemed urgent, and led to the persevering efforts of private individuals which culminated in the adoption of cooking and sewing in the grammar schools of a few cities.

Almost without exception the existing recognition of the value Intro-of Domestic Science as a school subject, utilitarian or educational, duction of is owing, in the first instance, to private enterprise, but before Domestic educational authorities would permit the introduction of the Science subject into schools, cookery lessons were given to public school due to children, from 1876 onwards, under the auspices of the Young Private Women's Christian Association, and other philanthropic bodies. Enterprise. The children of the poorest classes were those gathered in by these benevolent individuals; they were first instructed in the elements of needlework; simple training in housewifery under the name of " kitchen gardening "* followed, succeeded later on by lessons in plain cooking.

Sewing was adopted first in the public schools of Boston, which Intro-led the way in this matter, about 1840, though little was done duction and until 1865, when a lady furnished the materials for the children's development work and defrayed the expenses of a seamstress and of a dress- of the maker, each of whom was engaged to teach an advanced class of :— for half a day a week in the different schools. Eight years later (a) Sewing. a teacher was appointed to give her whole time to this work, and received an equal compensation with the regular teachers; in 1875 the important step was taken of appointing a special committee to supervise sewing in the schools throughout the whole city. At this promising moment the hopes of those interested were apparently doomed to disappointment, for the solicitor of the City Board of Education reported that it was illegal to spend public money for this purpose. Again private enterprise came to the rescue, and for the next twelve months the work was carried on entirely by private funds, until the legislature had passed a law authorising instruction in sewing in the public schools. To the present day, however, sewing is far from universally taught in the grade schools of the United States: and in quite a number of those where it is now found, it has been regularly introduced only within the last four or five years.

The germ from which the New York Cooking School has (b) Cooking. since developed came into being 30 years ago, when Miss Juliet Corson organised cooking classes for women of all social grades; public and private lessons being offered. The first public lesson to working women resulted in the formation of mission classes in cooking for children, and, about the same date, the Principal of Lassell's Seminary (Auburndale, Mass.) had sufficient enterprise

---

*In the United States the term " kitchen gardening " signifies the training of children in domestic work under the guise of play. The utensils provided are in the form of toys, and each household operation is conducted on a scale proportioned to the size of the utensil. Small children from five years old and upward appear extremely interested and happy when thus engaged, but I think this method of teaching Household Science, has, in all cases, been confined to private organisations; it has never been considered sufficiently educational for adoption even in the kindergartens of the public schools.

to invite Miss Maria Parloa to give a course of lessons to its
students. In 1879, this lady pioneered the first training course
in cooking to *teachers* at Chautauqua Summer Schools, but the
subject was not introduced into the public schools even of Boston
(which has been the most progressive city in this respect) until
1885. Philadelphia, Providence and Washington, rapidly
followed Boston's example, and to-day cooking courses in grade
schools are found in over fifty cities in the States, while each
year sees an increase in this number. The introduction of
sewing thus apparently preceded cooking, but its development
has followed very similar lines, and in numerous cities both
subjects are included in the curriculum. Meanwhile Domestic
Science on a far broader and more thorough basis, has been
gradually receiving recognition at the hands of High school and
college authorities, with excellent results. These indicate the
altered conception of the educational value of the subject since
the first awakening of interest in Domestic Economy some
thirty-five years ago. It was somewhat after this date that the
advocates for early introduction to, and training in, the domestic
arts pressed their point by calling attention to the advantages
these offer for the exercise of manual dexterity by girls. Un-
wittingly they made themselves responsible for the plausible
and still current belief, that to deal with plastic materials under
conditions where the attainment of the desired end (cultivation of strict accuracy and manual dexterity) by occasional
failure and repeated practice cannot be permitted on account of
cost or want of time, is of equal educational worth with the
manipulation of wood and iron carried on simultaneously by the
boys. This misunderstanding, in conjunction with the still
evident existence of the purely utilitarian spirit, has hampered
true progress in the treatment of Domestic Science throughout
a large proportion of the United States. Fortunately a powerful note of progress has been sounded during the last decade,
which has gained greatly in volume since the concentration of
effort resulting from the initiation, in 1899, of the Lake Placid
Conference of Teachers of Home Economics. The directly
educational value of the subject in schools, its great scope, its
intimate bearing on every phase of life, is now steadily gaining
recognition, while the field it offers for the application of
scientific principles, rather than for the mere acquirement of
manual dexterity, is forcibly emphasised by sound authorities.

The Lake
Placid
Conference
of Teachers
of House-
hold Econ-
omics.
(a) First
Conference.

Three or four years ago, Prof. W. O. Atwater (United States
Dept. of Agriculture) made the observation that "the Science of
Household Economics is now in what the chemists call the state
of supersaturated solution which needs to crystallise out. Sometimes the point of a needle will start such crystallisation." This
needle point would seem to have been introduced by the members of the Lake Placid Conference when they held their first
meeting in September, 1899. The initiators believed that the
time was ripe for some united action on the part of those most
interested in Home Science (or Household Economics); (1) because of the benefit derived from wise organisation and

co-operation; (2) because of the growing popular feeling that the study of Home Science was one of the most important questions before the nation; (3) because the real worth but often mistaken treatment of the subject demanded the direction and initiative of trained, enthusiastic experts. Invitations were, therefore, issued for a conference on this important sociological problem; and the generous hospitality of the Lake Placid Club (in the Adirondack Mountains, New York State), was offered to, and accepted by, twenty or twenty-five ladies and gentlemen, earnest students of the subject, to whom it has been extended for the same purpose each successive year. The cordial recognition of the great services rendered to Household Science by Mrs. Ellen H. Richards, Professor of Sanitary Chemistry in the Massachusett's Institute of Technology, led to her unanimous election as chairman of the conference, a tribute to the unremitting and tactful efforts, which, backed by her profound scientific knowledge, are responsible for a high proportion of the recent developments in this subject, whether in the social or educational world.

The conference devoted its first meeting to the selection of a suitable designation for its subject, such as should be simple and yet comprehensive enough to cover sanitation, cookery, and kindred household sciences and arts, whether the instruction concerning them were given in kindergarten or college. After full discussion, the name "Home Economics" was agreed upon as the best title for the whole general subject. When thus classified as a distinct section of Economics, it can take its place logically in the college or university course to which its dignity, scope and sociological value entitle it ; restricted to the narrower conception implied by the title of Household Arts, the conference was of opinion that it could not be suitably recognised as a part of a university curriculum. Though Home Economics was selected as the general descriptive term, it was agreed that other phrases might be advisedly used for subdivisions of the subject. Domestic Economy, for instance, might be appropriately reserved for lessons adapted to young pupils in kindergartens and grammar schools ; Domestic Science might be applied to it in high schools, where food and house sanitation should be studied by scientific methods, while Household or Home Economics appeared the title best suited for college courses. It was also at once emphasised that the teacher of Domestic Science and Household Arts should be an "all round" woman ; she should be qualified to bring a knowledge of many sciences and arts to bear on her work, and to this end a thorough practical training in each of these would be essential. The general opinion was in favour of intimate co-operation between special teachers of this subject with the other members of a school or college staff, and the desirability was pointed out of drawing the attention of educational authorities to the value of including some branches at least of Home Economics in school and college curricula, if only to combat the prevalent tendency to dissociate home life and interests from education, and thus, incidentally, to depreciate its dignity and influence.

At the second annual conference, held in July, 1900, a large proportion of the sessions was devoted to debates on courses of study ; (*a*) for public schools ; (*b*) for training teachers ; (*c*) for colleges and universities ; (*d*) for vacation and evening schools ; (*e*) for university and extension teaching, as well as for other agencies devoted to the scientific and sociological study of the home. In the course of her introduction to the special subject for one meeting, namely, "Courses of study for the Grade schools," Mrs. Ellen H. Richards referred to the need of fundamental work that will touch the lives of *all* the people, and showed that, under existing conditions, the only place where this can be done is in the Grade Schools, where she said the aims of the whole course should be to develop power in children and to guide them in the use of this power over their own environment, food, clothing and shelter. The quotation of recent statistics showed that at least 40 per cent.

(b) Second Conference.

of the pupils first enrolled drop out of school before the fifth grade ; and, though the National Commissioner of Education reports that "the increase in the number of high schools and in the number of students enrolled in them is something phenomenal," and highly satisfactory figures can also be quoted as to the growth in numbers of college students, it is but relatively few who as yet follow more advanced courses of study ; while, of these, the percentage who elect to devote definite attention during a part of these precious years to any aspect of sanitation, though on the increase, is still modest.   This opinion was not merely endorsed by this conference, but is shared by those responsible for the grade school courses in several important cities.

With a view to discover to what extent such teaching is given in the elementary and secondary schools of the country, an inquiry was addressed during the following year to the Boards of Education of a number of cities by a specially appointed sub-committee.   This *questionnaire* included the following points : (1) topics included ; (2) syllabus of courses ; (3) grades in which taught ; (4) time per hour, per week, per lesson ; (5) size of classes ; (6) cost of equipment and material ; (7) the value attached to the subject ; (8) the methods used to develop its value, either as manual training, applied science, or economics ; and (9) the methods used to correlate the subject to others.   Unfortunately only 25 replies were received, and these, in several instances, were not complete.   All but one course included cooking, however, in some form ; 13 included sanitation in part (as the care of plumbing and personal hygiene); 9 included sewing ; 10 included economics, but confined the subject chiefly to the economics of food supply ; few indicated appreciation of the value of time or of energy ; money value alone being taken into account.   Even these imperfect returns seemed to indicate that the workers placed the educational value first, one alone emphasised the utilitarian phase, though great diversity of opinion was reported as to the methods used to develop the value of the subject.   In their discussion of an analysis of these returns, the conference concluded that to take its proper place in educational work, the subject of Home Economics or Domestic Economy must be both narrowed and broadened ; narrowed till it shut out much that, though useful, is not of great educational value, in that it has not been correlated with other branches of study ; made broader, in that the subject of the hygiene of the home, including foods and sanitation, should be so woven into the sciences and economics that it will be the foundation for a liberal culture.

Another sub-committee of the same conference presented through its representative, Dean Marion Talbot, Professor of Sanitary Science in the University of Chicago, a report upon the existing courses of study related to Home Economics in colleges and universities ; the work of inquiry had been carried out by Mrs. Mary Robert Smith of Leland Stanford University. Circular letters were sent to 89 different institutions, asking what they offered in courses on domestic science or household economics, personal hygiene, sanitation, nursing, bacteriology, domestic architecture, etc. Out of the 89, 58 reported work in one or other lines ; 13 had nothing, and 18 did not reply.

One of the concluding resolutions at this second conference has already borne fruit.   It was resolved that "the time has come when public interest demands the recognition of Home Economics as a training of the child for efficient citizenship ; that the National Education Association be asked to consider and create a Department of Home Economics."   This resolution was passed in July, 1900.   In July, 1901, the Council of the National Educational Association included a "Round Table" of Domestic Science for the first time in the programme of its annual meeting.

(c) Third Conference.   It was my pleasant privilege to attend the third annual meeting of the Lake Placid Conference, where the 30 invited members included teachers or professors in every grade of educational institution, inspectors, and the presidents of the most prominent social organisations for the advancement of Hygiene and Domestic Science.   The representative character of the conference is apparent from the fact that its members were at work in at least 15 States, and held degrees from 15 different colleges.

The attention of the conference was concentrated chiefly on the consideration of a Report, prepared by a small committee and presented by the chairman, Miss Helen Kinné, Professor of Domestic Science at Teachers College, Columbia University. This report had occupied 3 years in its preparation and its suggestive, useful character may be best gauged by a perusal of the following extracts :—"While there is a growing appreciation of such work (*i.e.*, the teaching of Household Economics) in the schools, as evidenced by its introduction in many new places, there is also a sceptical attitude in the minds of many as to its value, a tendency to class it among fads, to regard it as one more of the new subjects that are over-crowding the curriculum. Even among superintendents, general teachers, and parents who are its friends, there is a lack of formulated opinion as to its value, and a tendency to throw responsibility on the special teacher, and consequently there is lack of vital connection with other school work. There is also no common understanding among special teachers of the subject, and little intelligent and interested discussion in general educational conferences. Yet statistics show that so-called Domestic Science, in some form, is taught in the elementary schools of more than fifty cities in the United States, in high schools and manual training schools supported by public funds, and that it is established in an increasing number of State agricultural colleges and universities. There are hundreds of teachers at work at good salaries, and schools of pedagogy and technical schools are sending out more workers each year. Hence the schoolman who takes time to consider the situation finds himself confronted by an extraordinary economic incongruity, the expenditure by School Boards of public funds for maintaining a subject about which they know little or nothing. The purpose of the report is to present the whole matter to principals and general teachers for discussion, by defining the subject, formulating a statement of its educative value, and proposing definite courses of study. It, therefore, propounds the problem 'What is Domestic Science and Art, or Home Economics?' Here are various household arts, such as preparation of food, making of garments and household articles, and keeping of things clean. In carrying on certain of these processes, particularly cooking and cleaning, we are working with forces outside ourselves, and when we ask what these forces are, and how they behave, we discover that here in these matters of daily life we are applying the principles of chemistry, physics and biology. In other processes, such as sewing, weaving, and basketry, we are dealing with form and colour, and so are applying the fine arts in the home. *Per se*, then, broadly speaking, our subject is one form of applied science and art.

" But home economics is more than the application of science and fine arts merely to the end that certain results may be correctly reached, or certain articles artistically made, for we must consider the place of these arts in the social order, and this brings us immediately to the thought of the home and its conduct ; *the home, as the place where the individual is given such physical and ethical surroundings, that he is made an effective human being ; the conduct of the home, on the material side, as the seeking to produce the best results with the least expenditure of energy, material, time, and money.* Here we have reached the study of economics ; the economics of home consumption. To sum up the whole matter, then, our subject consists of certain household arts and activities, based on a number of sciences, and leading to the study of economics."

The Report next discusses the value of the subject, which it presents from three points of view ; that of society, of the individual, and of the school in its attempt to train the individual for himself and for society.

" . . . Does society as a whole show any needs that such a study would meet and answer? Surely the most casual student of present social conditions must see that a large proportion of our population, both rich and poor, is in a poor physical condition, and that there is in consequence great economic waste ; for lack of vigour means lack of effective accomplishment, and also makes necessary large expenditure for remedial measures. With better shelter, food, water, ventilation, rational cleanliness and proper clothing, a check would be placed on this enormous waste, more real work would be

(d) Résumé of Report on Teaching of Household Economics. (Third Conference)

(*d.*) Résumé of Report on Teaching of Household Economics. (Third Conference) —*continued.* done, and there would be fewer patent foods, medicines, and hospitals.) Another common waste is through poor buying and extravagant use of materials." "To what," it continues, "are these things due? Doubtless to many influences, but potent among them are two : (1) Ignorance of women on these points in the management of the household ; and, (2) Ignorance of men and women together in the management of that larger household, the city. (1) Domestic and economic conditions have greatly changed during the last half century, and while men have met such changes in their business lives and adapted themselves to them, women go on in many respects in the ways which were adequate in the days of their grandmothers, but which are far from sufficient now. Again, the daughter from the family of small means must often take her place as a breadwinner outside the home, and the child of well-to-do parents is absorbed in her school life. Both, equally. enter upon their married life with little or no knowledge of the business of housekeeping before them. (2)(If all our citizens, both men and women, were alive to the physical and economic evils consequent on bad building, imperfect water supplies, defective disposal of waste, and dirty streets, these things could not exist.) No political organisation could hoodwink such intelligence into surrender of the right to sanitary surroundings. The teaching of Home Economics should go far to correct these errors, for it emphasises health as a normal condition, and gives knowledge of the physical conditions that will maintain this ; emphasises the home as the unit of society, and the management of the home as a business needing brain and special training ; shows how, on the economic side of marriage, the wife is the business partner, that her part as spender and manager is no less important than the husband's as earner, and that he cannot succeed if she fails to meet her obligations."

The Report next dwells upon the educational advantages to the individual consequent upon a right introduction of the subject into the school timetable. ("Experience offers evidence that children gain increased power of muscular control and expression through the hand work : they become self-reliant and useful to others by the capacity thus evolved, while the variety of occupation is not only agreeable at the time, but conduces to their social value. The subject also affords excellent opportunities for the development of the relating power, that is, for tracing cause and effect, and for the realisation that successful practice depends upon a firm grasp of underlying principles. Luck becomes a myth ; judgment as to time is developed, and good taste is formed in regard to colour and form, in furnishings and clothing. It becomes apparent to the most self-willed child, that in dealing with materials and forces it is not as *we* please, but as *nature* pleases, and to control her we must obey her. While, at first sight, it may seem a small matter for pupils to make a loaf of good bread, yet see what it involves. They are free individuals and may do as they please. They may please to pour boiling water on the yeast, forget the salt, refuse to make their muscles work effectively, let the dough stand a length of time convenient to themselves, and fail to manage the oven dampers ; what then ? Nature has gone quietly on her way and returns to them their just due ; their own careless, irresponsible selves expressed in a soggy, dark, sour, ill-shaped loaf of bread. We have here in concrete terms the whole matter of the limitation of the individual by his environment. (Through a series of such experiences there comes an understanding of what law means, and self-control, obedience, and freedom. . . . Taking the thought and hand work together, the subject gives the school a field where the knowledge and powers gained in other subjects may be applied to practical ends ; and conversely, it stimulates an interest in other subjects. This idea of application is an essential part of the plan that aims to make a close connection between school and home life."

The Report proceeds to consider the general order of the subjects included in Household Arts, and Economics, beginning with the lower elementary grades and running through the high school. Remembering the definition of the subject as a whole, as consisting of household arts based on several sciences and leading to the study of economics, the committee recommend that as, in the lower grades, the child is interested in the mere doing (the play element should enter largely into his activities), the art side alone should be given ; such processes as sewing, weaving, *(d)* Résumé basketry and cooking may be used as "forms of expression," with an of Report on occasional short series of cooking lessons.; " In the Upper Elementary, the Teaching of scientific aspect can be introduced ; sewing, cooking, cleaning, can be given Household in continuous courses ; the reasons why can be developed and principles Economics established. The economic aspect also arises in the necessary decisions (Third upon the best way to carry on a process in order to save time or strength, Conference) all other things being equal, or the best material to select for a given —*continued.* purpose. The health aspect finds its place by a study of cleanliness, not merely as the cleaning of things soiled by use, but, as the provision of clean air, clean water, clean food, and good drainage. In the high school, the activities must continue, but are less prominent, therefore the scientific aspect should be further emphasised, and the economic somewhat fully developed. The definite subjects of study are food, in its relation to nutrition ; clothing in its relation to health, and as embodying the beautiful ; the house with its artistic and hygienic furnishing, its sanitation and practical management ; the health of the household, as dependent on personal hygiene—this should comprehend the care of little children, as well as of those who are ill and injured. Thus, looked at as a whole, from the Primary Grades through the High School, the subject is seen to develop from the concrete doing through the scientific to the economic, but with no sharp dividing lines. This is not only the natural unfolding of the subject in itself, but it meets the natural interest of the pupil at each stage of his growth. First, we like to do, just for the pleasure of doing ; then we ask why ; and not until the mind is maturing do we care to balance values, and judge of the worth of things in relation to each other ; and here are the three phases of our subject, the art, the science, and the economic."

The Committee's next consideration was the arrangement of definite courses, where "it is necessary to have in mind some of the practical difficulties which arise in the arrangement of an ideal course ; and where the differences of opinion which exist among thoughtful special teachers must be clearly understood and be given due weight." These include the problems of the school itself. "Our first stumbling block is the fact that if we are to help the mass of our people by means of this subject, we must do it in the elementary school ; and if the work is to have real social value, we must enforce there those economic aspects that in an ideal scheme develop in perfection in the high school. The problem is to do this without over-crowding the school course, to make the work natural and interesting, and to avoid dogmatising. Our second difficulty meets us in the high school. In spite of the numbers of manual training high schools, and high schools giving so called English, scientific, or general courses, large numbers of our high school pupils are in college preparatory schools. The main purpose of the college preparatory is to put the pupil into college, and 'time is worth £1,000 a minute.' Of course, the manual training school gives an adequate amount of time to the home subjects ; the 'general' course may do so, and becomes a better course in consequence ; but the 'college preparatory,'—how can it? What it can or can not do depends on the dictum of the colleges. While it is encouraging to note the broadening of entrance requirements, in general, there is nothing as yet that really touches this subject. And is it not to these very girls, who are to spend four years as college students, removed from responsibility as to home life, that we need to give a bent toward the thought of home as a field for the use of their best powers?"

The opinions of special teachers are next taken into account. "While thoughtful teachers are agreed as to the purpose of this work, and have the same ends in view, it is but natural that they should differ as to the form of the work. The main points at issue occur in the lower element-ary and in the high school. There are some teachers who advocate, even in the first, second, and third years in school, continuous courses in cooking, and would, indeed, have it run through every year of the elementary. Others advocate an occasional short series of cooking lessons as expression work, specially in connection with a study of primitive life, equally with other hand work. It may be said for the former that they certainly touch

(d) Résumé of Report on Teaching of Household Economics. (Third Conference) —*continued.*

a large mass of children on the practical side, for the dropping out from school soon begins. Against this plan and in favour of the second, it may be said that this form of hand work is in itself more difficult and better suited to the older pupils, and that the youngest pupils are not ready to grasp the principles that need to be developed. Again, economy of time must be considered ; a subject may be good, but others, too, are good, and each subject should claim only that amount of time that makes it effective in connection with others for the child's development, rather than for its own complete unfolding. It would seem that cooking and cleaning need not require so much time as this first plan involves, when properly combined with other household arts and with all other kinds of hand work. It must be added that such work in the lower elementary is new, and is carried on in few schools. It is fortunate, however, that both of these schemes are in actual practice and that experience will argue for or against. The difference in opinion as to the high school courses is in regard to the amount of practical work and its relation to the other work of the high school. One attitude is this : that the hand work belongs strictly in the elementary school, because that is the time to develop self-activity and right habits of doing ; that if the household arts belong in the high school at all, they should be at the minimum and in connection with some other subject, not in consecutive courses ; as, for instance, in studying acids and bases in chemistry, baking powder could be made, and even baking powder biscuit ; or in physics, in studying siphonage, traps could be examined and cleaned. The main thought is to emphasise the scientific and economic aspect, by reducing the actual practice of the arts themselves, and by giving those arts directly in connection with the scientific courses. Another plan while emphasising and developing the scientific and economic aspects, would retain the practice of the arts in continuous courses, running parallel with the science and fine arts work, and closely connected with them. The advocates of this arrangement feel that in this way the girl's nature and likings are taken into account as they are not in the other. The first plan seems to assume a sudden change in the girl in passing from the elementary to the high school that really does not occur. Indeed, the first year high school girl is apt to be in a state of disorganisation, and is in the high school rather than of it, so far as serious and thoughtful work is concerned. She cares little for science *per se*, and nothing for economics, but is delighted still to plan, prepare, and serve a meal or trim a hat. Shall we not take her as she is, give her what she likes to do, and lead her through that doing to see what lies below it, and so develop her interest in science and in greater things? While the former plan may be the ideal one, the real girl seems to demand its modification. . . ."

To facilitate the criticisms and suggestions which it was the object of this Report to provoke, several tabulated schemes are included, illustrative of these various stages and methods of treating the subject. Its comprehensive character is further emphasised by the following extracts : " Certain practical considerations will suggest themselves as to the teaching staff, equipment, and cost of materials. First, as to the teacher. It is being demonstrated in a few schools that in the lowest grades the general teacher can carry on the various kinds of hand work without difficulty or overcrowding. In the 7th and 8th Grades it is desirable to have a special teacher for household arts, but teachers can be found who are able to combine the various kinds of work. In the high school, if the course is well developed, running through two or three years, and with large numbers of pupils, more than one special teacher is proved to be necessary ; and, so far, there seems to have arisen a natural division between the household arts that lean towards the sciences and those that lean towards the fine arts.

" Next, equipment and material. Up to the 7th grade most of the work, such as weaving, basketry, and sewing, can be carried on in the ordinary schoolroom. If cooking and cleaning are introduced below the 7th grade, some small amount of equipment is necessary. This, however, can be provided at a cost of from $30 to $100 (£6 to £20) for fifteen to twenty children, and may consist of two or three work tables, a few gas stoves, and utensils, and a cupboard for utensils and necessary food materials. Below the 7th grade the cost of all kinds of materials per child is from two to three cents (1d. or 1½d.) per lesson. For the work in the 7th and 8th grades, where cooking, housekeeping, and cleaning are taught, an extra room and special equipment, costing from $500 to $1,000 (£100 to £200), are necessary. In these grades cost of material for cooking and cleaning is four to five cents per child per lesson. In the high school cost of equipment will depend on the nature of the work, as indicated above. Equipments, ranging from $1,000 to $1,500 (£200 to £300), and even more, are put into our manual training schools, but effective work can be done with an equipment at $1,000 or less. But when the amount of money expended is too small, results must be unsatisfactory. The conditions are so variable that no fixed standard in equipment is possible. Apparatus should be good in quality but not excessive in amount. If too meagre, the work is restricted, and pupils do not learn the principles or value of good tools. If too elaborate, ingenuity is not developed, and extravagant standards are established. Cost of materials, too, is variable. Salaries of special teachers in elementary grades are $600 to $1,000 (£120 to £200) a year; in high schools, $800 to $1,800 (£160 to £360); this will vary in different localities, depending on cost of living governed by local conditions."

In conclusion, this suggestive and well-considered Report declares that "Good teaching of this subject is based upon the same principles as good teaching of other subjects, and the work should be in the hands of trained teachers, not of those who are familiar with the practical side of the subject only;" while, with compulsory briefness, it touches on the question as to the desirability of giving Home Economics to boys. "So far, boys and girls have shared in such work in the lower elementary grades, and in one school in the upper elementary also. Usually in the upper elementary the boys carry on heavier work in place of the domestic arts, and follow this by metal work in the high school. It seems necessary that boys as well as girls should understand hygiene and food values and their practical applications. If they do not share the household economic work with the girls, provision should certainly be made for this in their study of science, bearing in mind the responsibilities they assume later on as fathers, householders, or members of civic councils."

The consideration as to how far boys' education should include some introduction to the subject of Home Economics; and, in the event of its educational and sociological values being recognised, to what extent and in what form it should be presented, has assumed some prominence in certain minds, whose opinion is respected in the United States. Whether it be the immediate result of the co-educational teaching of the elements of Physiology and Hygiene during the first 7 or 8 years of school life, or whether the prevalent determination to attain the premier position among nations be the incentive, a realisation is evident on the part of both sexes that each is intimately connected with and responsible for the maintenance of the conditions essential to a healthy life. Some credit for this evident impulse to improve the conditions of home life is probably due to the State Board of Agriculture at Washington, which has carried on, for many years, true missionary work along lines at once simple and scientific, by the gratuitous diffusion of sound knowledge on the subject of food and diet in relation to the health of human beings. Then the desire to purify municipal politics, and to secure to each citizen in fact that which the constitution accords to him in theory, may

Influence of Lake Placid Conference. (a) Concerning the importance of home economics for both sexes.

also account for the growing appreciation that mere election by popular vote to a position of authority does not carry with it innate qualifications for the responsibilities assumed, but that previous preparation is demanded by honesty, if by no other motive. "Municipal Housekeeping," in which men play by far the more prominent part, is a common topic just now in many parts of the United States. As a consequence, opportunities have already been provided for students of both sexes in Colleges and Universities to follow courses in sanitation, chiefly in connection with the study of Sociology, Bacteriology, Household Science and Architecture. These assume that both have already received a slight, though practical, foundation in the elements of Hygiene in the Grade and High schools, where, obviously, such preliminary instruction is of great moment. As a matter of fact well-nigh every child does receive some teaching in the subject, but the time available is often limited, and the lessons may be not alone purely theoretical but confined to a very narrow presentation, so that at most, but a slight conception of its myriad ramifications through the whole structure of life is formed. It is against such unsatisfactory, contracted, lopsided teaching, that the Lake Placid Conference enters a protest. Two points hitherto often overlooked in the framing of school courses have been, the desirability of linking school and home life with ties of mutual interest, and the unrecognised importance attached by children to subjects included in their school programme. If home and the conduct of daily life be ignored by the teaching staff and find no place in the weekly studies, the scholars are apt tacitly to assume that they are of no account, that training in right methods is requisite only in school subjects, and that household duties do not demand, or are not worth, the exercise of qualities studiously cultivated in school practice for use in other phases of future life. Possibly these thoughts, too, as well as the point of early leakage from school, were in the minds of those responsible for the Report from which I have quoted at such length.

(b) On Women's Social Organisations.

As has been pointed out, the Lake Placid Conference conceives of Home Economics as a subject well-nigh as all-embracing as that comprehensive term, Hygiene. That this influence and these conceptions carry social weight is apparent from their echoes in the following quotation from a pamphlet on "Domestic Economy," widely circulated among, and approved by, the Ohio Federation of Women's Clubs, which numbers many thousand members.

"The question is frequently asked—'What is meant by Domestic Economy?' and the answer is confidently given—'Cooking and Sewing.' Such a conception is pitifully narrow. If domestic economy spans no broader horizon than this, there is just reason why educators should stop and count the cost, but cooking and sewing are only small parts of the subject, as are carbon and hydrogen small parts in the science of chemistry. To those of us who have most studied the subject, it is as broad as the world and as vital as life. . . . By political economy or national economy is meant all that bears most intimately upon state and nation; domestic economy then should include all that bears upon home life and human development, and if this is true it is the nucleus of every other economy in the world. No ology or ism but touches it. History, science, literature, language and economics are part and parcel with it, and link us to the past. Art is the stimulus to greater beauty and truer ideals for to-day, and sociology and religion are the beacon lights for the future. . . . Dewey says, 'After all, *life* is the great thing, the life of the child, not more than the life of the man,' and domestic economy means the conception and maintenance of life at its best. Its whole aim should be to create the best children, to place them in the safest environment, and to so train them that they shall develop into the most perfect type of men or women, physically, mentally, and morally. . . . To accomplish the desired result help must come from all sides, the ward school has its particular field, the high school may advance the work, the college and university must train the leaders, but back of all must stand the home and the men and women who are bearing the burdens of life to-day. When the parents of our country are convinced that a training for the most practical and sacred duties of life is needful for the truest development of their children, then from educators and statesmen will come a response to their call. . . . An improved home life is perhaps not all that is necessary to humanity, but if mothers and teachers were better informed concerning the actual needs of the human being, the result would be a superior race of men. From no source but from the homes can a nation recruit her citizens, and upon the training of her girls depend these homes. . . . We are yet to learn that there is power in correct living, and that nothing which pertains to life is trivial or unimportant."

The gradual formation of an intelligent public opinion on this subject, the promising growth of popular support in favour of its educational developments, are assisted by the action of this and other State Federations of Women's Clubs, and also by the influence of the National Household Economic Association, the Women's Educational and Industrial Union, the Association of College Alumnæ, and similar bodies.* These social organisations have done good service, not alone in the direction of securing a recognition of the school value of Domestic Science, but by the fact that the grounds upon which their advocacy is based is a realisation, by their members, of their own defective knowledge in this respect and of the price paid by those dependent upon them for their needless and costly ignorance.

Allusion has already been made to the three classes of opinion held and supported in the States as to the character, position, and methods to be employed in the teaching of Domestic Science or Household Economics, each of which finds representation in different cities and in schools of various types and grades:— *Three Schools of Thought as to Domestic Science Teaching.*

1. The utilitarian party, who desire to secure instruction for girls in cooking, sewing, cleaning and the elements of house sanitation, with the sole view of preparing the home makers of the future for the duties which will devolve upon them; and by this means to raise the standard of health and happiness among the people. The supporters of this opinion ask, therefore, that practical work in domestic subjects shall be included at an age which shall secure its advantages for all girls before "leakage" sets in, and that the courses shall bear as directly as may be upon the immediate economic necessities of the pupils; facility of accomplishment being more emphasised than reasons for results gained.

* See Part III. of Report.

2. The manual training advocates, who hopefully anticipate the attainment of two, or even three, ends; viz., the acquirement of such desirable faculties as quick observation, rapid correlation between hand and eye, careful precision and skilled fingers, by means of and coupled with increased command of the household arts. In addition they hope that a realisation of the dexterity and thought demanded by right manipulation will lend new dignity to the materials employed and to the home in which they find their natural place.

3. Those who have recognised the real educational importance of the subject in all its fulness and scope, when judiciously introduced into schools, quite apart from immediate utility or from the possible acquirement of manual dexterity. The supporters of this view consider the former conceptions incomplete, possibly mistaken, estimates of its real worth. To them its value lies in the field it offers for the application of scientific knowledge and for the exercise of the arts; in the strong social links it forges between school and home life at an early period; in the dignity it attaches to domestic matters at a later stage; and in the introduction which it involves to economic and sociological problems, when studied in its entirety by more advanced students.

Diversity of Educational Methods in Practice.
It will be well at this point to draw attention to, and to lay emphatic stress upon, the fact that no generalisation can be safely made upon educational methods in the United States. The elasticity permitted and independence possessed lead, as one result, to a diversity of detail in each city, often in each school of a city. This, while beneficial to those immediately concerned, is bewildering and discouraging to a " foreigner," who desires to form and to record an accurate conception of which method, among many, yields the most satisfactory results. It is possible to broadly classify the objects in view as utilitarian, manual training, or educational; but, in practice, the line of division is rarely defined with absolute clearness, and exceptions would almost equal the number which conform even to a very broad rule.

Under one or other title, and to a greater or less extent, Domestic Science finds a place in every type of educational institution. These may be classified under the main divisions of I. State Institutions, supported by taxation and controlled by the people, at which attendance is gratuitous; and II. Private Institutions, endowed by individual munificence, independent of popular control, at which the payment of fees is required.

The accompanying table will serve to convey some idea of the diversity of practice which obtains in Grade and High Schools with respect to the teaching of even two branches of Domestic Science. The particulars are adapted by kind permission from " Teachers College Record," for November, 1901, which contains a mass of interesting details upon the subjects therein grouped as Manual Training.

	Grade Schools.									High Schools.			
	I.	II.	III.	IV.	V.	VI.	VII.	VIII.	IX.	I.	II.	III.	IV.
Lewiston, Me.					S.	S.	S.	S.	S.				
Brookline, Mass.			S.	S.	S.	S.	S. Ck.	Ck.	Ck.				
Boston, Mass.				S.	S.	S.	Ck.	Ck.					
Concord, Mass.					S.	S.	S.	S.					
Dedham, Mass.				S.	S.	S.	S.						
Fall River, Mass.				S.	S.	S.	S.						
Fitchburg. Mass.							S.	S.	S.				
Medford, Mass.				S.	S.	S.	S.	S.	Ck.				
Natick, Mass.						S.	S.	S.					
N. Easton, Mass.	S.	S.	S.	S.	S.	S.	S.	S. Ck.		S. Ck.			
Waltham, Mass.					S.	S.	S.	S.	Ck.				
Hartford, Ct								S.		Ck.	Ck.	Ck.	
New Haven, Ct.					?. Ck.	S. Ck.	Ck.	S. Ck.					
Binghampton, N.Y.						S.				Ck.		S. Ck.	
Brooklyn, N. Y., M.T.H.S.										S. Ck.	S.		
Brooklyn, N.Y , Pratt Institute.										S.	S.	S.	Ck.
Ithaca, N.Y.						S.	S.	S.					
Jamestown, N.Y.	S.	S.	S.	S.	S.	S.	Ck.						
New York, N.Y.				S.	S.	S.	S. Ck.						
Newburgh, N.Y.			S.	S.	S.	S.							
Syracuse, N.Y.						S. Ck.	S. Ck.	S. Ck.					
Utica, N.Y.					S.	S.	Ck.	Ck.	Ck.				
Yonkers, N.Y.				S.	S.	Ck.							
Asbury Park, N.Y.	S.	S.	S.	S.	S.	S.	S.	S.	S.	S.	S.	S.	
Atlantic City, N.Y.					S.	S.	?.						
Camden N.Y.			S.	S.	S.	S.	S.	S.		S.	S.	S.	S.
Cape May, N.Y.	S.	S.	S.	S.	S.	S.	S.	S.					
Carlstadt, N.Y.				S.	S.	S.	S.	S.					
Garfield, N.Y.			S.	S.	S.	S.	S.	S.					
Hackensack, N.Y.			S.	S.	S.	S.	S.						
Hoboken, N.Y.						S.	S.	S.	Ck.				
Montclair N.Y.						S.	S.						
Newark, N.Y.						S.	S.						
East Orange, N.Y.					S.	S.	S.	S.		S.	S.	S.	
Orange, N.Y.				S.	S.	S.	S.				Ck.	Ck.	
South Orange, N.Y.				S.	S.	S.	S.	S.					
Passaic, N.Y.			S.	S.				Ck.					
Summit, N.Y.						S.							
Wilmington, Del.						S.							
Columbus, Ga.	S.	S.			S.	S.	Ck.	Ck.					
Cleveland, O.					S.	S.	Ck.	Ck.					
Toledo, O., Uk T.S.					S.	S.	Ck.	Ck.		Ck.	S.		
Champaign, Ill.		S.	S.	S.	S.					S.	Ck.		
Chicago, Ill.								S.					
Chicago, Farra School							S	S.					
Chicago, Jewish Fr. School.	S.	S.	S.	S.	S.	S.	S. Ck.	S. Ck.					
Minneapolis, Minn.				S.	S.	S.	Ck.	Ck.					
Kansas City, Mo				S.	S.	S.	Ck.	Ck.		S.	S.		Ck.
Menominee, Wis.	S.	S.	S.	S.	S.	S.	S.	S.		Ck.	S.	S.	Ck.
Oshkosk, Wis.					S.	S.	S. Ck.	S. Ck.		S. Ck.	S. Ck.	S. Ck.	S. Ck.
Carthage, Mo.							?.	S.		S.			
Moberly, Mo.						S.							
Denver, Cal, M.T.H.S.										S.	S.	Ck.	
San Francisco, Cal.				S.	S.	S.	S.	Ck.					
San Francisco, School of Mech. Arts.										S.	S.	Ck.	

Note.—The above particulars are derived from "The Economics of Handwork in Elementary and Secondary Schools" by *Louis Rouillion*, Table A. "Manual training subjects given in the various school years in the schools enumerated." *Teachers College Record*, vol. 2, No. 5, November, 1901.

S.—Sewing. Ck.—Cooking.

If, for convenience sake, the broadest English definition of Domestic Science be employed throughout this Report to cover the topics which that subject comprises in this country, it will be found to include the greater part of the ground occupied by the different designations of which use is made for describing the same subjects in the United States. I shall therefore com-

[margin note: Use of the term Domestic Science.]

prehend the following subjects under this generic term when
discussing their treatment and position in all grades of educational institutions, where they appear variously grouped under
the heads of Manual Training, Domestic Sciences, Domestic Arts,
Household Economics, Physiology and Hygiene, and Sanitary
Science :—

    (i.) Cookery.
    (ii.) Needlework.
    (iii.) Dressmaking.
    (iv.) Millinery.
    (v.) Laundry work.
    (vi.) Housewifery (which includes purchase of commodities).
    (vii.) Elements of Domestic and Personal Hygiene (including
        house sanitation).
    (viii.) Care of young children.

Scheme of the present report. A number of specimen schemes and syllabuses, typical of
Domestic Science and Hygiene courses and methods in each
grade of institution are included in the text and in the Appendix.
In the course of my comments upon these, I shall endeavour
to give a just view of the present position and treatment of
the subject, though time and space forbid the inclusion of much
suggestive material.

In conclusion, concise allusion is also made to the problems of
domestic service; for these, it is anticipated that at least partial
solution may result from the educational efforts recorded in
the following pages.

The Report is sub-divided as follows :—

Part I.—*State Institutions.*

A.—Primary and Grammar, or Grade Schools.
B.—High Schools.
C.—Colleges.
D.—Normal Colleges.

Part II.—*Private Institutions.*

A.—Kindergartens, Primary and Grammar Schools.
B.—High Schools.
C.—Technical Institutes.
D.—Women's Colleges.
E.—Universities.

Part III.—*Social Agencies for the Promotion of Domestic Science Teaching.*

A.—Women's Clubs.
B.—Philanthropic Agencies.
C.—Summer Schools.
D.—University Extension.
E.—The Domestic Service Problem.

PART I.

STATE INSTITUTIONS.

A.—GRADE (PRIMARY AND GRAMMAR) SCHOOLS.

As the Report is primarily concerned with State educational methods, this class of institution will be that first treated.

Domestic Science is frequently limited in the Grade Schools to the subject of cookery, and its accompaniment of the elements of cleaning. Needlework is more often included under Manual Training than under Domestic Science, and, in some cities, *e.g.* Cleveland (Ohio), Detroit (Mich.), and Toledo, *both* subjects are classified under the former head. Laundry work has not yet found a place in elementary schools; a great prejudice exists against its introduction, in spite of home washing being the rule in most families, especially in cities where the industry has not been absorbed by the Chinese. Housewifery, apart from that incidental to a cookery course, is rarely taught, but the inclusion is contemplated of definite teaching on simple house sanitation; probably this is now a fact in Philadelphia. Considerable time and attention are devoted to the outlines of domestic and personal hygiene, but as subjects apart from Domestic Science; they constitute the obligatory elements in the curriculum of practically all State elementary schools. Dressmaking and millinery are obviously too advanced for children in the grade schools, though the cutting and making of a simple blouse lends great attraction under some Boards of Education to the last year of the needlework course. The Care of Young Children is not usually dealt with at this period of school life. New York City is a direct exception to this rule, though incidentally scholars of both sexes get some insight into the subject, or, more precisely, gain some conception of the care necessary to ensure health, by means of repeatedly impressed lessons in the elements of hygiene.

Domestic Science Subjects taught in Grade Schools.

1.—*Cookery.*

Cookery is not yet an obligatory subject under every Board of Education, though it is becoming so in the majority of cities, as the result largely of the gradual removal of the difficulties which previously existed. These included parental objections, want of necessary accommodation, or of appropriations for the purpose, and considerations as to suitable employment for the boys while their girl companions were thus occupied. The subject usually finds a place in the time-tables of the 6th or 7th and 8th grades of the grammar schools, more generally in the last two. As the age for compulsory school attendance is 5 years, the average age when these grades are reached is 12 or 13. Weekly lessons are everywhere the rule during one, or more generally two, school years of 8 or 9 months each. At Brookline (Mass), where manual training and the domestic arts

Grades in which generally taught.

Length of Course and Methods of Teaching.

were developed and made increasingly educational during the last 10 years, of Professor Dutton's valuable service as Superintendent of schools, cooking is practised by the girls for 2 hours a week for three years in the 6th, 7th and 8th grades, and a three years course is available also at Menominee for girls who pass on to the high school. Here the last, or 8th grade, year in the elementary schools is devoted to the introductory stages of cookery, serving, housekeeping, and house sanitation ; the course being continued during the first two high school years. At Boston, Washington, Philadelphia, Toledo, and Chicago, the cookery course lasts two years, while in New York City it is confined to a year and a half, and at Cleveland (O.), and St. Louis (Mi.) to one school year. In these cities, however, the lessons are longer, $2\frac{1}{2}$ hours being the rule, as against the $1\frac{1}{4}$ hours at Toledo, Washington, and Chicago. Boston stands well with its 2 years' course of 2 hours lessons, but for the weekly loss of this half-hour at Washington some compensation exists in the small number (12) to which each class is limited, which favours careful individual guidance and supervision.

The number of scholars in a class is as variable as the length of the lessons. It is influenced by several factors. One of these is the almost impossible task, in some places, of keeping pace with the growth of the school population. In New York City, *e.g.* (a recognised proportion of whose children consists of very poor and ignorant emigrants), the Domestic Science Organiser (Mrs. Mary E. Williams), advises and sanctions classes of 40 or even 50 girls, in order to secure the advantage of some training for the largest possible number. The same cause and feeling are partially responsible for very similar conditions at Boston, though where possible the classes there are limited to 25, and an assistant is provided where this is not the case. Another factor appears in the relative proportion of boys to girls in any particular locality of a country where co-education is the accepted custom ; it is, for instance, responsible at the present time for the organisation of small classes at Washington, though their small size is in part due to the fact that this city is characterised by its large number of relatively small schools, less crowded classes being the result. At Chicago, where the influx of emigrants is large, the size of the Domestic Science classes varies from 18 to 32. The average number in most cities is 20, and the general rule is individual work on the part of each child. Group work—two or more —is only introduced when the article does not lend itself to much subdivision, or when the principle cannot be illustrated without sufficient bulk. To this rule New York City, Washington, and Cleveland are the three prominent exceptions. In these cities one-third only of the girls do practical work, the remainder make observations and take notes. Such large and numerous classes entail very heavy work on the teachers, especially where the work is individual, as at Chicago ; here nearly 600 girls pass through the hands of each teacher, weekly, allowing for four 1½ hour classes per day of 30 girls each; the additional strain of securing a thorough "clean up" by each class during the already brief lesson involves much nerve tension and physical fatigue. The 2 or 2½ hour lessons at Philadelphia, although they permit of the attendance of but a quota of girls from each school, reduces the number of weekly classes per teacher to 10, and the number of children to be individually known by each teacher to about 200.

It is of interest to note that in Philadelphia, cookery classes were first organised 15 years ago, in the Girls' High School; the experiment proved so successful that in two years a place was found for the subject in the grade school programmes; even now, it is only an "optional," or "elective," but, nevertheless, very popular subject.

The system of "centres" seems general. These are attached "Centre" in most instances to new schools, though the adaptation of System. basement rooms for this purpose is very common, in which case the light and ventilation are apt to be defective; still, great credit is due to organisers and teachers for the skilful care, thought, and personal trouble they spend to make the best of the second best premises. The Supervisor of Manual Training at Cleveland, Ohio (Mr. W. E. Roberts), has introduced a manual training centre method which presents various advantages, and has the merit of not being extravagant. A kitchen for girls and a carpenter's shop for boys are provided as an annex to the selected school buildings; the cost of building and equipment sufficient for classes of 20, respectively, averages £1,000; cloakrooms and sanitary conveniences are attached. Light, airy, suitably arranged apartments are provided, infinitely preferable to the more pretentious basement rooms frequently allotted to these purposes. This plan obviates the necessity for outside classes to enter the school building, and the proximity of the kitchen and workshop promotes mutual interest in each other's work among pupils who pursue all other studies together.*

The number of centres provided in each city depends upon the time Domestic Science has been adopted as a school subject; whether it is required of all girls in the selected grades; upon the size of the classes; and last, but not least, upon the funds available for building and equipment. At Boston, where the subject has been taught many years, 22 centres exist, each attended by girls from 5 to 7 grammar schools; these centres

---

* Significant of the strong development and recognition of the social spirit in the United States, is a pleasant little custom which prevails in the city of Cleveland for maintaining sympathy between boy and girl classmates. Permission is given at suitable intervals for the interchange of visits at these manual training centres. Simple hospitality is dispensed in their kitchen by the girls, as on the occasion of my visit to the Wade Park School, where preparations were in force to entertain the boys with cocoa and cake, prepared by the young cooks. Later on the courtesy would be returned, by an invitation from the boys to inspect their workshop, when each would present a small specimen of his skill to one of the girl visitors.

" Centre
System "—
continued.
are convenient in situation, but many of them are only adapted
rooms, basement or otherwise, though improvements now in
progress will gradually replace these with modern apartments.
At Chicago, where the subject was introduced in 1898, I found
11 centres; the same stage of adaptation is being gone through as at
Boston, with a like promise of better things, already fulfilled in
the newest schools. The accommodation, even with large classes,
sufficed for less than one-half of those eligible to receive the
instruction. At this date it is probably considerably increased.

Comparison with developments in New York City will
exemplify the rapidity with which these take place. In 1898 only
4 cookery teachers were employed by the Board of Education of
that city, though the subject had been tentatively introduced
into the schools some years before. In May, 1901, the supervisor
had 29 teachers under her charge, employed at 40 centres.
There the basement plan does not obtain, but the kitchens are
located on the top floor of the 4 and 5 storied buildings. This
plan involves much stair climbing on all concerned, and on that
account should be discountenanced unless lifts are provided, as
is customary in High Schools when carried up to this height;
in respect of light and ventilation such a position is admirable.
Five centres suffice for the needs of a less populous city, such
as Toledo, in spite of cookery being obligatory on all girls in the
7th and 8th grades since 1899; previous to that date it was
"elective.' Spacious cooking "laboratories" are attached to the
newest schools at Washington; hitherto, owing to want of space
and the number of centres necessitated by the small classes
and numerous schools, private houses have, in some instances,
been employed for the purpose, and are still in use; these are un-
objectional under the exceptionable conditions which obtain there.

Equipment. The small details of equipment are as variable as those of
all the other particulars recorded, but the broad general plan
is the same in all the cities I visited, or of whose courses
I obtained reliable information. Even this, however, is subject
to modification according to the method employed, either of
individual work or of practice limited to a small group, or by
the funds at the disposal of the organisers. Illustrations convey
the best idea of the prominent feature which most conspicuously
distinguishes an American school kitchen, or "cooking laboratory"
from the appearance familiar in England. It consists of a table
of varying length and form; three sides of a square to accommodate
20 students, as at the Pratt Institute and some of the Boston
school centres; or a short oblong, just sufficient for two, or at
most four, workers, as at the Ohio State University, the Toledo
Manual Training School or the Bradley Institute, Peoria, Ill.
Whatever the length, the table is usually of hard wood, from
30 inches to 33½ inches in height, about 25 inches wide, and
calculated to allow from 25 inches to 33 inches per pupil
according to size. I saw several instances where the front
portion was wood, either plain, polished, covered with metal,
slate or white glazed tiles, or coated with some vitreous
preparation resembling glass. Mr Louis Roubillion (Teachers

College, Columbia University) considers " that unglazed, vitrified, Equipment
white tile laid over asphalted paper, bound at the table edge by —*continued.*
a metal strip is perhaps the best, although somewhat expensive.'
At one high school each pupil is supplied with white American
cloth to protect the polished wood, and an asbestos mat upon
which to place her hot pans. The back half. of the table may,
or may not, be covered with sheet zinc; above this portion
runs an iron grid raised about 6 or 8 inches; this may be
continuous the whole length of a long table or be fitted in
sections of 12 to 18 inches. It serves the dual purpose of a
range which permits of individual cooking, and of a stand for hot
pans; bunsen gas burners, or gas rings, are fitted underneath
the grid, one for each pupil, and a considerable amount of the
cooking processes are conducted by these means. When gas is
not available, single burner oil stoves are substituted—one for
each pupil. Each pupil's place, about two square feet at the
table, is fitted as follows: slid immediately under the top are
two boards, one for bread or pastry, one for meat, etc., below are
two drawers, the deeper one usually provided with one or two
sliding trays. In this drawer is kept the small ware in constant

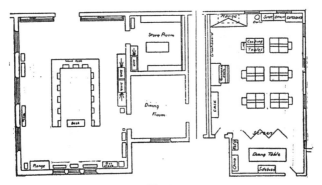

Fig. 1.

PLAN SHOWING HORSESHOE AND GROUP ARRANGEMENT OF
COOKING TABLES.

Figs. 1, 2, 3 are reproduced by kind permission from "The Economics of
Manual Training," Teachers College Record. Vol. II., No. 5, Nov. 1901.

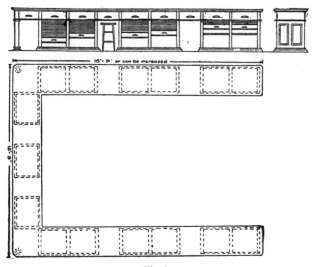

Fig. 2.

PLAN OF CONTINUOUS COOKING TABLE.

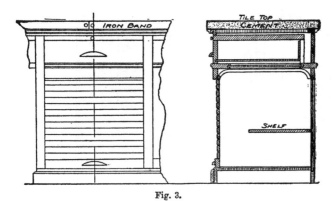

Fig. 3.

DETAIL OF FIG. 2.

FIG. IV.

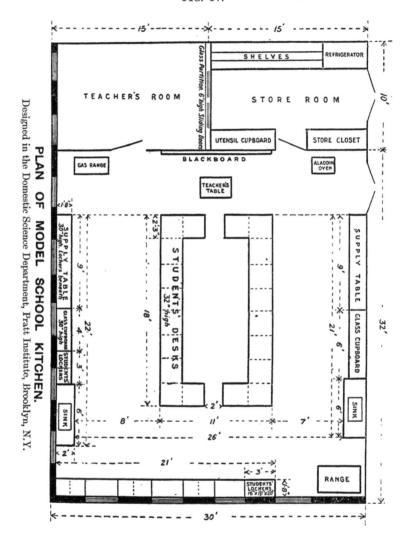

use, generally two knives and forks, two tea-spoons, two dessert Equipment spoons, two table-spoons, two wooden spoons, two plates, salt and *—continued.* pepper boxes, glass or metal measuring cup,* a small strainer, pattypans, and a box of matches. (Inexpensive appliances conducing to economic methods are freely provided, *e.g.,* " soap shakers," costing 5 cents; these consist of a small wire soap box at the end of a long wire handle, they are used for the rapid production of lather ; the smallest fragments can be utilised for the purpose without wetting the hands, while the handles projecting from the pans serve, upon occasion, to remind the careless that soap is going to waste.) The equipment in hardware, always simple, is usually sufficient for 20–25 individuals. I saw instances of admirable ingenuity exercised by teachers to improvise a supply for the needs of individual work under the stress of the large classes in some cities; but a crowded class-room is not the right opportunity to make such additional demands on an already hard-worked teacher, and the principle of demanding resourcefulness under such conditions cannot be commended. In the second and shallower table-drawer, note-books, recipes, and so forth, are kept. Below the drawers is a metal bin, used for either flour or potatoes, and a cupboard which usually contains a granite ware and a tin saucepan, a baking-dish, one or two china bowls of different sizes, and so forth. Between one drawer and the bin or cupboard is a sliding seat, of which prompt use is made, if a pause in active work occurs for the purpose of receiving directions from, or watching demonstrations by, the teacher. The dish-cloths, towels, etc., hang at one end of each table, while large utensils, such as a washing-up pan, hang generally at the other.

---

*The glass or metal cup measure is too prominent in all cookery teaching and recipes in the United States and Canada not to demand fuller description. It offers the unquestionable advantages of economical simplicity, cleanliness and uniformity in practice, and when of glass leaves little to be desired. Its usual shape is slightly facetted ; there are 4 broad and 8 narrow facets, and each of the 4 broad facets bears a scale on a different scheme of measurement, as follows :—

FACETS.

I.	II.	III.		IV.
½ pint even full.	Coffee cup or 2 Tea cups.	Table spoonful.		Sugar.
6 oz.		Sugar.	Liquid.	5 oz.
1 gill 4 oz.	even full 1 Tea cup.	4	8	4 oz.
3 oz.	Wine glass.	3	6	3 oz.
2 oz.		2	4	2 oz.
1 oz.		1	2	1 oz.

The one measure can thus be employed for fluids and solids, is uniform throughout the country, and is the accepted standard upon which recipes are compounded.

Equipment
—*continued.* In some recently fitted school-kitchens a small glazed earthenware sink finds a place in each cooking table, either at one end,
or dividing the table into two halves.   More generally the sink
accommodation is provided against an outside wall, and, in either
case, there is a good supply of hot and cold water available.   In
other respects the fittings closely conform to those customary in
this country, though occasionally a six-foot marble table is provided for the making of pastry or of very refined dishes.   The
universal custom is to expose all pipes, whether for the supply
of water or of gas, or for the removal of waste.   The plumbing
appears excellent, and, indeed, needs to be, in a country where
the climate necessitates the protection of soil-pipes within the
dwellings, and where sanitary fittings are furnished with far
greater liberality of supply and consideration for comfort than is
at present our habit.   Pipes are usually painted white, in a few
instances they are of polished metal; without exception they
are well managed, so that, far from being an offence, they are
pleasing to the eye, and contribute to cleanliness and convenience
of access.   A coal range and a gas range with ovens are found in
most schools; in Technical Institutes conveniences for cooking
by electricity are occasionally provided in addition.   An Aladdin
oven is a frequent feature, and is found very useful for
soup-making, or for processes requiring slow, steady and prolonged heat.   An ice-box of more or less pretension is considered
almost as great, if not a greater, necessity than a coal range.
Large cupboards are usually fixed against the walls; these are
usually glazed.   The "supply" cupboard contains the groceries,etc.,
in constant requisition, and specimens of preserves, canned fruit,
etc., often the handiwork of former pupils; the china cupboard
frequently displays a tasteful dinner and tea-service in addition
to bare necessaries; these are used in the "serving lessons," to
which marked attention is paid in all grades of cookery courses.
In closed cupboards, or on open shelves below the china, are
found the larger utensils in general use, and others more rarely
required—stew-pans, double boilers, moulds, cake-pans, and
cutters, ice-cream freezers, mincing-machines, coffee-mills, etc.
A third cupboard is often subdivided into lockers or small compartments; each member of each class has one assigned and
numbered, wherein to keep the cap and apron invariably required to be worn during class-work.   The making of these
articles constitutes, I was often told, a foretaste of good things
to come for small needlewomen, who thus anticipate during the
quiet hours of stitching the future active pleasures to be enjoyed
when young cooks.   Charts and drawings find a place on the
walls, and show the various cuts of meat, the proportion of
nutrient properties contained in different foods, and the amount
of certain nutriments which can be bought for a given price in
different foods.

A nice dining table, often with chairs *en suite*, is the rule, as
an essential equipment of the table-serving lessons.   Good
napery is provided in addition to the special china mentioned
above.   In many cases a recess, or a small separate room is

attached and utilised as a dining room, a great feature being Equipment
made of tasteful and suitable surroundings. The part of the —*continued*
room in which the table and china are placed is always noticeable for some appearance distinguishing it from the "kitchen"
air of the rest of the apartment. I do not know how widely the
opinion of the very successful Supervisor of cooking in one large
city is held, but it may be partially responsible for the homelike
atmosphere observable in many of these school kitchens. She
considers that the cookery room should be the "cosy corner"
of a school, the place for pleasant surprises and little
treats, to which a tired teacher or child can sometimes resort
for a cup of tea or other light refreshment. No doubt the
elasticity permitted to the schools under some superintendents,
and the invariable custom for all food cooked to be consumed on
the premises, usually on the spot, by the student responsible for
the dish, are also factors of some account in this characteristic.

In quite general use, too, are the sets of admirable wood
blocks, first designed and made at the Massachusetts Institute
of Technology, Boston, and now supplied by the Pratt
Institute, Brooklyn. Of these there are three sets in all; the
largest represents, in blocks of various colours, red, blue, white,
and yellow, and of various sizes, the proportions of water (blue),
proteid (red), fat (yellow), carbo hydrate (white), salts (grey), in
the bones, muscle, blood, etc., of a full-grown man. These can
be arranged in many useful ways; to illustrate, for instance, the
whole amount of each constituent in the body, or the *proportion*
of each in blood, bone, or muscle; their superficial area is 8 inches
× 8, and the total height $5\frac{1}{2}$ feet. The other two sets of blocks
are much smaller—superficial area, $3\frac{3}{4}$ inches × $3\frac{3}{4}$, total height 17
inches; but made to the same scale of proportion they illustrate,
respectively, the daily income and outgo of a healthy body the
colours being similarly employed to those in the large body blocks,
though others have to find a place—indigo blue for the daily in-
take of oxygen, brown for the daily outgo of urea, and so forth.*

Among the specimen Grade School Cookery Courses which I Typical
have selected to include in this Report are those in use in New Courses.
York City, Toledo, and Washington. They show the scope and
extent of ground covered where the amount of time expended, the
number of scholars in a class and the methods of practice are
somewhat diverse; it must be borne in mind that all are subject
to frequent revision.

In New York City the course at present consists of (a) New
weekly lessons for $1\frac{1}{2}$ years; the number of children legally York City.
allowed is 40, though, owing to the rapid increase of popula- Table I.
tion, 45 and even 50 names appear on some rolls. It is open
to girls in the 6th and 7th grades. In girls' schools, where
the whole class follows the course, two-hour lessons are usual,
but in mixed schools (by far the more general), the necessarily smaller class is nominally limited to $1\frac{1}{2}$ hours weekly,
though, in practice, the principal usually succeeds in allowing 2
hours for this popular lesson.

*For details and cost of a Model Kitchen equipment, See Appendix A.

To secure a measure of uniformity among the teachers in presenting both the scientific and practical sides of their subjects, Mrs. M. E. Williams, Supervisor of Cookery, has prepared a comprehensive outline for their guidance, though great elasticity is allowed in the details and actual ground covered. She advocates the method of prefacing each new department of practice with one theoretical lesson, to embrace experiments which bear directly on the principle of cookery involved.

This outline opens the course with instruction on air, fire, and water, the three essentials to life. Very simple experiments and demonstrations with air are carried out, e.g., testing it for carbon dioxide with lime water, subsequently comparing results with expired air and with that in which combustion has taken place. A short study of combustion follows; the series of demonstrations being conducted with the aid of a candle and lamp chimney, wood blocks, cards, and lime water, and so forth. This introduces an examination of the structure and management of kitchen ranges for coal and gas, time being devoted to the study of fuels, hard and soft coal, gas, kerosene, etc. Water and its most salient properties are then studied experimentally, subsequently to which cleanliness and cleaning introduce the girls to their first elementary lessons on moulds, yeasts and bacteria. Natural and artificial aids to cleanliness are illustrated by careful practice; the reason for each process and its constituent parts being carefully followed out. By this time it is anticipated that an intelligent, though, perforce, elementary insight will have been gained into matter, its nature, and changes; the importance of care and accuracy in details will have been impressed, while practical acquaintance will have been made with ordinary utensils and their uses, the principal methods of cooking and the accepted table of measures. A short time is then devoted to a consideration of the elements composing the human body, and of the part played by food in its growth and repair; the subject of food principles being thus introduced. These are classified as water, protein, fats, carbo-hydrates, and mineral matter. Simple starch foods are first cooked, the potato, cereals, wheat; then tissue building foods, as eggs and milk. Bread and bread stuffs follow, succeeded by meat and fish. The practice of frying and sautéing leads to a study of fats as valuable fuel foods, while the preparation of vegetables and fruits turns attention to the acid and salt supplying foods. Throughout, the experimental treatment and explanation of underlying scientific principles is consistently followed. For instance, at an early stage of the course, a potato is subjected to very careful examination, and a rough analysis is carried out to find "what it contains," the iodine test for starch is taught, and the results compared with those obtained with solutions of sugar, cornflower, laundry starch and salt; the effects of heat on albumen are closely observed, and their applications are demanded; milk and flour are subjected in turn to simple analysis, and the results discussed from the points of view of cooking, nutriment, and so forth. Bread making serves to introduce the action of acids on alkalies, and, more immediately, of an acid on baking soda; indeed the study of baking powders is entered into at some length for the sake of its many lessons. What yeast is, its growth, requirements, products, are all included under this study of bread. The principles of broiling, roasting, stewing, braising, frying, baking, soup making, are, of course, explained and illustrated in due order, and "made over" dishes, such as hashes, croquettes and mince, find a place. The practice of "canning" and preserving is made use of to present the germ theory and the effects of moulds on food stuffs.

Near the end of the second year the question is raised as to what constitutes a suitable diet, and experiments on cooked food with saliva, pepsin and pancreatic juice are carried out to demonstrate the processes of digestion. A short study of infant feeding and invalid cooking follows this physiological teaching. The course concludes with the cooking and serving of a simple, nutritious and economical dinner. The syllabus seems to me comprehensive, well-planned, useful, and educational; infinite care is taken to secure "intelligent doing," not mere mechanical practice.

TABLE I.

GRAMMAR SCHOOL COOKING COURSE, NEW YORK CITY, 1902.

Length of Course.	Scope of Course.	
	FIRST YEAR.	**SECOND YEAR.**
Length of Course, Two years.	AIR.—Why important to life; relation to combustion.	ANIMAL PROTEIN.—Theory and practice.
	FIRE.—Combustion; uses; fuels, varieties of, etc.	BOILING AND PARBOILING.—Practice.
Grades VI. and VII.		ROASTING.—Theory and practice.
	WATER.—Sources: characters; impurities, etc.	BROILING. — Simmering; theory and practice.
Average age, 12.	CHEMISTRY OF CLEANING. —Personal cleanliness; household cleanliness; aids to ventilation, sunlight, disinfectants; care of beds and bedding, floors, walls, ceilings, closets, traps, pantries, ice boxes, dish towels, etc.	STEWING.—Theory and practice.
		BRAISING.—Theory and practice.
Number in class, 40 to 50.		FRICASSEEING.—Theory and practice.
	THE HUMAN BODY.—Elements composing it, and where obtained.	FRYING.—Theory and practice.
One-third only do practical work.		MADE-OVER DISHES.—Theory and practice.
	FOOD. — Its function; food principles.	SAUTÉING.—Theory and practice.
METHOD.—	POTATOES (specimen of treatment)—.	FISH.—Theory and practice.
Theory, supported by experimental demonstrations of underlying scientific principles, precedes application in practice.	THEORY.—History; botany, note difference between sweet and white potatoes; composition; experiment showing water, starch test, cellulose, use of microscope; drawing—plant, tuber, starch grains; digestion of starch; salivary glands; action of saliva on glands; test saliva with litmus; pancreatic juice; food value of starch.	SOUPS WITH STOCK. — Theory and practice.
		BEEF-TEA, JUICE EXTRACT. —Theory and practice.
		VEGETABLES.—Theory and practice.
		SALADS.—Theory and practice.
	PRACTICE.—	DRESSINGS.—Theory and practice.
Lessons, 1½-2 hours weekly.	Boiled, Baked, Mashed, Cream } White, sweet. Compare nutritive value of same.	DESSERTS (sweets).—Theory and practice; method of treatment; their relation to food and diet; use and abuse; use of fruits alone, and in combination with other materials; reason for the indigestibility of pastry; use, composition, and adulteration of flavourings for desserts.
	CEREALS.—Theory and practice.	Custards.—Practice.
	BREADS.—Theory and practice.	Soufflés.—Practice. Gelatine Jellies.—Practice.
	YEAST. — Botanical classification; manner of growth, with experiments; use of microscope; drawings; fermentation—lactic, acetic.	Batter Puddings.—Practice. Cakes.—Practice.
		SAUCES.—Practice.
	FLOUR. — Other wheat preparations; theory and practice.	CANNING AND PRESERVING.—Method of treatment.
	PROTEIN.—Theory; digestion of; under what conditions most easily digested; mastication; gastric and intestinal digestion; experiments.	GERM THEORY. — Foreign matter in the air; dust, and what it contains; moulds, yeasts, and bacteria; show moulds on bread, lemon, cheese, jellies, etc.; fermented canned fruits; souring of milk, soups, uncooked and cooked food, etc.; use of microscope; food value of canned fruits compared with other foods; practice; canning of fruits in season; jellies.
	EGGS. — Theory and practice.	
	TEA, COFFEE, COCOA. — Theory and practice.	
	MILK.—Theory; nutritive value; care of; pasteurisation, sterilisation, cleanliness of utensils.	FREEZING.—Theory and practice.
		PHYSIOLOGY.—Alimentary canal; drawing showing salivary glands of canal; saliva, gastric juice, pancreatic juice; experiments with saliva, pepsin, and pancreatic juice.
	BUTTER.—Theory and practice.	
	CHEESE—Theory and practice.	INVALID COOKING.
	VEGETABLE CLASSIFICATION.	INFANT FEEDING.
	VEGETABLE PROTEIN.	COOKING AND SERVING OF A SIMPLE DINNER.—Table-setting, decoration, serving.

Details are largely left to the discretion of individual
teachers: *e.g.,* in a Jewish quarter, special care is given to showing
better methods of cooking the fish and coarser kinds of poultry
which form the staple diet of "Hebrews," as well as the right
methods of keeping and preserving fruit and vegetables, which
they consume in large quantities; or, in an Italian quarter, where
home made wine is the rule, the process, conducted under
conditions of scrupulous cleanliness, is introduced into the school
kitchen. Habitually the girls "can" and preserve fruit and
vegetables for use throughout the winter months.

The regrettable and very weak point in this course is that so
few pupils share in the actual practice work of each lesson. The
group method on a large scale is compulsorily adopted in all
schools, about one-third of the girls doing practical work, while
the remainder make notes and observations. The one-third who
are selected for the practice are subdivided into cooks, housekeepers, and scullery-maids, thus the actual number which
handles the food is very small, and no one child carries through
a dish from first to last. This incidentally prevents also the
formation of a true estimate of the time necessary for a single
individual to prepare either a dish or a meal, as the "housekeepers" are expected to put ready to the hands of the "cooks"
all the material and utensils they need at the very moment they
are required, while the "scullery-maids" remove and wash each
article immediately after use, by which means the final clearing
up is reduced to a minimum. The coincident demand upon the
attention of the observers is rather severe; they are expected to
concentrate their minds for over an hour upon processes in which
they take no active share. Excellent and most comfortable
"tablet" armchairs were provided in the kitchens of the New
York City schools I visited, but many children stood throughout
the time in order to see, as the large room had no raised gallery
to facilitate observation. The supervisor is well aware of the
disadvantage of the present system, but until far larger "appropriations" are made by the Board of Education neither staff nor
equipment can be supplied on the scale essential where individual
work at each lesson is the rule; meanwhile Mrs. Williams
believes that she does the greatest good to the greatest number
by pursuing the present policy. The interest aroused among
parents, the cordial support they accord to the subject, and the
facilities afforded to the girls for home practice, are all factors in
the formation of a public opinion which will presently insist upon
the provision of further opportunities for each girl in every
school. The system of alternate demonstration and practice
lessons, such as is the rule in England, is quite the exception in
the United States, even if it be anywhere found. In New York
City it is the custom to demonstrate part of the time more or
less early in the course, but only to do so just enough to secure
right manipulation at each step by beginners. In the "bread"
lesson, for example, the teacher would begin the kneading; if
"omelettes" be the subject she would make one first; but if the
process be simple, the girls would carry out the whole under her

direction, and this is the ordinary plan with lessons on the (a) New York City —*continued.* cooking of vegetables, or the broiling and roasting of meat, etc. Marks are given for conduct; no examination is held, knowledge being tested by the prevalent custom of revision. It is usual to inquire and to record which girls have practised at home what has been learnt at previous lessons, and samples of home work, to which special encouragement is given, are brought habitually for criticism or approval. Experience shows that home applications are general, even in well-to-do homes where competent servants are kept.

High qualifications are demanded of the special teachers, and it is proposed to insist in future upon a college degree, plus a special course in cookery of at least one year. Teachers must be licensed under the New York State Examination Board, after passing a successful qualifying examination, of which the following is a specimen paper :—

EXAMINATION FOR LICENCE TO TEACH COOKING.

NEW YORK BOARD OF EXAMINERS.

19th October, 1899.

Time, three hours.

1. (*a*) Describe the structure of a coal range, stating the use of each part.

    (*b*) Describe the operating of such a range.

    (*c*) Describe your method of teaching the structure of a coal-range and the use of its parts.

2. Which is more easily digestible, a crust of bread well browned or a boiled potato ? Give reasons in full, indicating the chief physical, chemical, and physiological processes involved.

3. Describe your method of giving a lesson on meat soup as regards (*a*) instruction, (*b*) laboratory management. Give reasons.

4. (*a*) Classify the food principles.

    (*b*) State the nutritive function of each food principle.

    (*c*) State with reasons the approximate proportion of each food principle in the average daily ration.

5. Discuss impurities in drinking water and in ice, treating (*a*) their kinds, (*b*) their source, (*c*) their effects, (*d*) household precautions or counter-agents, with reasons.

6. (*a*) Show how in the matter of language instruction, the cooking teacher may co-operate with the regular teacher.

    (*b*) Suggest specimen themes for compositions drawn from your subject.

    (*c*) How would you correct such compositions ?

    (*d*) What directions would you give regarding note-taking and the keeping of note-books in your class ?

    (*e*) Frame two arithmetical problems such as you would give pupils in connection with their cooking lesson : in measure and proportion, and in cost of food.

7. (*a*) Classify the cooking processes with reference to the mode of applying heat.

    (*b*) State the approximate temperature of the several processes.

(c) State in degrees Fahrenheit the proper temperature for baking a loaf of bread ; muffins ; meat. Give reasons.

(d) Give two ways in which the temperature of the oven may be approximately determined without the use of a thermometer.

The salaries for teachers of cooking and sewing are as follows : First year, $900 (about £180), with a rise of $100 (£20) a year for the succeeding three years, making a maximum of $1,200 (about £240). Supervisors of these subjects receive $1,500 (£300) the first year, and progress by annual increase of $100 to the maximum of $2,000 (about £400). The Supervisor in New York City gives personal instruction at the Teachers' Conferences on the division of the work in the different grades, and teachers are required to give, in turn, a lecture from some subject chosen from the excellent little manual in use, " The Elements of the Theory and Practice of Cooking." Free use of the blackboard during each lesson is advocated, also composition and dictation lessons on the class subjects. In addition to the use by teachers of the State Board of Agriculture's Food Bulletins, Professor Atwater's " Principles of Food and Diet " is employed as a reading book in each class ; Mrs. Williams also desires and ensures that pupils should be familiarised with quotations on cooking, cleaning, and housekeeping from the best authors, to emphasise the dignity of the subject, and to illustrate the high estimate attached to home life by the most eminent writers. Valuable books of reference, both for teachers and pupils, are provided in the school libraries, and care is taken to keep these abreast of the progress made by investigation and research in this line of work. To afford useful stimulus and assistance to her staff the Supervisor periodically conducts parties of these special teachers to visit manufactories of food products, such as flour mills, cream of tartar works, canning and baking establishments, or tea and spice importing works.

(b) Toledo. Table II.　　In Toledo, cooking is an obligatory subject for girls of the 7th and 8th grades of the grammar schools. The average age is 13, and the average number 30 in a class ; the otherwise excellent work being done has its practical value seriously neutralised by the limited time allotted for the lessons. One and a quarter hours per week is the period assigned to all classes of manual training, and though this may suffice for deriving some of the advantages offered by sewing, chip-carving and carpentry, it is quite inadequate for cooking classes, where girls first receive a small amount of theoretical instruction, then prepare and cook a dish, and subsequently clear up the utensils employed in the lesson. A one-year course of $2\frac{1}{2}$ hours weekly lessons, such as is provided in Philadelphia, is on many accounts preferable to half the lesson period for two years, as is the case at Toledo. The syllabus finds a place in this Report for two reasons—(1) Because the City Superintendent of Instruction states that, in spite of its shortcomings, the influence of the Domestic Economy course in the public schools is distinctly apparent in the homes of the people, a statement amply confirmed by several teachers; the Superintendent is

satisfied that not only are families served with better food, but
houses are cleansed and their inmates refined because of this
training. In four years it covers the field of the selection, making and care of the wearing apparel of a family; instructs girls in
the art and economy of the purchase, preparation and serving of
meals, and demonstrates some of the elementary principles of
those sciences and arts which underlie housekeeping and the
beautifying of homes. (2) Because, though the syllabus
drawn up by Miss Matilda Campbell of the Manual Training
High School has naturally much the same scope as that generally found, it approaches the subject in an educational as well as
a utilitarian spirit, and deals more directly than is usual with
the municipal protection of food and water by means of the
Public Health enactments. The experimental demonstrations
are on lines similar to those in the New York City Course, but,
apparently, rather more detailed attention is given to the various
methods employed for the preservation of food; the useful
question of adulterations and sophistications is raised on several
occasions, while some possible causes of water pollution are not
only discussed, but pupils are incited to make their own outside
observations and to bring reports for discussion. The chemistry
of cleaning is introduced towards the completion of the course,
rather than at its commencement, which, conceivably, might
lead to more intelligent appreciation of its principles. An experienced eye, however, quickly detects the compulsory limitation
of choice to rapidly-cooked dishes, and trained teachers will perceive that time does not permit the whole preparation of even
these to be carried through in class, though here, as in New
York City, general, well-justified reliance seemed to me to be
placed on home practice. The girls work in groups of two and
the equipment is good, but materials are cut down to an unwise
limit. Each teacher is responsible for 20 classes a week, and
receives poor remuneration, $360 per annum (about £75). No
normal training in addition to their special subject is required
at present of teachers, indeed, it could not be at the existing
salary.

With the exception of the syllabus, which is framed on some- (c) Phila-
what old-fashioned conventional lines, Philadelphia offers a delphia.
favourable contrast to the conditions obtaining in respect of the
cooking classes at Toledo. The first permanent cooking centre
for grammar schools was established in 1889. In 1901, 13
school kitchens were in operation, and provided instruction for
about two-thirds of the whole number of girls eligible to attend.
The course extends through the nine months of one school
year; each weekly lesson averages 2½ hours, and is open to
6th grade scholars. The system gives each teacher of cooking
10 classes a week, and about 250 girls attend each centre; the
actual number in a class is variable—the inevitable result of co-
education in the schools. There is keen competition to be
among the selected quota from each school; indeed, the children
coming from the best houses are often among the most eager
applicants.

TABLE II.

TOLEDO GRAMMAR GRADE SCHOOLS.
SCHEDULE OF COURSE IN COOKING.

	1st YEAR.	2nd Year.—Cont.
Length of Course, Two Years.	INTRODUCTION, History and importance of cooking. TABLE OF WEIGHTS AND MEASURES (illustrated). BOILING OF WATER, TEMPERATURE, etc.	EGGS. Composition and food value. Effect of heat upon albumen. Test for fresh eggs -preservation of. Soft and hard cooked.
Average age, 13.	COMBUSTION, different fuels used, making and care of a fire. Effect of cold and boiling water on food principles in starch and albumen.	SOUP.—Made from meat. Amount of meat : slow cooking. Stock. MEAT.
No. in class, 30	CEREALS. VEGETABLE CLASSIFICATION. Seeds Shoots Flowers Roots Stalks Fruits Tubers Leaves Fungi Composition and food value.	Review cuts of meat. CHICKENS. How to buy. How to prepare for cooking. FISH.
Grades VII & VIII.	FRUITS. Composition and food value. RECITATION AND REVIEW (typical treatment). Milk, its composition and food value.	How to tell fresh fish. Composition and food value. Practice. REVIEW MAKING BREAD. DIGESTION OF FOOD.
Lessons, 1½ hours weekly.	Analysis : Fat shown by making a small amount of butter. Casein, by action of rennet and acids. Milk sugar with alcohol test. Danger of disease from milk. Introduce opinion of Health Officer as to some sources of contamination. Sterilization and its object. SOUPS, economy of as food. Composition and food value of TEA, COFFEE and COCOA. Lessons on the CUTS OF MEAT. STEWING. Economy of thus using cheap cuts of meat. Preservation of meat by different methods. Smoking, salting, freezing, cold storage, etc. BROILING. Direct application of intense heat to cut surface of fibrin of meat. How to retain the juices of meat. Evils of frying meat. Composition & food value of meats. BAKING POWDER. Composition. Chemical union of acid and alkali, liberating CO_2 : adulteration with alum and starch. Proportions of acids and alkali. BREADS. CAKES. INVALID COOKING. Neatness and daintiness of service. Thorough cooking of starchy foods. Low temperature cooking of albuminous foods. Practice. CHEESE. Manufacture, composition and food value. TABLE SETTING AND SERVING. Cooking and serving of a simple dinner by each class. FREEZING.	Experiments with artificial digestion. FRYING. PASTRY. WATER (typical treatment). Surface wells. Deep wells. Its source { Rivers and brooks. Springs. Rain water. Test of hard and soft water. Reasons for boiling { For cooking purposes. To destroy germ life. Danger of surface wells. Pupils investigate wells in their neighbourhood and report. Possible sources of contamination. SALADS. DESSERTS. Use and abuse. Use of fruits alone and in composition. Adulteration of flavouring extracts. CHEMISTRY OF CLEANING. Materials { Soap. Salsoda. Washing Powder Ammonia Sapolio Dirt { visible { Dust Grease, etc. Invisible { Germs Bacteria Disinfectants { Natural { Fresh air. Sunlight. Heat Artificial { Carbolic acid. Corrosive sublimate. Sulphur fumes. FLOUR.—Manufactured flour. Spring wheat. Winter wheat. Analysis of. Separating starch and gluten. Burn flour to show presence of water and mineral matter. Yeast.—Where found. Method of Growth. Chemical caused by its growth. FERMENTATION { Lactic. Alcoholic (Illustrated.) Acetic TABLE SETTING AND SERVING. Daintiness, cleanliness, quietness, carefulness.
	2nd YEAR.	
	CLASSIFICATION OF FOOD. USES of food in the body. THE HUMAN BODY. Elements and compounds composing it. Growth. Food, its function, waste and repair : heat and energy. Typical foods of different nations.	

The course comprises instruction in the usual processes, economy, cleanliness, method, promptness, and the development of executive ability being the primary objects; the high standard demanded of the special teachers obviates any risk of disparagement. of the importance of the intellectual value of Domestic Science. A manual is provided for the use of the pupils, which contains a very extensive variety of dishes, including delicate invalid cookery, the selection from which is left to the judgment of the teacher. The recipes are generally distributed, legibly printed on cards, for use during the lessons, which minimises the large amount of time otherwise absorbed by note making, which is then limited to a record of methods or other observations. The girls work either individually or in groups, according to the particular recipe to be carried out. Both oral teaching and practical demonstrations are given by the teachers; the proportion of time devoted to the two depends upon the subject under consideration, and a little upon the individuality of the teacher; the whole period is never devoted to teaching or demonstration except at the introductory lesson The teacher actively directs the pupils' work, and where group work is for some good reason inevitable, she divides it so far as may be among the members of the group in such a way that each member may take part in each step of the process. Periodical "quizzes" are conducted by the teachers, and examinations form part of the curriculum; table setting, and the cleaning of room, sink and utensils constitute a part of such tests. The equipment, with the exception of the necessary plumbing, is left entirely to the discretion of the Supervisor, Miss Wright; while very simple it seems complete. All cooking teachers are required to be graduates of the Drexel Institute, and their sound scientific training must gradually influence school methods; the Supervisor is also hopeful of securing by degrees more connection with physiology and other suitable subjects now included in the regular school course. Numerous instances of home applications were advanced, and each child is systematically called upon to say what she has done at home each week during the interval between the classes.

At Washington, cooking is an obligatory subject for girls (d) Washington, D.C. in the 7th and 8th grades, the total number of lessons in the two years' course is 72, of 1¼ hours' duration. The classes Table III. are held at centres, each of which serves a weekly average of 200 pupils. As has been said, the number in each class rarely exceeds 12—an arrangement supported by the Supervisor, Miss Emma Jacobs, for various reasons, to which I have referred below. In the new schools large cooking laboratories are provided; well fitted, spacious, with an air of great comfort. The arrangement of lessons varies somewhat each year, though in substance the syllabus is the same; that employed the first year is repeated in a more extended form during the second. All recipes are written from memory after the article has been made, except in such cases as soup stock and bread, when it is impossible to complete the entire process in the

(d) Washing ton—continued. lesson period; these recipes are, therefore, dictated. The outlines of an ox, sheep, calf and lamb are supplied to each girl

TABLE III.

WASHINGTON, D.C., GRAMMAR GRADE SCHOOL.

SYNOPSIS OF FIRST YEAR OF COOKING COURSE.

PARTICULARS OF COURSE.	INTRODUCTORY.	BOILING.	STEWING.	BROILING.	BAKING.	FRYING.
Length of Course, Two Years.	(1) Definition.	Definition.	Definition.	Definition.	Definition.	Definition.
Grades VII. and VIII. (Girls).	(2) Purposes.	Materials. { MEATS.—Fresh beef, mutton, fish, poultry. Cured beef, pork, fish, tongue. Soup, beef, lamb, mutton, fish, poultry.	Materials. { Meats. Vegetables. Fruits.	Materials. { STEAKS.—Veal, beef, sirloin, tenderloin, porterhouse, flank, round.	Materials. { Bread (raised by yeast) bread (raised by the union of soda with an acid.)	Materials. { Fish. Oysters. Poultry. Batters. Cakes.
No. in Class, 12.	(3) Processes.	VEGETABLES.—Large potatoes, beets, onions. Small beans, peas, grains.	Kinds. { Haricot. Ragout. Salmi. Chowder. Fricassee. Pot-pie. Braising.	CHOPS.—Pork, lamb, mutton.	Bread (raised by entanglement of air).	UTENSILS.—(Kettle, pan).
Lessons 1¼ hours.	(4) Incidental and general information respecting materials, sources, processes of preparation and combination, care and selection of materials.	DOUGHS.—Dumplings. Roly-poly puddings.		FISH.—Shad, salmon, cod, salmon, oysters, clams, bread.	Meat, beef, mutton, pork, fish, poultry.	PRESERVING. { By sugar (fruits).
A Syllabus, substantially the same as that employed in the first year is repeated in a more extended form during the 2nd year.		LIQUIDS.—Custards, sauces, beverages, tea, coffee, cocoa.		UTENSILS.—Gridiron, broiler, spit, toaster.	Cake (loaf, small). Pies, puddings, vegetables.	By vinegar (fruits, vegetables).
		UTENSILS.—Tin; copper; earthen; iron, plain, galvanised, tinned.				Kinds. { By salt, smoke, ice (meats).

attending the classes : these she fills in and numbers as the joints (d) Washington—*continued.* so defined are cooked or described. The market price is recorded of each article used, and the variation in price of certain articles is also shown, as the date of each statement is recorded for subsequent comparison; pupils are called upon at intervals to compute the cost of meals from data so collected; the recipes provided give quantities sufficient for six persons. Knowledge is tested by revision lessons, which are very liberally introduced; specimens of home efforts are also invited and constantly brought for criticism, while the practical value and influence of the work are evidenced by the frequent letters of approval received from mothers, grateful for the assistance gained in home life from school tuition. The lessons seemed spirited and most practical, and were evidently enjoyed by those who took part in them. There are no demonstrations in the English sense of the term. Miss Jacobs believes that better results attend work performed by the pupils under careful supervision; she therefore allows only one-third of the twelve girls to work at the same time, two as cooks, two as housekeepers, while the remaining eight watch, criticise and make notes. Those who are selected to work, do so, following the explicit verbal directions of the teacher, who can at once see and correct an awkward or imperfect movement. If a pupil fails to secure correct manipulation the teacher will guide the child's hand, and show how the muscles must be controlled, for instance, in the kneading of bread. If the children are likely to have acquired a poor method of holding an implement or using the muscles in some familiar home process, the teacher would show the correct and better way of doing the work before giving her directions, as when beating white of eggs to a stiff paste. The fact that no teacher can watch at once the work of 20 children and be sure that each is doing the work with accurate facility is one of Miss Jacob's strongest arguments in favour of the Washington system. "Our children," she writes, "are able to work from dictation, because from the first day they enter school they are trained to obey directions which call into play the muscles of the hands and other parts of the body in the execution of orders. Manual training begins for them in the Kindergarten, and the work for each grade calls into play more groups of muscles and other powers. I do not mean to say that the manipulation in the cooking classes is all that could be desired, but with only two girls at work the teacher secures better results; thus something more perfect is presented to the class without having to use every alternate lesson for demonstration on her part."

High qualifications are demanded of the teachers; graduates of the Pratt or Drexel Institutes, or of some first-class training school are preferred. Details of the lessons and personal observation show the attention devoted to learning the "reason why," to basing practice on intelligent knowledge, and the importance attached to thoroughness. Frequent revision, even at the expense of fewer recipes, is preferred to mere mechanical compliance with a stipulated programme. · The intelligent efforts to connect the Domestic Science work with the language, literature and plan work (geography) throughout the grades are largely due to Miss Jacob's influence; *e.g.* in the Nature work, under animals, the bee, hen, duck and rabbit (creatures of food value to mankind) are discussed and studied; under plants, the development, growth and fruition of the bean and pea and their uses in the daily diet, are observed and noted; under institutional life, ice, ice wagons, ice houses, markets, their produce, how and why sold, find a place. In number work, simple exercises in the application of the number of pecks in a bushel, quarts in a gallon and so on, are based on articles in common family use. In language work, work done in and around a home is often the selected subject, with the direct object of arousing interest in the right fulfilment of home duties. The formation of good habits in the protection and right care of food is fortunately promoted by the stringent milk regulations in force in Washington.*

Cost of Classes.   To summarise accurately the expenditure involved by Grade School Cooking Courses is impossible; the cost of equipment is much affected by the prices which rule in a particular city or State—labour is much dearer in the east than in the west, to the extent of almost doubling the cost of some articles, such as tables—metal work is subject to almost equal variations, and the " appropriations " granted bring in another element of uncertainty. In Chicago, given a suitable room, $150 (£30) suffices to equip a class of 24 well; but, were other figures quoted, they would admit of no really accurate comparison. In more than one city the cooking tables were made by the boys as part of their manual training course. The cost per head per lesson is much more generally the same, one cent represents a fair average. At New York City the cost varies from $\frac{3}{4}$ cent to $1\frac{1}{4}$ cents; at Boston it must not exceed $\frac{3}{4}$ cent; at Chicago $1\frac{1}{4}$ cent is the rule; at Detroit, $1\frac{1}{2}$ cent is allowed. This means that the quantities for individual work are very small, though, as a whole, food stuffs, and especially vegetables and fruit, are cheaper than in England. Each class eats on the spot the food it has prepared, unless request be made to take specimens away from the centre for display to the Principal or teacher at the school attended. This custom is prevalent throughout every grade of institution. I still remember the novel impression it conveyed to me, as a complete stranger, on the occasion of my visit to the Pratt Institute shortly after my arrival in the United States. I had watched the class of normal students engaged in the preparation of a suitable meal for a child of 18 months; immediately the processes were complete and had been criticised by the teacher, each drew out her sliding seat, sat down and, with the most businesslike air, disposed of her handiwork. The English

---

* No person or company is permitted to send milk into the city who does not conform to the requirements as to air space, cleanliness, protection of the milk, etc., in the cow byres and dairies from which the milk is despatched. The rules are stated to be rigidly enforced.

method of selling the food cooked excited very severe comments: the general opinion was that only by eating her production could a student of any age test its quality and really gauge its short-comings or good points. To require children to handle, smell, see, savoury or sweet dishes, and then to turn their backs upon them was considered a relic indeed of Puritan days. As each Grade School Course includes the making of cake and ice cream (the latter really almost a national dish), on some occasions a truly festive spirit pervades the kitchens. The usual plan is to conclude the whole course with the cooking and serving of a simple three-course dinner, to which are invited some members of the Board of Education, or the Principal and a few of the staff; the young cooks are responsible for the provision, for a given sum, of a suitable and seasonable meal, in sufficient nutritive proportions. The dainty ways and quick perceptions observable in American girls make them deft at the table service upon which such stress is laid during the cooking courses, and "table manners" are by no means neglected. I was glad to hear emphasis laid upon daily care and method rather than upon the occasional display for which this concluding dinner might otherwise set a precedent.

Salaries are a variable quantity, though Toledo is fortunately *Teachers.* conspicuous in its very low scale of remuneration. Those in force at Chicago seem to me a fairly usual average: *i.e.* $500 (£100) the first year, rising by annual increase of $50 or $100 to $900 (about £180). The tendency is for the salaries of special teachers to rise. As each year the standard of training is some-what raised, the Normal and Technical Institute classes are followed by a higher class of women; superintendents also realise the value to the work of "all round" as well as of "special" knowledge, and demand evidence of a good general education as well as expert knowledge. The grade school teacher of cookery is not one apart, she is as highly trained and qualified as any one of her colleagues, and shares their lives and interests. I have reason to believe that the teachers at the Hyde School, Boston, are not unique in their frequently voluntary meetings to discuss the inter-relations between the various subjects for which they are severally responsible, so that intelligent interest may be stimulated by co-ordination of subjects in all the various classes, cookery taking its place on equal terms with history, literature, or languages.

2.—*Needlework.*

Needlework is not an accepted "constant quantity" in a *Of recent* United States public school programme as it is in Great *and limited* Britain. It is not unusual to learn that the introduction of the *adoption.* subject, for so limited a period as even one or two years out of the eight which constitute the full curriculum, coincides only with the comparatively recent adoption of manual training into the schools of such cities as Detroit or Cleveland, and it would be possible to name important towns where no instruction at all in sewing is included in elementary school work.

Various causes are assigned for this fact: (1) There are those who attribute it to the very rapid development of the country, with which its system of education, in spite of its great elasticity, finds it no easy task to keep pace; but a few years since, in many districts the distance to be accomplished to reach a school made the attendance so limited in time that only subjects which could not be acquired at home found a place in the time table. (2) The sudden advancement of industrial fortunes coincident with the country's growth threw the mental perspective of the masses awry, so that parental and public misconceptions of the value and dignity of manual occupations bulk yet as large obstacles to the universal introduction of needlework into the Grade schools. (3) The world-wide, slow-dying delusion that book-learning is the only agent of culture, and that attention should be concentrated upon the printed page during school hours, is still responsible for the continued existence of a monotony of method under some Boards of Education by whom the intellectual stimulus derived from variety of occupation is as yet imperfectly recognised.

Methods of Teaching and Length of Course.

Outside New England the present rapid adoption of needlework as a school subject seems to me the direct outcome of an evident reaction in favour of almost any form of manual occupation. The shortcomings for purposes of absolute exactness in manipulation inherent in the employment of finely-woven, pliable materials, which also make considerable demands on eyesight, and favour "coaxings" to conceal slight inaccuracies, are overlooked or condoned, in view of the other facilities offered. One of the most attractive of these is the small expense incurred by the employment of needlework as a branch of manual training for girls, where boys enjoy the superior advantages, for the special educational object in view, of wood and metal work. To maintain, so far as possible, the parallelism of the two employments, several directors of the subject in different cities have adopted the method of dealing with the various stitches as so many "exercises," to be carried out on pieces of unbleached calico from $4\frac{1}{2} \times 4\frac{1}{2}$ inches square to 9×5 inches in size. These are then fastened into a book, to be retained by the pupil; usually written descriptions, and very frequently excellent pencil sketches, are appended of the position of the hand in sewing, for instance, or the fixing of the material for a bias seam. Unless the acquirement of the usual stitches be followed by their sufficient application to a suitable garment, these "exercises" are decidedly unsatisfactory. All difficulties of manipulation are emphasised by the use of such small pieces of material, insufficient in themselves to provide space for real practice or to reproduce ordinary conditions of employment; and the learner only experiences the discouragement attendant on most first attempts, unmitigated by the subsequent realisation of the power gained through repetition and constant application. This from the utilitarian point of view. From that of manual training, does not the real worth of any "exercise" adopted for this purpose depend upon sufficient time allowance to favour, if possible, to ensure, the individual development of accuracy, facility and skill; does it not almost presuppose sufficient opportunity for repetition, so that success be gained by sturdy strides of independence, though these involve a few bad falls, rather than by carefully guided, faltering, unstable steps, as of an infant, whose leading strings have spared it any hard tumble, but have robbed it at the same time of the healthful spirit of active self-reliance? I am by no means alone in the opinion that these "sample" books, if desired, should form the apex, not the base, of such a course, when their contents would serve to demonstrate the skill gained by long practice on actual garments, rather than the painfully executed handiwork of untrained fingers.

This, at best unsatisfactory, method seemed to me to be carried to an extreme at Toledo, in spite of the undoubtedly good intention of the organiser; all the 5th and 6th grade pupils receive 75 minutes manual training instruction per week. The special teachers visit each school in pairs, a teacher of woodwork and a teacher of sewing together. The mixed classes are divided, and the boys do chip-work on one side of their ordinary class-rooms, while the girls learn to sew upon the other side. The course for each term contains a certain number of problems and pieces, with the object of allowing a pupil to progress slowly or rapidly according to ability, and to secure for each child a fair share of individual attention. Thirty pieces of needlework must be completed during the two years; as a consequence, very small samples of each stitch or its application are possible, and the results, as observed, did not appear very satisfactory. The boys were interested, eager, and happy; the girls uninterested, bored, and rather careless. This introduction to "Manual Training" is succeeded in grades 7 and 8 by cooking for the girls and by carpentry for the boys; the change of attitude among the girls was significant and striking.

The length of these sewing courses as well as the methods adopted are variable; that advocated in "Scientific Sewing and Garment Cutting," by Antoinette Wakeman and Louise M. Heller, illustrates one in common use (this seemed a favourite book with teachers). The latter lady is the originator of a system of cutting out generally adopted, which is guided by simple, easily-comprehended, mathematical principles.

This manual provides for sewing practice throughout the eight public school grades; an exceptional arrangement at present, for there are still cities where girls get no training in needlework under high school age. The usual length of grade school course is two years, though Philadelphia and Brooklyn cover approximately the ground dealt with in Miss Heller's book, during the five years needlework is taught in their schools.

The custom seems general of employing coarse canvas for beginners, and at no period of the grade school course is the use of fine material approved; coloured thread on a cream-toned material is generally employed during the first stages. The methods of instruction and usual scope of practice closely resemble those usual in this country, but I think greater emphasis is laid on the artistic side; grace of form, taste in colour, selection and combination are dealt with at every stage. Large frames with coarse canvas are supplied for the teachers' demonstrations, and a very liberal use is made of the blackboard for illustrative purposes. Satisfactory importance is attached to cleanliness and care in keeping of materials.*

Specimen Courses.

I include a few notes on the courses and methods I observed in different cities, but, as I have already said, there is too wide a diversity of detail in practice to permit of generalisations, while the tenor of the whole is closely allied to what has been long established in England.

(a.) Brookline, Mass.

At Brookline (Mass.) needlework is continued throughout the grades in a few schools where French and Latin are not taught. In the other schools an hour a week is devoted to it from Grades III. to VI. inclusive. The co-educational system is here consistently enforced: boys share these classes with the girls and prove themselves very adept in the use of the needle. An excellent example of home work recurs to my memory in the form of a neatly patched knee in a cloth knickerbocker, executed by the small boy wearer. At this particular school one room was set apart for sewing. The actual method of instruction by the motherly teacher might be described as "old fashioned," but the results secured and the interest aroused spoke volumes for its merits, plus, of course, the personality of the instructress. She mentioned with gratification the increased neatness and attention to personal appearance apparent after a few weeks' attendance in her classes, and referred also to the influence on posture and carriage which follows the making and fitting of simple blouses by the girls in the upper grades. Additional and useful interest is lent to these sewing lessons by the use of a well-proportioned doll, equal in size to a child of three or four years of age, upon which garments of every description are fitted by their makers, who are thus stimulated to accuracy in measurement, care in cutting out, skill in fitting, and to a generally business-like attitude in their manipulation of materials.

---

*Miss Heller describes an inexpensive case in which work and materials can be kept ; which, with modifications for convenience, was to be noticed in several schools.

It consists of a series of nine wooden shelves arranged between two standards, 4½ × 1 ft., placed against a wall. Arranged in tiers of seven on each shelf are strong pasteboard boxes, furnished with small brass rings, so that they can be drawn out with ease. Each box is 12 ins. long by 8 wide by 5 deep. On the front part, beneath the ring, is pasted a slip of paper bearing the name of the pupil whose work is placed in the box. The innate mechanical ability of the Americans shows itself in many little neat, simple devices of this kind, which economise trouble and promote order and cleanliness. At Buffalo, the boys make work-cabinets for the girls' use as part of their manual training. In some Philadelphian schools a simple labour saving appliance is in use, devised and made by one of the staff (Miss Trumble). A piece of stiff card is fitted about 1½ ins. below the surface of a wooden (cigar) box, the card being perforated with rows of oblong holes. At the conclusion of each sewing class the box is carried round by one of the pupils ; each of her companions drops her pair of scissors into one of the slits, the number of which corresponds with the number of scissors in use. The whole number are thus rapidly collected and ready for the next occasion, the absence of a pair is immediately detected, while the scissor blades are protected from damage and dust.

To arouse a similar active spirit of self-help in their sewing (b.) Boston.
classes seems the object of many Boston teachers. At an exhibit
of the year's needlework in one school I saw not only creditable
sewing, especially in the execution of buttonholes, but undergarments and blouses cut out and made at home almost without any
assistance or supervision ; these gave evidence of personal selection
on the part of the maker, combined with efforts to produce what
would be of service at home and satisfactory to the teacher at school.

In the schools of Cleveland, Ohio, manual training includes (c.) Cleve-
sewing, and the whole is under the charge of a male supervisor, land, Ohio.
a not infrequent occurrence ; the work is considered to be
developing satisfactorily. In the earlier grades simple clay
modelling, cutting and pasting of paper into cubes, prisms, etc., is
the rule for both sexes. Subsequently boys have drawing, knife
and wood work, while girls have sewing in grades V. VI. and VII.,
and cooking in Grade VIII. The sewing course covers running,
basting, overcasting, hemming and stitching. These are applied
in grade V. to small model aprons, pillow-slips and laundry bags. In
grade VI., in addition to "review lessons" of stitches previously
learned, corners are "mitred," patches prepared and hemmed,
bands cut and stitched, ruffles gathered and sewn. In grade VII.
buttonholes are made, garments brought from home are darned
and patched, and simple garments are cut out in calico and print.

In Philadelphia, 40 instructors in sewing work are under the
direction of a most able woman supervisor, Miss Kirby. Each of (d.) Phila-
her staff has an assigned district comprising adjacent schools ; delphia.
about 60,000 girls are eligible for, and receive these lessons : Table IV.
boys share the instruction in some schools and are among the
brightest pupils. The course covers six grades (III. to VIII.).
The City allows 6 cents per annum for each child engaged in
sewing. There are two lessons a week of 35 or 40 minutes each.
Every pupil is provided with needles, pins, thimble, scissors,
buttonhole scissors, cotton, dressmakers' scales, emery bags,
drafting paper and calico. Very free use is made of the blackboard by teachers, who endeavour, by question and answer, to
enable each pupil to grasp the underlying principles of their
work. The genuine enthusiasm aroused speaks volumes for the
excellence of the teaching ; great pleasure and pride, of a purely
disinterested character, are taken by the children in this subject,
for neither marks nor promotion depend upon the proficiency
displayed. The reward for progress takes the form of permission
to make some dainty and attractive article, such as an
embroidered petticoat, a smocked frock, a Liberty hat for a
younger member of the family, or some special garment which
appeals to the fancy of the young seamstress. In each grade I
saw specimens of really exquisite needlework, which seemed the
rule rather than the exception. Instruction in how to draft and
cut paper patterns is given systematically throughout the course ;
the elder girls manifestly enjoy the cutting and fitting of a
simple dress and blouse, which form the subject of their last year's
needlework. All the course is carried through in the ordinary
class-rooms ; table accommodation is provided for the cutting out.

TABLE IV.

GRAMMAR SCHOOL COURSE IN NEEDLEWORK, PHILADELPHIA.

LENGTH OF COURSE, SIX YEARS.	THIRD YEAR.		FOURTH YEAR.		FIFTH YEAR.	SIXTH YEAR.	SEVENTH YEAR.	EIGHTH YEAR.
	FIRST HALF.	SECOND HALF.	FIRST HALF.	SECOND HALF.				
Grades III.–VIII.	POSITION.—Of the body, of the thimble finger; of the hand. DRILL.—Threading the needle; taking stitch; holding the scissors. SEWING.—Hemming, basting, fastening a new thread. OVERSEWING. CUTTING. (Pupils who sew reasonably well may bring towels, wash-rags, and similar articles to be hemmed.)	Review work: SEWING.—Running seam; backstitch seam; backstitch and running seam; half backstitch seam. Raw edges of all seams to be overcast. Sewing bags, pillow-slips, oversleeves, iron-holders, and bibs to be made. DRAFTING.—Bibs and simple straight bodices with strap over the armhole.	Review work: SEWING.—Reversible seam; square patches; sheets and tablecloths to be hemmed. Pillow-slips, dust caps, pen-wipers, under bodices with seam over the armhole to be made. DRAFTING.—Yokes; under bodices with seam under the arm; covers to fit books.	Review work: SEWING.—Gathering, darning. Making plain aprons, children's dresses with yokes, aprons with bodice and skirt. Books to be covered; worn garments to be mended; shoe buttons sewed on. DRAFTING.—Under bodices with underarm and shoulder seam; drawers; children's dresses with yokes; infant's nightdress.	Review work: SEWING.—Making narrow hems and fells. TUCKS. STOCKING DARNING.—Patching and angular dress darning. FRENCH FELLS.—Angular patch. FINE GATHERING. BUTTON-HOLES. DRAFTING.—Drawers, combing capes, shoe bags, stocking bags, aprons, under bodices, and plain skirts to be made. DRAFTING.—Drawers, under bodices with one dart and one spring to fit the hip.	Review work: SEWING.—Special attention to be paid to button-holes. Bias seams of all kinds. GUSSETS.—Stockings re-soled. HERRING-BONE STITCH AND FEATHER STITCH for flannel garments. CIRCULAR PATCH. GORED SKIRTS, chemises, blouses, nightshirts and flannel skirts. DRAFTING.—Chemise, gored skirt, dress sleeve, nightshirt, blouse.	Review work: SEWING.—French gathering; button-holes with tailor finish; cutting, fitting, and making plain garments. Special attention given to nightdresses, corset covers, and men's shirts. DRAFTING.—Corset-covers, nightdresses, men's shirts, and night shirts.	Review work: SEWING.—Cutting, fitting, and making garments of all kinds. Special attention to men's shirts and to dresses to fit pupils. DRAFTING.—Dress bodices, skirts, and sleeves.

In Washington, sewing is taken for 1½ hours a week during (e) Washing-
4 years of the school life. The number in each class averages ton.
25 for plain sewing, 18 for the cutting and fitting of plain
dresses; special rooms are provided for these latter classes at
convenient centres, and excellent practical training in more than
mere dressmaking is the result of the method adopted. Mathematical precision is required in the patterns designed and
drafted, "while attention is directed also to the development of
the activities and creative faculties" through drawing and colour
design. The teacher gives frequent "talks" on the processes of
manufacture, illustrated with samples of the various processes
to which each material is subjected, and the girls gain a working
knowledge of how to distinguish good from bad materials. As a
rule, pupils bring a sufficient number of home articles in need of
careful darning for ample practice when that stage is reached in
the course, and the girls are quite commonly enthusiastic enough
to cut out and make blouses for themselves at home, which they
subsequently wear at school for the approval of the teacher and
the admiration of their friends.

The salaries of sewing teachers are, as a rule, similar to Teachers.
those earned by teachers of cooking. At Boston, for instance, the
maximum for both is identical, $936 (£187); but, whereas, the
minimum salary for a teacher of cooking is $532 (£106), subject
to an annual increase of $48 (about £10) that of the sewing
teacher depends on the number of "divisions" for which she is
responsible; thus, in the Annual Report by the Boston Board of
Education, it is stated in School Document No. 2, 1900, that the
salary for a teacher of sewing in one division is $144 (£28), in two
divisions, $240 (£48), three divisions, $336 (£67), and so up to
eleven divisions $880 (£176) the maximum is $936 (£187) for
teachers of over eleven divisions.

The custom of employing specially trained women seems invariable; frequently they are required to be graduates of the
Pratt or Drexel Institutes, or of some other institution of recognised standing. The special training is as a rule supplementary to the general preparation demanded of all teachers;
it includes a knowledge of common textiles and their manufacture, ability to design, draw and draft patterns, practical
acquaintance with sewing machines (hand and foot, of various
makes), the details of needlework, and a certified familiarity with
educational principles as applied in the teaching of sewing.

Although it is a general and advantageous custom to include Dress-
the cutting and making of a simple blouse in the majority of Making,
grade school sewing courses (while in one or two cities the Millinery,
cutting and making of a "housemaid" skirt is utilised to intro- Laundry
duce elder girls to the use of the sewing machine), the instruc- Work not
tion so given could not be described as dressmaking. Grade
Neither that subject, nor millinery, nor laundrywork, have Schools.
yet found a place in the United States elementary schools.
Dressmaking or millinery would be out of place where compulsory school life ends at 13 or 14; of the time devoted to needlework the whole must be expended on the acquisition of its

D

elements. Considerable diversity of opinion prevails as to the
desirability of introducing laundrywork into the grade schools.
Parental opposition appears to be pronounced, and those who
advocate its inclusion are forced to recognise that the time is
not yet ripe. This is the more strange in that most women of
all classes take a more active share in housework than is usual
in this country, and the washing of ordinary articles is generally
done at home; the charges at a public laundry are very high,
double or even treble those general in this country; but it must
be confessed that the results seem to compensate for the cost:
professional laundry work is more of a fine art, more akin to
the best French clear starching than it is in England.

3.—*Housewifery.*

Method of
teaching
Housewifery
in Cookery
Lessons.

Housewifery, as a separate subject, does not appear in
Grade school courses. Great attention is given in the cooking
courses to the cleaning of kitchen fittings and utensils, and to
the cleaning of floor and furniture. A usual method employed
is, towards the conclusion of each lesson, to divide the girls into
groups of two or three; of these one group will wash utensils,
another rinse, a third will dry, a fourth will clean the stove or
sink; another group will put each article in its place, while one
group is told off to superintend and inspect the work of the rest
of the class. As an instance of what care will do, apart from the
incidental training in good methods, I saw saucepans in excellent order in one Boston school which had been used for 9
years by 13 classes weekly with 30 girls in each. The causes
and sources of household dirt, and the reasons why the different
cleansing agents attain their object are usually treated in detail;
experiments are made with the cleaning of metals with different
materials, and their effectiveness is compared; *e.g.*, tarnished brass
articles are rubbed respectively with rottenstone, with rottenstone and water, with rottenstone and oil, with vinegar or with
lemon juice; the results are turned to account for the inculcation of underlying scientific principles, which are thus thoroughly
brought home to the children, who seem to gain an intelligent
comprehension of some of the physical and chemical changes of
matter, to be able to differentiate elements from compounds,
and to understand practically some of the relations and properties of acids, bases and salts. The staining of steel, the
corrosion of tin and other metal ware by potatoes or fruit; the
action of the acids in meat or fruit upon the tins in which they
are preserved when these are opened to the air; the unwholesome
products liable to be so formed; all afford endless opportunities
for the application of these principles, once their existence is
realised, and should foster " systematic knowledge of things pertaining to the home." The subject of " Living and Dead Dust"
treated on similar experimental lines, introduces girls to an
elementary conception of the causes which favour the development of moulds, yeasts, and bacteria; *e.g.*, a piece of bread,
cheese, or some cooked fruit, is exposed to the air for a few days,

covered sufficiently to be kept moist, and the resultant growth Method of
is examined with hand lens and microscope, comparisons being teaching
instituted with specimens kept entirely protected from the air, Housewifery
or allowed to dry. in Cookery
    Methods of household cleanliness outside the kitchen are Lessons —continued.
included in some cookery courses: at Brookline (Mass.), for
instance, a bed and simply furnished room are provided in
one school cooking centre, where the airing and making of a
bed, with the daily care of a bedroom, are taught by demonstration and practice. This is, however, exceptional; such instruction when given, is most usually theoretical, and is ordinarily
deferred to the more advanced High school course.

    Great stress is laid in all cooking courses upon the cost of food
materials, and the relative nutrient properties of food stuffs of different qualities and of various prices, specially in connection with the
different cuts of meat. Thanks to the work of Professor Atwater
and his assistants and to the liberality of the State Department
of Agriculture, a vast amount of more reliable information upon
diet and food-stuffs is gratuitously available in the United States
than in Great Britain, and this is turned to excellent practical
account by good teachers in the schools. It is not the custom
to entrust the outside purchase of commodities to the children
composing a class; to send untrained girls to select articles, a
judgment of whose qualities they are not competent to form, is
regarded as unprofitable. The teacher, without exception,
discusses the price of her own purchases, her reason for selection,
and the signs by which she has been guided; she will also
occasionally take her class to the market and draw their attention
to the choice available and, to the features which should
influence a wise choice. Towards the end of their course the
girls are called upon to practise the drawing up of a plan of a
day's or a week's meals, which must contain a definite amount
of nutriment for a given sum; from a series of these exercises
one menu will be selected for preparation, which is then probably
served to school managers or parents as the finale of the school
year. Reference has been already made to these little functions,
which consist usually of a three-course breakfast or dinner.

    Table service and "table manners" are dealt with very practi-
cally and with repeated emphasis. The girls waiting on the
several occasions when refreshment was served to me during
visits to schools, gave evidence that their dexterity was the
outcome of studied and intelligent practice: the natural
deftness of the American girl makes her an apt pupil where
taste and neatness are demanded. The higher standard of
living which prevails generally in the United States may
account for a rather different attitude towards this part of
the training from that usual in this country, where, so far,
such teaching is confined to our primary schools; nevertheless, in cities like New York, Boston or Chicago, where some
quarters are given up to the poorest and most recently arrived
emigrants, I found dainty methods and refined "table manners"
inculcated and exercised with reiterated care, and not by any means

in the cooking classes only—the "Good Habits Talks" deal constantly with the subject.

4.—*Hygiene.*

An Obligatory Subject. The obligatory inclusion of the elements of Hygiene and Physiology in the time-table of all primary and grammar schools in almost every State of the Union is the direct result of the persistent and successful efforts made to obtain legislation on the subject by the Women's Christian Temperance Union, which advocates this method of arming the rising generation against subsequent temptations to excess in the consumption of either stimulants or narcotics. The extent of this vast influence, which has imposed uniformity in even one particular upon a national system priding itself upon its elastic independence, is not easily appreciated in a country such as ours, where centralisation is the rule, as far, at least, as elementary education is concerned; and though there are some wise and thoughtful minds who question the realisation of the ideal by this means, there certainly appeared to me to be a promise of good fruit, not so much directly from the occasionally crude inculcation of so-called "temperance" doctrines, as, indirectly, from the coincident lessons on good habits, and the simple, reiterated instruction on the beauty and complexity of the human body and its functions. **Attitude of Teachers ; Methods of Teaching.** To these lessons so many hours must be devoted for so many weeks each year for the seven or eight years of elementary education; the very text books employed must, in most States, be submitted to the Council of the Temperance Organisation, before circulation in the schools. Both requirements are really working for good, though at a regrettable expenditure of friction and irritation on the part of those who disapprove of the compulsory introduction of highly debateable topics. The "Good Habits Talks" in the lower grades are not only very popular with the little ones, for they deal chiefly with familiar surroundings, and with that centre of deepest interest to the young child—his own self—but they are found to offer a broad field for the cultivation of other subjects. As these simple lessons gradually develop in the higher grades into more specific treatment of hygiene and physiology, direct stress is laid on the dignity of the body, and its dependence upon environment for the attainment of perfection, emphasis being meanwhile given to the claims of home life in all its relations. Such teaching demands previous acquaintance with the subject by the teachers, especially as the tendency is to encourage practical illustrations; consequently more care is now devoted to the study of hygiene and physiology in the Normal schools and State colleges, with undeniable advantages to the students and their prospective pupils.

The irritation and soreness which followed the adoption of these coercive measures are, though visibly existent, gradually giving place among some of the more thoughtful and intelligent to a recognition of the undoubted value of the subject, when shorn of the questionably desirable obligation to include specific instruction upon the effects of alcohol and narcotics upon the Attitude of human body. Its educational possibilities show themselves to Teachers ; be ample. It excites interest, exercises observation and reason, Methods of links school lessons with daily life, promotes reverence for the Teaching body, suggests reasons for everyday· customs, and lends them a —*continued.* new dignity, fosters good habits, and affords a convenient gathering ground for the clans of nature work, geography, history, science (elementary or advanced), art and physical exercise. Manual work and field trips, both desirable in a well-planned curriculum, are almost essential elements in its study, while in the upper grades, in skilled hands, the first principles of economics and sociology open young eyes to a wider social world than has been hitherto conceived. Already a respectable proportion of superintendents, inspectors and teachers are agreed as to the undoubted claims of hygiene to recognition on other than reforming grounds; while none but affirmative answers were offered to my persistent inquiries as to its attraction for and influence over the children. The somewhat hot partisan spirit apparent in a number of the recognised text-books, to which exception is taken by principals and teachers alike, results also in the more general employment of that preferable method, which discards implicit reliance on the printed page in favour of more apparently spontaneous instruction by the teacher. In some cases the modified laboratory method adopted enables pupils to gain their information at first hand, chiefly by direct observation of the concrete object, though this plan is yet in its infancy. The details of these State laws vary slightly as to numbers of hours and weeks per year that the instruction must find a place in the time-table: the minimum period appears to be 10 weeks, the maximum 6 months annually, with five, four, three or two weekly periods of instruction, given to both sexes, of each grade, in every public school.

A fair presentation of the whole movement and a well-balanced review of the questions involved may be found in the "Educational Review" for March and June, 1902. Superintendent W. B. Ferguson (Middletown, Conn.) takes for his text the recent modification of the State law which was carried a few months ago, and his remarks embody my own impressions of the best educational thought on the subject as I heard it expressed during my recent visit.

In the course of this article Superintendent Ferguson traces the history of what he describes as "one of the most remarkable movements in modern times. The Connecticut statute of 1893 resembled in its general features the statutes of several other States : it was less stringent than the law of New York, Illinois, or New Jersey, but more exact than that of Massachussetts or Pennsylvania." The statute has been in force eight years. "The hope entertained by the Women's Christian Temperance Union of effecting a thorough temperance reform in society by teaching the children the effects of alcohol on the human body rests upon the old Socratic philosophy that knowledge of evil ensures the avoidance of evil, that people do wrong from ignorance only." . . . This instruction was to be given in connection with Physiology and Hygiene, but "temperance was to be made the chief object." The writer points out that the first great

Attitude of
Teachers ;
Methods of
Teaching
—*continued.*

mistake made by the temperance leaders was to compel publishers to revise their text books on "Physiology" and to incorporate in them chapters on narcotics. "These books, therefore, instead of being scientifically accurate, contained statements that contradict both science and the everyday observations of men."

Superintendent Ferguson deals admirably with one reason for the general disapproval of these "endorsed" Physiologies by intelligent teachers, namely "the emphasis placed upon facts—or assumed facts—that appeal to fear, and to negative teaching chiefly, to the disregard of facts that appeal to manliness and the moral nature, and to the omission of much that should be given to emphasise the beauty, nobility, and strength of a temperate life. The poverty, crime and misery of the drunkard are hysterically held up to the gaze of the children, but the steady hand, the distinct speech, the quick senses, the healthy body, the clear brain, the success and happiness of the temperate man are scarcely mentioned. Says Professor S. T. Dutton of Columbia University : "We do not teach hygiene by the study of disease, cleanliness by the observation of filth, nor purity by the contemplation of vice. . . . We teach truth, kindness, generosity by pointing to men and women who exemplify those virtues." Froebel's injunction was so "to fill the mind with the beautiful that there will be no room for the ugly." . . . We do not contend that the evil effects of alcohol and tobacco should never be pointed out to children. They should be, but chiefly in order that by contrast the nobility, strength and success of the temperate life may be made more impressive. . . . This temperance education law had been tried in Connecticut eight years with results that were unsatisfactory to both teachers and temperance leaders, when, suddenly, the widespread opposition to the law that had been gathering force among the educators became manifest and made itself felt in favour of radical modifications. . . . It was suggested that a committee of school teachers be appointed to confer with the officers of the temperance organisation of the State, with eminently satisfactory results. . . . Great honour is due to the temperance people of Connecticut, especially the W.C.T.U., for manifesting a broad-mindedness and a spirit of conciliation which made agreement with the teachers possible. They placed duty before policy, good teaching before any desire for a "perfect" law, and the interests of the children before the fear or pleasure of anybody. The future will show, we believe, that in winning the respect and confidence of the teachers by uniting with them in support of a more reasonable temperance education law they "builded better than they knew." . . . If this statute be compared with that of 1893, the following chief difference will appear, the present law does not require temperance instruction below the fourth grade, nor in the high school ; it does not require the use of text books below the sixth grade, nor the use in any grade of books that devote any definite portion of space to narcotics. Neither does it require the use of text-books by the pupils. All these requirements were definitely specified in the statute of 1893."

It seems probable that similar action will be gradually taken in other States, for which reason I include a reference to the preliminary report of the Committee of the New York State Science Teachers' Association, which is distinguished by its temperate tone, and by its recognition of the unquestionable advantages to be gained if the desired instruction be wisely and scientifically imparted.

The opinions and recommendations submitted in their preliminary Report on "School Instruction in the Effects of Stimulants and Narcotics " by this Committee deals with (1) the discrepancies which exist on this subject between the scientific text books used in Universities and Medical Schools and the "endorsed" text books employed in the public schools; (2) the extreme complexity of the problem involved; (3) a résumé of the opinions of upwards of 200 teachers regarding the present

required methods of teaching physiology; (4) the Committee's
conclusions from their investigations, and (5) their recommendations. No doubt is raised as to the great importance of the
proper study of physiology in both grade and high schools
"because of the practical teachings of hygiene that may be thus
widely diffused," but it is pointed out that so far there is no
evidence " of a marked change of sentiment in the young either
for or against the use of" stimulants and narcotics, while "by
the unpedagogic methods employed (frequent and unnecessary
repetition, the exhibition of charts showing morbid physiological
conditions, etc.) it succeeds only in cultivating in children an
abhorrence of the beautiful and useful science of physiology;"
therefore the recommendations urge modification of the existing
arbitrary laws;—freedom for teachers to decide as to the
character and content of their instruction in physiology and
hygiene; broad truthful teaching on the subject of alcohol and
narcotics until this modification has been effected, time being
devoted to a treatment of the subject from the moral and
economic rather than the physiological standpoint. I have
dwelt thus in detail with the present attitude of the teaching
world towards this question, because of its importance to us in
Great Britain. Daily evidence of the want of self-control in the
use of stimulants confronts even the least observant among us ;
the necessity for checking the continuance of a menace to the
nation's health and prosperity is generally recognised ; the most
effectual methods of inculcating self - control, and removing
causes contributory to its destruction or inhibition are yet to
seek. I believe that our great neighbours across the sea are on
the right road when they include in their school curriculum
lessons in self-respecting patriotism and such a practical
acquaintance with the body and its working as to stimulate
the acquirement of hygienic habits. It will be readily recognised
that meanwhile, and in spite of its limitations, this legal
obligation to include the elements of physiology and of personal
and domestic hygiene in the curriculum of all Primary and
Grammar Schools throughout at least seven - eighths of the
United States results in the devotion of much more attention
to these subjects than would otherwise be the case. As the
primary object has hitherto been to secure to each boy and girl
simple teaching, impressed by constant repetition, on the pernicious
effects of alcohol and narcotics on the human body, the laws
usually demand that one third of the specified time be set
apart for this immediate purpose. Originally the coincident
lessons on the structure, functions, needs and possibilities of the
body were included to supply reasons upon which to base the
special instruction. My observations gave me the conviction
that in the hands of the greater number of superintendents,
principals and teachers, the first has become last; every allowable minute, and possibly a good many more, is devoted to
instilling the general principles of healthy living, the
"temperance" teaching is reduced to a minimum and often
given under protest—wisely so, in the opinion of some who are

qualified to be the best judges. To give lessons of apparent and desirable simplicity on a highly complex subject to immature minds is an achievement possible only to the few, as, for instance, to such rare brains as those of Professors Huxley and Tyndall. The average well-intentioned, but often indifferently qualified, hard-worked teacher is liable to be led into one of two dangers, rash, exaggerated dogmatism, or commonplace, unimpressive, even ridiculous platitudes, neither of which methods attains the really good object.

The subject of Personal and Domestic Hygiene usually, therefore, takes its place not as a branch of domestic economy, but as one among others, in the general school programme; this is the case at Cleveland (Ohio), Buffalo, Washington (D.C.), or Lynn, (Mass.); but it is not uncommon to find it first brought before children in their language or object lessons, or in the nature study course, which last would seem, for good reasons, the most suitable position. These latter methods have been adopted in Philadelphia and Boston among other large cities. Occasionally this teaching on the physical structure and development of the body is connected with the course on "Conduct and Government," or with that on "Manners and Morals," which find a place in the time-tables of some Boards of Education. The most evident advantage which arises from the obligatory prominence assigned to physiology and hygiene is that boys and girls alike share the instruction, whereas if the subjects appear only as incidental to Domestic Economy, as in England, girls alone devote time or attention to their study, and that to a scant degree. As a rule, all the children appear to enjoy these lessons, if at all suitably given, but if there be a preponderance of interest it is on the side of the boys; this is not the observation of a prejudiced witness, it is the confirmed opinion of experienced school authorities.

Typical Courses.

The course at Cleveland, Ohio, has been selected for presentation, because it offers a good illustration of an intelligent method of treatment when physiology forms the backbone of the course and hygiene appears chiefly in the form of applications. The course of study in the Public School of Lynn, Mass., is given as an example of a scheme which starts with the habits familiar to the little ones in home life, supplies reasons for their adoption,

(a) Hyannis Table VI.

and leads up to the structure of the body only in the later years. The third selected course (Hyannis Normal School) also approaches the subject from the familiar side of home habits and is of interest on two accounts (1) as an illustration of the quick observation which enables educators in the United States to remark, appropriate and adapt to their school use, material put into shape in other countries; (2) the fact that this scheme embodies very closely my own views of what should be taught to every child in every school. The original was drawn up four years ago by request of the Council of The Sanitary Institute, with the hope that it might find a place in the Board of Education's Day School Code, a hope not destined to be realised. It was therefore the more satisfactory to find it had been meanwhile successfully adopted in some Massachusetts schools, where it has answered its desired ends to a degree which warrants its employment as a model for students in the Practice school of one of the best Normal colleges.

The children in Grade I. at Cleveland make acquaintance with the human body by first having their attention turned to the appearance, position, number, form, use and beauty of its external parts : this suggests the idea of care being desirable, and emphasises one form of that care, viz., cleanliness. Upon this a talk on the skin and its uses follows naturally, and the proper care of hair and nails is a practical point emphasised. The use of the different senses is then taught objectively, and is incidentally useful as a language lesson also : the children must not only touch objects, and name the sensation, for instance, but must mention other substances and the "feeling" they induce ; so with the parallel exercises on sight, smell, taste, sound. The first year's teaching concludes with very simple lessons on why and what and where and when we should eat and drink. In order to comply with the legal requirements, it is suggested to teachers that "they should make a simple statement that people should not use very strong drink if they wish to have good health." Grade II. revises the previous instruction, with considerable amplification, *e.g.*, attention is called to the relations of the parts of the body to each other, and to the purpose of life ; "the neck turns the head, the arms help the hands to reach, to carry," etc. Prominent bones are identified and named (skull, spine, ribs, hip bones) ; the relations of bones and muscles to bodily posture serve to throw light on motion, and to bring in the application of the need for exercise, rest and sleep. The direct purpose of the lessons on the special sense organs in this Grade is to train the children to greater acuteness in distinctions between sounds, colours, forms, distances, flavours and muscular efforts. The idea of growth and nutrition is next connected with food, also the advantages of cooking food are discussed. Table manners as well as table setting are practised as well as preached ; talks on the lungs and on air, with rudimentary ideas on ventilation, introduce another useful topic.

In Grade III. the same points constitute the basis of instruction. The children find, name, and suggest the uses of many more bones. The connection between food, posture, and good physical development is carried further. The special sense organs are subjected to simple tests, and the pleasure derived by their means is emphasised. Various forms of food, right and wrong methods of preparation and consumption, some idea of the process of digestion and the reasons for habitual care of the teeth again culminate in a talk on table manners and arrangements. The mechanical aspect of breathing is discussed, and the good or ill effects of impure air and out of door exercise, together with suitable means of domestic ventilation, find a place. In Grade IV. the instruction substantially follows similar lines, but assumes a less colloquial form, though the importance of simple treatment is emphasised ; thus, in treating of the heart and circulation, teachers are advised not to touch on the subject of cavities or valves at this stage, but practical applications to assist the formation of good habits are to be invariably included. The outline of work in Grade V. is preceded by the following "General Suggestions" for the course of study in the remaining grades :—

"Never lose sight of the practical side of the subject ; it will profit a child but little to know about bones, for example, if after all he lets his shoulders droop and his spine become unnaturally curved. Pupils should study their own bodies as much as possible. They should find out by actual examination how many bones they have in the arm, hand (not wrist), leg, foot (not ankle), ribs, etc. They should study heart beats, pulse in wrist, neck and temple, weight and height ; chest measure and expansion in inches ; motion of the different joints ; the wonderful motion of the hand and arm ; of the head upon the backbone ; of the whole trunk upon the hip joints. The sight and hearing of pupils may be tested roughly, also sense of touch. The microscope and apparatus in the 8th Grade are free to the teachers of the 5th."

(marginal note:) (*b*) Cleveland, Ohio. Tables V. and VII.

TABLE V.

GRADE SCHOOL COURSE IN PHYSIOLOGY AND HYGIENE. CLEVELAND, OHIO.

GRADE I.	GRADE II.	GRADE III.	GRADE IV.	GRADE V.	GRADE VI.	GRADE VII.	GRADE VIII.
PARTS OF THE HUMAN BODY. Position, number, use, beauty, special adaptation, care. THE SKIN. Use, appearance, structure, care. THE SPECIAL SENSE ORGANS. Their uses taught objectively—what is learnt by touch, sight, smell, taste, sound. FOOD AND DRINK. Simple lessons on what food is, etc. Care of teeth.	PARTS OF THE HUMAN BODY. Amplification of Grade I. Relation of parts to each other, and to the purpose of life. BONES AND MUSCLES. THE SPECIAL SENSE ORGANS. Amplification of Grade I. Main points of structure. Purpose of lessons to the training of senses to greater acuteness. FOOD AND DRINK. Amplification of Grade I. General introduction to growth and nutrition. Why food is cooked. Table setting and table manners.	BONES AND MUSCLES. Find bones, discuss shape and reasons. Bone for bones. Bone growth and habits of posture. Exercise and rest. THE SPECIAL SENSE ORGANS. Pleasure derived from senses. Simple tests of sight, hearing, taste, etc. FOOD AND DRINK. Solid and liquid food. Outline of digestive process. Care of teeth. Meals and Manners, etc. BREATHING. Mechanical aspects. The lungs and their work. Pure and foul air. Value of exercise. Ventilation of bedrooms.	BONES AND MUSCLES. Composition, growth, repair, uses, motion and locomotion. Joint structure. THE SKIN. Construction, uses, baths. FOOD AND DRINK. Digestive process. Manner, time, quantity, frequency of eating. Influences of alcohol and tobacco. CIRCULATION AND RESPIRATION. Work of heart and blood vessels. Respiration. Air and its impurities and purification.	ORGANS OF MOTION. Study bone structures. "Passive" strength. "Active" strength of muscles. ORGANS OF REPAIR. Introduction to study of metabolism in body. THE BLOOD. Composition. Microscopic appearance. Absorption by lacteals. THE LUNGS. Use. Structure. Deep and shallow breathing. Pure air. THE SKIN. Study of hair, nails, etc. ORGANS OF PERCEPTION. Study of tongue, nose, eye, etc.	PHYSIOLOGICAL EXPERIMENTS. To show why bones are hollow. To show animal and mineral parts of bones. Study of fresh bone. Study of fresh muscle. Study of muscle action on sheep's leg and in own bodies. Experiment to show action of diaphragm in respiration. Card models illustrating action of intercostal muscles. Review digestion. Study absorption. The heart and its functions. The nervous system. Location of chief centres, etc.	PHYSIOLOGY AND PHYSICS. Blending of life and matter. Physical & chemical } changes. Experiments. PHYSICAL FORCE. Experiments. THE CIRCULATION AND THE LAWS OF LIQUIDS. (Pressure, capillary attraction, speed, etc.) Experiments. RESPIRATION AND ATMOSPHERIC PRESSURE. (Combustion and Respiration. Physical properties of air, principle of barometer, etc.) Experiment. Dissect sheeps' lungs. Ventilation. DIGESTION AND ABSORPTION. Combination of physical and chemical processes. Effects of alcohol on human body.	THE EAR AND SOUND. Simple Anatomy of Ear. Sound.—(Wave motion, telephone, musical pitch, velocity of sound, etc.). THE EYE AND LIGHT. Simple anatomy of eye. Light.—(What it is, how it travels, velocity, etc.). GENERAL SENSIBILITY AND HEAT. Nerves of Sensibility. Heat.—(What it is, how produced, etc.). Experiments. THE NERVOUS SYSTEM AND ELECTRICITY. Simple anatomy of brain, spinal cord, etc. Cf. a nervous impulse or liberation of energy with electric discharge. Elementary study of electricity. Experiments.

TABLE VI.

GRADE SCHOOLS.—OUTLINE COURSE IN ELEMENTARY PHYSIOLOGY AND HYGIENE. HYANNIS, MASSACHUSETTS.

GRADE I.	GRADE II.	GRADE III.	GRADE IV.	GRADE V.	GRADE VI.	GRADE VII.	GRADE VIII.	GRADE IX.
THE HOME.—Shelter, parts of home; use of each part.	THE HOME.—Materials and necessaries; air, light, space, warmth, etc.	THE HOME.—Choice, aspect, soil, surroundings, comforts, etc.	CLEANLINESS— 1. Of person. 2. Of clothing. 3. Of home. 4. Of school-room. 5. Of town. 6. Of hall and chambers.	EXERCISE.— 1. Use of exercise. 2. Kinds of exercise. 3. Forms of exercise. 4. Time for exercise. 5. Amount of exercise. 6. Place for exercise. 7. Regularity of exercise. 8. Variety of exercise. 9. Dress for exercise. 10. Effect of exercise. 11. Results of exercise. Rest; public Gymnasia.	AIR.—Properties of air; ... causes; ... out of air; ... of ... pure ... and ... ventilation, ... light; ... methods of home ...	FOOD AND BEVERAGES.—Review Grade III. Composition of foods; starch and sugar, fats, proteids; examine milk, cheese, butter.	PERSONAL HYGIENE.—Review of the hygiene that directly relates to the care of the body.	HEALTH OF COMMUNITY— ... laws of ... for ... and cities.
CLEANLINESS.—How homes are kept, how persons are kept.	CLEANLINESS.—Of home, of person, of clothing.	CLEANLINESS.—Of home, of person, of clothing.					1. ...	1 Cleanliness.
DIRT DANGERS.—What makes dirt; effects of dirt.	DIRT DANGERS.—What dirt is; where it comes from.	EATING.—Foods, Classes, and varieties; for different ages; regularity and variety.	CLOTHING.— 1. Uses and materials; advantages—clothes for various seasons; making of clothing; cleaning of clothing.		BREATHING.—Why, how; Organs of breathing; need of breathing; helps, hindrances.	BEVERAGES.—Water, properties, ... impurities...	2. ... 3. (Grade VI.).	2. ... 3. Pure air and water.
EATING.—Meals; when, what, why.	EATING.—Manners, methods.	SLEEPING (rest).—Other resting periods.			Review circulation and exercise.	alcohol... of ... hygiene of eating; risks to food; ...	4. Hygiene of ...	4. ...
SLEEPING.—When, how, why.	PLAYING.—When, where, why.	HEALTH PRESERVATION.—Five laws of health; importance and examples of each.					5. ... (a) in ...ing—fresh air, clothing; (b) in eating—regularity, etc.. ...; (c) in work; (d) in ...ation.	5. ...
HEALTH PRESERVATION.—A treasure, and how to guard it.	HEALTH PRESERVATION.—Mother Nature and her laws.							

Interest in the study of the organs of motion is stimulated by comparisons between the motions of different animals, as horse, fish, worm, man, bird ; the activity of muscles with observations on the results of use upon known substances, leads naturally to the topic of the organs of repair and the material furnished in the form of food, drink, or air. After a review of the processes of digestion, the fact that the digested matter must enter a " common carrier" which has "the right of way" over the entire body, introduces the subject of the blood, and to some teaching on absorption by the lacteals and lymphatics. This and the remaining subjects for this Grade (the lungs, skin and organs of perception) are but lightly treated, as they are repeated in far more detail in Grade VI. Here digestion is reviewed, and absorption is taught more fully. The structure and functions of the heart and the circulation of the blood occupy a great portion of the allotted time, but the concluding lessons are devoted to a preliminary study of the brain, spinal cord, and great sympathetic nervous system, especially to their great importance as instruments of mind and centres of nervous force. Prior to this period most illustrative material is found in observations made by the children, but at this stage teachers are urged to employ simple experimental illustrations, especially "during the winter months, when there is less to observe out of doors." (A few specimens of such illustrations may prove suggestive.)

"To illustrate why bones are hollow : Take a sheet of foolscap paper and roll it into a cylinder about an inch in diameter, holding in shape by means of strings or rubber bands ; support this cylinder in a horizontal position by placing a support under each end. Now place weights upon the middle, noting how much it sustains before breaking. Next, take the same kind of sheet of paper and fold or roll it into a solid bar : support and load as before. Notice the result.

"To show the animal part of bone : Soak a clean bone, as a rib, in strong vinegar or dilute muriatic acid until it becomes flexible. Mineral matter has disappeared.

"To show what part of a bone is mineral : Weigh a small bone accurately, then roast it for about three hours on a hot bed of coals. Remove carefully and weigh again. Animal matter has disappeared. Notice what proportion.

"Saw a bone through lengthwise. Notice the structure of ends, middle, and outside part.

"To show the structure of muscles : Take a piece of lean meat that has been boiled ; pick it to pieces with needles, showing connective tissue and the larger and smaller muscular fibres. Place one of the smallest fibres under a microscope and notice the markings.

"To show the action of the flexor and extensor muscles : Procure the front leg of a sheep. Remove the connective tissues which surround the entire leg, and carefully separate the muscles from each other, loosening up the tendons to where they are attached to the bones. By pulling the different muscles, their function in life can be nicely shown. It will be seen that many muscles act together to cause the same movements : that other muscles are antagonistic.

"Have children notice the swelling of muscles when in action on their own bodies. Let them find the muscle, or set of muscles, which makes certain movements : as, extending the arm, bending the arm, extending or bending the index finger, turning the head to left or right, chewing, etc. Show the muscles as the power acting upon the bones as levers of different classes."

Further suggestions include how to make models to show the principle upon which the diaphragm acts in respiration, or to illustrate the action of the intercostal muscles. Most teachers find no difficulty in improvising or adapting many more of the same kind to meet the need for concrete demonstrations.

The method adopted in the remaining two Grades brings out well a point yet dimly perceived in this country, which is, nevertheless, susceptible of far fuller development than is accorded to it even in this instance at Cleveland, Ohio, viz., the valuable field afforded by hygiene and physiology, not alone for the acquirement of the theories of physics and chemistry, but for their application under most favourable and attractive circumstances. The syllabus opens as follows— (b)Cleveland
Ohio—
continued.

"We do not know what life is, but the mechanism which life has woven and built around itself conforms to the same laws and principles which hold in the physical world, and cannot be well understood without some reference to physical laws. The following outline is an attempt to suggest lessons which will be a blending of the two great departments of science, physiology and physics, life and matter—and the two thus brought together become one, viz., physiology, since all matter and its laws are but subservient to the one great thing—Life.

"As a preliminary to these lessons the teacher should place the minds of the children in the right attitude towards the work. They should know that it is the human body that forms the central figure in all these lessons, and their thoughts should be continually brought back to that fact."

The following is the outline :—"All the manifestations of life, whether individual or national, can be reduced ultimately to certain changes. All changes are of one of two kinds : either changes of place or of composition : the former are known as physical, the latter as chemical. The teacher will illustrate physical changes and chemical changes. Let the children classify the following changes : water evaporates ; dew forms ; coal is mined, transported, thrown upon the fire, burned ; unsupported bodies fall to the ground, trees grow, sugar dissolves in water, a match ignites by friction, gunpowder explodes, water boils, iron melts, iron rusts, grape juice ferments, apples decay, cherries ripen, blood circulates, food digests ; animals inhale air, a certain part unites with the blood, the blood repairs worn-out tissues ; animals feel, children think, sudden news quickens the pulse, etc. Physical force. Muscles exert force. What force is. Other kinds of force than muscular force, as cohesion, adhesion, gravitation, magnetism, electricity, etc. How force is measured ; units of force ; as, pounds, ounces, etc. Weigh many things on spring scales or other kind. Educate the muscular sense by having pupils estimate the weight of many things after *lifting* them.

"By exerting force, muscles produce motion. Some kinds of motion, as uniform, accelerated, retarded, pendulum movements, etc.

"The circulation and the laws of liquids.

"The heart fully explained as to its shape, size, walls, cavities, valves, interior, by means of dissections of heart of ox or sheep. The circulation carefully and minutely traced through both the pulmonary and systemic circuits.

"The circulatory system compared with the distribution of water in a city ; the heart, arteries and capillaries and veins having their analogies more or less perfectly in any city supplied by a pumping station.

"Study, in connection with the circulation, the effect upon liquids when subjected to pressure ; also capillary attraction.

"Respiration and atmospheric pressure. Why we breathe ; the relation of air to the blood. Show nature of oxygen and carbon dioxide. Experiment with lime water to show that breathing and burning give rise to same products. Relation of plants and animals as regards the air. Show simple experiments in atmospheric pressure. Connect the facts of the physical properties of air with the organs of breathing, showing that it is a purely physical process. Teach the mechanism of breathing ; ribs, intercostal muscles, abdominal muscles, diaphragm, trachea, bronchial tubes, air cells, and how all operate together, thus forming the respiratory apparatus.

"Dissect lung of sheep, showing lung tissue and air tubes.

(*b.*) Cleveland, Ohio —*continued.* "Perform, if possible, the experiment with mercury and barometer tube to show the principle of the barometer.

"Ventilation. Why necessary : how performed.

"Digestion and absorption. Relation of these processes to the blood.

"Digestion is performed by a combination of physical and chemical processes, while absorption is identical with the taking up of moisture by the roots of plants. The effect of alcohol upon the body in general and in particular should receive a large measure of attention."

THE SUGGESTIONS FOR GRADE VIII. ARE GIVEN IN FULL.

The Ear and Sound.

"Teach as much of the anatomy of the ear as is found in any elementary physiology.

"The ear constructed with reference to sound.

"Sound. What it is. Wave motion shown by rope. How sound is produced. Show by using tuning fork, small bell or large glass dish, that a sounding body is vibrating. Show how sound travels through the air : string telephone : experiment to prove that sound will not pass through a vacuum. Velocity of sound in air : echoes. Musical sounds : pitch, loudness.

"Having studied the ear and sound to some little extent show how the former is adapted to receive the latter : trace a sound wave from a distant bell through the air, into the ear, through its different parts until the ends of the auditory nerve are excited.

"Test the hearing of pupils.

"What knowledge is brought to us by the sense of hearing.

The Eye and Light.

"The anatomy of the eye. The eye-ball and its surroundings. Muscles to move. Why located where it is. The cornea, sclerotic coat, choroid, iris, lens, retina, aqueous and vitreous humour. Drawings of eye made. Light and what it is. Travels in straight lines (nearly) through the air. Velocity : how found. Reflection.

General Sensibility and Heat.

"Why our sense of heat should be distributed over the entire body. What heat is? Various ways of producing by mechanical action, by combustion.

The Nervous System and Electricity.

"The anatomy of brain, spinal cord, nerves, sympathetic system, taught by use of chart. Do not go too deeply into structure of brain, a very general notion only. Show that the nerves bring all parts of the body into a sympathetic relation. A nervous impulse is a discharge or liberation of energy analogous to the electric discharges : not identical but having an analogy so near as to make the study of electricity in place in this connection : occupies time. Experiment.

"Teach paralysing influences of alcohol and narcotics upon nervous tissues, and especially upon the brain. Discuss other physiological reasons why stimulants and narcotics should not be used : also moral aspects of drinking alcoholic stimulants."

Throughout the whole eight years teachers are incited to maintain a close connection between nature study and human physiology; applications are also required and introduced in his classes by the Physical Culture Instructor. At the teachers' quarterly meeting when this among other subjects is discussed between the supervisors and their staff, unremitting efforts are made by the former to present suitable suggestions of how associations may be created between these subjects and daily life, either by judicious co-relation with other subjects, or by the constant diffusion of a general atmosphere of healthful habits around and among the children. Teachers are also furnished with a list of suitable books of reference: "Physiology for Little Folks," "The House I live in," and Blaisdell's "Our Bodies" for the earlier grades: Huxley and Youman's "Physiology," and Shaw's and Gifford's and Avery's "Physics" for the later.

The complete curriculum at present in force in the Grade schools of Cleveland, Ohio, is detailed, as it appears to be a good specimen of such time-tables, and brings out clearly the proportion of hours devoted each week, throughout the compulsory school life, to the various studies, mental, moral, physical, manual, and so forth, upon which the attention of the children is concentrated. Hitherto sparse attention has been given to physiology in the Cleveland Normal School, a defect to repair which no pains is spared by the Superintendent of the City Schools. Admirable and exhaustive courses of lectures to the teachers are given by the Medical Officer of Schools, Dr. R. Leigh Baker, or by other authorities, and the sincere interest exhibited in the lessons by their supervisors must prove a useful impetus to good work.

The school course at Lynn (Mass.) also shows the position assigned in the time-table to civics, elementary science, and morals and manners, as well as to hygiene. This last subject is divided into two parts: the first treats of good habits, of what the children do daily; the second takes up the study of physiology. Teachers are advised to begin by brief and simple conversations, to direct children to their own experiences and observations at home, at school and elsewhere, and to bring out the elements of healthy living: eating, drinking, working, resting, sleeping, playing, cleanliness. It is intended that children should then be led to see what parts of the body are brought into use through the actions noticed; to see why these parts are useful, how they should be cared for, and why exercise, rest, and pure air are necessary. Among the many suggestive "Notes to Teachers" the following is one of the most valuable:—"In order to impress upon the children the importance of correct living, the teacher must practise in school what she teaches. She should see that the schoolroom is kept clean, that the heat is properly regulated, that the air is kept pure by proper ventilation, that the children are not subjected to dangerous draughts, that the light is suitable, that the physical exercises, songs, and other diversions are used at the right time, so far as these things are under her control or influence. She should see that the children observe the hints on cleanliness of person or clothing, that they take proper care of themselves and their garments, etc."

(c.) Lynn, Mass. Tables VIII. and IX.

TABLE VII.

CLEVELAND PUBLIC GRADE SCHOOL WEEKLY TIME TABLE.

Grades I–IV (h. m.)

Grades	I.	II.	III.	IV.
Reading	9 10	8 5	8 45	5 35
Spelling	1 —	2 5	1 40	2 5
Language				
Constructive Work				
Composition				
Nature Study	2 5	2 55	2 25	1 15
Literature				
History				
Industries				
Conduct and Morals				
Geography	6 40	6 40	6 40	6 40
Physiology and Hygiene	0 25	0 25	0 25	0 25
German	0 25	0 25	0 25	3 20
Arithmetic	2 30	3 35	3 45	6 10
Manual Training	0 40	1 0	1 0	0 45
Drawing	1 0	1 0	1 0	1 5
Penmanship	1 30	2 5	2 5	1 30
Music	1 6	1 15	1 0	1 5
Physical Culture	0 50	0 50	0 50	0 50
Recesses	0 25	1 40	1 40	1 40

Grades V–VI (h. m.)

Grades	V.	VI.
Reading	3 15	3 15
Spelling	1 15	1 15
Language		
Constructive Work	1 15	1 15
Animal study (1st mth.)		
Plant Study (7th, 8th and 9th months)		
Industries (3rd and 5th months)		
History with Conduct and Civics (2nd, 4th and 6th months)	1 15	1 15
German	2 0	2 0
Literature & Composition	2 20	2 5
Physiology & Hygiene	0 40	0 40
Geography	3 55	3 55
Arithmetic	3 55	3 55
Manual Training	1 0	1 0
Drawing	1 10	1 10
Penmanship	1 10	1 10
Music	1 10	1 10
Physical Culture	0 50	0 50
Recesses	1 40	1 40

Grades VII–VIII (h. m.)

Grades	VII.	VIII.
Reading	2 5	2 10
Spelling	1 10	1 1
Language		
Grammar	3 10	3 0
Composition on General Subjects / Special Composition (VII) — General Composition (VIII)	0 40	0 40
Elementary Science		
Physics (VII) / Botany (VIII)		1 5
Botany (VII) / Physics (VIII)		
Astronomy		
Lauer Literature	1 20	1 5
German	2 40	2 40
Physiology & Physics	0 40	0 40
History	2 40	2 40
Arithmetic	4 25	5 0
Manual Training (VII) / Penmanship, Book-keeping, and Manual Training (VIII)	1 0	1 40
Drawing	1 10	1 15
Penmanship (VII)	1 10	
Music	1 10	1 15
Physical Culture	0 50	0 50
Recesses	1 40	1 40

TABLE VIII.

LYNN GRADE SCHOOL CURRICULUM.

	I.	II.	III.	IV.	V.	VI.	VII.	VIII.	IX.
Reading.	Reading.	Reading.	Reading.	Reading.	Reading.	Reading.	Reading.	Reading.	Reading.
Spelling.	Spelling.	Spelling.	Spelling.	Spelling.	Spelling.	Spelling.	Spelling.	Spelling.	Spelling.
Vertical writing.	Vertical writing.	Vertical writing.	Vertical writing.	Vertical writing.	Vertical writing.	Vertical writing.	Vertical writing.	Vertical writing.	Vertical writing.
Arithmetic.	Arithmetic.	Arithmetic.	Arithmetic.	Arithmetic.	Arithmetic.	Arithmetic.	Arithmetic.	Arithmetic.	Arithmetic.
Hygiene and physiology.	Hygiene and physiology.	Hygiene and physiology.	Hygiene and physiology.	Hygiene and physiology.	Hygiene and physiology.	Hygiene and physiology.	Hygiene and physiology.	Hygiene and physiology.	Hygiene and physiology.
Manners and morals.	Manners and morals.	Manners and morals.	Manners and morals.	Manners and morals.	Manners and morals.	Manners and mora's.	Manners and morals.	Manners and morals.	Manners and morals.
			Geography.	Geography.	Geography.	Geography.	Geography.	Geography.	Geography.
Language.	Language.	Language.	Language.	Language.	Language and grammar.	Language and grammar.	Language and grammar.	Language and grammar.	Language and grammar.
History stories.	History stories.	History stories.	History stories.	History stories.	History (American narratives).	History (American narratives).	History of the United States.	History of the United States.	History of the United States.
							Civics.	Civics.	Civics.
					Elementary science.	Elementary science.	Elementary science.	Elementary science.	Elementary science.
Observation lessons on place and position.	Observation lessons on place and position.	Observation lessons on place and position.	Observation lessons on place and position.	Observation lessons on place and position.					
Observation lessons on natural and physical phenomena.	Observation lessons on natural and physical phenomena.	Observation lessons on natural and physical phenomena.	Observation lessons on natural and physical phenomena.	Observation lessons on natural and physical phenomena.					
Observation lessons on people and occupations.	Observation lessons on people and occupations.	Observation lessons on people and occupations.	Observation lessons on people and occupations.	Observation lessons on people and occupations.					

TABLE IX.

LYNN GRADE SCHOOL—COURSE IN HYGIENE AND PHYSIOLOGY.

Grades I. and II.	III. and IV.	V.	VI.	VII.	VIII.
Simple talks on topics treated in detail in subsequent Grades. Teachers are directed to lead the children to do daily, and to train daily living, by giving them correct general notions on this point as far as they can comprehend.	HOME.—Its people, and what they do. EATING.—The meals. FOOD.—Various kinds. HOW TO EAT.—Manners at table. SLEEPING.—When; how much. WORKING.—At home; at school; with hands and head; why. PLAYING.—Why; how. RESTING.—When; why. CLEANLINESS.—Of person; of clothing; of rooms. BAD HABITS. *Note.*—Children should be led to see what parts of the body are brought into use through the service and exercise noticed; to see why these parts are useful; how we should care for them; how to avoid injury and properly to exercise them. Children are trained to see that *exercise, rest,* and *good air* are always necessary. Teachers must attend to the use of daily breathing and physical exercises in the school.	Extend work of Grade IV., and emphasise its importance. FOODS.—Their kinds; quantity; adaptation to special purposes; cautions, etc.	DIGESTION.—Organs and processes with effects of drinking and smoking habits. Hindrances to digestion; cautions. ABSORPTION AND CIRCULATION.—Organs and processes; hygiene of; cautions.	RESPIRATION.—Organs; processes; hygiene of. NERVOUS SYSTEM.—Growth; hygiene; exercise; cautions. In Grades VII. and VIII. suggestions should be given in	SKELETON AND MUSCULAR SYSTEM.—Structures; uses; hygiene; repair; cautions. SPECIAL SENSES.—Light; smell; taste; hearing; touch. cases of accidents.

The lessons are illustrated at first by using the pupils (c) Lynn, Mass—continued. themselves, the school buildings, or common objects easily obtainable. Charts and experiments are employed in the higher grades, but it is not usual to make use of fresh animal tissues or organs, as it is at Cleveland. Advantage is taken of opportunities offered for correlation with the "Observational Lessons" on natural and physical phenomena, and on people and occupations, as well as with the Nature Work and Elementary Science later on. This inter-relating method is turned to account also in connection with the history, geography and civics taken in the upper grades. The details of all courses are left to the discretion of his staff, by Mr. O. Bruce, the Superintendent of the Lynn Schools, so that the personal equation of the teacher may find expression, and the special needs or interests of the class be consulted. Two demands he makes, and expects to have met; the one, that each lesson be well prepared and presented, in order to arouse, direct and maintain a wholesome interest among the children—the other, that his staff and their school houses shall be living object lessons of hygienic practice to the town.

Similar good methods and terms of advice to teachers are (d) Massachusetts. found under other Boards and Superintendents. The Massachusetts Board of Education, *e.g.*, in its published "Course of Studies for Elementary Schools" suggests the following as a method of teaching physiology and hygiene to children which has been tested and proved successful by experience:—

Section 1. The Whole Body.

Position. Teach the pupils to observe their own and others' positions while sitting, standing and walking. Teach them to desire and to strive to be erect. The lessons on height and weight should be to this end. Height. Each pupil should know his height. Mark the height of a pupil on an unused blackboard or door jamb : record the date, the height, and weight, beside the mark. Do the same for three or four pupils. Repeat the measurement at regular intervals. Encourage other children to have the same done at home by their parents or by older children. Have children compare their growth during different intervals. All the lessons should tend to producing and retaining correct posture and carriage. Weight. Do the same as for height. The practice of measuring height and weight should be continued through the period of growth.

The External Parts of the Body.

Pupils should touch and name the parts in regular and irregular order. Care of parts. Each child should be taught to take proper care of his hair, eyes, nose, mouth, teeth, hands, feet and nails. Cleanliness of the body, and the clothing should be insisted upon daily before the school exercises are begun.

The Senses.

Teach by simple experiments what each sense is, the parts that are prominent in structure and delicate in sensibility, the uses of the important parts, the knowledge gained by each alone, and the care of each sense. Avoid in experiments all sources of error, such as learning through touch what ought to be known by hearing.

In Section II. which comprises the next three classes, attention is directed to the limbs and structure of the body, the following extract indicating the method advised :—

Section II.   The Limbs and Walls.

Skin, muscle, tendon, blood, blood vessels, nerves, fat, bones, joints, ligaments, cartilage.

Sources of knowledge. The body. At home—fur, raw and cooked beef, leg of a fowl, veal, lamb. At the market—sides and cuts of beef, mutton and pork, bones. At school—shank of beef, bones, pictures, diagrams, books.

What to teach. The organ : its chief characteristics and its name ; its position and uses ; how it should be cared for ; the effects upon it of alcohol and narcotics.

Method. 1. Find what is known. 2. Teach pupils to observe the organ ; to observe its uses ; to learn its care from experience, home training, from knowledge of use, from reading. 3. Contribution of facts. Selection and arrangement of facts by pupils. 4. Oral and written descriptions, drawings with and without objects, according to outline. 5. Reading of selected articles. Suggestions. Observations of corresponding parts in other animals. (Teach to put a piece of sticking plaster on a wound ; to cleanse and bandage a cut ; to assist one who is weak.)

The remainder of the course is devoted to the consideration of food, air, clothing, removal of waste, exercise and rest, the necessary illustrations being gathered by the pupils and added to by the teacher ; the nutritive, digestive, circulatory, respiratory, motory and nervous systems being considered and studied in Section III. by the higher grades. Teachers are exhorted to avoid technicalities as far as possible with the younger pupils, to make use of numerous simple experiments, and to let rules for the proper care and use of the different organs, systems or functions of the body be repeated and re-enforced. Special attention to the interdependence of vital processes is advocated, and the ideal of a strong, wholesome and unabused body as best fitted for successful and happy living is kept constantly and conspicuously in the foreground. In consequence of the law which requires special instruction in schools as to the effect of alcoholic drinks, stimulants and narcotics on the human system, these subjects appear in each section of the course, but the teachers are cautioned to deal only with the more serious consequences, just enough to attain the purpose of mentioning them at all, to refrain from assertions of what is uncertain or sincerely doubted by high authority, or likely to be repudiated by the pupil when he is mature enough to judge for himself. If the children thoughtlessly incline to make merry over the weakness, or folly, or misfortune of persons visibly under the influence of alcohol, their teachers are advised to lead them to a truer and more serious attitude towards such things, dwelling on the personal effort and capacity necessary to form good habits and to avoid bad ones, and showing by illustration, that the man needs a strong and beautiful body if it is to be sound and well balanced. Special delicacy of treatment is pointed out as necessary in those unfortunate cases where children find themselves between the safe teaching of the school and the counter practices and influences of home.

(e) Washing-
ton, D.C.
Good methods and wise counsels to teachers find admirable illustration at Washington, where the enthusiasm, on occasion limited elsewhere to supervisors, extends to most members of the staff. This is largely due to Mrs. I. G. Myers, who has been responsible for many years for the Normal School curriculum and has also had an intimate connection with the schools themselves.

The following extract from the "Outline of Work for 1901" speaks for itself as to the personal practice which it is assumed should accompany the teachers' precepts:—

"To the teacher—

"Study the ventilation of your own building and schoolroom. Know how to secure the best possible fresh air conditions for the children and for yourself. Test this frequently by going from the room for a minute, returning sensitive to vitiated air. Keep a fraction of the mind on temperature, to see that it is the proper one. Have a watchful care to the adjustment of shades, for the best distribution of light. Be mindful of the seating of pupils having defective sight, so that their defects may lessen by fostering care. The direct aim of the early study of physiology is the intelligent care of the body. The formation of healthful and refined habits is the end to be secured."

In Grades IV., V., VI., VII., and VIII. advantageous place is found for the elements of sanitation. The skin, nails, hair, and teeth are first studied in Grade V., then appears the following note : "Study the conditions of a healthful schoolroom : sunlight, its effect ; dust, its dangers ; fresh air, its value ; temperature, what it should be. Let the responsibility for this care gradually pass from the teacher to the pupils, by whom in turn, it should be sustained, with intelligence and conscience." In Grade VI. sanitation comprehends "The care of the sleeping room ; a kitchen sink, use, construction, care, risks from want of care, etc." In Grade VII. air and ventilation are required to be treated experimentally and "practically ; " and sewer gas, its nature, effects, and dangers, is considered in connection with the city regulations for plumbing. The physiology in Grade VIII. is confined to a simple general study of the nervous system : the sanitation concerns itself with the sources of diseases, germs and their conditions of development, a study of simple disinfectants (sunlight, soap, and water, par excellence), and concludes with an introduction to municipal sanitation (sanitary dwellings, street cleaning, sewerage, garbage, contagious diseases, etc.). Appended is this suggestion : "Combine this unit with the study of city government ; " the force and worth of which note is appreciated when the fact is recalled that boys of 13 or 14 constitute half the pupils who come under this instruction. No text-books are suggested for use until Grade IV., then "The Child's Health Primer" and Stowell's "Essentials of Health" are named as suitable ; but long and valuable lists of reference books are appended for the teachers' use throughout the course, all of which are available at the teachers' library. Among books on general physiology, Foster's, Colton's, Tracey's, and Bertha Brown's find a place, with Ball's "Care of the Teeth," Mercier's "Nervous System and the Mind," Rosenthal's "Muscles and Nerves," and Lagrange's "Physical Exercise ; " Billing's and Morrison's excellent books on Ventilation and Heating, and Prudden's "Dust and its Dangers" and "Story of the Bacteria" are also included, besides the Annual Reports of the Health Department and references to articles in current literature.

Practical methods and field trips are advocated, and unusual trouble is taken to inter-connect this with other school studies. The much talked-of principle of correlation is practised with most encouraging results in the Washington schools, though all concerned are aware that but the first steps along this right road have yet been taken.

At Philadelphia the Good Habits Talks find a place among object lessons in the four primary grades. *(f)* Phila-delphia.

In view of the well-recognised fact that eating and drinking bulk largely in a small child's mind, the conversational lessons open on articles of food and drink (bread, beef, mutton, coffee, tea, butter, cheese, rice, fruits), and from what natural objects these are obtained, followed by a similar treatment of common articles of clothing. In Grade III. the care of the human

(*f*) Phila-
delphia—
continued.

body, by means of cleanliness, clothing and breathing fresh air, gives occasion for much useful talk, so that by the time Grade IV. is reached (the children being from 9 to 10 years old), curiosity is aroused as to the general structure of the body and the means by which it receives sensations. During the remaining four years the physiological and hygienic aspects of the study are well balanced in treatment, as is evidenced by the written notes of the more advanced grades. By the courtesy of Miss Wright, one of the Board of Education Supervisors, I have been furnished with a large number of notes made by pupils in Grade VIII., executed without previous notice in the ordinary course of work, and handed to me without revision as they left the writers' hands. Of these, forty papers are on the nervous system ; they are clear, well expressed, and, as a whole, satisfactorily accurate ; the plentiful introduction of pen and ink drawings illustrate the facility attained in this mode of expression by an American child. Each paper contains a verbal sketch, illustrated, of the cerebro-spinal and sympathetic nervous systems, and highly creditable drawings of the under surface of the brain, showing the cerebrum, cerebellum and medulla oblongata ; each paper concludes with the hygienic applications to be made of the knowledge gained, couched in evidently original language :—— "It is the worry in many cases that causes nervous sickness." "To keep our body in health also tends to keep the nervous system in health, as the blood which nourishes the nervous system must be pure and good. . . . The nervous system can be easily abused, sitting up late at night, overtiring the body, reading cheap novels and going to the theatre too much all tire the brain." The following extract from one of the best papers illustrates the danger, to which reference has been made as so liable to arise from well meant efforts to simplify a complex, and, as yet, incompletely understood subject ; though the general tenour is excellent some of the daring assertions on the part of the pupil are inaccurate and misleading. "The use of narcotics, strong drink and opium all tend to weaken the nervous system. The alcohol gets into the blood, takes away all the healthful parts of the blood and it gets into the nerve tissue which is very watery, and the alcohol dries up the water and takes its place, and when the alcohol is once in the nerve tissue it is very hard to get out, so for this and other reasons, alcohol should be avoided by every sensible person. Opium and all other drugs should be equally avoided, the craving is very hard to get rid of and will often be inherited by the victim's innocent children. The opium has a deadening effect that is very dangerous, often resulting in death ; all the patent medicines and cough cures often have a form of opium in them, and they should be avoided as a household remedy, as the effect on children especially is very dangerous."

Even more striking is another set of papers from the same school for the variety in verbal expression of identical facts and the really beautiful pen and ink drawings of the structure of the ear, including separate illustrations of its parts. The evident grasp of the theory of sound, in addition to the fitness of the human ear for the transmission of sound waves, is most apparent, and the remarks on the care of the ear are simple, rational, common sense. A third set of papers deals with the eye and also merits high praise. Sketches enter even more fully into these notes, and are used with great effect to illustrate and assist to shorten written descriptions. It is evident that the hygienic applications have been well impressed, though a number of the writers wisely omit any notes on the effects of alcohol and tobacco on the eye, which are reported by others in words similar in substance to the following extract from one paper :—

"Effect of Alcohol on the Eye.—It in a general way dulls or weakens the nerve. Alcohol is known to produce congestion of eyes. It irritates the delicate linings of the eyelids and lessens the acuteness of vision.

"Effect of Tobacco on the Eye.– Tobacco smoke irritates the eyes. It causes sharp pain of the eyeball. Smokers often have confused and feeble vision due to partial paralysis of the optic nerve."

These papers are home-work on an assigned subject which had been previously studied in class, and rank as " Composi- tions; " the sketches are allowed to be copied from diagrams or objects. The execution of these careful drawings has various values, in addition to the inevitable mental impression received of relation of parts, of form and of structure ; accurate observa- tion, neatness, precision, manual dexterity, reliance upon means other than verbal for expression, the employment of facility gained in another branch of study, are all called into play. The method appears in general use. I have specimens of similar, though less advanced, notes collected in the course of a visit to some schools at Providence, Rhode Island, where pencil illustra- tion rather than verbal description is relied upon. Bone structure, the mechanism of a joint, the shape and arrangement of the teeth, the position of the organs in the thorax and abdomen are drawn ; and usually six or seven written lines are considered to supply the necessary letterpress.

Good papier-maché models and anatomical charts are provided Illustrative under some Boards of Education, but a majority of those teachers Methods. whose previous training or post-graduate courses enable them to approach the whole topic from its practical side. confirmed my own opinion that one illustration from life or a familiar object, one demonstration on animal tissues, such as the leg of a rabbit or the eye of an ox, is worth more as a means to convey a true conception, to arouse active interest, or to stimulate subsequent observation than the free use of costly models. The extent to which this " better " way is followed depends upon the attitude of the Supervisors or school principal, and the capacity and en- thusiasm of the teacher. The same spirit which has prompted the rapid introduction of the " laboratory method" into high schools and colleges is permeating the whole world of education, with a promise of good things to come for this as for other suit- able subjects.

Special lessons upon the care of young children are not The Care of usual in the public schools, though exceptions to the rule exist Young in New York City, Washington, and very probably elsewhere. Children. In respect of sensible clothing, England can learn with advan- tage from the United States where babies, from birth, have necks, arms, and legs completely and continuously protected. The artificial feeding of infants is chiefly in the hands of physicians, who write individual prescriptions to be " made up " at milk laboratories instead of at chemists' shops; and this cus- tom was, in my experience, a reason frequently advanced for not giving instruction on the subject of " bottle fed " babies in schools. At Buffalo the use of tube bottles is forbidden by law. I do not know whether such enactments have been made elsewhere, but in this city the result within a comparatively short time was to reduce the rate of infantile mortality by one- half. At the New York cookery centres the girls learn how to

sterilise and pasteurise milk ; how to modify cow's milk to meet
the needs of infants at different age periods ; how much food to
give and how often to feed; what are and what are not the
right shapes for feeding bottles. They also learn how to make
barley water and foods suitable when the child begins to require
other than milk diet. " What Baby must not have," needs to
be well impressed in the poorest quarters of that city as well as
in our own towns. Regular instruction is not given at Washington, but Mrs. I. G. Myers occasionally takes the elder girls alone,
at one or other school, for personal instruction in nursery
hygiene as well as in the wise care of their own health.

B.—HIGH SCHOOLS.

To confine the following remarks to the teaching of the
Domestic Sciences and Arts, and Hygiene in the public high
schools is to omit, for the present, reference to some excellent
examples of secondary school courses supported by private endowment, e.g.—those at the Pratt and Lewis Institutes, which
will be treated in Part II. Nevertheless, adherence to the
division of educational institutions into the two groups of
those maintained by State funds or from private resources will,
it is hoped, enable those unfamiliar with the intricacies consequent upon this parallel dual system to assign to each its just
relative proportion to the mass of good work accomplished
by both.

Curricula.   Domestic Science is classified, almost without exception, as
Manual Training under all Boards of Education into whose
high schools it has been introduced. The reason for this is
found substantially in the system of co-education. If the girls
of a division devote so much time per week to a subject from
which boys are excluded, their occupation during these " periods "
must be of a character inapplicable to girls. Manual training is
widely recognised as desirable for both sexes and is therefore
conveniently, if not quite accurately, extended to cover cooking,
sewing, laundry and table service, as well as its more legitimate
subjects, work with clay, card, wood, or metal. It must always be
borne in mind that a proportion of authorities maintain the
" training" value of all these occupations to be equal. In large
cities which support several high schools, one of these is usually
set apart for the express purpose of offering special facilities in
manual training to both sexes, and is so denominated; not that
all Manual Training High Schools necessarily include domestic
subjects in their curricula, but they do so in many cities, and, I
believe, to an annually increasing extent. At Providence (Rhode
Island), at Ann Arbor (Mich.), and in the early days at
Philadelphia, cookery and even sewing, appeared in the time
tables of high schools before adoption into the grammar schools :
but Brookline, (Mass.), offers an illustration of the more
general tendency, viz., to include an introductory course in both
subjects in the elementary schools, and to encourage further
study and practice in the high schools.

As a rule, high schools provide a choice of courses for their
students, usually from five to eight in number; these

are described as General, Classical, Scientific, Latin-German, English preparatory, Commercial, Manual, etc. The base of most of them is very similar during the first two out of the four years of high school life, by which means differentiation or specialisation is postponed until about 16, and premature specialisation avoided at 14 years of age. Domestic Science may constitute a required subject in the General, Technical, or Manual Training courses, as it does, *e.g.*, at Brookline (Mass.), or it may be an "elective," open to all girl students, as at Ann Arbor and Muskegon. When house sanitation plays a prominent part this section of the course is occasionally thrown open to boys, as is the case at the Toledo Polytechnic School.

The scope of the whole course is often very comprehensive, as the arts are included to an extent not usual in this country (considerable time being devoted to the practice of design, clay modelling, drawing, and to some study of colour), while it would be hard to find one scheme which does not require, or include in itself, a study of general chemistry, elementary physics, and an introduction to the first principles of bacteriology; some suggestions on economic and sociological problems are also brought forward, with a view to widen the girls' horizons and to prepare them for their future positions and obligations. It is evident, therefore, that valuable opportunities await those who approach such courses in the attitude of mind anticipated by the experts responsible for their formulation. During her four years' study an intelligent girl devotes time to theoretical and experimental work in chemistry, physics and biology, usually with special reference to their practical household applications, which she at once proceeds to test in her cookery, laundry and cleaning practice. Her hands and eyes are trained in the studio, so that she may bring skilful manipulation, habitual accuracy, and an eye for form and colour to her classes in sewing, dress-making and millinery. She is called upon to make personal observations on sanitary house construction, and then to repro-duce, or to originate, the plans for a healthy dwelling; here she is required to have good reasons for all her details and to be as practical in her knowledge of plumbing possibilities and risks as she is in her scheme of colour decoration for the rooms. Cal-culation of cost must be carried out with care and the economics of family life studied. She is trained to realise that mere provision of food and clothing does not fulfil the housewife's duty; meals at reasonable cost must furnish requisite nutriment in wholesome, varied forms, with the details of which she should be familiar; clothing must fulfil many more requirements than mere surface show—how to ensure these constitutes a part of her study. She perceives how responsible is the woman for the expenditure of a household, and gets her first glimpse by this means into the sociological problems of to-day. Time has to be found for gaining an insight into the special care essential for infants and invalids; while, most wisely, the study of literature, and, if possible, of one or two modern languages, maintains, throughout, the necessary connection with the wide world of

Scope and Value of Domestic Science Courses.

Scope and
Value of
Domestic
Science
Courses—
continued.
experience, thought and culture, of which each home reflects a part.

Needless to say, the realisation by the pupils of all these ideals is not as yet contemplated in every high school; but, where the effort is made, there is already warranty of eventual attainment. At this age period, more than at that of any other, the mental attitude of teachers is quickly observed by scholars, who are impressionable in a high degree to standards of thought set up by those under whose influence they spend a third of their time. The fact that highly qualified professors of both sexes manifest an unfeigned interest in the right conduct of homes and give cordial attention to studies which bear on the scientific and artistic regulation of domestic life carries great weight with boys as well as girls in the high schools where these courses have reached their best development. It is believed that this fact impresses a wider circle than the students alone, and will bear good fruit among parents by its contribution to the dignity of home life; in any case its influence is active at the moment when the unrest of adolescence is prone to manifest itself in a contempt for familiar surroundings and in impatience with the claims of the family circle. Further, such a course serves the useful purpose of revealing their vocations to girls who are discouraged by their distaste or want of capacity for literary, artistic, or purely scientific studies, in which their companions already display a promise of future proficiency, or from their inability to reach an accepted standard in other lines of school work. The combination of scientific theory with its prompt application to familiar processes; the union of mental with manual activity; the school links constantly forged with home interests; the sense of power acquired in the performance of daily duties, hitherto complicated by the rule of thumb system, accompanied by its irritating and uncertain element of chance; all appeal with an often unsuspected force to the undeveloped Marthas of the school world, who find here an outlet for their latent capacities, and whose perpetuation—no longer " careful and troubled about many things "—through knowledge thus attained, will be of unmixed benefit to the human race.

In contrast to such comprehensive courses (details of three of which are included), it is quite possible to find high schools where the term Domestic Science is confined to practice classes in cooking or sewing, and where no direct inter-relation between scientific principles and domestic methods is worked out. Of these, that at Ann Arbor (Mich.), is an average specimen. Or there may be a sort of compromise between the educational and the utilitarian methods, of which the courses at some of the private high schools afford illustrations. Significant of the awakening appreciation of the possibilities and claims of the subject is the following extract from the 21st Annual Report of the Superintendent of Public Schools of the City of Boston, dated March, 1901; its tenour has aroused considerable hope among those in the city who have desired for some years past to see a course established in Household Economics, and who regret that the 3,000 girls in attendance at the half dozen high schools have hitherto had no officially recognised opportunity for instruction under this head, at an age when they are able to bring to it an interest and intelligence more developed than that possessed by pupils in the grammar grades: "The next piece of legislation relative to high school studies that may suggest itself is the establishment of courses in Household and Industrial Science and Arts for girls. Whether such courses would better be provided for in a separate high school or in connection with existing high schools is a debatable question, but either method would be feasible. In former reports I have advocated the establishment of a separate high school, which should be for girls what the Mechanic Arts High School is for boys. At the same time I am persuaded that, if good courses in Household and Industrial Science and Arts were offered as 'electives' in the existing high schools, the same practical results could be secured. The addition of such 'electives' would be an easy matter if the general system of elective studies which I now advocate should be adopted." It is possible that the activity of private enterprise in this direction in Boston may in part account for the delay in providing courses similar to those so well supported in other cities. Further on in the same interesting document Superintendent Seaver points out that the choice of studies under the elective system can be scarcely too wide, as chemistry, physics, drawing etc., "do not always furnish the best training for all minds; there are always excellent pupils who would do better to omit one or other of these subjects and give the time to studies better suited to their capacities, thus leaving school with some real scholarship."

As in the grammar grades, Personal and Domestic Hygiene are most usually, if not invariably, treated as a definite school study under the title of Physiology, in which both sexes share. The subject is obligatory in only a minority of the States, but often finds a place in high schools where much attention is given to biology, of which it forms an appropriate and valuable development.

The course of Domestic Science study at the Brookline (Mass.) High School is detailed in this Report for two reasons: first, because the whole school system in that city has attained so high a level of excellence (largely due to its late superintendent, Professor Samuel Dutton, now Superintendent of the Horace Mann School, Teachers College, New York City), that if a subject appears in its school r ra es, the educational value and practical possibilities of that study are, virtually, guaranteed. In the next place, its schedule demonstrates the feasibility of finding an honourable place in an undeniably liberal scheme of secondary education for subjects whose absence from the time tables of corresponding schools in this country is excused or condoned on the plea of want of time, want of educational value, or want of attraction to parents and pupils.

The educational history of the town of Brookline has been a source of satisfaction to its inhabitants for the past ten years: School Committee, Superintendent, and teachers have worked freely, and few restraints have been placed on a reasonable display

Typical Domestic Science Courses:— (a) Brookline, Mass. Tables X and XI.

TABLE X.

BROOKLINE HIGH SCHOOL, MASSACHUSETTS.—GENERAL COURSE.

Institution and Course.	Entrance Requirements.	Scope of Course.	Methods.	Length of Course.	Fees and Finance.	Equipment.
Brookline High School. General Course. Principal— D. S. Sandford, A.M. (Yale).	A Brookline Grammar School education, or Entrance Examination.	**FIRST YEAR.** Hrs. per wk. English Composition - 1 English Literature (half year) - 5 Ancient History (half year) - 5 Mathematics (Algebra, Geometry) - 4 Art - 2 1 Zoology and Botany - 4 Latin (elective) - 4 French (elective) - 4 Bookkeeping (elective) - 4 Manual Training (elective) - 4 Domestic Science (elective) - 4 **SECOND YEAR.** Hrs. per wk. English - 2 Mediaeval History - 3 Art - 3 2 1 Mathematics (elective) - 3 Latin (elective) - 4 Physiology or Physical Geography (elective) - 4 French (elective) - 4 German (elective) - 5 Manual Training (elective) - 4 Domestic Science (elective) - 4 **THIRD YEAR.** Hrs. per week. English Literature - 3 Modern History - 3 Physics - 4 Art (elective) - 2 Mathematics (elective) - 3 Latin (elective) - 5 French (elective) - 4 German (elective) - 4 Mechanical Drawing (elective) - 4 Manual Training (elective) - 4 Domestic Science (elective) - 4 **FOURTH YEAR.** Hrs. per wk. English Composition - 2 English Literature - 3 Chemistry - 4 Political Science - 3 Art (elective) - 2 Mathematics (elective) - 3 Latin (elective) - 4 French (elective) - 3 German (elective) - 5 Manual Training (elective) - 4 Domestic Science (elective) - 4 History of Art (elective) - 1	The curriculum of the school is broad and full. This General course … two … fair academic training in the school. The great range of electives allows each student to follow the lines of his … likes.	Four years.	None for … in Brookline. Public Funds. $100 per annum for … non-resident … fee.	The school buildings are spacious and … The school furniture and appliances are all of the most approved kinds.

of individuality and inventiveness. Nature study has been in- (a) Brook-
troduced, manual training and the domestic arts have been line, Mass
developed and made more educational; new school buildings —continued.
have been erected with modern appliances for comfort and
sanitation, and the old ones have been enlarged and improved.
Free kindergartens, increased provision for public health and
hygiene, improved tenement houses, the exclusion of children
from work in mills and shops, with additional public support of
such " culture forces " as libraries, museums, music, lectures, etc.,
these, and other social developments, have all supplemented and
supported school influences. The High school is a source of special
pride to the community, and it is earnestly desired that its
curriculum should be a good example of the avowed aim of those
responsible for its initiation, viz., not so much the acquisition of
knowledge as the development of power and the building of
character. " While knowledge is not the *end* it is still recognised as a powerful *means*, and if only partial success has been
attained it is rather because of the incompleteness of its adoption
and application than of any fault in the aim."

The curriculum of this school is broad and flexible; certain
subjects are required, others are elective; there are four courses
of study in all. The "constants" occurring in each, although
in varying proportions, are English, history, mathematics, the
natural sciences, art, and physical training. Three courses, the
classical, sub-classical, and *technical,* furnish a good preparation
for all who wish to enter college, scientific or technical schools, and
candidates select these according to the requirements of the institution which they expect to enter; the *general* course, in which there
is a greater range of " electives," provides for those who complete
their education in the high school. Manual training and
domestic science and art, for boys and girls respectively, appear
in each year of the technical and general courses; they are obligatory in the technical, and elective in the general course; zoology,
physics, chemistry and physiology are also " elective " subjects.

The work in Domestic Science is largely an application of
other sciences to daily life; the ultimate object of its pro-
moters is, while training the pupil in scientific method and in
an appreciation of economic values, to give the home its legitimate position among our social institutions, to arouse interest in
the familiar processes and environment of home life, and to show
that home making is a worthy occupation for the most gifted.

The food problem, as approached by the cook and as exemplified in the kitchen, is selected for the first year's work, because
experience shows the average girl of 14 or 15 to be more interested
in this department of the subject than in any other; but, as a
knowledge of general chemistry is essential to an even superficial
understanding of every-day processes, the second year is devoted
to this subject and its applications. The third year is concerned
chiefly with a study of the house itself, its construction, its
sanitary arrangements and their care, its furnishing and
decoration. An excellent opportunity is given, and improved,
for correlating the work of this year with that of the Art

TABLE XI.

BROOKLINE HIGH SCHOOL, MASS.—SCHEDULE OF DOMESTIC SCIENCE COURSE.

Institution and Course.	Entrance Requirements.	Scope of Course.	Methods.	Length of Course.	Fees and Finance.	Equipment.
The High School, Brookline, (Mass.) Domestic Science. Miss Alice Smith.	Graduates from Primary and Grammar Schools approved by the Principal. Admission: examination required of Candidates outside Brookline.	1st Year. General Subject—Food and its preparation (Practical Cooking), in connection with simple chemistry and physics. 2nd Year. (a) General Chemistry. (b) Household Applications (analysis of food stuffs and of cleaning materials). 3rd Year. General Subject—The House. Situation and surroundings. Domestic Architecture. Modern American Houses. House Sanitation. Furnishing and Decoration. 4th Year. General Subjects— (a) Household Biology (Bacteriology of air, water, milk.) (b) Sociological and Economic problems of the home (study of division of income, etc.), also a few lessons on Emergency work and Home Nursing. Art, Physics, and Biology are "obligatory," Zoology and Physiology are "elective" subjects for students of Domestic Science.	Aim. The development of power and the building of character; to train the pupil to appreciate the dignity of home life, and to arouse interest in familiar processes. The work in Domestic Science is largely an application of other sciences to daily life. So far as possible the work is carried out practically by each individual. Special attention is paid to the inter-relation in this course of such subjects as physics and economics; the director of drawing is careful also to correlate the art work with household requirements. "Field work" comprises visits to well-planned houses, steam laundries, chocolate and other factories, shops, marketing, etc.	4 years: forms part of the general and technical courses.	None for Residents. Public Funds. £5 per annum for Students non-resident in Brookline.	The General Laboratories are used for all purposes except cooking. The School is a modern model building, and the kitchen, while simply equipped, contains all that is required for individual work by 20 to 30 pupils in a class.

department. Other of the topics, such as ventilation and (*a*) Brookheating, involve principles of physics, and here also the effort is line, Mass made to apply work already done in that department, and to —*continued.* bring to students without that training the knowledge of some of its elementary principles. The fourth year is largely given to the applications of biology to every-day life. As this comprehends an elementary study of bacteriology, the theory of disease causation is naturally introduced, and the practice includes some simple home nursing and emergency work. A short subsequent course in invalid cookery gives opportunity for a review of the principles learned in the first year. The latter part of this, the last year, is spent in the discussion of problems of home making rather than of housekeeping, many of which are looked at from the economic and social as well as from the domestic standpoint. For example, the following selected topics belong both to Political Economy and to Domestic Science—the consumption of wealth; food, in its relation to labour power; the housing of the poor and its relation to good citizenship; municipal sanitary regulations; expenditure *versus* saving; domestic service (as a part of the general labour problem); the work of superintending a home compared with other economic occupations; child labour, etc. Evidence of the thoughtful inter-relation of studies, for which this school is notable, is also apparent in the following selection from some of the topics suggested for theme work in the English department—the life and work of Count Rumford; the influence of Pasteur on modern science; yeast fermentation in its relation to bread-making; the manufacture of flour; experiments with albumen, dust, bacteria and butter-making; the Brookline water supply; the system of ventilation in the Brookline High School; an ideal room. This method serves at least three ends; facility of verbal expression is acquired in respect of subjects studied chiefly in the laboratory or by observation; girls are stimulated to study the history and development of existing domestic customs; and intelligent application of principles acquired in one department is demanded in another. Physiology, chemistry, physics and economics are also closely affiliated by cross-work reference throughout the course. Miss Smith, who is in charge of the present promising class, spares no pains to secure the co-operation of her colleagues in order to maintain continuity in theory and practice, and finds an ample reward for her efforts in the increasing interests and greater womanliness of those who include Domestic Science in their studies. Throughout the course visits to well-planned houses, steam laundries, chocolate works and other factories connected with food and clothing processes, are made whenever practicable or desirable, in order to broaden the outlook of the students and to impress on their minds the points under discussion.

I subjoin a concise synopsis of the ground covered and a few suggestions of the methods adopted in the courses in chemistry, physics, geology and art; the course in general household cookery is a somewhat extended treatment of the grade school syllabus.

(a)Brookline, Mass—*continued.* The General Chemistry includes : A study of the air and its gases. Chemistry of respiration. Water : its composition, distillation, solvent power. Hard and soft water. Hydrogen. Acids, bases, salts. The halogens and their compounds. Sulphur and phosphorus. Carbon and the chemistry of combustion. Fuels and illuminants. Dyeing of cloth. Starch, sugar, albumen, fats. Chemistry of fermentation and of digestion. Study of the metals. Action of acids and alkalies upon the common metals and their compounds. Simple qualitative analysis.

To this succeeds the " Household Applications " previously mentioned.

" The General Physics Course is governed by three permanent aims :— (1) that which it has in common with the general chemistry, viz., to develop in the pupils steady, persistent, logical thinking ; (2) to make them fairly intelligent in reference to their own scientific environment ; (3) to teach them to apply the elements of algebra and geometry to the problems of daily life. Incidentally it is anticipated that the sense of appreciation will be aroused for all that modern science has done and is doing for the comfort and convenience of the race." As the average manual offers few opportunities for any original independent thinking, and contains so little of anything like a practical application of physics to the phenomena of daily life, the head of the department substitutes special notes of his own—still in manuscript form—in which students are told as little as possible directly, but are given, practically, a series of original exercises in mechanics, optics and electricity, to work out by the aid of a set of simple apparatus, their mathematical instincts and their own brains ; the intention is that these shall then be applied to the affairs of daily life in continuous sequence, suggested by questions, problems and references. This thoroughly practical aim takes the form, for instance, in hydraulics, of directing attention to the water-meter, the simple motor, and the turbine, rather than to the lifting pump, the ram and the breast wheel, as the average man is more likely to see and use the former than the latter series. In optics again, the camera, the opera-glass, and the spy-glass are dealt with more fully than the telescope and the compound microscope, for the same reason. Throughout, continual reference is made to the current literature of the day and to the features of Boston and its vicinity. The work in physics is distributed somewhat as follows :—September, October, November—mechanics, including hydrostatics and pneumatics. December, January, February — optics. March, April, May —electricity. June — review. Towards the close of the school year special topics are suggested for more exhaustive treatment than is possible in the regular classroom work. Each pupil is expected to choose one or more of such topics and to present an illustrated paper upon the subject selected, at the end of the year. Among the topics recently suggested may be mentioned the following :—mechanics of the clock ; the bicycle ; the sewing-machine. Consumption of gas, water and electricity in the household. Testing a water-meter. The fire-alarm system of Brookline. School-room ventilation. The long-distance telephone. The gas-engine. The horse-power of an electric motor.

These courses, each of which extends over an entire year, are required of the Sub-classical, the Scientific and the Manual training pupils. The time is equally divided between laboratory and lecture-room work, to both of which two periods per week must be devoted beside the usual preparation. Complete notes are kept by the pupils of the laboratory and lecture work, which are inspected from time to time by the instructor.

The course in Zoology is planned on lines of equal practical value. Observation of living animals and a study of their external anatomy, expressed by drawings and oral or written descriptions ; constant use of the simple microscope and occasional use of the compound ; field trips, study of text and reference books, investigation of special topics, the making of collections, represent the method of study. All the work is carried on in well-lit, airy rooms ; the physics laboratory, 40 feet by 23, deserves special mention for its well thought out arrangements and equipment.

The same spirit can be traced throughout the Art work, under the direction of Miss Irene Weir, who bases her method upon the facts that the principles of art form the basis of good taste, and good taste concerns itself with every act and duty of daily life. In a recent paper on this subject she expressed her view as follows :—"From the economic standpoint alone the most important object which any course of art training can attain is to establish in the mind of the child principles of good taste ; from the standpoint of the child's own well-being, the power to do a thing well, which is art, requires the full and complete training of hand and eye and a concentration of brain energy scarcely excelled by any other mental process. The average child is not going to become either painter or architect, but will work in some sort of industrial occupation, or help in the production of marketable goods, or dress in good or bad taste, and make and have a home where order and beauty prevail, or where disorder and inartistic confusion reign. These things, therefore, are of primary value which tend to the improvement of the home, the comfort, well-being and harmony of the family, the order, security and beauty of the city, and finally, the best and happiest life of the individual ; and in good taste is found the broad foundation stone upon which these things rest." So her students are first trained to comprehend, and then required to apply, the principles of art in form, colour, design and composition to "homely" objects and ends, in the highest significance of the word.

The part of the Domestic Science Course at present least developed as regards practical work, is that concerned with House Sanitation, though time is freely spent on "field trips.' After all, this method offers by far the best practice, especially as a course of physics is obligatory the previous year ; pupils are thus prepared to make their observations on building construction, pipes, water supply, and sanitary fittings, with an intelligence based on a practical, though elementary, knowledge of the subject. Their art training should have already developed some ideas as to house plans and room decoration. About one-fourth of the whole time is devoted directly to the study of Domestic Science during the four years' course; zoology or physiology, physics, chemistry, and art absorb a full third ; the remaining hours are devoted to English literature and composition, history, mathematics, and one modern language, though, in the general course, book-keeping is also an elective subject.

The four years' course of study in Domestic Science is confined (*b*) Providence (R.I.). to one of the three High schools in Providence (Rhode Island), dence (R.I.). viz., that devoted to manual training, where it is carried on Table XII. under the direction of Miss Abby L. Marlatt. At present this training is available only for 25 girls a year, at an average age of 15 years. Here, again, marked attention is given to the correlation of subjects; *e.g.* in the Household Arts Course, suitable and original designs must be prepared for the dress and hat, the making of which forms part of the sewing practice ; in the study of house construction, the plan and elevation of a simple dwelling are demanded of the student, subsequent schemes in colour for its internal decoration being duly carried out. In mathematics, problems are given for the calculation of the cubic capacity of various shaped rooms, of the velocity of entering and out-going air in different systems of ventilation, and of the amount of air provided per hour per person under different conditions of atmosphere and propulsion.

TABLE XII.

MANUAL TRAINING HIGH SCHOOL, PROVIDENCE, RHODE ISLAND. DOMESTIC SCIENCE COURSE.

Instruction and Course.	Length of Course.	Fees and Finance.	Methods.	Equipment.	Scope of Course.
Manual Training High School, Providence, R.I. Domestic Science Course. Professor, Miss Abby L. Marlatt.	4 years of 38 weeks each. Average age, 15–17 years. Students are required to be 15 years of age on entrance.	None. Public funds.	Marked attention is given to the correlation of subjects. The first year's work is carefully joined on to and out of the previous years. Through out the whole course the same method of linking study with work, and the work with the home, is carried out. The plan of setting pupils for individual tasks to work out for themselves is largely used.	The building laboratory is fitted with all conveniences for work and runs in one site of the room, with the chairs for the cookery apparatus. There are well-spacious, pupil work rooms, and also a large reference library.	Physics .... 2 years or 57 weeks, ¾ hour daily. General chemistry .. 1 year or 38 weeks, ¾ hour daily. Chemistry of foods and Physiology of digestion (Analytical) .. 1 year or 19 weeks, ¾ hour daily. Physical matter of .. ½ year of 1 year or 19 weeks, ¾ hour daily. Botany .... 1 year or 38 weeks, ¾ hour daily. Psychology ...... 1 year or 19 weeks, ¾ hour daily. Household (and the repairs and household supply) 1 year or 19 weeks, ¾ hour daily. Science of cooking 1 year or 38 weeks, 4½ hours weekly. Sewing .... 2 years 100 hours in all. Millinery .... 2 years 70 hours in all. Dressmaking .... 2 years or 19 weeks, 4½ hours weekly. Laundry .... 1 year 60 hours in all. Household .... 1 year or 19 weeks, 4½ hours weekly. Modelling ...... 1 year 45 hours in all. Drawing and design 4 years or 152 weeks, ¾ hour daily.

A free hand is given to the singularly capable instructor, who (*b*) Provi-
has deservedly gained the confidence of the principal, and who dence
is responsible for the four years' course of study in Domestic (R.I.)—
Science detailed in Appendix B, which is noteworthy on several *continued.*
accounts. In the first place actual manual work is practised in
three out of the four years; elementary and advanced carpentry in
the first and last years; basket-weaving, modelling in clay and
wood, and wood-carving in the first, second, and fourth. Book-
keeping, elementary rhetoric, trigonometry, the elements of
psychology, and the science of photography appear as academic
subjects in conjunction with mathematics, geometry, physical
geography, and German. General chemistry, physics, botany
(which includes elementary bacteriology), and civil government,
are carried on in direct relation with the Domestic Science work,
and the Art course is well graduated to the same end. That the
elements of psychology should be included in a course for girls of
this age (15 to 19) is justified by Professor Huxley's
strongly expressed conviction that by this means only can a
properly proportioned introduction be given to a study of the
laws of Nature which underlie all the processes of life.*

It is found that the introduction of some practical Emergency
and First-aid work appeals strongly to girls on coming to the
High school, so this is introduced in their first year; but the
more responsible study of home nursing and the use of domestic
disinfectants is delayed till the conclusion of the course (the
fourth year), when it is illustrated practically by demonstrations
at the Rhode Island Hospital, to which Miss Marlatt conducts
her class. Reference to the schedule of the course will show that
the year's work in physics precedes, while that in general
practical chemistry runs parallel with, the practical cookery
course. In any case it is believed that this arrangement is the
best, but here it is of special service as Miss Marlatt is also
Professor of Chemistry. Hitherto, the girls have come with no
previous preparation in practice, as cooking is only to be introduced into the grade schools of Providence this autumn (1902).
The cooking laboratory is furnished with single tables for each
student, which are provided with Bunsen burners and stands,

---

* Readers will be familiar with the plan of his "Introductory" Science
Primer, wherein he pointed out that "a definite order obtains among
mental phenomena just as among material phenomena. . . . Moreover
there is a connection of cause and effect between certain material
phenomena and certain mental phenomena. . . . All the phenomena of
nature are either material or immaterial, physical or mental; and there is
no science except such as consists in the knowledge of one or other of
these groups of natural objects and of the relations which obtain between
them." (Introductory Science Primer, pp. 93, 94. Macmillan. 1880.) So
in his own masterly way, even in this elementary outline of the vast field
of science, he leads his young readers from an observation of material
objects (mineral bodies and living bodies) to the conception of immaterial
objects as perceptible in mental phenomena ; and, though his great gift for
expressing the complexities of scientific principles in most simple words is
given to but few, this should not condone the omission of an integral part
from a great whole, or discourage those who desire to present it in suitable
form to intelligent students.

drawers to contain the necessary utensils, a sliding seat, and
hooks at the side upon which the pans are hung; coal and gas
ranges as well as Aladdin ovens are provided, and glazed cupboards contain the china and glass. A bench fitted with the
conveniences for chemical work runs the whole length of one
side of the room (this enables problems to be dealt with on the
spot as they arise in cooking practice); the drawers beneath
provide accommodation for necessary apparatus. A small museum
contains specimens of food stuffs in the various phases of manufacture and other objects of practical interest, which include a
complete set of very beautifully mounted common household
pests, such as the red ant, cockroach, clothes moth, bug, etc. A
good reference library for the use of the girls also finds a place.

In the third year the study of food analysis and digestion is
dealt with at length, and creates a demand for the fourth year
course in analytical chemistry and bacteriology. In this senior
year the course also deals with the hygienic and sanitary problems illustrated in home and public life; the sanitation of soils,
the study of house plans, of plumbing, of heat and ventilation;
with considerations of a sanitary food supply, and of the risks
from food adulteration, or from insects injurious to food; a study
of moulds and bacteria then leads on to the causes of disease
and rules for hygienic care of the sick as well as of the sound.
This work, though in part experimental, is largely done by means
of home study of assigned topics; the details of her " topic " are
worked out by each pupil from observation, experiments or
reference books. Miss Marlatt thus aims to foster habits of
independent study and independent thought.

Miss Bowen, a graduate of Pratt Institute, who is responsible
for the sewing, has her difficulties increased by the fact that the
girls come to her with little or no knowledge of needlework.
Time, therefore, only permits, as a rule, of the practice of each
stitch on small samples of material in the first year; application,
in the form of a completed article, is compulsorily limited to the
making of one blouse, for which the pupils are allowed to use a
simple pattern of Butterick's; and of a " raffia " hat, braided, sewn,
shaped and trimmed by themselves. It will be observed that for
three out of the four years as much time is given to modelling
in clay or wood, or to carpentry, as to the use of the needle. In
the second year a simple cotton dress is made. All the available time in the third year is devoted to dressmaking, but
"advanced" wood-carving and carpentry absorb two-thirds of
the whole period in the fourth year, leaving but one-third for
"advanced" dressmaking. I account for this under two heads;
(1) the conviction that variety in manual occupations is of much
value in its development of dexterity and consequent reduction
of merely mechanical repetition; (2) the, to me, apparent fact that
young people in the United States are quicker in perception and
performance than their contemporaries in England, and are more
usually disposed to "give their minds" to what they are called
upon to do. Much care is given to a clear comprehension
throughout of the "reason why," and attention is called to the

keeping of accurate notes, which are illustrated with usually excellent drawings. The needlework classes are carried on in a spacious, well-lighted room, which measures 28 by 32 by 14 feet, and accommodates 45 pupils. The furniture is easily adjustable. 10 hand-sewing machines are provided, 5 of which are single thread Singer's. Each girl has a large and a small box stored in a numbered locker in which to keep her work materials and any article in the process of completion, as, for instance, hats in the millinery course. Large hanging cupboards are provided for skirts. There is no better evidence of the genuine interest aroused by the course than the emulation which exists among the students to complete not only a simple dress during the fourth year, but a more elaborate muslin gown in which to attend the graduating ceremony—a function of great importance in the life of an American student of either sex. The custom of making her own dress for this great occasion is habitual in High Schools and Technical Institutes among girls who attend sewing courses; and even in the grade schools of cities where the subject is taught through several years I found a similar ambition present among the little "graduates," though, as yet, rarely realised.

The daily school session is from 9 a.m to 3 p.m. with a half-hour recess for lunch, which is served in the building. These hours are divided into "periods" of 45 minutes; all "periods" in manual work are double that length. No Domestic Science, as such, is taken the first year, but $1\frac{1}{2}$ hours is devoted to Manual Training or Household Art on alternate days in this, as in each year of the course. Domestic Science claims $1\frac{1}{2}$ hours on alternate days throughout the remaining 3 years, and to art work 45 minutes is assigned daily for the whole period. Thus a liberal half of the school life is left free for academic studies.

Miss Marlatt subjects the schedule of this course to constant revision in the light of her growing experience; meanwhile it embodies some of the best, if not the best, High school work accomplished on these lines in the United States.

It is the intention of those who have the interest of the school (c) Hackley. most deeply at heart, to frame all the work of the Hackley Table XIII. Manual Training School on a similar educational basis—to present all the studies in the way which shall best mould and shape character and so further the all-round development of the pupils, while the ideal of good health is kept prominently in view. When domestic subjects were introduced into the High school five years ago, parents as well as children were unfamiliar with any branches of manual training. It was felt that to make the desired favourable impression, sufficient time must be devoted to them, not merely to ensure their presentation on the above mentioned educational basis (which the initiators considered the only right way), but to be assured of enough practical results to interest and please the public generally. It is a still popular idea to regard this work largely from the standpoint of utility, and ignorantly to taboo educational value of work which does not make some practical showing. The growing interest of the public at Muskegon is evinced by the increased attendance on

TABLE XIII.

MUSKEGON, MICHIGAN, HACKLEY MANUAL HIGH SCHOOL.—SCHEDULE OF DOMESTIC SCIENCE AND ART COURSE.

Institution and Course.	Entrance Requirements.	Scope of Course.	Methods.	Length of Course.	Fees and Finance.	Equipment.
Hackley Manual Training High School, Muskegon, Michigan. Dom tic Science and Art. Miss A. M. Thomas.	Graduates from Primary and Grammar Schools.	SHORT COURSE.— Cooking Sewing Laundry Home Sanitation Emergencies and Home Nursing Drawing Gymnastics } Two double High School periods of 45 minutes each per week, for six months. } Two single periods per week for one year. LONG COURSE.— Domestic Science Domestic Arts Drawing Gymnastics Light Bench Work Wood Carving } Two double periods per week for three years. } Two single periods per week for three years. Other High School studies bearing on Course— FIRST YEAR.—(a) Physiology; special attention paid to hygiene, digestion, and assimilation; Bacteriology, the germ theory; (b) Physical Geography. SECOND YEAR.—(a) Biology; cellular theory; microscope work; study of lower forms of life, advancing to the vertebrates; Specimens—cray fish, fresh-water mussels, turtles, fish, birds, rabbits and cat; (b) Botany—seeds; foods, oils, and starches; grains, plants; roots, stems, leaves, flower, and fruit; families. Bacteria and fungi. THIRD YEAR.—Chemistry; course in elementary chemistry; some simple organic work is given; experiments and study of fermentation; soap making, etc. FOURTH YEAR.—Physics. A course in Physics as laid out by Carhart and Chute's Elementary Text Book, adapted to suit the needs of the class; this includes the chapter on Heat, together with various original experiments.	Aims—(1) To give a thorough understanding of the principles of each subject; (2) To ... the basis for woman's work as well as man's; (3) To present the work on the ... of true ..., to ... further all-round de... ... they in measurement, careful manipulation, neatness, g d methods, system in ..., are all carefully considered in the manual ..., also the "time" element as ... as the quality of results. Pupils work individually. Table ... and elementary dressmaking enter into both courses.	Short Course, ... , to be extended to ... years. ... y ... Manual Training required to entitle pupils to a High School Diploma. The "Long ..." entitles to a Manual Training High School Diploma plus the ordinary High School ...	None. Public Funds.	Sufficient, and suitable for individual work.

visiting and exhibition days, and by hearty parental expressions
of appreciation. The figures showing the increase in the numbers
of those who elect the long course in Manual Training, which are
quoted later, are sufficient evidence that so far the experiment
has met with success. A general system of "electives" has
lately been arranged, which enables any pupil following a General
Language, or other course, to substitute manual training subjects
for certain literary studies in the third and fourth high school
years; two hours of manual training work then count as equivalent to one hour of academic training. In such instances the
pupils are allowed to select the branches of manual training they
prefer; hitherto emergencies, home sanitation, home nursing,
table service and laundry in Domestic Science, and elementary
and advanced dressmaking in Domestic Art have been the popular
subjects. Sometimes the girls choose light bench work and
wood carving in the boys' department, and, occasionally, turning.

The Domestic Science work has been divided into two courses,
termed the Long Course and the Short Course. The length of
each lesson in cookery, sewing, or laundry, is two high school
"periods" of 45 minutes each; for lessons in home sanitation, emergencies and nursing, and drawing and gymnastics,
one such period. The Short Course consists of two lessons per
week for an entire year. One half year is devoted to cookery
and the other half to sewing; this division is not based entirely
upon psychological reasons, but is to a certain extent necessary
in a school of this size. Theoretically it may seem better to
give an entire year to each subject, but practically it is found
to be impossible with the average teachers and average
equipment. The experiment has been tried of giving one lesson
per week in each subject during the entire year, or two per week
on each subject for half a year, and the latter is found to be far
better. The Short Course also includes two lessons per week in
drawing and two lessons per week in gymnastics. Two years of
the Short Course manual training is always required for a pupil to
be entitled to a High School Diploma, and, in almost all courses,
three years is required for graduation.

The Long Course is four double periods per week, for the first
three years at least; two in Domestic Science, two in Domestic
Art, three single periods in drawing and two single periods in
gymnastics. This course is designed for those who have a special
liking and aptitude for manual training branches, and endeavours
to cover the ground thoroughly. The pupil who completes this
course receives, upon graduation, not only the High School Diploma,
but a Manual Training School Diploma as well. The work was laid
out when the High School course covered four years; last year
this was extended to five; probably the same amount of
Domestic Science work will now be extended over this longer
period, and less time will be devoted to it during the last two
years. Up to the year 1900 the Long Course classes were not
very large, about 10 per cent. only of any entering class of girls
chose this study, but, in 1901, it was elected by 72 new pupils

(c.) Hackley out of 95; in July, 1901, only the natural "shrinkage" was
—*continued.* reported, a strong testimony to the growth of interest in the
subject.

Reference to the schedule will show the efforts made to
bring a knowledge of the principles of the Special Sciences to
bear upon the subjects which involve practical application of
these principles. Miss Thomas hopes that much closer correlation
will gradually be effected; meantime, the training as detailed in
the following outlines should have a strong influence towards
the elevation to a new dignity of those branches of manual
labour with which the woman in the home comes most directly
in contact.

COOKERY.—First year: short course. First half year: long course; two
lessons per week for one half year. This comprises a course in elementary
cooking of a strictly economical character along lines slightly in advance of
those followed in grade schools. It opens with a brief study of the chemical
elements of combustion illustrated by experiments; the kinds of fuel and
their comparative costs, based upon the locality, etc. The foods cooked are
taken up with regard to the food principle which they represent; and their
comparative food and market value considered; the effect of heat and the
chemical and physical changes which occur are carefully noted; the use of
each in the body, their digestion and assimilation. In this manner the
foods are classified. The value of combining different foods to make a
complete one is also studied. These food principles, taken in their natural
sequence, are illustrated by the cookery of vegetables and cereals; eggs in
various ways; soups; stewed, broiled, and roasted meats; fish, both fresh
and dry; the use of "left-overs," the commercial and food value of legumes,
and their importance as substitutes for meats. The utility of economy of
food material, of time, of labour, and of fuel in its preparation, is brought
before the pupil, as is accuracy of measurement, careful manipulation,
neatness, method and system in execution.

COOKERY.—Second year: short course. First year, second half: long
course; two lessons per week for one half year.

The preparation of batters and doughs; the different methods of making
them light, and the comparative value of each, illustrate the uses of soda
and sour milk, soda and cream of tartar, and various kinds of baking
powders; next in order comes the study of the yeast plant, its growth and
requirements; experiments with yeast, with tests of the different temperatures to which it can be submitted, and the conditions most suitable to its
growth. This is followed by lessons in practical bread making from the
different varieties of flour, and discussions on the nutritive value and
digestibility of the different breads. The preparation of a few inexpensive
cakes and sweet dishes concludes these lessons.

COOKERY.—Second year, first quarter: long course; two lessons per
week.

This course is pursued by pupils who wish to acquire a more technical
knowledge of cookery, and consists in lessons in jelly making, canning,
pickling, and preserving; the preparation of salads and desserts (sweets),
and other made dishes.

LAUNDRY.—Third year: long or short course; two lessons per week
for one quarter.

This course is planned to give the student an intelligent
understanding of the general principles on which cleaning processes are
based. In addition to the practical laundering of cottons, linens, woollens,
coloured materials, stiff starched and fine articles of clothing, attention is
paid to the care of plumbing and the ventilation in a room used for
laundry purposes, and to the value of all materials used with a view to the
best varieties and their most economical use. The removal of stains by
neutralisation and natural bleaching processes; the advantages of the use
of soft water; the composition of soap, the harm which results from the
use of a strongly alkaline quality, or of a too large quantity; and the risks

which accompany the application of inferior blueings, are each shown by (c.) Hackley
experiment. The setting and restoring of colours in the laundry, and the —*continued.*
cleaning of embroideries and fine laces are also discussed ; and, in all
practical work, the time element as well as the quality of results obtained
is considered.

TABLE SERVICE.—Third year : short course : fourteen lessons, balance
of quarter employed in canning and pickling. Long course ; one quarter of
two lessons per week.

The classes who pursue this work take up : (1) The consideration of
various menus, the food value of the dishes, and the comparative cost and
nutrition of each ; the combination of various dishes to form a meal, which
shall be a well balanced one, of both material and labour at the smallest
expense ; the importance in the variety of meals, and the avoidance of a
daily routine ; (2) the equipment and care of the dining-room, china closet
and pantry ; (3) the care of silver, glass, china and steel ware ; (4) the
arrangement of a table at different meals and the duties of a waitress at
each. Correlated with the above mentioned work is the practical work of
cooking and serving meals ; pupils take the places in turn of cook, waitress,
hostess and guest ; (5) the arrangement and packing of simple and
nutritious lunches for school children, which are now thought worth very
careful consideration as a factor in growth and well-being.

EMERGENCIES.—Fourth year : short course. Third year : long course ;
four single periods per week for one quarter.

This syllabus includes lectures, recitation and practice work, review of
physiology (especially circulation and the structure of the blood vessels) ;
the treatment of wounds of varied severity ; improvised bandages, com-
presses and tourniquets ; the treatment of burns and scalds ; the temporary
treatment of sprains, dislocations and fractures ; and the methods of
utilising material at hand for improvised splints, bandages, slings, pads and
stretchers ; the treatment of unconscious conditions ; practice in the various
methods of using bandages, both emergency and roller.

HOME NURSING.—Third year : long course ; four lessons per week for
one quarter.

This embraces the usual topics : talks on the best methods of caring for
patients in their own home ; ventilation of rooms ; precautions against
draughts ; the necessary care and precautions regarding nursing contagious
disease, and disinfection of clothing and room ; bed making ; the arrangement of draw-sheets ; moving of helpless patients ; prevention of bed sores ;
preparation of fomentations and poultices ; baths of various kinds.

INVALID COOKERY.—Third year : long course ; two lessons per week for
one quarter.

The various kinds of liquid diets are here discussed, and their uses in
different diseases ; koumiss and peptonised milk are prepared, also broths
and teas ; nutritious, cooling, and stimulating drinks ; convalescent diet ;
simple and dainty " desserts " suitable for an invalid ; the equipment, arrangement, and preparation of an invalid's tray are also considered.

HOME SANITATION.—Fourth year : long course ; four single periods per
week for one quarter.

Under this subject is considered the location of the house ; the condition
and quality of the soil and its drainage ; the construction of the cellar,
and the importance of sanitary conditions in cellars ; the evil effects of
impure air in cellars ; the disposal of house refuse in country, village, and
city ; house drainage ; the modern system of plumbing ; the defects in
many systems ; the bad effects of sewer air, and precautions against its
getting into a house ; the water supply, sources of contamination, suggestions for improvement. In like manner is discussed the heating, lighting,
ventilation, and general care of a house from a sanitary standpoint ; also
the sanitary care of food.

DIETARIES.—This work is planned for the fourth year. The values of
foods are studied more in detail than in the other courses, and the food
values of rations at a limited cost are estimated to meet the needs of
persons of different ages and occupations.

DOMESTIC ART.—At present the Needlework course takes up the hand-sewing at the point where the pupil left it in the grade schools.

HAND-SEWING.—First year : short course ; first half year : long course ; two lessons per week.

The sewing lessons are supplemented by talks on the position of the body while sewing, and the evil results of incorrect positions ; the manner of holding work, and the direction from which light should fall. Special attention is paid to practical repairing and mending, to darning of stockings and flannels, patching and piecing, together with the sewing on of buttons and the making of button-holes. Correlated with this work are short lessons on weaving and the manufacture of the different materials used, as thread, thimbles, needles, shears, cotton, silk, and wool. These are illustrated by cases of materials which show the different steps in the process.

MACHINE-SEWING.—Second year : short course. First year, second half : long course, two lessons per week for one half year.

Here the practical application is required of what has been learned in the previous sewing course. The use and care of machines is taught, and models, illustrative of all kinds of machine work, such as tucking, placing ruffles, embroidery, and lace insertions, are made. In this, as in all other branches of this work, the time element is considered, and the question of saving labour, when not necessarily required, is dwelt upon ; thus, a pupil is discouraged from putting several ruffles where one will answer, or from making tucks in ruffles, which will be difficult to iron and cause unnecessary labour. After this preliminary work, drafting is taught by a system of simple measurements, and a white petticoat is drafted and made, during the making of which the various uses of the machine, taught in the previous lessons, are put into practice.

MACHINE SEWING.—Third year : short course. Second year, first half : long course ; two lessons per week for a half year.

The practice of drafting by a system of measurement is continued. The uses of patterns are taught, and the changes and variations required by the average patterns on the market ; the shrinking and preparation of cloth for making is practised ; and a blouse is cut, fitted and made.

ELEMENTARY DRESSMAKING.—Fourth year : short course. Second year, second half : long course ; two lessons per week for a half year.

In this course simple drafting is continued, and an unlined muslin dress is made, previously designed by the pupil.

DRESSMAKING.—Third year : long course ; two lessons per week for one year.

A system of dressmaking by a chart is now introduced, and pupils practise how to measure, draft, cut and fit linings for and to each other ; after which, a lined, boned and trimmed dress is made. A study of textiles and the material suitable for different occasions is continued throughout the course, and designs are made for all the garments.

MILLINERY.—This is designed to occupy part of the fourth year in the long course, but as yet (1901) no teacher has been employed for the purpose.

DRAWING.— Two single periods per week. First year : freehand, nature work, and still life, composition book covers, composition book illustrations. Second year : freehand composition, charcoal and water colour studies. Third year : charcoal work, historic and antique ornament, pen and ink sketches. Fourth year : clay modelling, water colour, advanced composition. Throughout all the different lines of work special attention is paid to note-taking. This gives the pupil practice in expressing facts briefly, and in logical order, and provides useful material for future reference.

(*d*) Toledo.   The Toledo Manual Training School was opened in the autumn of 1884 in rooms set apart for the purpose in the Central High School of the city ; it is now installed in its own imposing, finely-situated building. The initial instruction was limited to classes in woodwork and drawing for boys. In 1887 the

(d) Toledo—
continued.

directors realised the necessity of providing a practical course of instruction for girls also, and the Sewing and Cooking departments were established. Four courses of manual training instruction are planned for students of high school grade, which include Domestic Science and Art for young women; either of these courses may be taken in connection with any regular high school academic course of study, in order to train head and hands to work together, and thus contribute to the ideal that the academic education secured by students in the purely literary school may be put to practical use. Though the directress is thoroughly imbued with the desire that the training shall be educational, not merely technical, she has not yet achieved the introduction of such thoroughly scientific methods as those which distinguish Miss Marlatt's High School course at Providence. The Domestic Science and the Art courses are similar in the first two years; no fees are enforced, except a small sum for laboratory requirements. One and a half hours a day are devoted to manual training throughout the four years' course and are variously apportioned according to the demands of the subjects entering into the particular year's curriculum. Classes are limited to 20 in number, but, and this deserves special note, boys have the opportunity of optional attendance at the 10 lectures on House-planning and Sanitation, of which some are glad to avail themselves. The result of this attendance was shown me in a simple house plan prepared at these lectures, which was being executed by the boys in the Woodwork Department on a scale of $\frac{1}{4}$ inch to 1 foot; the plumbing was to be carried out by the same young artisans in their metal work course, and the model will then be available for demonstration on house sanitation, being planned to permit of convenient division for this purpose. In spite of the large size of the building, the class-rooms and studios now suffer from overcrowding, and extensive additions were to be made during the summer vacation (1901).

It appeared to me that the "art" side of the domestic training is especially well thought out in this course, for which reason the following details are introduced: freehand drawing, clay modelling, and sewing, constitute the work in the first year; the freehand drawing, with the pencil as a medium, takes up the subjects of light and shade from still-life groups; clay modelling covers work in simple ornament and plaster of paris casting. The work in sewing consists in the drafting, fitting, and making of linen undergarments, the making of blouses, dressing jackets, or plain gowns. In the second year, freehand drawing is continued, with charcoal as a medium, working from still-life groups, the ornament, and the mask. Considerable time is devoted to the study of design.

In the third year the student is given the choice between a Domestic Science or a Domestic Art course. In the Domestic Science work, the freehand drawing is continued with the aim of developing the student's idea of taste for the beautiful in the home. The clay modelling is omitted, and the subjects of

(d) Toledo—
continued.

dressmaking and fitting of garments comprise the year's work. If the Art course be elected, freehand drawing is continued; and the subjects of millinery and art needlework receive very practical attention. The autumn and spring terms are usually devoted to millinery work, while the winter term is occupied in the study of decorative art needlework, which consists of work in drawn linen and silk embroidery. The fourth year of the Art course is devoted to the study of freehand drawing, and water-colour from still life and nature ; clay modelling is continued by study from life, and the making of glue and wax moulds for plaster casting is included.

The needlework room is well proportioned and abundantly supplied with presses, sewing machines, dress stands, and other conveniences. The teacher works in close collaboration with the director of the art classes, so that as students are led on to the use of colour and the selection and graduation of shades, application of this knowledge is required in the production of simple designs for patterns of materials, hats and dresses, on a good bold scale. In the dressmaking course individual attention is freely given, and pupils are not required to keep abreast of each other. They usually make three dresses of different materials and styles in the year; Storey's system of dress-cutting being employed. In the session devoted to plain needlework, a corset cover, petticoat of more or less elaboration, full drawers, dressing jacket, and dainty nightdress apparently represent the work accomplished.

(The equipment for a typical High School Course in Dress-making will be found in Appendix C.)

The practice is individual throughout the Domestic Science work. Knowledge is tested by revisions, periodical demonstrations by two students to the rest of the class, and occasional written "quizzes" by the teacher. The study of household economics, the chemistry of cooking, and the care of the home form a very important branch of the work in this second year of the course, and are based upon a study of elementary biology ; it is hoped that physiology will be introduced very shortly. The cooking laboratory is a spacious room on the fourth floor of the building, in all ways satisfactory except as regards light, for the windows are very low. The cooking tables accommodate groups of four; they are of the prevalent type, provided with drawers, the basins and pans in most frequent use finding places upon the shelves beneath. The sink accommodation is ample, and a large coal range is provided in addition to the gas rings fitted at each end of the tables. It still happens that some girls first enter the course quite disposed to despise it and to resent the time expended upon it, but subsequent genuine interest is almost invariably developed, and the voluntary opinion is often expressed that this class has proved the most attractive in the year's work. The keen and growing appreciation by the boys of the crumbs of sanitation they are allowed to gather from the full meal supplied for the girls, promises two results; first, that a more complete training in the subject will, if possible, be organised for those who desire it; second, that the girls become at once more alive to the advantages of the course.

In illustration of a method but little followed, brief reference (*e*) Ann is made to the Ann Arbor High School, where Domestic Science Arbor. is practically confined to the narrow limits assigned to it in many Grade schools. At Ann Arbor, sewing is taken in the fourth, fifth, and sixth grammar grades, and cooking in the seventh and eighth, where both subjects are classed as "manual work," which is meantime actually carried on by the boys during the parallel five years in the form of card, knife, and subsequently bench work. A short time ago voluntary classes were formed in the High School, in bench work for boys and in cooking for girls; these are planned to build on the foundation that has thus been laid, and to continue the work so far as the facilities of the school and the needs of the pupils may indicate to be wise. The work is "elective," but, once entered upon, must be continued through the term, unless a re-classification is granted. The cooking equipment is sufficient for a class of 24, but the accommodation provided in a cramped, dark, questionably ventilated basement room does not offer attractions to young girls of 16 or 17, especially as the adjacent manual training room for boys is in every way superior. Opportunity is given in the third year of each of the six alternative courses of study to lay a scientific foundation in Household Economics by the inclusion of biology, physics and chemistry in each curriculum, but there were no evident indications that the indispensable correlation is demonstrated. A conveniently-arranged and well-lighted biological laboratory is provided for individual work; its equipment includes compound and dissecting microscopes, paraffin heater, tank for aquatic plants, air-tight chests for preserving specimens, and a good provision of glass ware, chemical reagents, etc. The physical and chemical laboratories are in every respect up-to-date, and secure to each pupil the advantages of actual experimentation, so that the "willing mind" alone is required to organise a satisfactory course in Domestic Science here as elsewhere.

The detailed accounts of these selected High school courses Summary. will have indicated their usual scope: plain household cooking, housewifery (which includes the chemistry of cleaning, the purchase of household commodities, the intelligent calculation of nutritive food values, the arrangement of family meals, the plan, structure, and sanitation of a dwelling-house), needlework, dressmaking, millinery, a short course in laundry work, some knowledge of home nursing, the preparation of invalid food, and last, but by no means least, an introduction to the science of economics, in order that, as women, these girls may be fit for the responsibility of intelligent, just expenditure of the family income. Housewifery may be, and is often, subdivided, so that sanitation assumes its rightful position of a distinct and important subject; but, as in the grammar grades, personal hygiene (the structure and care of the body) does not enter into these Household or Domestic Science or Art courses. It must be sought under the shelter of biology or physiology, where; as in the more elementary schools, it is studied together by the mixed classes and well nigh without exception, by the laboratory method.

Physiology and Hygiene Courses. Physiology and hygiene are *obligatory* in the High schools of very few States; it is their value, as fit developments of, and conclusions to, a course in biology which usually accounts for their presence; the opportunities afforded, by hygiene especially, as a field for the application of observations in economics and civics, as well as for the theories and principles acquired in the study of chemistry and physics, also gives them a position in some of the leading High schools, which is of good omen for their more general adoption eventually. It suffices to mention New York City, Cleveland (Ohio), and Detroit, (Mich.), to support the statement that an honourable place is found by the highest educational authorities for these studies in their High schools. They may appear as "elective" in the second year of two out of the six courses (modern languages and English) as at the Detroit Central High School; or in the last year of four out of the six courses (Business, Scientific (three in number), Latin-English, German,) as at Cleveland, or they may be obligatory for all first year students as in the Peter Cooper High School, New York City. The time allotted to their study, and their position with respect to the other sciences is also variable. The time may be daily periods for five months or bi-weekly periods for one year (nine months). At the Cleveland High schools physics must, and biology may, be taken the previous year ; civics and chemistry run concurrently with physiology when "elected;" the preceding course in biology is of special excellence and completeness. At Detroit, botany, and usually zoology, precede physiology, to which chemistry, physics, and economics succeed. In New York City three periods of 50 minutes a week are assigned to botany and zoology during the year and two such weekly periods are allotted to physiology. Here physics and chemistry again succeed the biological course. Without exception, individual laboratory work plays a prominent part in the method pursued. In consequence of my visit to the United States taking place in the late spring and early summer, most laboratory work in physiology was concluded for the year, but I was fortunate in finding some (a) Detroit. Table XIV. still in progress at the Central High School, Detroit. Here a student of physiology gives one or two hours respectively on alternate days to botany and physiology. Latin, rhetoric, algebra, and history constitute the companion studies which may complete a typical weekly programme, though this depends on the special course elected. Professor Louis Murbach is responsible for the biology at this school, and has the advantage of a spacious, well-lit, well-equipped laboratory for his classes in botany, zoology, and physiology. Here he is able to demonstrate his conviction (well expressed in an article on "Physiology in the High School," published in *The Physician and the Surgeon*, December, 1900), "that schools should institute exact mental discipline, therefore, when instruction is given in physiology, it should not, and need not, be mere teaching to avoid bad habits,

to shun disease, or to acquire a (dangerous) smattering of medical (a)Detroit—
knowledge, it should take its place as a part of natural science; *continued.*
for, if properly taught, it inculcates scientific methods of investigation, and is of real value in mental development." Professor
Murbach illustrates in his class-room "what is generally known
as the strength of the laboratory method, which lies in the
student's contact with the material studied, and his independence,
forced, if necessary, in getting his knowledge from the material,
in its classification, and in building up principles therefrom."
Questions are set which the pupil must answer from experiment
or specimen; "all text books whose head-lines embody the
conclusions of their experiments are strictly banished, otherwise
the chief aim of biological studies and their value in science
training is defeated." Necessary information is gained through
discussion of experimental and observational work, and consultation of indicated authorities in the excellent library. A strong
point of this practical course lies in the inexpensive equipment
with which the excellent results are accomplished. "When the
course was initiated," writes Professor Murbach "one alcohol lamp,
six test tubes, a microscope, a skeleton, and some reagents constituted the stock in trade; at its existing state of evolution the
following is found sufficient: a compound microscope, dissecting
lenses, one for each student, a skeleton, a thermometer, a lacto-
meter, retort stands, forceps, needles, Bunsen burners or alcohol
lamps, test tubes, porcelain crucible, evaporating dishes, glass and
rubber tubing, glass and porcelain dishes, models of eye, ear, and
heart, gelatine for culture, and reagents such as nitric acid, ammonia, caustic potash, copper sulphate, formaline, pepsin, pan-
creatin, rennin, peptone, and beef extract." With his other
attainments Professor Murbach combines an exceptional
facility for the devising of simple apparatus and the ingenious
employment of "makeshifts," which he places at the disposal
of science teachers less fortunately equipped than himself;
of even greater value is the resourceful atmosphere he developes
in his laboratory and the spirit of self-help he arouses in his
students. I wish that space permitted me to give more than
the following brief synopsis of this course, for though its scope
can be indicated, it is in the method that the training lies,
with its subsequent influence on action in the form of good
habits, for continued emphasis is laid upon hygienic application along the wholesome lines of sound common sense.

"The organs of the body actually studied in the laboratory
are the following: the kinds of bones in the body—long, short,
flat, correlated with their functions, kinds of joints, places of
attachment of muscles; the lever functions of long bones,
with some simple problems of lifting weights, support of the
body's weight in walking; the heart, from models and specimens;
the circulation as seen in a frog's foot or mesentery; finally,
the general appearance and position of the internal organs in
a freshly killed frog or guinea pig. The latter may be in
form of demonstration to groups of pupils. The ear, from
model and discussion; the eye from models; specimens also

TABLE XIV.

CENTRAL HIGH SCHOOL, DETROIT.—SCHEDULE OF COURSE IN HYGIENE AND PHYSIOLOGY.

Institution and Course.	Entrance Requirements.	Scope of Course.	Methods.	Length of Course.	Fees and Finance.	Equipment.
Central High School, Detroit. Physiology and Hygiene. Professor Louis Murbach.	Primary and Grammar School Certificate.	Study of Air and Water. Study of Bacteria and Yeast. Study of Cells and Tissue Structure. Study of Food Stuffs in Foods. Study of Digestion. Study of General Physiology. Study of Special Senses. Study of Personal Hygiene. Study of the Origin of Diseases (immunisation, isolation, disinfection). Emergencies. The following courses in the school curriculum bear on the intelligent study of these subjects. 1st Year Physiology. 2nd Year { Botany. Zoology. 3rd Year { General Chemistry. Elementary Bacteriology. 4th Year Physics.	Laboratory Method. Pupil works out all data, then draws his own conclusions. The student comes in close contact with the material studied; the system enforces the personal classification of knowledge individually acquired, and the building up from this of principles. The two main objects are; (1) to familiarise the pupils with man's place and part in nature; (2) to cultivate habits of careful observation, reflection and inference. Each student is provided with specimens for study, and a set of directing questions to guide his observations. When individual study is complete, recitations are held for better understanding the underlying principles.	Five months. Two hours a day. Taken in second or third year of the four years course.	None. Public funds.	Work carried on in well equipped biological laboratory. The apparatus considered necessary for this course comprises — a compound microscope, dissecting ..., lactometers, ... test stands, Bunsen ..., test tubes, porcelain ..., tion dishes, glass and porcelain dishes; re-agents, such as nitric acid, ammonia, caustic potash, ... sul..., ..., pepsin, pancreatic juice, rennin, peptone, and ... ext ...; a ... ..., ... of eye, ear, heart.

are brought into the laboratory work if time permits; this study is either followed or preceded by a few experiments on skin sensation. Besides these laboratory exercises, the following subjects are included: respiration (with some experiments), circulation, excretion, bacterial origin of diseases, immunisation, isolation, disinfection, antiseptics, hygiene, emergencies, and what may be done before the physician arrives".

To those already familiar with Professor J. E. Peabody's (*b*.) New suggestive "Laboratory Manual for Practical Physiology York City. Classes" it will appear self evident that the course for which Table XV. he is responsible at the Peter Cooper High School, New York City, should be a model of its kind. The following remarks will be couched chiefly in his own words (recorded in an article contributed to the "Journal of Applied Microscopy," III., No. 7), as, in consequence of the short time at my disposal, I was unable to visit the school, though I received much reliable testimony as to the high character and utility of the work carried out under Professor Peabody's supervision; and have had the advantage of subsequent correspondence with, and much kind assistance from him. The principal aims of this course are these: (1) to give to each pupil some knowledge of the normal functions of the organs in his own body; (2), to make him so familiar with the structure of his organs and tissues that he will get this understanding of their function (anatomy is therefore subordinated to physiology); (3) to acquaint the pupil, so far as time allows, with the general biological principles involved in nutrition, growth, relations of animals and plants, and evolution. . . .

The number of boys and girls in each division is usually about 35. The physiological laboratory is situated in the north-east corner of the school building. Its dimensions are 21 by 27 feet, and it is lighted on two sides by large windows. The greater part of the floor room is required for the ten laboratory tables, each designed for the use of four pupils. The tables are made of white wood, the lower portion being finished with shellac. The top is soaked successively in solutions of logwood and of iron, and melted paraffin is then rubbed into the wood with a hot iron. This treatment gives a dull black finish that is not affected by acids, alcohol or stains. Unlike varnished desk-tops, these do not reflect light into the eyes of the pupils. The desks are arranged in the room so that the pupil faces the north windows when doing laboratory work. He therefore has the best possible light for the microscope and for the object he is studying. Revolving chairs are used, which can be easily raised or lowered according to the needs of each pupil. When recitations are held or class demonstrations given, the boys and girls turn their chairs to face the instructor, and since the desks in this position are on the right side of the pupil, notes can be taken easily. By this arrangement it is possible to convert the laboratory into a recitation room without any loss of time. Half of a fifty minute recitation period may be devoted to microscopic work,

then the specimens may be pushed aside and the attention
of the class directed to recitation.   The seven teachers of
biology use, in common, the apparatus and supplies belonging
to the Department, a partial list of which follows: thirty-six
compound microscopes, each provided with rack and pinion,
fine adjustment, double nose-piece, iris diaphragm, two eye-
pieces, and a two-thirds inch and a one-sixth inch objectives;
magnifiers and dissecting microscopes; steam sterilizer, hot
air sterilizer, and Petri dishes for bacteriological work; fourteen
specially prepared wall charts, twenty-five prints of photo-
micrographs from each of forty-five negatives, skeletons and
dissected preparations, glass ware, chemicals, reference books.

The pupil begins the study of each topic with laboratory
work, considering when possible the organs and tissues of
his own body.   In studying the mouth cavity, for example,
he writes in his note book the answers to questions found in the
Laboratory Manual used by the classes.   Some of the laboratory
work is done at home, the written reports being discussed at
the following recitation.   Text-book lessons in Martin's "Human
Body" supplement the facts gained by laboratory work.   In the
study of the different organs, continual reference is made to
the structure and functions of other animals; for example,
after the consideration of the bones and teeth of man and of
the animals in the school museum, the classes are taken to the
American Museum of Natural History to study other mammalian
skeletons.   Groups of eight to ten pupils gather round the
different specimens, each pupil answering in his note book
the questions, of which a specimen is given below.   The facts
gained from this observation are discussed at the museum,
and the boys and girls hand in at the next recitation a
written account of some of the animals studied.

Comparative study of the Mammalian Skeleton.
A.—Spinal cord.

1. How many vertebræ are found in the neck (cervical) region?
2. How many vertebræ bear ribs (dorsal vertebræ)?
3. How many vertebræ in the lumbar regions?
4. Can you determine how many vertebræ have united to form the
sacrum?
5. How many vertebræ in the tail (caudal vertebræ)?
6. In what region of the spinal column are curves noticeable? How do
they differ from the curves in the human skeleton?
7. Are spinous processes specially developed in any region? Can you
suggest any reason for this?

"Repeated demonstrations from the wall charts by the pupils
help to fix in their minds the relative position in the human
body of the various organs of digestion, circulation and excretion
which they are studying.   Considerable microscopic work is
done during the laboratory periods.   Some of the photomicro-
graphs are then distributed and the discussion of the pictures
serves to make clearer to the students the structures they have
been examining."

The outline of the course opens with some introductory
lessons on the chemistry of air, of the human body, and a study

of acid and alkaline reactions; the study of living substances (*b*) New York City. – *continued.* (protoplasm) follows,–then that of foods and of digestion. To this succeeds lessons on the blood, skeleton, muscles, heart and circulation, respiration, excretion and the nervous system (from which the special senses are omitted), while a few concluding hours are given to a study of yeasts and bacteria.

A general idea of the method of study may be gained from the following specimen extract from the syllabus :—

"Study of respiration.

(1) Laboratory work.

(*a*) Drawing of lungs, wind-pipe, and larynx of calf.
(*b*) Demonstration of action of lungs from model.

(2) Text-book.

(*u*) Structure and function of (*a*) lungs, (*b*) diaphragm,
(*c*) larynx.

(3) Applications.

(*a*) Principles underlying ventilation.
(*b*) Relation of clothing to respiration.
(*c*) Hygienic habits of breathing."

Laboratory work first; the consultation of text-books next; hygienic applications to daily habits and the details of community life in conclusion : these are the main lines for work and guidance, and this is the method of which the sound value is testified to equally in Detroit as in this New York City High School by the visible interest of the girls and lads, the results on conduct, the evidence afforded of mental discipline, and by the manual dexterity acquired.

Among the most practical parts of the whole course are the eight lessons devoted to the study of bacteria.

Culture dishes of nutrient gelatine are exposed to the air, others are exposed to the city water, while a certain number of the dishes are kept closed. After several days the dishes are distributed among the pupils, and the colonies of mould and bacteria are studied and figures made. Home work on the growth of bacteria in milk is one of the applications of the subject to everyday life. After experiments in methods of sterilization, the boys and girls are asked such questions as the following :—

1. From all your experiments, state (*a*) what conditions seem to favour the growth of bacteria ; (*b*) what conditions seem to hinder the growth of bacteria ?

2. Why should fruits be cooked before canning ?

3. Why are foods kept in the refrigerator in summer time ?

4. Why should the prohibition against spitting in public places be rigidly enforced ?

5. Why should sweeping be done as far as possible without raising a dust ?

6. Why should the teeth be brushed often ?

7. Why should the refuse be removed from the streets every morning early, especially in summer time ?

8. Why should wounds be carefully cleansed and dressed at once ?

9. In what ways do bacteria prove to be of benefit to man ?

10. In what ways do bacteria prove to be "man's invisible foe ?"

A course in general biology is to be put into operation next year, which will combine much of the work now done in the separate courses in botany, zoology, and physiology.

Five periods a week are to be devoted to this subject, the main outlines of which are planned as follows : " Introductory experiments in chemistry and physics will give the pupils some first hand knowledge of chemical elements and compounds, the process of oxidation, and the principles of capillary attraction and evaporation. The remainder of the first half year will be devoted to the study of botany, emphasis being laid on the physiological functions carried on in seeds, seedlings, roots, stems, leaves, flowers and fruits. In the second half year the basis of the work is to be the physiology of the human body. Each function will, however, be considered from the comparative standpoint. For example, in studying the subject of respiration the following topics will be considered in addition to those now included :—

" 1. Study of (*a*) skin of earthworm ; (*b*) gills of fishes ; (*c*) lungs of frogs, reptiles, birds and mammals.

" 2. Comparison of respiration in animals living (*a*) in water, (*b*) in moist places ; (*c*) in the air."

This proposal meets with my entire approval, for it is by thus placing man in his relation to less highly developed forms of life that a most desirable admiration for the marvellous beauty of the human body is aroused, and the equally essential senses of self-respect and personal dignity are developed. The value of such High school courses as these at Detroit and New York, followed by lads and girls of 15 to 17 years of age, appears to me to be incalculable in its future influence for good on the homes of a great city and a great nation, and no visitor to the class-rooms could fail to be impressed with the unaffected and practical interest of the young people. Placed, as the subject is, in its natural setting as a part of the great study of life in its many manifestations, and turned to account as it also is as a field for the application of the laws of natural and moral science (physics chemistry, psy   , economics, civics), no opening is afforded for morbid introspective employment of the physiological facts acquired in the laboratory. A thoroughly wholesome tone pervades the class-rooms, and the most noticeable influence on the personality of the students is stated to be a more intelligent recognition of the needs of the body, and a greater disposition to give the necessary attention to its right performance of vital functions.

How " time " can be legitimately found for this invaluable study by both sexes, during high school life is apparent from the particulars of the five alternative courses at the Peter Cooper High School.*

C.—COLLEGES.

Before entering upon a review of the College Courses in Household Science and Hygiene, it seems advisable to refer somewhat fully to the history and aims of these institutions.

History and Development. In his exhaustive paper on the "American College" (No. 5 *Monographs on Education in the United States*, edited by Dr. N. Murray Butler), Professor Andrew Fleming West opens his subject by telling his readers that the American College has no exact counterpart in the educational system of any other

---

* *See* Table XV.

TABLE XV.

COURSES OF STUDY FOR THE HIGH SCHOOLS OF MANHATTAN AND THE BRONX, NEW YORK CITY.

Classical.	College and Normal Preparatory.	Scientific.	Modern Language	Commercial.
FIRST YEAR.	FIRST YR.	FIRST YEAR.	FIRST YEAR.	FIRST YEAR.
Biology	Biology	English		English
English				French or
History		French	French	
Latin		Physiology	Physiology	
Mathematics				
Physiology				SECOND YEAR.
SECOND YEAR.	SECOND YEAR.	SECOND YEAR.	SECOND YEAR.	
	English			Book-keeping &
History	French or German	Physiography or	French	
Latin	Latin		Matics	
	Mathematics			
			THIRD YEAR.	English Language or
THD YR.	THD YEAR.	THIRD YR.	English	Physics
French or German	French or		French	Book-keeping &
Greek	Latin	or Latin		Typewriting
Latin	Mathematics	and Economics		
Mathematics				
	FOURTH YR.	FOURTH YEAR.	FOURTH YEAR.	FOURTH YEAR.
M. YR.	Latin		English	
		or		
Greek	Electives:			Typewriting
		History		Law
Latin		M		
	Latin			
	Mathematics			
	Physiography			

NOTE. Physical training, two periods a week, is prescribed for all pupils; but half the time allotted to physical training in the third and fourth years may be given to elocution.

History and
Develop-
ment
—*continued.* country. " The elements which compose it are derived, it is true, from European systems, and in particular from Great Britain; but the form under which these elements have been finally compounded is a form suggested, and almost compelled, by the needs of our national life . . . notably different from the old world schools." He then traces the history and progress of this important factor in the national system of free education, concluding this portion of his paper as follows : " Still, in order to understand the precise nature and unique influence of the college in American education, it is not necessary here to trace step by step the story of its development, for in its various forms of present organisation it reveals not only the normal type which has been evolved, but also survivals of past stages of development, instances of variation and even of degeneration from the type, and interesting present experiments, which may to some extent foreshadow the future."

On a later page Professor West draws attention to the fact that " the American College, as contrasted with European schools, is a composite thing—partly secondary and partly higher in its organisation. It consists regularly of a four-year course of study leading to the Bachelor's degree. Up to the close of the Civil War (1861–1865), it was mainly an institution of secondary education, with some anticipations of university studies toward the end of the course. But even these embryonic university studies were usually taught as rounding out the course of disciplinary education, rather than as subjects of free investiga-tion. Boys entered college when they were 15 or 16 years of age. The average age of graduation did not exceed 20 years . . . With but few and unimportant exceptions, the four-year course consisted of prescribed studies. They were English literature and rhetoric, Latin, Greek, mathematics, natural philosophy, and political economy, and often a little psychology and metaphysics. Perhaps some ancient or general history was added. French and German were sometimes taught, but not to an important degree. At graduation the student received the degree of Bachelor of Arts, and then entered on the study of law, medicine, or theology at some professional school, or went into business or into teaching in the primary or secondary schools. Such was, in barest outline, the scheme of college education a generation ago. At the present time things are very different. With the vast growth of the country in wealth and population since the Civil War there has come a manifold development. The old four-year course, consisting entirely of a single set of prescribed studies leading to the one degree of Bachelor of Arts, has grown and branched in many ways. It has been modified from below, from above and from within. The better preparation now given in thousands of schools has enabled colleges to ask for somewhat higher entrance requirements, and, what is more important, to exact them with greater firmness. The age of entrance has increased, until at the older and stronger colleges the average is now about $18\frac{1}{2}$ years. A four-year course leading to a Bachelor's degree remains, although in some quarters the increasing age of the students is creating a tendency to shorten the course to three years, in order that young men may not be kept back too long from entering upon their professional studies . . The four-year course, however, no longer leads solely to the degree of Bachelor of Arts, nor has this old degree itself remained unmodified."

" With the foundation of schools of science which aimed to give a modern form of liberal education based mainly on the physical and natural sciences, and yet only too often gave, under this name, a technological course, or a somewhat incongruous mixture of technical and liberal studies, the degree of Bachelor of Science came into use as a college degree. . . . Still other degrees of lesser importance also came into vogue and obtained a footing here and there to mark the completion of a four years' college course. . . . The organisation of such courses was naturally embarrassed by grave difficulties which are as yet only partially overcome. . . . The present drift, however, of opinion and action in colleges which offer more than one Bachelor's degree is more reassuring than it was some twenty years ago. There is a noticeable tendency, growing stronger each year, to draw a sharp line between liberal and technical education, and to retain undergraduate college education in liberal studies as the best foundation for technical studies, thus elevating the latter to a professional dignity comparable with law, medicine, and divinity . . . and if this happy result can be considered assured, then the undergraduate college course, the sole guarantee of American liberal culture, will have a good chance to organise itself in accordance with its own high ideals, however imperfectly it may have realised these ideals in the past. Another hopeful tendency which is gradually gathering strength is to give the various Bachelor's degrees more definite significance by making them stand for distinct types of liberal or semi-liberal education. . . . Three such types are now slowly evolving out of the mass of studies with increasing logical consistency. . . . First comes the historical academic course, attempting to realise the idea of a general liberal education, and consisting of the classical and modern literatures, mathematics and science, with historical, political and philosophical studies added, and leading to the Bachelor of Arts degree. The second is the course which aims to represent a strictly modern culture, predominantly scientific in character, and culminating in the degree of Bachelor of Science. As this course originated in the demand for knowledge of the applied sciences in the arts and industries of modern life, the ideal of a purely modern liberal culture, predominantly scientific was not easy to maintain. . . . Conscious of this difficulty, many schools of science have been giving larger place in the curriculum to some of the more available humanistic studies. Fuller courses in French and German have been provided for, and the study of English has been insisted upon with sharper emphasis Economics, modern history, and even the elements of philosophy, have found a place. . . . The college of to-day provides a four years' course, consisting generally of a mixture of prescribed and elective studies in widely varying proportions . . . and, at the

Methods of
Instruction.

end of the course, there is a multiform instead of a uniform Bachelor's degree, or, in some instances, a " simple Bachelor's degree of multiform meaning," while the average age of the students has increased at least two years."

In Section VII., which deals with Modes of Instruction, Professor Fleming West records that " Instruction is still mainly conducted by recitation and lecture, the recitation finding its chief place in the earlier, and the lecture in the later, part of the course." But other forms of instruction are included . . . " In all except the elementary courses in science, the laboratory plays a most important part, and even in the lectures in the introductory courses in physics, chemistry or biology, full experimental illustration is the rule. Then, too, the library serves as a sort of laboratory for the humanistic studies. Students are encouraged to learn the use of the college library as auxiliary to the regular exercises of the curriculum. Certain books are appointed as collateral reading, and the written examination at the end of the term often takes account of this outside reading." The combination of these three methods seems to exercise a stimulating effect on the eager students, and acts, I was told, as a spur to the indolent ; it also offers just what is desirable in the treatment of Household Science with advanced students.

Form of
Government.

"The form of government is simple. A college corporation, legally considered, consists of a body of men who have obtained the charter and who hold and administer the property. Where a particular State has established a college or even a university, which regularly includes a college, the members of the corporation are commonly styled regents, and are appointed by the State to hold office for a limited term of years. But most colleges have been established as private corporations. In this case the title is vested in a board of trustees, sometimes composed of members who hold office for life, or else composed of these associated with others who are elected for a term of years. . . . The president and professors usually hold office for life. In some places provision is beginning to be made for the retirement of professors on pensions as they grow old. Instructors and sometimes assistant professors are appointed for a limited time, such appointments being subject to renewal or promotion. In the larger colleges the president is assisted in his administrative work by one or more deans. By immemorial tradition the president and faculty are charged with the conduct of the entire instruction and discipline. They have the power to admit and dismiss students. The conferring of degrees belongs to the corporation, but this power is almost invariably exercised in

Sources of
Income.

accordance with recommendations made by the faculty. . . . In State colleges the income is derived from taxation, in others from endowments, often supplemented by annual subscriptions for special purposes. . . . State colleges receive few private gifts. But the private colleges are cut off from dependence on the State, and have to rely on these (private gifts). This stream of

Students'
Expenses.

private liberality flows almost unceasingly. . . . The expenses of individual students vary greatly. In some places there is no charge for tuition; in others they must pay as much as $100 or $150. In little country colleges the total cost for a year often falls within $300; in the larger old eastern colleges, drawing patronage from all parts of the land, the student who must pay all his bills, and receives no aid in the form of a scholarship, can hardly get along with less than $600 or $700, exclusive of his expenses in the summer vacation. . . . Moreover, many colleges possess scholarships which are open to able students who need temporary pecuniary help. The young American of narrow means, if he be of fair ability and industry, can almost always manage to find his way through college."

According to the last available Report of the United States Commissioner of Education (1899-1900), there are now 480 Universities and Colleges (excluding those for women only) ; it must be borne in mind that a considerable number of these are independent of State endowment or control. About 72·5 per cent. of the total number are co-educational ; in fourteen over 1,000 students are enrolled.

Of the State universities, or colleges, as they are variously described, about thirty have already initiated courses in Household Science, the subject being based upon a course of study which qualifies for a Bachelor of Science degree ; and as many more have introduced some more or less organised form of this work into their curricula. The Household Science department is usually housed in the college of agriculture, but its students follow general courses in science, art, literature, languages, and so forth, with the students in the other colleges. The idea that domestic subjects have any claims to associate on terms of equality with the studies carried on by college undergraduates savours of suspicious novelty and questionable stability to English minds, so that the statement that their claims to post-graduate study have sufficed to gain them honourable recognition in universities of such standing as Columbia and Chicago will be suggestive of a degree of unconventionality, possible only in a new world untrammelled by age-long traditions. That the movement is not merely an evanescent outcome of a passing fad, or the product of inexperienced or unbalanced womanhood is indicated by the fact that, without exception, it has received the cordial, active support of the other faculties in colleges where it has been inaugurated. Professors of chemistry, biology, geology, art, architecture, psychology, economics and sociology, voluntarily devote time, ability, and influence to further the initiation and success of these courses, not in one, but in all the universities where the subject has been introduced.

Province and History of Courses in Household Science.

Its claims for consideration and for organisation as a college study have been briefly recorded by Miss Isabel Bevier, Professor of Household Science at the Illinois State University, in an address given a few months ago ; and no woman is better qualified to "state a case," for, under her highly qualified organisation, what promises to be a model university course is being gradually evolved. Before transcribing her remarks I would remind my readers of Professor Fleming West's opinion quoted above, that a sharper line is being drawn annually in college science courses between liberal and technical education, and that liberal studies are emphasised in undergraduate college education as the best foundation for technical studies, in

Province
and History
of Courses
in House-
hold Science
—*continued.*

order to elevate the latter to a high standard of professional dignity. Bearing this in mind it becomes conceivable, and to some thinkers apparent, that to institute a university course in Household Science does not threaten to lower the college in which it is pursued to the humbler footing of a cooking school ; on the contrary, it raises the whole complex question of the right nutrition of the human race to its legitimate status in the kingdom of science. Miss Bevier was invited to answer the inquiry, " What do you mean by Household Science, and what is its province in a State University ? " The following extracts embody the gist of her reply : . . . " It has been said that Household Science includes the study of the agents, the materials, and the phenomena of the household. One needs to pause a moment and repeat the words to appreciate the largeness of the subject—the agents, heat, light, sound, electricity, colour; the materials, the air we breathe, the food we eat, the water we drink, the houses we live in—who will complete the list ? It is well to remember that principles are universal, while their applications are special and peculiar. The general laws of heat are as true for the modern range as for the steam engine. The painter, the decorator and the dyer have each a technical interest in colour, but the woman who would give beauty and personality to her home by a harmonious blending of colour cannot disregard these same principles. By Household Science we mean very largely applied science. Just at this point it seems to me is the weak spot, perhaps it were better to say the uncultivated field, in the education of woman. Our colleges for men long since recognised the value of science and its application. This fact is illustrated by the increase of our technical schools until they number over sixty, and the students in technical courses of college grade number over 20,000 young men. Women have been rather slow to recognise the close relation science sustains to the affairs of the home, and by some strange oversight provision has not been made for them to apply their science in a kingdom peculiarly their own. Is there any good reason why the girl should not apply her knowledge of chemistry to bread, and of bacteriology to the processes of fermentation ? I am co-educational enough to believe, generally speaking, that the system which proves most successful in the training of boys will have a similar result with their sisters. I believe it is our privilege to profit by their experiments. They have tested successively the classical school, the manual training school, the technical school ; and our universities stand to-day because men have felt that the highest development, the truest unfolding of the human spirit, was to be accomplished not by any one kind of school, but by the correlation of the best elements of each. This brings us directly to our topic—the province of Household Science in a State University. I answer :—to provide a place and an opportunity for the correlation and application of the arts and sciences to the home. I know of no one place which affords so many opportunities for the application of science. Neither do I know of a place more fateful for good or evil in the life of the individual or the nation, than the home. As the equipment and advantages of the university greatly exceed those of a single college, so are the opportunities of the Household Science department greatly multiplied. In no other institution to my knowledge can the department have the inspiration and help of expert workers in so many different lines, as well as the advantage of illustrative material of so many different kinds. The college of science can reveal to the students some of the mysteries of the laws of life. The college of liberal arts can give them a truer conception of their own place and work in the world by a study of the history and literature of other peoples and tongues. The eye can be trained to recognise beauty of colour and outline and the hand to express it, by the work of art and design. The architect and decorator can show how to construct and adorn ' the house beautiful.' A wise selection and correlation of work in these various lines, with the special work of the Household Science department, affords an unusual opportunity for that symmetrical development so greatly to be desired in educational training."

The fact that an annual increase takes place in the number of girls willing to devote four years to these courses speaks for the growing recognition of their educational equally with their social value; for the American girl of 18 is eager to learn, she desires "culture," and would not forego its anticipated attainment for the most "useful" course in the world. Show her the possibilities and advantages of a combination of the two, and the practical side of her character welcomes the opportunity to increase her command of the tools she is called upon to wield throughout her daily life, and to thereby lighten and brighten her tale of work; her social instincts are stimulated by the increased worth and happiness she can add to human existence, and her intellectual abilities find satisfaction in the scope afforded for their profitable exercise. The innate mechanical instincts characteristic of the American of to-day furnish an "energy" for application far more conspicuous than is the case with the descendants of older civilisations.

The first college course in the subject was organised in 1875 by Miss Lou. C. Allen, in what was then described as the "Industrial" University at Champaign (Ill.), now the University of Illinois. Her object was to place instruction in household arts for young women upon a level with instruction in agriculture, horticulture, and the mechanic arts for young men. Miss Allen was made Professor of Household Science, constituted a member of the Faculty, and carried on the classes for several years. The department was only abandoned after this period of good work, because, on Miss Allen's marriage, no suitable person could be found to take her place. Some work in Domestic Science was started in the Kansas State Agricultural College the same year (1875); at first in the form of lectures only, but, later, practical work was introduced, and in 1878, Mrs. May B. Welch, the wife of the President of the Agricultural College, induced the trustees to open a definite Household Arts Department, which for some years she herself conducted. The continuity of this course has been uninterrupted: at the present time one year's study of the subject is obligatory on all female students, while a complete four-years course is open to those who desire to avail themselves of such opportunities. Thus, tentatively, the movement began; and its present phase of hopeful development is the outcome of quiet perseverance, strenuous effort, and assured conviction on the part of the college women who have pioneered its passage into the universities. To them is now accorded the well-earned encouragement of increasing support from the public, from the press, and from their male colleagues. This is accorded on the grounds of the value of a comprehensive, practical knowledge of household economics as a factor in the promotion of national efficiency, of the home happiness and stability which must underlie such efficiency, and for its recently recognised worth as a focus for the application of the sciences and arts.

Three specimen college courses have been selected for reference in this Report as typical of the leading features which distinguish those at present organised. That at the State University of Illinois is framed to prove that, as to laboratory work and methods generally, the subject is of an equal educational value with other

Typical
Courses in
Household
Science—
continued.

branches of science and art, capable of holding its own with any
course of advanced study. The second, at the Ohio State University, is an illustration of the methods followed when the
course approximates more closely to that of a high class
Technical Institute: and the third, at the Michigan State Agricultural College, is frankly technical in character. Did space
permit, much suggestive material could be gathered from a close
study of other excellent courses, those, for instance, at the State
Agricultural Colleges of Colorado and Kansas, or at the State
Universities of Minnesota and Missouri, all of which are conducted by women of ability and good qualifications, with the
assistance of the leading professors of their respective colleges
and universities.

The broad features have a certain similarity in all those of
which I have secured particulars. The full course occupies four
years: the scope of subjects is wide, made purposely comprehensive to introduce general culture studies: the aim is to show
the foundations of science and art upon which domestic economy
is well and truly laid: the method is that known as the "laboratory," which constitutes a valuable mental training in addition
to its scientific value. The anticipated results are the elevation
to its true dignity of home life and its constituent parts; a
gradual repression of the sins against sanitation which are
inimical to the perfect development of the individual and an
economic tax on the community; a substantial gain to the
nation at large in the increased efficiency, physical, mental, and
moral, of its units.

The variety in detail is wide; a two or one year's course may
be obligatory, and is almost invariably optional, for young women
whose tastes or time do not allow the full four years' course to
be undertaken; or short winter courses are available which aim
to impart a certain amount of definite information in the limited
time at the students' disposal. In these, scientific must give place
to more utilitarian methods, but the worker learns better ways
of doing, and forms a centre for the subsequent formation of a
more enlightened "public opinion."

The scope of the full courses is usually on the following lines:—

SCIENCES.—Obligatory: chemistry, physics, biology, physiology,
sanitation; with geology, meteorology, bacteriology and psychology as "electives."

ARTS.—Obligatory: drawing, design, architecture, cooking,
sewing, dress cutting and fitting; with music, painting, millinery,
etc., as "electives."

GENERAL CULTURE STUDIES.—Obligatory: English literature,
history, modern languages, botany and physical culture; of which
one modern language and botany would be "electives."

The laboratory method is invariably emphasised, but the
actual manipulation of foods or of materials is, by some authorities reduced to a minimum, because of the belief that, with brain
trained to habitual observation, accuracy and reflection, with
hand skilled through brush, pencil and laboratory work to give

quick and reliable response to mental suggestion, with muscles strengthened and co-ordinated by intelligent physical culture under careful supervision, principles acquired and based upon sound reasoning can be applied with a precision and certainty which should ensure rapid success. The home life of the student should afford abundant opportunity for repeated practice, when circumstances have probably removed her from the chances of other scientific or artistic training for which she has peculiar facilities in her college days.

In respect of these courses, the Western colleges preceded those in the Eastern States, where the State authorities for higher education seem, as yet, hardly awake to the importance or possibilities of the subject. I am partly inclined to attribute this apparent inattention to its claims for recognition in State colleges, at least in New York State, Pennsylvania and Massachusetts, to the excellent courses available at the Pratt and Drexel Technical Institutes, and to other similar outside opportunities for advanced study, such as that offered at the Simmons Technical College for Women at Boston (Mass.), which meet the existing demand.

The University of Illinois is situated in the eastern central part of the State between the cities of Champaign and Urbana, 128 miles south of Chicago; the country round is a rich and prosperous agricultural region, while the combined population of the cities is about 15,000. The University was opened March 2, 1868, with some 50 students. During the first term the number increased to 77, all young men, but, in March, 1870, the trustees admitted women as students, and during the year 1870–71, 24 availed themselves of the privilege. Since that time they have constituted from one-sixth to one-fifth of the total number. Applicants for admission to the freshman class must be at least 16 years of age. Entrance may be made at any time, provided the candidate is competent to take up the work of the classes then in progress, but all are advised to enter in September. Admission to the freshman class of the University may be obtained in one of three ways : (a) by certificate from a fully accredited high school ; (b) by examination ; (c) by transfer of credits from some other college or university. Persons over 21 years of age, not candidates for a degree, may be admitted to classes, after satisfying the president and the professor in charge of the department in which such classes are taught, that they possess the requisite information and ability to pursue profitably, as special students, the chosen subjects. Such students are not matriculated ; they pay the tuition fee of $7·50 a term, in addition to the regular incidental fee of $12.

The government of the University is vested by the trustees primarily in the President of the University, in the Faculty, in the Council of Administration and in the Deans. The President is the executive head of the University. The University is divided into 11 interdependent colleges and schools. For some years past one scholarship from each county has been awarded annually, upon competitive examination, to males throughout the State, and considerable satisfaction was experienced in the spring of 1901 when the Board of Trustees granted to the daughters of farmers a privilege similar to that previously enjoyed only by their sons. The fees for matriculation, laboratory work, etc., are very small, and a tuition fee of $7·50 only, a term, is demanded. The University does not furnish board, but there is a dining hall in the basement of the University Hall, under university supervision, where good meals may be obtained at reasonable rates. The immediate control of this dining hall is entrusted to the skilled management of a graduate of the Boston School of Housekeeping (now incorporated in the Simmons Technical College), who ensures that the food is not only varied, but nutritious, wholesome, and proportioned to the require-

(a) State University of Illinois.

Table XVI.

(a) State
University
of Illinois
— *continued.*

ments of normal diets; indeed, the food provided must meet with the approval of the Professor of Household Science, Miss Isabel Bevier, whose dietary studies in connection with Professor Atwater's work have been published among the United States Food Bulletins. The charge for table board in this dining hall is fixed at $3·50 (about 14s.) a week, for which three full meals daily, including Sunday, are supplied. "Fraternity" or "Sorority" houses are a popular form of lodging among students; in the case of girls, 9 to 14 often select a chaperon and equip one house between them; they almost invariably perform personally all domestic duties, which, however, owing to the arrangement just described, do not include cooking.

All the courses are open to all the students, though it is necessary that the professor in charge be satisfied concerning the fitness of the applicant to profit by his selection. A full course equals 5 "credits," each of which is the equivalent of one hour's recitation and two hours' preparation (this may be laboratory work), for 5 days in the week; this works out at about 15 to 19 hours a week. All physical training is extra, though it is accepted for "credit" by some of the professors. Students graduate with the degree of Bachelor of Arts, Science, Literature, &c., according to the line of study they elect to follow.

The course in Household Science* is followed in the College of Agriculture, a large, well-planned building, opened in May 1901. The department occupies the entire second floor of the north wing, and is well supplied with laboratories, apparatus, and a mass of illustrative material, such as charts, specimens of various kinds of building material, and exhibits illustrating the chemical composition and products obtained in the manufacture of certain foods. The students have access also to the museum of the Architectural department, as well as the benefit of close association with the Art department. A chemical laboratory is attached to the kitchen for the immediate application of science to home problems in chemistry or bacteriology. Adjoining this is a room which will gradually acquire the appearance of a museum, consequent upon the accumulation of a large collection of specimen foods, utensils, apparatus, etc., connected with the course. One room is devoted to the study of Household Art: here are found full-sized illustrations of window decoration, of wall-papers, parqueterie flooring, etc., which afford materials for colour study in drapery and room decoration, and for the cultivation of a taste too often conspicuous by its absence among a large section of the community. A small collection of artistic tiles and sample vases, selected for grace of form as well as for beauty of workmanship, is also being made, with a view to training the mind and eyes of students who bring only the crudest ideas of art from their remote rural homes. No limit is set to reasonable and wise expenditure in the equipment of this or other minor departments essential to the completeness of the whole scheme.

The studies peculiar to the Household Science course can be taken in two years, given adequate previous preparation, but a full four years is requisite to gain the degree of Bachelor of Science. Forty female students entered the Household Science department on its initiation in September, 1900, one male student also followed it throughout, while others of his sex were so much interested that there is a prospective demand for a course in Sanitation planned to

---

* *See* Table XVI.

meet masculine needs. Meanwhile, Miss Bevier has worked to meet (*a*) State University of Illinois —*continued.*
the needs of two classes of students; (*a*) those who specialise in
other lines of work, but who desire a knowledge of the general
principles and facts of household science; (*b*)those who wish to make
a speciality of household science by a comprehensive study of the
affairs of the home, together with the arts and sciences whose applications are directly connected with its management and care.

Though still in its infancy, this course promises to be of great value in
the opportunity it offers for combining a liberal education with a basis of
pure and applied science. By the judicious correlation of the distinctive
household science subjects with some of the regular courses given in other
colleges of the University, excellent facilities are provided for a study of
their applications to the affairs of the household, while the oneness and
interdependence of all knowledge is accentuated. "Woman's education
here seems to me to have swung to one extreme and to be now coming
back to a more normal and sensible ideal," writes Miss Bevier, in a reply to
a request on my part for further particulars of her guiding principles when
she framed this course; "in my own college days we were just feeling that
the one thing to do was to share the privileges enjoyed by the men : to
study and do everything they did. So, in the course in trigonometry, as
the men had surveying, we girls diligently walked along too, sighted,
measured—the boys being gallant enough to carry the chain and various
other impedimenta. I think we might have gone to the studio with much
greater advantage and learned something about form and colour in those
hours. If Harvard can devise a scheme, as it has done, by which their men
who wish to enter a professional course after their college course, can finish
the studies of the college course in three years, I believe it is entirely
possible to give to girls in two years the sciences that must form the basis
of any intelligent study of the home problems, together with a little application in those first years and a great deal of application in the third year.
A fourth year student should then be ready and competent to do some
investigation worthy of the name, while she is also at liberty to enlarge her
horizon by a study of economics, education or psychology."

The required studies are household science, botany, bacteriology, zoology, physiology, chemistry, physics, mathematics, art
and design, domestic architecture, elementary decoration, German and physical training; the "electives" are English, French,
economics, history, psychology and education. No laundry
work is included, no practice work in housewifery, no needlework or dress cutting, as it is Miss Bevier's creed that it is a
study of the principles of these home industries, rather than
their technical application, which belong to a university course.
In botany, zoology, and physics, the general regular courses for
all students are followed. In chemistry, after the first elementary
and experimental course, qualitative and quantitative analysis
is taken up, with the elements of organic chemistry, to which a
course on household chemistry forms the conclusion. In this,
analyses, planned on special lines for these students, of baking
powders, vinegars, syrups, sugars, soaps, wall-papers, etc., are
carried out; an examination is also made of materials used in
the household ; individual work is demanded throughout.
In bacteriology, the general introductory course is followed,
supplemented by special applications to those ferments, yeasts,
moulds, etc., related to household work. Physiology is studied
with the agricultural students, and is practically illustrated by
demonstrations, dissections, and discussions carried out by
Professor Kemp; students make their own sections of tissues,

TABLE XVI.

SCHEDULE OF HOUSEHOLD SCIENCE COURSE, STATE AGRICULTURAL COLLEGE, UNIVERSITY OF ILLINOIS.

Institution and [ ].	Entrance Requirements.	Scope of Course.	Methods.	Length of Course.	Fees and Finance.	Equipment.
[State] Agricultural College, Urbana, [Ill]. Household [Science] Course. [ ] Miss Bevier.	At least 16 years of age. (a) By [certificate] from a fully [accredited] School. (b) By examination. (c) By [ ]... [ ] other [ ] age or University. Persons [over] 21, [ ]... may be [ ]... [ ] the President and the Pr[ ] in charge of the [ ]... that by [ ] [ ] informa-tion and ability to [pursue]... [ ]. Such students [ ] an [ ].	The aim of the Course is to [give] a liberal [ ] with a [ ] of [ ] and [applied] Science. [Hold] [ ]. General [ ] often with other students in the regular [ ], [ ], by a [Special] [ ] on [ ] istry and [ ]. Bacteriology, [ ], [ ], Art and Design, [ ] [ ], } Special Courses. [ ] Train-ing, } General Courses. English, French, [etc.], [ ], } Elective Courses.	The [ ] is planned to [ ] the true lines of [ ] Science on [ ] [ ] to [ ] belong [ ]... rather than [ ] [ ]... [ ] no [ ], [ ] cutting. Laundry [ ], to [ ] [ ] [ ], will shortly be [ ]ded. All practical work is indi-vidual. Students of Botany, Zoology, and Physiology, make and mount their own sections of tissues, and be-come expert in microscopy. Books of reference are [ ] ferred to any [ ] [ ] [ ] [ ] [ ] bear-ing on the work of a [ ] [ ], month, or [ ], are [ ] by [ ] [ ] [ ] the [ ] of [ ] students, [ ] [ ] [ ] the [ ] reading being provi[ ] [ ] in the fine library.	Short Course 2 years, [ ] [ ] [ ] [ ] [ ]-paration. For B.Sc. De-gree, full 4 [ ] Course [ ].	Small [ ] [ ] [ ] and labora-[ ] work. Tuition fee $750 a [term]. [No] funds. [ ] [ ] [ ] from [ ] [ ] [ ] in the [ ] awarded an-nually by [ ] [ ] [ ] to a [ ] and student.	No [ ], [ ] [ ] on reason-able [ ]. The [ ] [ ] [ ] of one entire [ ] [ ] of the [ ] agricul-tural [ ]; it [ ] [ ], [ ], and ex-[ ] art, [ ], and the [ ]bits [ ] of textiles and [ ] [ ] [ ], [ ] [ ] [ ] [ ] and [ ] [ ] in the [ ] of [ ] [ ], [ ] [ ] [ ] also have, [ ] to the museums of the Archi-tectural [ ], and of the Art [ ].

mount and investigate them microscopically. Dean Ricker, of the Department of Architecture, has taken much interest in the preparation of a special and suitable course in house planning, sanitary construction, and history of architecture, which is usefully supplemented by his unusual collection of illustrative lantern slides and by the number of models and specimens of stones, bricks, fixtures and fittings, arranged in the architectural museum. Professor Frank Frederick, who is responsible for the art course, requires his students to devote their first term to the acquirement of facility in accurate drawing, freehand, perspective, cast outlines, etc. Lectures on colour and design, with accompanying exercises, form a portion of the course, while shading, wash and charcoal sketches and rapid drawing from life, constitute the second part of the art studies. Students are advised throughout to consult books of reference rather than to confine their reading to any single text-book ; bibliographies bearing on the work of a given term, month, or week, are prepared by Miss Bevier for their use, in which references to articles in current journals and reviews find a place among those to standard authorities. Every facility for the necessary reading is provided in the Library, which is quite the most imposing building in its architectural features among the group on the extensive campus ; within also it is interesting on account of its fine proportions and the beauty of its colour scheme and fresco decorations.

The class of women from which this Household Science Department draws its students is largely agricultural ; the daughters of Illinois farmers constitute the greater proportion of those who come under Miss Bevier's influence and supervision ; so far she finds that, though her demands necessitate very hard work on the part of her students, it is not over severe or impossible of accomplishment. The year which has elapsed since my visit has given promise of increased vitality, and the cordial co-operation of the other professors concerned has been not only sustained but strengthened.

The Ohio Agricultural and Mechanical College was established by law in 1870, but was not opened until 1873 for the reception of students. Five years later the Legislature passed an Act which, amongst other changes, provided that the institution should be subsequently designated as "The Ohio State University." Up to this time but one appropriation had been made by the State for its support ; with the reorganisation came a larger and broader view of the State's relation to public education, and since that time the Ohio State University has shared with other public educational institutions a more generous support by the State. The governing body of the Institution is a Board of Trustees, appointed by the Governor of the State and confirmed by the Senate, for terms of seven years, as provided in the law organising the University. The original endowment has been supplemented, and the objects of the University promoted, by a permanent annual grant from the United States, under an Act of 1890 ; by special appropriations of the General Assembly ; and, in 1891, by a permanent annual grant from the State, which grant was doubled by the legislature of 1896. In accordance with the spirit of the law under which it was organised, the University aims to furnish ample facilities for education in the liberal and industrial arts, sciences and languages, and for the thorough technical and professional study of agriculture, engineering in its various departments, veterinary medicine, pharmacy and law. Through

(b.) Ohio State University. Table XVII.

6490.　　　　　　　　　　　　　　　　　　　　H

(*b*) Ohio
State
ni ersity
—*continued.* the aid which has been received from the United States and from the State, it is enabled to offer its opportunities with a slight charge for incidental expenses, to all persons of either sex who are qualified for admission. The University has now over one hundred instructors, and 38 departments of study. Six of its 30 courses are offered by the College of Agriculture and Domestic Science and lead to the degrees of Bachelor of Science in Agriculture, Bachelor of Science in Horticulture and Forestry, and Bachelor of Science in Domestic Science. There are two free scholarships from each of the 88 counties of the State, in Agriculture, Domestic Science, and Veterinary Science.

The former President of the University, Dr. James Canfield, now librarian of the Columbia University, New York City, did excellent pioneer work in his ardent advocacy of the necessity for a general teaching of hygiene and household economics; it was to him that this course owed its initiation in 1896, and through him that Miss Perla Bowman (now Mrs. W. Gibb) was selected to organise it. The results justified his choice; Miss Bowman worked unremittingly to frame such a course of study as should exemplify the connection of history, science and art with home life; her object was the production of well balanced, cultured women, endowed with the power of facing and solving home life problems. Experience showed her that at first girls must be taught to appreciate the value of life, and then only can they be stimulated to acquire the knowledge how to maintain life at its best. In accordance with her advice two courses are offered in Domestic Science; the shorter (two years) is planned for those who can give but a limited time to university training, and the longer (four years) is of a more exhaustive character; it requires a more advanced standing for entrance, and leads to the degree of Bachelor of Science in Domestic Science. A certificate of attendance is given for the two years' course, which includes the same practical work as does the four years', but demands fewer allied subjects and less general culture. Experience shows that this short course appeals especially to country girls who have had the equivalent of two years' high school work. The minimum time spent in class-room work is 15 hours a week; this represents at least 30 hours' work, exclusive of 4 hours a week physical training during the whole two years, for each "credit" hour presupposes 2 hours actual work. From 50 to 60 students have completed this course, their ages varying from 18 to 21 years. The complete four years' Domestic Science curriculum includes domestic art, botany, zoology, chemistry, physiology, bacteriology, drawing (freehand, architectural, and plan drawing), horticulture, psychology, economics, physical culture, history, and English literature; French and German are optional. The actual work in Domestic Economy absorbs a little less than one-third of a student's time. It consists of sound and advanced training in cookery, under first-class instructors, with great stress laid upon the comparative nutritive value of foods, the effect of cooking upon their digestibility, and the construction of economical, nutritious and varied diets. The accompanying study of household economics comprises laundry work in addition to the study of much that pertains to

the planning and sanitary care of a house; disinfection, home (*b*) Ohio
nursing, and emergency work are also included, as well as a State
practical knowledge of domestic accounts. The scheme of University
Domestic Art embraces studies and practice in colour schemes *—continued.*
and all forms of household decoration; there is constant practice, under competent instruction, of plain sewing, dressmaking
and millinery, with much drafting and cutting of patterns;
while attention is consistently directed to the production and
manufacture of materials, equally with their choice and treatment; the study of line, form, colour and texture runs parallel
with the whole practical course. The schedule (Table XVII.)
shows the scope, plan and aim of the whole scheme.

The subject of bacteriology is first taken up generally, in its relation to
man and his immediate surroundings, students are taught to make nutrient
media, and to work reliably with the microscope : in the laboratory they
learn the isolation of pure cultures, how to distinguish the various bacteria
met with in food and water, and the mechanical examination of water,
milk and air. Food adulteration is somewhat fully treated by Professor
Weber, who gained his experience as State Inspector and Food Analyst,
and who has an extensive and most interesting collection of specimens of
artificial and adulterated foods. Professor Kellermann endeavours through
the method he pursues in his course on botany to train students to exercise
their reflective powers, and to employ individual effort, rather than to rely
on their teacher or text book ; he seems to possess the gift of stimulating
them to work out their own applications, economic and artistic, and spoke
to me of good thesis work done by his Domestic Science students, especially
in connection with fungi and moulds ; in fact he had selected the writer of
one of these to act as his assistant for the year. Professor Gordy, then in
charge of the department of Psychology and Pedagogy, took special interest
in his share in the promotion of the course, from his firm conviction of the
paramount influence of the home upon national life and character ; and I
learnt from him with interest that their introduction to these subjects
seems to open up a new world to many of the students.

The marriage of Miss Bowman at the completion of the first four years
of the course, which necessitated the election of a successor, may probably
somewhat influence the methods ; but the foundation for future development seemed firmly laid. The majority of students who have hitherto
entered this department come from quite rural districts ; they are often
ignorant of conventions too common for their existence to be recognised
among a town population, though quickly attracting attention if omitted
from the conduct of daily life, so the course had to be planned to develop
social refinements and amenities, as well as to impart a knowledge of
scientific and artistic principles, and to afford opportunity for the acquirement of manual dexterity. I was furnished with many instances of the
good work already accomplished ; that increased contentment with home
life which apparently accompanies ability to modify its conditions, and the
development of a new spirit in the pursuit of philanthropic ends, were two
forms reported to be especially evident. At the date of my visit (June,
1901), all the Domestic Science graduates had either married or returned to
home life, with the exception of one who had gained a Fellowship in botany
in the university over the heads of several candidates from the College of
Science.

The character of the work done, and the progress made, have been
tested up to the present by the professor in charge of each department, at intervals left to his discretion, but the graduation thesis of
each student must be accepted by the general Faculty, and the
time for the final examination is fixed by the executive clerk,
usually at the end of the term. Miss Bowman employed the

TABLE XVII.

STATE UNIVERSITY OF OHIO. COLLEGE OF DOMESTIC SCIENCE AND AGRICULTURE.—SCHEDULE OF DOMESTIC SCIENCE COURSE.

Institution and Course.	Entrance Requirements.	Scope of Course.	Methods.	Length of Course.	Fees and Finance.	Equipment.
State University, Ohio. Agricultural and Domestic Science College. President, Rev. W. Oxley Thompson, D.D., LL.D. Domestic Science Courses— (1) four years. (2) two years. This course offers the same practical work, as (1) but fewer allied subjects are studied and less general culture is demanded.	At least 16 years of age. 1. By certificate from preparatory department of college or normal school. 2. By examination. 3. By graduation certificates from certain High schools approved by the University.	Agricultural Chemistry - 5 terms, 10 hrs. per wk. Botany - 3 " 10 " Zoology and Bacteriology - 3 " 6 " Physiology - 3 " 6 " Chemical Physiology - 1 " 6 " Hygiene and Physical Training - 6 " 4 " Domestic Economy - 9 " 8 " Political Economy - 2 " 6 " Horticulture - 3 " 4 " Drawing— Freehand - 3 " 5 " Mechanical - 1 " 4 " Architectural - 2 " 4 " House Designing - 1 " 4 " English Composition - 3 " 5 " English Literature - 3 " 4 " U. S. Political History - 2 " 6 " Theory of Education - 3 " 6 " French or German - 6 " 8 " Thesis - 3 " 4 "	The course aims to supplement the work of other departments. The study of languages, arts and sciences is combined with a practical consideration of the economic problems which are linked with sanitation and hygiene, and are also directly connected with home life. The Laboratory method is employed wherever permissible.	(1) Four years, each divided into three terms leading to the degree of B.Sc. in Domestic Economy. (2) Two years course, leading to certificate of attendance.	No fees, except certain nominal fees for laboratory work. State funds.	The Science and Biological Laboratories are somewhat limited for the large numbers, but two new buildings are on the point of erection. There is a Spacious Cooking Laboratory and Dining Hall, in which the arrangements aim at duplicating home conditions while they suggest better arrangements.

usual method of giving oral or written " quizzes " to her students (*b*) Ohio State University —*continued.*
at varying intervals.

The following " quiz " in bacteriology was furnished me as a typical example, and serves to indicate the lines followed :—

1. What can you say of the importance of food preservation ?
2. Why in the study of food preservation should we consider bacteria ? Will any other agent cause food to spoil ?
3. Classify bacteria as regards appearance. How do micro-organisms reproduce ?
4. Give a definition for yeast ; for a ferment ; for a mould. What are the fungi ?
5. Are fermentation and putrefaction synonymous terms ? Are bacteria animals or plants ? Support your statement.
6. Give the six divisions of bacteria, as distinguished by their varying properties.
7. What do you understand by anærobic and ærobic bacteria ? What kinds of substances would furnish the best food for each class ?
8. What elements are needed by bacteria ? What conditions particularly affect germ life ?
9. What are spores ? How do they develop ? What may be said concerning the rapidity of germ multiplication ?
10. How may fermentation be checked ?
11. How is this principle of excess of bacterial produce being harmful to the germ applied in inoculation ?
12. Name the principal organised and unorganised ferments.
13. In what class of substances may yeast fermentation take place ?
14. Give the names of the active agents, and the successive steps in the reduction of cellulose to cane sugar in a plant.
15. Do the same, giving reactions, in reduction of starch to grape sugar in the body.
16. Give the reaction when sugar is fermented by yeast ; lactic acid is changed to butyric acid ; when stearine is acted upon by steapsin and changed to glycerine and stearic acid. Give reaction when lactose is attacked by lactic acid ferment.
17. On what mediums are ferments most active ? How does this answer affect the keeping properties of sour fruits ?
18. What is meant by amylolytic ferment ? What is meant by proteolytic ferment ? Name the principal ones of each class.
19. Suppose that a green pear hangs on a tree ; trace the chemical changes which would occur during its ripening and decay, if it were unmolested.
20. Name the different methods by which foods have been preserved.
21. To what man are we particularly indebted for our knowledge of food preservation ? What is the difference between pasteurisation and sterilisation ?
22. What is the action of a rich syrup in preserving food ?
23. What is the active principle in jelly making ? Why do not over ripe or over cooked fruits make good jelly ?
24. How do you explain the preservatives of vinegar, salt, bright hot sun, smoke, cold, heat, antiseptic substances ?
25. What are the most common preservatives used ?
26. Do you recommend their use ? If not, why ?
27. What can you say of the relative food and money values of canned and fresh foods ?
28. What are the arguments in favour of home canning and preserving ?
29. What do you know of the food laws with regard to canned or preserved fruits ?

An evidence of the interest excited among the students by this study is found in the fact that, among the subjects selected for their graduation theses last year were :—The Edible Fungi of Ohio, the Study of Mould in Preserving, and the Bacteriological Examination of Water.

The department is situated in Hayes Hall where there is a
spacious cooking laboratory with a dining-room adjoining, each
fitted with good appliances, $1,000 having been recently ex-
pended to make the department thoroughly efficient. The aim
of the equipment is to duplicate home conditions, while, at the
same time, suggesting better arrangements. To this end great
care and attention has been expended on the dining-room, its
furnishing, use, maintenance, and so forth. The science laboratory
accommodation has been latterly somewhat cramped, owing to the
rapid increase of numbers, which has resulted in overcrowded
classes, but the erection of two new buildings, Physics and Law,
will shortly relieve this congestion. Individual practice work is
the rule throughout the course, except that the dissections in
the general physiology course are carried out by the professors.
This is in part due to the specially crowded conditions of these
classes. Physiology is *required* in *all* the agricultural, veterinary,
horticultural, and domestic economy courses; it is *elective* in all
arts and science courses.

Dr. Thompson, who succeeded Dr. Canfield as President of the
University, anticipates still further developments in the near
future. It was proposed some months ago, and the resolution
was at once adopted by three out of the six Faculties, that a
course in public sanitation be organised, open to students of
both sexes, to meet a growing demand for opportunities of study
on the part of general students who desire to secure a sounder
acquaintance with the questions of sanitary reform, and to equip
themselves to play a more intelligent part in philanthropic
undertakings. President Thompson is in full sympathy with
the proposal, and expressed the hope that this year may see the
resolution adopted by the remaining Faculties.

(c) Michigan State Agricultural College.
The courses in Domestic Science and the Domestic Arts at
the Michigan Agricultural College may be taken as typical of the
best offered in a high grade Technical college. A broad, general
education in English, mathematics and science is provided for its
students, in addition to which, it gives a thorough technical
training in agriculture and related sciences to students in the
agricultural course; in shop work and mechanical engineering to
students in the mechanical courses; and in cookery and domestic
economy to students in the women's course. Wherever possible
the laboratory method is followed.

There are four full courses. Three of these—the agricultural
course and the four years' mechanical course for men and the
domestic economy course for women—require four years for
graduation; and one—the mechanical course for men not
qualified to pass the examinations for entrance to the four years'
mechanical course—requires five years. Each full course leads
to the degree of Bachelor of Science. Besides these the college
offers seven special short courses of from four to eight weeks, in
dairy husbandry, creamery, cheese making, live stock husbandry,
fruit culture, floriculture and winter vegetable gardening, and
sugar production.

The aim in the long courses is to take the student from the high school, or from the end of the 8th grade school year, and to carry him or her through four years of general and technical training, making science the main feature of the college work, and applying it to practical use at the earliest possible moment along the lines of technical training essential to each course. General culture studies are introduced to develop "poise," self control and patriotism, and to enlarge and dignify life in all its aspects. In the special winter courses the object is to impart in the shortest possible time a certain amount of definite information; they are designed chiefly for adults. General culture is not attempted, but efforts are concentrated on the teaching of methods of procedure which can be applied at once to bread-winning. The women's course is designed to give a thorough practical education with special reference to home-making.

(c) Michigan State Agricultural College— *continued.*

Its duration is four years, and it embraces the following subjects: English, mathematics, literature, history, modern languages, botany, chemistry, physics, physiology, entomology, drawing, graphic art, history of art, cooking, domestic science, sewing, cutting and fitting, laundry, physical culture, music, painting, millinery, floriculture, fruit culture, bacteriology; zoology, history, economics and political science, geology, meteorology, physics, and psychology are "electives." The course is considered suitable also for young women who desire to prepare for teaching technical or advanced courses in high and other schools. Candidates for admission must not be less than 15 years of age, and entrance examinations in elementary subjects are required. Candidates over 18 years of age may be admitted without examination, provided that they make arrangements to pass the entrance examination within one year. The average expenses per annum are $136. The college owns four handsome dormitories, one for women and three for men; lodging can also be had in the neighbouring town of Lansing. Board at the college is in the hands of the Students' Club Boarding Association, and is managed by the students. There are six clubs, and each club fixes its own rate of living. The cost varies from $2 to $2.60 per week for young men, and from $1·60 to $2·10 per week for young women. An independent boarding club is run for young men at an expense of about $1·50 per week.

In the Domestic Science course the common facts are correlated in their bearing on household matters; the various occupations and methods necessary to conduct the home in comfort and health are discussed, and stress is laid on practical demonstration. Considerable time is devoted to laboratory work in general, advanced and invalid cookery; a waitress's course, and lectures on household economy are included. The opportunities for practice work are unusually extensive. Students are encouraged to act as waitresses in the large dining-room of the women's building until they acquire the necessary proficiency to direct the serving of dinners of several courses, while those specially interested in catering for large numbers of persons are permitted to make use of the facilities provided by the kitchen attached to the women's dormitory. The kitchen laboratory provides accommodation for the work of 20 students at one time; four tables are subdivided into five compartments, each of which is provided with the usual fittings: conveniences for cooking by electricity, as well as by other mediums, are installed; a private dining-room and the necessary offices are attached. The large laundry

(c) Michigan is furnished with a dryer, wringer, ironing tables, and 18
State porcelain-lined stationary tubs, each of which has hot and cold
Agricultural water laid on. The equipment bears evidence throughout of
College— the study of a wise economy in strength and time.
continued.
•   The Domestic Science students have also two courses in
household bacteriology: the object of the first is to open various
subjects to an examination which should yield a better understanding of the questions involved. The function of yeast in
bread making, a careful survey of milk and its products with a
view to a comprehensive knowledge of their bacteriological and
hygienic significance, the fermentations which occur in vinegar
and canned foods, are leading features of the course. Food preservation in its various forms is also studied from the bacteriological side. A second course is planned to permit of a more
detailed and careful study of the various features of hygienic
work: it includes a study of the causal agents of the more
common infectious diseases, as well as of the action and mode of
application of antiseptics ; while further consideration is
devoted to the hygiene of water, milk, and soil, and some
practical aspects of sewerage and drainage, light and ventilation
are dwelt upon and studied. Three hours a week are devoted
to human physiology and anatomy by the agricultural and
women students during two terms : part of this time is spent in
actual dissection and in the study of the histology of the
tissues; these lessons are supplemented by lectures covering the
principles of hygiene and sanitary science, and of the restriction
and prevention of disease : the department is well equipped with
microscopes and dissecting apparatus. The course in Domestic
Art is carried on in a specially fitted, well equipped and well lit
apartment : it includes sewing in all its branches, dressmaking,
art needlework, and millinery; courses in modelling and manual
training in woodwork also find a place. Drawing is introduced
at an early stage, as it has proved to be a most excellent means
of developing and sharpening the faculty of observation, especially where this has been previously neglected. Some of the
numerous mediums employed in graphic arts are next studied,
such as charcoal drawing, black and white work, pen and ink
work, oil and water colour. A series of lectures on the history of
art, (considered under the three heads of architecture, sculpture,
and painting), conclude the year's work. The study of economics
and political science is elective ; in this course, the training of
citizens, industrial reforms, and problems of population, receive
careful examination, and are correlated with the study of hygiene.
        The short Household Economic course, which is confined to one year,
comprises sanitary science, emergencies and home-nursing, household
accounts, and the principles of everyday art applied to the furnishings of
a house and the treatment of floors, walls and ceilings. A special course
of laboratory exercises and lectures in domestic physics is provided for all
women students in their second year ; it includes determinations as to the
specific heat of various substances, the heat of vaporisation and liquefac-
tion, tests of various forms of thermometers, and a series of comparative
tests as to the efficiency and economy of gasoline, kerosene, alcohol, and
electric heaters, for household use ; a previous study of elementary and
general physics is imperative.

The Household Science courses in the State universities of Reference to Courses in Household Science in various State Universities. Colorado, Iowa, Kansas, Minnesota, Missouri, Nebraska, Utah, and twelve or fourteen similar institutions in other States exemplify variations of the three above detailed. In each case the health and well-being of the nation appears to have been the root cause for the initiation of the course. The proper care of humanity is recognised as a study possessing dignity and worth, and though the interdependence of mind and soul upon physical conditions is appreciated by but a minority of either the students or the public from which they are drawn, yet the leaven is at work which assigns a high place among the sciences of the day to Household Economics, and which also recognises that, by means of this instruction young women are trained to be more healthful, more economic, broader and more appreciative home makers. Influenced as are the details in each college course by the mental attitude of the organiser, by the needs of the students, the sources from which they are drawn, and by the special characteristics of the college (that is to say whether university, technical or utilitarian methods be pursued), there is one broad guiding principle to be traced throughout, viz., that institutions for the higher education of women must offer training adequate for the responsibilities of life, as most women *ought* to meet them, and sooner or later must meet them; a training which shall be broad, which shall supplement established principles, which shall send women to their work cultivated in the fullest significance of the term, and prepared to make life fuller, brighter and better for all with whom they come in contact. For which reasons the very variety presented is, in my opinion, advantageous; the scientific course offered at the University of Illinois, the more utilitarian methods pursued at the University of Ohio, the purely technical training at the Michigan Agricultural College, are each creating, or responding to, the demands of different sections of the community. The last course, which was first established, met and meets the needs of its clientèle; the desire to co-ordinate the science and art of home making with other work of a university grade is realised with some completeness in the newly organised course at Urbana; the cruder conditions of public opinion did not permit of this when the sister course at Columbus was inaugurated but four years previously. It is the opinion of the best informed that it is the highest type which will prevail and gradually draw the others up to its level; if this be the case it will be largely due to the unremitting efforts and example of certain members of the Association of College Alumnæ, to whom great credit is due.

In college life, as during the period of elementary education, Courses in Hygiene. the advantages of a study of personal hygiene, and to a certain extent also of domestic sanitation, are shared by the two sexes; though, in this case, the motive is other than that of a desire to promote a distaste for the use of stimulants and narcotics. Emphasis is laid in most, if not in all, college courses, upon the absolute necessity of maintaining (or, if necessary, of developing) sound health, by means of a judicious regulation of the hours

devoted to study, recreation, exercise and rest. The great
educational advantages to be derived from a good physical
development and a highly trained muscular system are presented
to each year's freshmen; and the custom of requiring a definite
amount of physical culture from all students, preceded by a
carefully conducted physical examination, seems quite the
general college rule. This examination is repeated annually and
the results recorded ; the measurements are outlined on specially
prepared charts, and are accompanied by other desirable data
bearing upon family and personal history, habits (such as
condition of the digestive organs, hours of sleep, etc.), the
standard of the sense organs as to sight, hearing, and so forth ;
naturally these charts are accessible only to the professor in
charge of the gymnasium, and to the individual whom they
concern. The examination and records are framed, in part, to
arouse an intelligent interest among the students in the improvement of their own physique and to stimulate them to a careful
performance of any remedial exercises recommended ; in part to
facilitate the accumulation of reliable statistical material, upon
which, in due time, necessary reforms can be based. It is realised,
however, that an intelligent being should be possessed of good
" reasons for the faith that is in him,' and for the practice which
should spring from that faith ; consequently lectures on personal
hygiene, given by the professor of physical culture, constitute an
integral part of these gymnastic courses (to which more detailed
reference is made in my Report to the Council of The Sanitary
Institute on the " Teaching of Hygiene in the schools and colleges
of the United States of America "). By both these means, theory,
as given by lectures, and practice, as carried out in the gymnasium,
the attention of the greater part of the college population is
directed to the right care and development of the body, to its
dependence on good habits and environment for the fulfilment of
its functions, and to the duty laid upon each to cultivate
symmetry, mental and physical, for personal advancement and
for the welfare of the community. If safeguarded by discretion
and pursued with perseverance and accuracy the results should
be far reaching, for this method of introducing the subject
extends to every student on the register, not merely to those
following this or that course. It is true, the instruction on
personal hygiene is theoretical, in the sense that it is given in pure
lecture form ; but the young people are called upon to make
their own observations and applications, not in the more or less
artificial atmosphere of the gymnasium, but in the conduct of
their daily life, which, in the case of some colleges, is subjected to
advisory suggestion on the part of their instructor. This may be the
survival of the " strong paternal anxiety and oversight " exercised
formerly over students by college Faculties, to which Professor
Fleming West refers in his previously quoted monograph.

At present, a more definite course in general hygiene is not
usually available for college students, though signs of a growing
demand are perceptible. This made itself felt six years since at
Michigan State University, at Chicago University, and in one or

two other instances. To the general course in Sanitary Science at Chicago University reference will be made in Part II. of the Report; particulars of that at the Michigan State University are here detailed.

The University is a part of the public educational system, governed by a Board of Regents, who are popularly elected for terms of eight years' service. There are seven departments, each with its own special Faculty. The only fees are for matricula- tion, incidental expenses, and diplomas. Courses on hygiene, physiological chemistry and bacteriology are provided for medical students, but until the course on Hygiene and Household Economics was initiated by Dr. Eliza Mosher (Dean of Women) in the Department of Literature, Science, and the Arts, only these specialised and extensive courses were offered. This general course receives a satisfactory amount of support from the students, about one-third of the attendance consisting of young men; the total number is considerably influenced by the hour appointed for the lectures, as the subject is " elective " and must give way in the time schedule to those which are obligatory or imperative. Up till last year the lectures were illustrated only by demonstration, but Dr. Eliza Mosher anticipated the early appointment of an assistant professor, who would conduct and superintend individual practical work in a suitably equipped laboratory. The first term is devoted to a study of (*a*) Personal Hygiene; this includes the structure of the body; the phenomena of nutrition; the influences which favour or retard body metabolism; foods and their adulteration; and to (*b*) Household Economics, into which enter house construction, furnishing, decoration and cleansing. The second half of the course deals with (*c*) Domestic, and (*d*) Municipal hygiene. Under (*c*) a study is made of the chemical constituents, nutritive values and comparative costs of foods, together with practice in the consideration of dietaries for the sick, as well as for the sound; in (*d*) school sanitation finds a place. Personal observation showed the unquestionable interest aroused by this course, carried on, as it is, by a woman of strong personality and wide experience; one, too, who is able to completely dissociate her sub- ject from its pathological aspect, and to present it from the stand- point of perfect, not defective, physical development. A perceptible effect on the opinions and habits of the young people is reported as the course continues to exercise its good influence. At the con- clusion of each year Dr. Mosher conducts an examination of her students by means of written papers and *viva voce* " quizzes."

(a) Michi- gan State University. Table XVIII.

I was unfortunately unable to visit the State University of Indiana, at Bloomington, where a valuable and suggestive short pioneer course in hygiene is given to women, each spring, by Dr. Rebecca Rogers George; the keynote of the whole is stated to be the elevation of home life, and of all its contributing factors, to a more scientific and higher moral basis. The ten lectures concern themselves with the following topics :—

(b) State University of Indiana.

    (*a*) The chemistry of food stuffs, their proper proportions and combinations.

TABLE XVIII.

SCHEDULE CF COURSE IN HYGIENE.—STATE UNIVERSITY OF MICHIGAN.

Institution and Course.	Entrance Requirements.	Scope of Course.	Methods.	Length of Course.	Fees and Finance.	Equipment.
Michigan State University, Ann Arbor, Michigan. Hygiene and Household Economics. Dr. Eliza Mosher. Mixed class, about one-third male students.	High school certificate or its equivalent. Written entrance examination. The course is open to all students at the university.	Personal Hygiene { Structure of body. Phenomenon of nutrition. Metabolism. Household economics, foods. { Nutritive value, cost, dietaries, adulteration. House construction, furnishing, decoration, cleansing. Municipal hygiene—which includes school sanitation. The above can be supplemented by courses in Chemistry—general and analytical. Physics—General Biology and Bacteriology.	The practical work in this course is limited to demonstration, but the contemplated appointment of an assistant professor will coincide with the introduction of individual practice, such as accompanies the supplementary courses. The ingenious and skilful employment of clay as an illustrative material was of interest in this course: cells, bones, organs, postures of the body, plumbing details, were rapidly moulded by the demonstrator and exhibited, attached to glass-covered blackboards. A specially mounted skeleton — with springs—and models of the internal organs made in thin silk, assist to a marked degree in the illustration of Dr. Mosher's lectures.	One year. Two classes weekly.	Only for matriculation, incidental expenses and diplomas. State funds.	The classes are held in an ordinary Lecture Theatre. An ample supply of diagrams and models for demonstration is provided.

(*b*) The physiology of digestion.

(*c*) The channels and means for promoting elimination from the body.

(*d*) Respiration and ventilation.

(*e*) The anatomy and physiology of the reproductive organs and their purpose in the scheme of creation.

(*f*) The pathology of the female reproductive organs, with such means of relief as lie within the reach of all.   '

(*g*) The social relation of the sexes.

(*h*) The profession of motherhood.

This course is " elective," but each girl who takes it and passes a successful examination is given a " credit," as for any other course.

Dr. Rebecca George writes, that "believing the present system of education tends towards the production of teachers rather than of home-makers, these lectures have been given for the past four years to offset, in a way, present educational tendencies, and to impress upon girls the dignity of household science and the sacredness of wifehood and motherhood." The results thus far have been most gratifying ; " eager interest without a sign of vulgar curiosity has been the rule during each of the four years' work, and not a few have testified to the value of the knowledge so obtained two and three years after their student life has closed." Few can dispute that, through the judicious introduction by skilled hands of such suitable preparation for the highest duties to which girls are called lies the right road of escape from much needless, costly suffering among women, much ignorant maiming of child life, many saddened homes, much social evil. The transmission of the highest manifestation of life, in so perfect a form as may be, lies at the root of all hygiene ; and at the right time, in the right way, it should surely be assigned a dignified and carefully safe-guarded position in the study of the right conduct of life. (See "Training of the Young in Laws of Sex," Hon. and Rev. Canon Lyttelton ; Longman, Green & Co.)

D.—NORMAL SCHOOLS.

Normal courses of training in domestic subjects are almost invariably post-graduate; they are followed, to a great extent, in private Technical Institutes, to a small degree in those State Universities in which Household Economics have been adopted on educational lines; in the future it is probable that the proportion of students in each class of institution will be fairly balanced, since the college courses are now making rapid growth in quality and quantity.   *Framingham State Normal School Course in Household Arts. Table XIX.*

The excellent two years' course at the State Normal School at Framingham (Mass.), holds an almost unique position, and the history of its development is not without interest. It originated in the establishment in Boston of a department for the study of household arts, under the name of Boston Normal School of Cookery, by the late Mrs. Mary Hemenway, in 1887. Its graduates so easily found positions as teachers in public and private schools, as well as in public and philanthropic institutions, that its usefulness was rapidly proved. In June, 1898, the trustees of the Mary Hemenway estate offered the school to the State Board of Education, with the very generous proposal that, if the offer were accepted, Mr. Augustus Hemenway, her son, would thoroughly furnish and equip such a department, as a memorial of his mother, in which project he was joined by his

Framing-
ham State
Normal
School
Course in
Household
Arts—
continued.

sisters, Mrs. Louis Cabot and Mrs. Wm. E. C. Eustis. . The Board
was quick to appreciate the worth of such a gift, together with
its far-reaching beneficence. The Normal School at Framingham
was selected as that best fitted to receive it, on account of its
proximity to Boston, its two boarding halls, which attract
students from a distance, and the many grammar schools in the
town, from which pupils could be drawn for its practice school;
for the object always in view has been to provide for the
adequate training of teachers of the various household arts,
especially of cookery in its different forms. Existing arrangements enable any pupil who graduates from the regular Normal
course to take the course in Household Arts in one year; or
any graduate of the two years course in Household Arts can take
the Normal course in one year; thus the usual term of training
is, in either case, lengthened by one year; those students who
qualify in Household Arts only complete the course in two years.

The wise aim of the instruction in all branches is to teach the
students intelligent, thoughtful self-reliance; for, to those responsible for the instruction given, it appears obvious that the
equipment of actual knowledge which a student takes with her
from any school such as this can be but limited; therefore, they
feel that judicious training in accurate thinking and working
must be the main object of the teacher, if the student is to reap
the highest benefit from her stay in the school. The courses in
chemistry are particularly well adapted to give this training,
since a large part of the two years of study is spent in actual
work in laboratories, where the student discovers for herself the
absolute dependence of results on the character of her work and
on the methods she has employed; as disciplinary work alone
the value of such study cannot be overrated, but it also has a
direct and permanent practical value in the Household Arts.
These courses form a progressive series, and are intended to
prepare the students in a systematic way for an intelligent comprehension of the underlying principles of cookery, of laundry
work, of dyeing, of cleaning, etc., as well as of those involved in
the management of foods, fires, fuels, illuminants, ventilation,
and the like.

Considerable time during the first year is devoted to the study of
general chemistry, in which the fundamental principles of the science are
taught by means of experimental lectures, 60 in number, and by class-
room recitations. In connection with this course, the student has 120
hours of practical work in the laboratory. Systematic and extended
instruction in qualitative analysis is given in the second half of
the first year, so that by the end of this year students are prepared to begin
the more exact discipline of quantitative work. The work in quantitative
analysis consists of a brief course in volumetric analysis and in gravimetric .
analysis; both of these courses include class-room as well as laboratory
work. An elementary course is given, in conclusion, in organic chemistry;
this deals with the structure of carbon compounds, and with the interactions
between the different classes of those compounds which are most frequently
used. Not so much time is given to physics as to some other studies, yet
it has a definite place in the curriculum.

The instruction consists of lectures, recitations, and demonstrations upon the fundamental principles of matter and energy,

mechanics, hydraulics, and the elementary forces—heat, light, and electricity. To biology, as to physics, only so much time is allotted as is believed to be absolutely required to furnish a sound basis for physiology, hygiene, and bacteriology; the course consists of lectures, recitations, and laboratory work.

The beginner is introduced to the use of the microscope, and learns to examine plant and animal bodies, and to resolve them into elementary organs, tissues, and cells. Constant practice in drawing is required, and such subjects are dealt with as the structure of living things ; the elementary living stuff (cytoplasm) ; first principles of nutrition, digestion, foods, and feeding ; the sources of starch, sugar, etc ; and the interdependence and interrelation of the organic and inorganic world.

The chief interest of the class in the study of physiology centres naturally in nutrition and related subjects. Somewhat more than half the time is therefore devoted to such questions, while the remaining heads are treated in less detail.

Some time is given to the quantitative side of metabolism. This becomes a very practical matter, as it throws light upon the value of the different food stuffs, the extent to which one may replace another, and the relation of the diet to tissue building, muscular work and heat production ; finally, the usefulness of the condiments, stimulants and mineral matter in the food is discussed. The concluding lectures deal with the central nervous system, the sense organs and the principles of personal hygiene. Miss Clark, who is responsible for this course, emphasises throughout the hygienic aspect of physiology ; she attaches comparatively little value to the use of models or diagrams, but prefers to rely on fresh specimens ; the use of the microscope also is required to a moderate degree only, in order to stimulate careful observation of natural objects with the naked eye, and to prepare students for good work in schools where equipment is perhaps compulsorily limited ; the cultivation of great facility with blackboard illustration is very carefully encouraged. The text books in use are "Physiology for High Schools," by Macy Norris, Blaisdell's Series of Physiology Manuals, and Thornston's "Human Physiology." The ordinary Normal student receives three lessons a week for twelve weeks, the Domestic Art student has the advantage of two weekly lessons for one year.

Bacteriology and the study of micro-organisms, and of fermentation, especially of yeasts, constitute a prominent feature in the final year. The students learn how to make their own culture media, how to examine milk, water, air, ice, dust, etc., and how to test the efficiency of filters, sterilizers, and germicides.

The Course is arranged as follows :— ·
Bacteriology and micro-organisms of fermentation.
Classification of micro-organisms.
General biology of bacteria.
General physiology of bacteria.
Bacteriology of water and ice.
Bacteriology of air.
Bacteriology of earth and dust.
Bacteriology of drainage.
Bacteriology of milk.
Bacteria concerned in vinegar making.
Bacteria concerned in lactic acid production
Bacteria concerned in dairying.
Bacteria concerned in nitrification.
Testing of domestic filters.
Testing of disinfectants for household use.
Bacteriology of food preservation.

TABLE XIX.

STATE NORMAL SCHOOL, FRAMINGHAM NORMAL COLLEGE.—SCHEDULE OF HOUSEHOLD ARTS COURSE.

Institution and name.	Entrance Requirements.	Scope of Course.	Methods.	Length of Course.	Fees and Finance.	Equipment.
State Normal School, Framingham, Mass.) ... f or courses ... (1) A general two years ... (2) A three yrs' ... (3) A ... one yr ... ... (4) A two yrs' ... Arts to provide for training of ... of various household arts, especially cookery in its different forms. Principal, Mary ... Professor of ... Ms. L., etc.	Candidates must be ... in ... good moral ... (1) Present certificate of good moral ... (2) ... of a High School ... (3) Pass a written ... which embraces ... the following ... of Scientific Geography, Physiology, Hygiene, Physics, Chemistry, Botany.	Physics (Elementary). Chemistry — General - 133 hrs. Qualitative - 114 " ... - 342 " ...ic - 19 " ...logy - 57 " ...ol gy - 60 " ...my - 152 " Food and Dietetics - 38 " Laundry - 30 " Teachers' Conference - 76 " Practice School - 456 " ...y - 57 " Art of Study - 57 " At... - 114 " Singing - 78 " ... - 228 " ... - 57 " "Field work" ...	The ... of the ... is to ... and the ... of ... It is realised ... ... the teacher's ... ... in Biology, Bacteriology, and Phy... the use of ... milk, ...	Two years, but any pupil who ... from the regular Normal ... take the Household Arts ... of the Household Arts Course can ... the ... in one ...	Free to inhabitants of Massachusets, but an annual charge of $60 is made to those from other States. State Endowment. Free text books; charge made for stationery only.	All ... light, large, ... ept ... day, ... in the ... The ... ... not for Household ... is the gift of the Hemenway ... The ... is ... containing ... ences—a ... of ... nearly ... ship. The Science laboratories are well equipped for individual work. The Domestic Art Students are required to wear white in the kitchen, and blue overalls in the Laundry.

Bacteriology of Pasteurising.
Bacteriology of canning.
Bacteriology of pickling, etc.
Yeast, general biology and physiology.
Yeast, cause of fermentation of bread and drinks.
Yeast, compressed.
Yeast, wild.
Yeast, fungi related to.
Moulds, general biology.
Moulds, structure and physiology.
Moulds, fermentations caused by.
Moulds in relation to food substances.
General phenomena of putrefaction and decay.
Relation of bacteria to infectious disease.
Epidemics, etc.

The subjects which have thus far been described have had to deal with the scientific side of the subject; their practical application finds a place pre-eminently in the Household Arts laboratory. The work is arranged to be educational as well as technical, and therefore includes both the theoretical and practical aspects of the subjects.

To illustrate the character of this instruction, the following outline of courses in the Principles and Practice of Cookery and Laundry work is given:

The practical work of cookery is presented in four courses on the following lines :—

(1). Household or plain cookery.

(2). Advanced cookery, including preserving, canning, and the making of jellies, jams, and marmalades.

(3). High-class cookery.

(4). Special cookery for those very ill (therapeutic cookery), and its application for hospital nurses in training schools.

In the first course the five "food principles" or "nutrients" are carefully considered, viz., water, mineral matter, carbohydrates, proteids or albuminous fluids, and fats. The principles of the science and art of cookery are developed by general rules and formulæ, so far as practicable, and special attention is given to their application by individual practice. The subjects of the course are developed as follows :—

FUELS.—Principles of combustion, conditions for sustaining ; use and costs of the ordinary fuels.

Construction of both gas and coal ranges, with practice in the use of such apparatus, and in the building, regulation, and care of coal fires. Principles and experimental work relating to the Aladdin oven. The chafing dish.

FOOD-STUFFS.—Introductory. General composition of the human body. Classification of nutrients needed, and a study of the different food-stuffs as the source of supply.

MILK AS A TYPE.—Experiments to illustrate its constituents and properties.

WATER.—Considered as a cooking medium, with experiments. Thermometers are standardized, and used in the boiling of water and the cookery of starch, sugar, albumen and fats.

MINERAL MATTER.—The various salts of food materials.

CARBOHYDRATES.—Sources : (a) Starch—composition ; experiments ; cooking temperature. Practical application to cookery of starchy food-stuffs, as corn, flour, rice, tapioca, sago, macaroni, etc. ; the cooking of such starchy foods as grains, vegetables ; the use of cornflour and flour in the making of sauces and thickening of soups. (*b*) Sugars—compositions the cooking of cane sugar ; the use of thermometer ; the degrees of heat required for different results, as in soft and hard caramel (for colouring soups and sauces) ; also for soft and hard sweets, as in French cream candies or fondant and glacé fruits. Practical tests for the same. Practical applications, including the preparation of dishes containing starch, sugar and fruits in various combinations, are then made.

PROTEIDS or albuminous foods. Albumen—sources ; type, white of egg. This subject is studied and experimentally developed by the same general methods as the cookery of starch, and the principles of its cookery are applied to the making of various dishes, as soft and hard cooked eggs ; poached and baked ; combined with milk in other forms, as in creamy eggs, and soft and baked custards of different kinds ; the combination of milk, starchy and albuminous food materials in dishes for breakfast, luncheon or dessert ; the cookery of albumen, as applied to the cooking of fish, poultry and meat ; methods of their cookery ; objective points ; heat transferred. In connection with meat cookery, the albuminoids are considered.

ALBUMINOIDS.—Sources ; gelatine, prepared in the form of food stocks, brown and white.

PRINCIPLES AND RULES FOR CLEARING STOCK—Soups : stock and vegetable ; milk and cream. Gelatine dishes : commercial gelatine, kinds, costs and uses ; plain jellies ; jellies with egg or egg and cream in different combinations, as used in the making of wholesome puddings.

FATS.—Sources ; constitution ; effects of heat ; use and importance of the dietary.

BATTER AND DOUGH MIXTURES.—(1) Expansion by air and moisture; as effected by heat, to make porous. (2) The application of these principles to the preparation of popovers and Yorkshire pudding, wheat and gluten wafers, cream and sponge cake. (3) Expansion of batters and doughs by use of chemicals, as cream of tartar and soda, or other acids, or acid salts with the alkaline salt, soda, in combination. Objective points : principles and properties ; experiments ; application to the preparation of breakfast bread-stuffs, gingerbread desserts and cake. (4) Baking powders : general composition of standard powders ; chemical reactions and products, with applied principles of chemistry ; formulæ, with practical applications to the preparation of bread-stuffs, cakes and sweets.

FERMENTATION.—Fermentation by yeast, and its application to the preparation of bread, rolls, and biscuit, also for breakfast muffins and gems. Experimental work with flour of different kinds.

FROZEN DISHES.—Principles ; general rules ; sherbets ; ice-creams (1) plain ; (2) fancy, with simple and richer combinations.

PRACTICAL LAUNDRY WORK.—The course consists in the examination of fabrics, as cotton, linen, woollen, and silk ; effect of hot and cold water.

THE USE OF CHEMICALS as cleansing agents ; namely—soaps, washing-powders, soda, ammonia, and borax.

REMOVAL OF STAINS, as fruit, tea and coffee, iron-rust, etc.

HOUSEHOLD LINEN.—Preparation for the laundry ; cleansing, drying, and starching, hot and cold processes ; folding, ironing ; special : embroideries and laces ; blueings : kinds, composition (tests with experiments), and use.

In addition to the foregoing outline of instruction, the pupils are trained in the preparation of dietaries at given prices for varying numbers of persons, how to judge of meats and how to buy them, by visits to meat shops, where the butcher cuts up the meat before the class, at the same time giving practical instruction. Students are also required to visit grocery establishments and meat markets, and to make themselves familiar with the supply and demand of staples and their prices. Each pupil, by conference with the superintendent of the boarding halls, learns how to prepare the ménu for a large family, according to market supplies and prices. She is also expected to take her turn in presiding at the dinner table in one or other of the boarding halls, and to carve the joints. As the boarding halls offer ample facilities for demonstration of the science of Household Arts in daily living, the pupils, though not required to do household work in the ordinary sense of the term, are expected to qualify themselves as future teachers of Household Arts or as superintendents in institutions by availing themselves of all such opportunities for practical work as the Principal can from time to time provide for them.

Sanitary science, including home sanitation, is carefully studied during the second year, during which a course in the study of psychology, conducted by the Principal, Mr. H. Whittemore, is included in the curriculum. A course of practical instruction is also given in home and school emergencies, and in the detection and recognition of common school diseases, especially those which are considered contagious. The practice classes consist of girls in the eighth and ninth grades of the Framingham schools, who come for weekly lessons to the Normal school. These pupils are divided into a number of classes, under the care of, and taught by, the Household Arts department students. Each senior has charge of one class during a whole year, and has thus ample opportunity to make a practical application of her own acquirements and to learn how to instruct others. The junior students are required to act as assistants to the seniors when they are teaching; and to aid in the instruction and general management; in this way they have a year's observation to prepare them for the more responsible work of teaching in the senior year.

That the intention of the course to excite thought and to demand the exercise of individual mental powers is fulfilled is quite evident to the observer; and it is easily credible that considerable development of character follows upon such training; special stress was laid, in the course of conversation, upon the noticeably broadening influence it exercises on the temperament of the majority of the students. No doubt this is partly due to the excellent aims and good influence of Mr. Whittemore, a liberal-minded and experienced man, who has held the position of Principal of the Normal School since the department of Household Arts was taken over by the State in 1898. A pleasantly refined and cultivated home atmosphere is perceptible in his own house, where students eagerly avail themselves of boarding vacancies.

All the rooms, residential and scholastic, are light and large, except the laundry, which, on the occasion of my visit, was improvised in the basement of the Principal's house; thanks to the ingenuity exercised, the work was adequately carried on; but, by now it has doubtless been transferred to suitable quarters. The Hemenway Memorial kitchen is planned on a princely scale, replete with unusual conveniences, and actually adorned

by the fine specimens of plumber's work which enter into the
equipment. The pipes for hot and cold water for heating
purposes and for gas are all in bright metal, in every case
" exposed"; fortunately, in the dry, clear air of New England,
they need polishing but twice a year, and are rapidly dusted at
daily intervals. Each cooking table is fitted for eight students,
but in actual practice four is the usual number by whom they
are used. Drawers contain the usual fittings, including, in this
instance, a spatula and rubber moulds for candies; the pans are
chiefly steel agate ware; there are the usual shelves with kneading and pastry boards, and, of course, sliding seats. Four stoves
are fitted for coal, wood, gas and gasoline respectively. The
glazed earthenware sinks have hinged drainers which can be
closed, flush with the wall, when not in use. Two Aladdin
ovens are employed in the baking of bread and cakes or in the
preparation of soups. There is a large Pasteuriser for milk and
an incubator for bacteriological tests, an " Eddy" ice box, a
Chamberlen steam cooker, and an ample provision of glazed
cupboards and drawers, all in perfect order. The very spacious
room has one end fitted for the children's practice lessons, the
other is set apart for the use of the normal students; there is
also abundant space for a dining table and lecturer's desk. No
expense was spared in any particular in the equipment of this
memorial kitchen, and the workmanship is so good that, at the
time of my visit, not a cent had been spent on repairs of any
kind during the three and a half years the kitchen had been in
use. The necessity for equipping a kitchen on simpler lines, as
a useful adjunct to a complete training, will be realised by
practical teachers, and I believe this has now been provided.

The students are required to dress in white for kitchen work,
large blue overalls being worn in the laundry. The personal
equation of each student is closely studied throughout the
course, and although the staff usually arrange monthly tests of
various kinds to ascertain progress, actually more importance is
attached to daily observation of conduct. An instance of this was
given to me by Miss Nicholas, directress of the course, where
failure to graduate was due, not to technical shortcomings, but to
faults of disposition, which, in the opinion of the professors,
rendered this student unfit for the teaching profession. Her
attention had been privately, tactfully, and repeatedly drawn to
certain shortcomings, but as either the will or the power to
amend or control were absent, the sense of responsibility towards
her future pupils left no alternative to those who were entrusted
with the issue of the desired certificate but to refuse to confer it.

Thirty-two normal students were taking this course in 1901,
twenty-two of whom were entered in 1900 ; a smaller
number is considered preferable in order that careful individual
attention may be bestowed and the thoughtful observation of
character be carried on, to which reference has just been made.
Twelve is considered a satisfactory number for each year's entering class, but the excellence of the course brings its own penalty
in the eager demand for admission.

The following paragraph from the "School Circular and Report" seems to me a fair statement of the value and of the high estimate formed of its graduates, whose services are in immediate request.

"Many of the alumnæ of the school are employed in the Boston public schools, others are instructors in Normal and High schools, at the Armour and Drexel Institutes, superintendents at the Johns Hopkins and other hospitals and asylums, or else in training schools from Boston to Kansas, Denver and California. All over the country they are scattered, wherever education has sufficiently advanced to recognise that Household Arts is scientific. Such women have graduated from something more than cooking classes, or from schools in Domestic Science. They have won diplomas from the point of view of education, rather than from that of self-support. They have taken the word arts as the resultant term in the application of science to industry. They have gone forth to teach and direct, until in time it will be realised that proficiency in Household Arts is to be examined, rated, and certificated as is now literature and mathematics."

As I have said, four courses are open to candidates for admission to this Normal school : a general two years' course; a three years' course for those who wish to broaden the work offered in the regular course; a special course in one year for experienced teachers and college graduates; and this two years' course in Household Arts. All the requirements for admission to the Normal school in regard to examinations, written and oral, tuition, testimonials, and other regulations are enforced equally in this department (Household Arts); the written examination consists of papers upon certain groups of study.

The science group includes and requires an elementary knowledge (1) of physical geography, *i.e.*, the mastery of the elements of this subject as presented in the study of geography in a good Grammar school, (2) physiology and hygiene, the chief elementary facts of anatomy, the general functions of the various organs, the more obvious rules of health, and the more striking effects of alcoholic drinks, narcotics and stimulants upon those addicted to their use, (3) physics, chemistry and botany, the elementary principles of these subjects so far as they may be presented in the courses usually devoted to them in High schools.

Candidates for admission must be 16 years of age, and must present certificates of good moral character and of the equivalent of a good High school education. To persons who live in Massachusetts tuition is free, but to those from other States an annual charge of $50 is made. Text-books and reference books are furnished free; the only expense is for stationery and such books as drawing books, that are destroyed in use. From time to time pupils are advised to buy some book which is thought by the teacher to be indispensable as a part of their outfit for the work in the schoolroom, upon which they are soon to enter; all such books are furnished at cost price.

The Normal school, with its surrounding residences for students, is beautifully situated on a wooded hillside, surrounded by a considerable amount of land used for various forms of recreation and commanding a view over rolling wood-clad hills, broken by the vast reservoir from which the Boston water supply is drawn. The copses round provide materials for nature study under most favourable conditions, while golf, tennis and basket ball are enjoyed in the ample grounds. There are two

boarding halls, Crocker Hall and Normal Hall, which are made
as homelike as possible.　They are thoroughly warmed by
hot water, lighted by electricity, and furnished with the best
sanitary and lavatory arrangements of hot and cold water.　Each
hall has two rooms set apart for the use of the students, one as a
reception room for friends who call, the other for their sole
use.　The students' rooms have each a piano; and there
is also a small library.　The cost of board is $80 (£16) per
term, $160 (£32) a year; this is inclusive.　In cases of illness
or other unavoidable absence, the expense of board is shared
between the State and the boarder.　These rates are made on
the basis that two students occupy one room; an extra charge
is made when a student has a room to herself.

Provision is made for a physical examination of all candidates
for admission to Normal schools in the State of Massachusetts,
and a student may be subjected to a re-examination at any time
during the course should his or her physical condition suggest
the need; the same precaution in the interests of all concerned is to be found to an increasing extent elsewhere, though the
praiseworthy custom is not yet generally adopted.　All students,
unless specially excused, are required to devote a specified period
to exercise in the gymnasium throughout the entire course, for
which purpose a suitable costume must be worn; attention is
also paid to the out-door life of the students, each of whom is
expected to take a certain amount of out-door exercise daily.
Special arrangements are made for the lunches of day students;
hot soup, cocoa, rolls and fruit are supplied at cost price in a
pleasantly fitted room.　Everywhere there is evidence that
honest efforts are made to give the most favourable conditions,
opportunities and assistance to students who desire to equip
themselves to become teachers; the rest may be truthfully said in
the words of the school catalogue, "to rest with the student herself."

Sewing and Cooking Courses.　Occasionally courses in sewing and cooking form a part of the
manual training courses which enter into the curriculum of, I
believe, the majority of State Normal schools; of these I may
cite that at Worcester (Mass.), as an example; the results are
stated to have been satisfactory, although but one lesson a week
is given in each subject.　For this two reasons are advanced:
(1) that the nature of the work admits of home practice, which
is consistently encouraged, so that the actual time of study is
much extended; (2) that as these household arts are studied in the
senior year the maturity of the pupils is a probable factor in
their interest and progress, in spite of the limited number of
lessons.　Whether, with the more general introduction of
needlework into the Grade schools, instruction in methods of
teaching sewing will enter into the training of all women
teachers, or whether the subject will continue to be assigned
to specialists, does not yet appear.　I incline to the latter
opinion, because needlework is more generally classed as
manual training than as an ordinary school subject.　With
the exception of physiology, hygiene and some emergency
work, therefore, the Normal student in the United States must

seek her domestic science training (outside New England) at a
State University (where even a four years' college course will
scarcely give time to combine it with other studies if general
teaching be her ambition), or in the form of a post-graduate
course, either at one of these colleges or at a Technical Institute
of high standing.

The emphasis laid of recent years upon the study of psychology Physiology
by Normal students, with special reference to child life, together and Hygiene
with the obligatory requirements as to the teaching of physiology Courses.
in grade schools to which detailed reference has been made, have
indirectly acted as a stimulus to the study of hygiene—the
sciences depending one upon the other for application and practice. Consequently, in those States to which my observations
were confined, I gathered the impression that this important
subject is likely, by degrees, to assume its rightful position in
the equipment of teachers. The attention devoted to biology and
physical culture is contributing to the same end; whether Normal
students resort to State Universities or to their special schools for
the necessary training. A marked feature in the ten State
Normal schools in Massachusetts is the care centred, not only on
the physical well-being of the pupils, but on the instruction by
which they will be enabled to deal practically with questions of
hygiene, as they present themselves in daily life. For instance,
in addition to the entrance requirement which demands a
medical certificate of good health, no pupil is allowed to remain
whose physical condition is considered unequal to the exactions
of the work. Efforts are made to counteract any tendency to
overwork, over-excitement or hurry ; careful oversight is
exercised, and in numerous cases individual advice is given.
Thus in addition to the theoretical instruction in the conditions
essential to a healthful life, students are trained and assisted to
realise these by personal practice.

The position, construction, lighting, heating, ventilation and (*a.*) Salem,
equipment of many Normal schools can be described only by one Mass.
word—magnificent. That at Salem, for example, stands in a Table XX.
splendid position on an open, elevated spot, from which its
numerous lofty windows command views over a wide expanse of
country and an arm of the Massachusetts Bay. This new building was completed in 1896 ; it has three stories and a basement ;
its frontage of 180 feet is balanced by two wings, each 140
feet, running from north to south. The interior finish throughout is of oak, and the wide, handsome corridors are adorned by
many good pictures and other artistic decorations provided by
the State, by past and present students and teachers, or by the
generosity of private individuals. Model schools (for 300 children), gymnasium, lunch and dressing-rooms, library, class, and
assembly-rooms, offices and laboratories, all gave me an invigor-
ating sensation of light, air, space and fitness. Two years spent in
such environment must exercise beneficial effects on the 225
students and, thanks to the influence of the staff, these should
"action" in good habits.

The third floor is devoted chiefly to the various departments of science — physics, chemistry (elementary and advanced), botany, geography, mineralogy, zoology, etc.   All
students must devote three 40-minute periods a week to
zoology and physiology in their second year; to botany two
weekly periods are assigned during the first year.   Here, as
elsewhere, it is found of great advantage to lay this preliminary
foundation in practical biology; the dissection and comparison
of the various forms of animal life contribute to a so much better
understanding of human physiology.   Fifteen students carry
on individual laboratory work at the same time.   Each has
separate equipment, which includes both compound and dissecting microscopes.   Specimens of the lower orders of life, such as
hydras, star-fish, clams, fish-frogs, etc., are furnished to each
student, and at the close of the 20 weeks' work in zoology, which
is the threshold of the course in human physiology, a dissection
of a cat is made for each section (*i.e.* 15 students) of the class.
There is a liberal supply of Auzeau models, and the Auzeau life-
sized mannikin is taken repeatedly to pieces for demonstration
purposes throughout the physiology course.   The " recitation "
method is largely employed for the theoretical work: topics for
study are allotted to groups of students, and then discussed.
Miss Alice Warren, Professor of Biology and Physiology, is unquestionably successful in her power of eliciting individual
opinions, impressions and proposed applications; "to help
practice" is a prominent object in her theoretical instruction.
Martin's " Human Body"(advanced edition) and Colton's "Experimental Physiology" are recommended text-books ; but the free
consultation of authorities, to be found in the excellent library,
is encouraged here as in most other institutions for higher
education.   The students have access also to the Peabody
Academy of Science, one of the finest collections of its kind in
the country.

As many living forms as possible are kept in the class-room.
By this means, those who are to become teachers are instructed
as to what creatures may be provided, and how they should be
cared for.   In the spring, opportunities are given for the pupils
to become familiar with the common birds and their songs, as
one aim of the course is to prepare the students so to instruct
children, as to foster in them a greater love and sympathy for
animals, a consciousness of what we owe to them, and an increasing interest in observing their habits, their uses and their
intelligence ; in no better way can they be brought into a close
relation with out-door life.   The course in physiology is conducted throughout as a continuation of the previous biological
work.

The course is intended to fit teachers to secure and preserve
a sound body for themselves, through an intelligent appreciation
of the structure, arrangement and function of the different
systems and organs, and to enable them to train children under
their care to form habits which will conduce to a healthy, free
action of their own bodies.   For this purpose special stress is

TABLE XX.

THE STATE NORMAL SCHOOL.—SALEM, MASSACHUSETTS.

Institution and Course.	Entrance Requirements.	Scope of Course.	Methods.	Length of Course.	Fees and Finance.	Equipment.
State Normal School, Salem, Massachusetts. General Course. Principal, Walter P. Beckwith, A.M., Ph.D. Professor of Physiology and Biology, Miss Alice Warren.	Candidates must be 16, and must— (1) Present certificates of good moral character. (2) ri...ce of a good High School education. (3) Pass a written examination, ...th embraces one paper upon one of the ...llowing groups of ...sees:— Physical geography, physiology and hygiene, ...stry, or botany.	SCIENCE COURSE.—Physics, 20 weeks of junior year. Botany, 40 ...ks of junior year. Chemistry, 20 ...ks of senior year. Hygiene and Physiology } 20 ...ks of senior year. Two 40- ...ute periods of labor...ry ...k in one or ...ther subject per ...ek. The course includes in addition— Literature, ...toric; geometry; algebra; miner-alogy; geography; music; gymnas-tics; reading; ...ing. } 2 years. Also— Psychology; peda-gogy; language; grammar; arith-metic. } in the senior year.	The laboratory method where possible. In every department, practical, individual observations are carried out, advancing from simple to complex, and connected with theoretical study. The science students carry out their work in groups of 15. In Biology, each student has a separate equipment and specimen. The course is arranged to give in the first year, work ...h des most to ...hen the students' knowledge of ...tes, leaving the application chiefly to the review of grammar school ...tes in the second year. Special ...ss is laid upon the needs of children and the formation of good ...bits.	2 years of 40 ...ks each. Except in ...ses of students believed ...be of good ...rt, who, from inadequate or previous lack of thorough training, cannot ...ate the course in this period. Their work is re-arranged upon the ...sis of tak-ing an extra term or year, as the case requires.	No fees. Public funds. Non-residents of Massachusetts. $100 a year. (£20)	The chemical and ...al labora-tories are ...el-...ely ...ed, and ...te for individual work. The equipment includes a ...lim-sized Auzeau ...tn, ap-pliances for ...my, biology, and physiology, ...teen microscopes, and equipment for individual work in zoology and ...tany.

laid on hygiene. The subjects of food, clothing, bathing and rest are considered, as well as the effect of muscular action upon the organism as a whole and upon the special organs. At intervals the pupils prepare lessons suitable for the grammar and primary grades, and conduct them in class. Miss Warren requires constant examples of application to the needs of children and to the formation of good habits; and she told me she is already, after five or six years, able to perceive results which prove that her efforts are productive of good. Graduates from her classes, now employed in primary or grammar schools, are noticeable for the hygienic influence and practice they have brought with them to their work. In conjunction with other members of the staff, Miss Warren exerts herself to secure, so far as possible, correlation between the various branches of study, and to adhere throughout to true pedagogical lines. At Salem, as at Framingham, I was impressed with the pains taken to form a just estimate of the personal fitness of each student for the selected vocation; in both colleges, a similar sentiment obtains, viz., that intellectual acquirements constitute but a part of the capacity to act as a teacher, for which each certificate granted acts as a guarantee.

(b) Hyannis, Mass. Very similar methods for the study of physiology and hygiene are employed at the State Normal School at Hyannis, (Mass.), where these subjects are included in the science group both of the two and the four years' course; the good provision of biological, physical, and chemical laboratories permits of eminently satisfactory work. The natural science course includes geology and geography in addition to chemistry, physics, biology, and hygiene, and is supplemented by a study of psychology, pedagogy, school organisation, and methods of teaching English, mathematics, drawing, and vocal music.

Six months in the first year are devoted to chemistry and physics respectively; zoology precedes physiology in a similar way in the second year; four hours a week, of which two hours are laboratory work, are devoted in turn to each of these subjects. The laboratory equipment includes a drawer with instruments for each student, also a glazed stoneware sink and a bunsen and batswing gas burner; eight or nine compound microscopes are provided. Each student makes any models he desires to employ in practical work for himself as part of the manual training. Nearly all specimens are worked at individually. The Professor of Biology and Mathematics, Miss Bertha M. Brown, a graduate of the Massachusetts Institute of Technology, is unusually interested in the hygienic treatment of physiology in schools of all grades, and encourages a very free introduction of experimental and practical illustrations by her students in the Elementary Hygiene which they teach in the Practice School.* The outline of each lesson is submitted to her before it is given, and the proposed method of handling the topic is discussed. Six weeks' observation work, and fifteen weeks of teaching are required of each student in the regular two-year course. She told me that most gratifying results follow the methods she has adopted with her students as regards influence on the character of the young people, the perception by them of personal possibilities and responsibilities in respect of health promotion, and the awakening of a desire on their part to impart such hygienic information to their own little pupils, as shall in turn arouse the children's interest, and stimulate them to right action.

---

* See Table VI., p. 59 above.

I was informed on reliable authority that the Boards of Education in some of the most prominent cities are no longer satisfied with proofs of a theoretical acquaintance with hygiene from the members of their teaching staff, but hold them severally responsible for the maintenance of wholesome conditions in their class-rooms, require of them intelligent co- operation with the medical inspectors in safeguarding the health of the children, and call upon them to inculcate good habits in those committed to their daily charge; when with these duties is combined that of the definite instruction of their pupils in hygiene and physiology, it is readily conceivable that facilities must be afforded to Normal students for a thorough practical grounding in these subjects. Hence the few theoretical lectures on School Hygiene hitherto provided in most Normal schools no longer suffice to meet the demands on teachers which arise from this broader conception of the significance of that hard worked, much-misunderstood word Education. I received repeated assurances that the admirable courses and methods for training teachers in hygiene and physiology which I visited and observed in different centres in Massachusetts and Ohio, were not confined to certain favoured cities, but may be truthfully considered typical of a perceptible movement towards the general introduction of similar practical teaching into all Normal colleges. For this indication of progress various reasons are advanced; perhaps the two of most weight are: (1) that the training is rendered compulsory by that wider view of the scope of school education to which I have just referred; and (2) a keener realisation of the fact that the State owes it to her children that they shall grow up to maturity sound and well developed in body as well as in mind. Besides these I may also mention the gradual development of a more intimate popular interest in school conditions, evidenced by the attractive and valuable co-operation which exists in some cities between parents and teachers; the perception by authorities that precious time and money are lost when, owing to the teacher being ignorant or hampered in the exercise of his discretion, children carry on their studies under insanitary conditions ; and a growing appreciation of the educational advantages offered to pupils of all ages by the study of practical hygiene which constitute it one of the most, if not the most, generally valuable subject in the time-table.

The profound belief in education which permeates the great American people must be witnessed to be realised. It is to education that they look to weld their many millions into one coherent whole, of which the units shall be sturdy, resourceful, well-balanced citizens, to whose hands the honour and prestige of a great nation can be safely confided. In this ambition to be in the forefront of the world's nations may be found, in my opinion, one powerful motive for the initiation of the whole movement recorded in these pages. The well-being of a nation hinges on the physical, mental, and moral status of its people; while to each state and city is entrusted the responsibility of protecting its inhabitants from moral or physical ills, and of developing .

their mental powers. It is a commonplace to add that, unless
State efforts be aided and supplemented by individual support,
they are futile.   Authorities recognise, therefore, that in
educational institutions for all ages, provision must be made
to train children in an intelligent and practical knowledge of
health rules, to be applied in private and in public duties, *i.e.*, in
every.relation of life.   It will have been noted that the obligation
to acquire an elementary knowledge of personal and public
hygiene is at present laid upon both sexes in all State schools
and in most State colleges, while for girls the opportunities of
gaining a useful working knowledge of domestic science promise
to become abundant.   But what seem to me of equal, if not
of greater, promise in this connection, are the educationally
organised courses in the public High schools and the recognition of the social and national importance of Household
Economics by its installation among other subjects of university rank in State universities.   By the High school courses
the young people are imbued at a most impressionable age with
a conception, hitherto often absent, of the dignity and worth of
Home, and will, it is believed learn to appreciate its claims; they
are intelligently familiarised with the world in which they must
shortly play a part of greater or less influence, and their scientific, artistic, literary and manual training studies are usefully
and attractively associated with daily duties and social interests.
By means of the college courses it is anticipated that, in addition to
the general advantages just enumerated, the resources of modern
science and art will in future be more utilised for the improvement of home life; trained intelligences will be brought to bear
upon vexed domestic problems, upon diet, expenditure, and
service, so that in years to come a complete and harmonious
system will be evolved from the present faulty and discordant
methods.   It has been well said by Dr. Mary E. Green, late
President of the National Household Economic Association, that
" Household Economics once properly understood by the women
of the country will make possible to each individual the health,
happiness and development which are his due."   The United
States now offers to its women of all ages, free of charge, the
opportunities essential to the gaining of this understanding.

PART II.

PRIVATE INSTITUTIONS.

Side by side with the State system of education in the United **Introductory.** States there exists a parallel system of schools and of institutions for higher education; these are supported entirely from private sources (fees and endowments), unrestricted by State legal regulations. The governors or directors of these private institutions are thus independent of any popular or outside control; free to initiate new departures and at liberty to test original theories by practical experiment. As a rule, this power and independence are not abused; the standard of instruction is such that graduates from private High Schools or Colleges take equal rank with those under State control; while it suffices to mention the names of Columbia University or of some of the best-known Technical Schools, such as Pratt, Drexel, Armour or Lewis, to indicate the leading position occupied by institutions which owe their existence to the lavish generosity of individuals. The vast sums with which many of these private schools and colleges are endowed enable them, indeed, to set a desirable standard in respect of buildings, equipment, and staff; the freedom to express many new ideas in practice serves as an outlet for the rapid flow of original conceptions characteristic of the present stage of national development; and, though it may be permitted to question the immediate result to the juvenile subjects of some few scholastic experiments, the cause of education will probably derive eventual benefit from efforts which are invariably well intentioned, though occasionally eccentric in expression. This is not the place in which to attempt to detail the causes which have led to the gradual growth of this dual system of schools in the United States, it must suffice to say that both are complete throughout, from Kindergarten, Primary and Grammar Grades to High School, Technical Institute, College and University. In a large number of instances, the curriculum of the private Grade and High schools is identical with that sanctioned by the official Boards of Education in the various States and cities; but, as has been stated, certain others are prominent in the public eye on account of the originality of their practice and the suggestiveness or efficiency of their methods. Deviations from accepted canons are less obvious in private Colleges; on the contrary, these and the great Technical Schools often "set the pace" for State-aided institutions by the high standard they attain in systems tested by experience.

The several grades of these private institutions and their recognition and treatment of the various subjects upon which I was commissioned to inquire will now be dealt with in practically the same order as in Part I., with a view to facilitate reference and to preserve similarity of arrangement :—

(A.) Kindergartens, Primary, and Grammar Schools.
(B.) High Schools.
(C.) Technical Institutes.
(D.) Women's Colleges.
(E.) Universities.

A.—KINDERGARTENS, PRIMARY, AND GRAMMAR SCHOOLS.

No allusion was made to Kindergartens in Part I. of this Report because, so far as I could learn, the methods of teaching Domestic Science subjects which obtain in certain experimental school kindergartens, with the primary object of strengthening home affections while training social instincts, have not yet been introduced into those under State Boards of Education; it is to the former I now propose to refer. The Monograph on "Kindergarten Education," by Miss Susan E. Blow[*] records the growth of the movement in favour of their establishment, with all it owes to Dr. W. T. Harris, National Commissioner of Education; and reveals the existence of fully-developed systems of public kindergartens in 189 prominent cities and 15 States. "The history of the Kindergarten in America," writes Miss Blow, "is the record of four sharply-defined movements; the pioneer movement whose point of departure was the city of Boston; the philanthropic movement, whose initial effort was made in the village of Florence, Massachusetts; the national movement which emanated from St. Louis; and the great maternal movement which, radiating from Chicago, is now spreading throughout the United States, evolving a more enlightened and consecrated motherhood, and thereby strengthening the foundations and elevating the ideals of American family life." In these concluding words are found the key-notes with which those in charge of the Kindergarten and Primary classes at the two experimental schools attached to Chicago University endeavour to harmonise the methods they advocate. They believe that by taking advantage of a little child's strong affections and instinctively personal standpoint he may, through his social interests, be made intelligently acquainted with the world in which he lives; family ties may be strengthened in the process, and home life dignified: while such a desire to know the "reason why" for daily facts is awakened, that, in its gratification, real scientific habits of mind are acquired.

Thirty years ago Dr. W. T. Harris drew attention to the fact that "at the age of three years the child begins to emerge from the circumscribed life of the family and to acquire an interest in the life of society and a proclivity to form relationship with it. This. increases until the school life period begins at his seventh

Marginal notes:

Growth of Kindergarten Movement.

Connection of Domestic Science with Home and Social Interests.

---

* No. 2, "Monographs on Education in the United States," edited by Professor N. Murray Butler.

year. The fourth, fifth, and sixth years of transition are not well provided for either by family or by social life in the United States." It is upon the training and development of this social instinct in childhood, upon the provision of suitable educational opportunities during this transition period, that great stress has been laid throughout their school programmes by two of the leading educationalists of recent years. By written and spoken word, Dr. John Dewey and the late Colonel Francis W. Parker have asserted their conviction that all school work should connect on the social side with the life without ; and that this connection can be fitly and profitably made by means of suitable occupations carried on throughout the period of school life. " By occupation," writes Dr. Dewey, " is not meant any kind of ' busy work ' or exercises that may be given to a child to keep him out of mischief or idleness when seated at his desk. By occupation I mean a mode of activity on the part of the child which reproduces or runs parallel to some form of work carried on in social life."* In the Chicago University Elementary School these occupations are represented by the workshop with wood and tools, by cooking and sewing and by textile work. To those to whom this conception is unfamiliar, a careful perusal of Dr. Dewey's book " The School and Society," and of his article on the " Psychology of Occupation " in the " Elementary School Record '" will result in a better comprehension of his thesis. The limits of space forbid more than the most concise references to Dr. Dewey's writings, or to Colonel Parker's ideals and methods. Careful abstracts of a year's work in the schools where the views and methods of these leaders of educational thought are subjected to the test of practice, are furnished in Tables XXI. and XXII. They are included in this portion of my Report as affording the best illustrations I can offer of the means by which the domestic, equally with other sciences and arts, may be educationally employed to make schools for our children of all ages a " genuine form of active community life, instead of places set apart to learn lessons."

Dr. Dewey's opinion, shared, I believe, by the late Colonel Parker, must be borne in mind while studying these school programmes, viz., that " those subjects and that material develop the young intelligence of the child which (1) forge social links between school and home ; (2) can be acquired largely in the first instance through the exercise of the bodily activities ; (3) are so interwoven with family life as to appeal to the limited, familiar experience of a young child ; and (4) demand thought, yet by their simplicity permit that thought to function in actions, habitual or suitably acquired at the special period of life at which the lesson requires them." Dr. Dewey also maintains that the educational material should stimulate efforts directed to

Marginal note: Domestic Science and Arts at the University of Chicago Experimental Schools.

---

* " Psychology of Occupations." The Elementary School Record. A series of nine Monographs, published by the University of Chicago Press. 'The School and Society," John Dewey, University of Chicago Press.

the acquirement of technique, even though at considerable personal cost, and that each subject must possess inherent continuity in itself, adapting it for progressive development, consistent with the several periods of child growth. Further, both authorities agree that veritable correlation of each subject with the whole school programme is an essential qualification, not "through devices of instruction which the teacher employs in tying together things in themselves disconnected," but through wise selection, by which real, organic continuity of subject matter is ensured.

Elemen-
y School
ble XXI.

In the University Elementary School at Chicago, therefore, the Domestic Sciences and Arts appear throughout among the Occupations for all groups included in the Time-Table, from which it is Dr. Dewey's object to secure the absence of mere mechanical routine repetition, and to ensure the presence of conscious, intelligent action and habits of reflection.

> * "Occupations, so considered," he writes, " furnish the ideal occasions for both sense-training and discipline in thought. The weakness of ordinary lessons in observation, calculated to train the senses, is that they have no outlet beyond themselves, and hence no necessary motive. Now, in the natural life of the individual and the race there is always a reason for sense-observation. There is always some need, coming from an end to be reached, that makes one look about to discover and discriminate whatever will assist it. . . . . The same principle applies in normal *thinking*. It also does not occur for its own sake. It arises from the need of meeting some difficulty ; in reflecting upon the best way of overcoming it ; and thus leads to planning, to projecting mentally, the result to be reached, and deciding upon the steps necessary and their serial order. This concrete logic of action long precedes the logic of pure speculation or abstract investigation, and through the mental habits that it forms is the best of preparations for the latter. . . . Now, there can be no doubt that occupation work possesses a strong interest for the child. A glance at any school where such work is carried on will give sufficient evidence of this fact. Outside of the school, a large portion of the children's plays are simply more or less miniature and haphazard attempts at reproducing social occupations. There are certain reasons for believing that the type of interest which springs up along with these occupations is of a thoroughly healthy, permanent, and really educative sort ; and that by giving a larger place to occupations we should secure an excellent, perhaps the very best, way of making an appeal to the child's spontaneous interest, and yet have, at the same time, some guarantee that we are not dealing with what is merely pleasure-giving, exciting, or transient. In the first place every interest grows out of some instinct or some habit that in turn is finally based upon an original instinct. It does not follow that all instincts are of equal value, or that we do not inherit many instincts which need transformation, rather than satisfaction, in order to be useful in life. But the instincts which find their conscious outlet and expression in occupation are bound to be of an exceedingly fundamental and permanent type. The activities of life are of necessity directed to bringing the materials and forces of nature under the control of our purposes ;

* " The Psychology of Occupations," Elementary School Record.
University of Chicago Press.

of making them tributary to ends of life. Men have had to work in order to live. In and through their work they have mastered nature, they have protected and enriched the conditions of their own life, they have been awakened to the sense of their own powers, have been led to invent, to plan and to rejoice in the acquisition of skill. In a rough way, all occupations may be classified as gathering about man's fundamental relation to the world in which he lives ; through getting food to maintain life ; securing clothing and shelter to protect and ornament it ; and thus, finally, to provide a permanent home in which all the higher and more spiritual interests may centre. It is hardly unreasonable to suppose that interests which have such a history behind them must be of the worthy sort. However, these interests as they develop in the child not only recapitulate past important activities of the race, but reproduce those of the child's present environment. He continually sees his elders engaged in such pursuits. He daily has to do with things which are the results of just such occupations. He comes in contact with facts that have no meaning except in reference to them. Take these things out of the present social life and see how little would remain—and this not only on the material side, but as regards intellectual, æsthetic and moral activities, for these are largely and necessarily bound up with occupations. The child's instinctive interests in this direction are, therefore, constantly reinforced by what he sees, feels and hears going on around him. Suggestions along this line are continually coming to him ; motives are awakened ; his energies are stirred to action ; it is not unreasonable to suppose that interests which are touched so constantly, and on so many sides, belong to the worthy and enduring type."

(*a*) Elementary School —*continued.*

In other passages of his writings Dr. Dewey advances further arguments in support of these methods and subjects pursued in his school, and throws more light upon the educational value of the Domestic Arts for young children. He points out that it is natural to young children to begin with the home and occupations of the home, to proceed next to the study of occupations outside the home, that is, to the larger social industries, after which they are prepared to study the historic development of industry and invention, so learning the steps of progress and development.* " There are," he writes, " distinct phases of child growth to which the periods of organised school work should correspond." The first, from four to eight years of age, is characterised by that directness of social and personal interest (upon which, as has been stated, Dr. W. T. Harris lays much stress) as well as by directness and promptness of relationship between impressions, ideas and actions. The demand for a motor outlet for expression is urgent and immediate. During this period the constructive work should therefore combine activities which include an immediate appeal to the child as an outlet for his energy, while leading up in an orderly way to a result ahead ; habits of working for ends may thus be formed, while present occupations are gradually recognised to be a sequence of steps, which permit the accomplishment of something beyond. In the second period, which extends from eight or nine years old to eleven

---

* " General Introduction to Groups V. and VI." The Elementary School Record, p.49 .

or twelve, the aim should be to recognise and respond to the change which comes over the child from his growing sense of the possibility of more permanent and objective results and of the necessity for the control of agencies for the skill necessary to reach such results. The mere play of activity no longer satisfies. Hence the recognition of rules of action . . . . and of the value of mastering special processes so as to give skill in their use. . . . There is a conscious demand in the tenth year for ' something hard ' to do, something which will test and call out power, efficiency. The third period comes when the child has a sufficient acquaintance of a fairly direct sort with various forms of reality and modes of activity ; when he has sufficiently mastered the methods, the tools of thought, inquiry and activity appropriate to various phases of experience, to be able profitably to specialise upon distinct studies and arts for technical and intellectual aims. This interest in technique, in acquiring skill, demands a sufficient background of actual experience ; the introduction of technique must come in connection with ends that arise within the child's own experience, that are present to him as desired ends, and hence as motives to effort." . . . . * " Hitherto the school has been so set apart, so isolated from the ordinary conditions and motives of life, that the place where children are sent for discipline is the one place where it is most difficult to get experience— ' the mother of all discipline worth the name.' The world in which most of us live is a world in which everyone has a calling and occupation, something to do. Some are managers, some subordinates. But the great thing for one as for the other is that each shall have had the education which enables him to see within his daily work all there is in it of large and human significance. . . . All the media necessary to furnish the growth of the child should centre in the school. Learning certainly, but living primarily, and learning through and in relation to this living. When we take the life of the child centred and organised in this way we do not find that he is first of all a listening being ; quite the contrary. Still, in the ordinary schoolroom all is made for listening. The attitude of listening means, comparatively speaking, passivity, absorption ; there are certain ready-made materials of which the child is to take in as much as possible in the least possible time. There is very little place in the traditional schoolroom for the child to work. . . . The difference that appears when occupations are made the articulating centres of school life is not easy to describe in words ; it is a difference in motive, of spirit and atmosphere. As one enters a busy kitchen in which a group of children are actively engaged in the preparation of food, the psychological difference, the change from more or less passive and inert recipiency and restraint to one of buoyant and outgoing energy is so obvious as fairly to strike one in the face. Within this organisation is found the principle of school discipline and order. . . . The

---

* " The School and Society." Lecture I.

moment children act they individualise themselves; they cease
to be a mass, and become the intensely distinctive beings that we
are acquainted with out of school. This is the change which is
gradually coming into our educational systems, and is shifting the
centre of gravity. Now the child is more and more becoming the
sun about which the appliances of education revolve: the centre
about which they are organised. . . . The child is already
intensely active, and the question of education is the question of
taking hold of his activities, of giving them direction."

* Dr. Dewey considers that the active impulses available in the
school may be roughly classified under four heads: (1) The social
instinct, shown in conversation; (2) the constructive impulse,
shown by the child's impulse first, to "make believe," afterwards
to construct objects; (3) the instinct of investigation, which seems
to grow out of both the former, and leads to the enquiry as to the
"why" of things; (4) the expressive impulse, which is the combined outcome of the communicative and constructive instincts.
That home interests and domestic occupations afford exercises for
the expression and satisfaction of each of these is evident to
careful students of Table XXI.

Of the educational worth of these instincts Dr. Dewey writes
as follows † :—" A question often asked is: if you begin
with the child's ideas, impulses and interests, all so crude,
so random and scattering, so little refined or spiritualised,
how is he going to get the necessary culture and information ?
If there were no way open to us except to excite and indulge these
impulses of the child, the question might well be asked. We should
either have to ignore and repress the activities, or else to humour
them. But if we have organisation of equipment and of materials,
there is another path open to us. We can direct the child's activities,
giving them exercise along certain lines, and can thus lead up to the
goal which logically stands at the end of the paths followed. ' If
wishes were horses, beggars would ride.' Since they are not, since
really to satisfy an impulse or interest means to work it out, and working it out involves running up against obstacles, becoming acquainted
with materials, exercising ingenuity, patience, persistence, alertness,
it of necessity involves discipline—ordering of power—and supplies
knowledge. Take the example of the little child who wants to make
a box. If he stops short with the imagination or wish, he certainly
will not get discipline. But when he attempts to realise his impulse,
it is a question of making his idea definite, making it into a plan, of
taking the right kind of wood, measuring the parts needed, giving
them the necessary proportions, etc. There is involved the preparation of materials, the sawing, planing, the sand papering, making all
the edges and corners fit. Knowledge of tools and processes is inevitable. If the child realizes his instinct and makes the box, there is
plenty of opportunity to gain discipline and perseverance, to exercise
effort in overcoming obstacles, and to attain as well a great deal of
information.

"So undoubtedly the little child who thinks he would like to cook
has little idea of what it means or costs, or what it requires. It is simply
a desire to 'mess around,' perhaps to imitate the activities of older

---

* "The School and Society." Lecture III.
† "The School and Society." Lecture II.

people. And it is doubtless possible to let ourselves down to that level and simply humour that interest. But here, too, if the impulse is exercised, utilised, it runs up against the actual world of hard conditions, to which it must accommodate itself ; and there again come in the factors of discipline and knowledge. One of the children became impatient recently at having to work things out by a long method of experimentation, and said : ' Why do we bother with this ? Let's follow a recipe in a cook-book.' The teacher asked the children where the recipe came from, and the conversation showed that if they simply followed this they would not understand the reasons for what they were doing. They were then quite willing to go on with the experimental work. To follow that work will, indeed, give an illustration of just the point in question. Their occupation that day happened to be the cooking of eggs, as making a transition from the cooking of vegetables to that of meats. In order to get a basis of comparison, they first summarised the constituent food elements in the vegetables, and made a preliminary comparison with those found in meat. Thus they found that the woody fibre or cellulose in vegetables corresponded to the connective tissue in meat, giving the element of form and structure. They found that starch and starchy products were characteristic of the vegetables, that mineral salts were found in both alike, and that there was fat in both—a small quantity in vegetable food and a large amount in animal. They were prepared then to take up the study of albumen as the characteristic feature of animal food, corresponding to starch in the vegetables, and were ready to consider the conditions requisite for the proper treatment of albumen, the eggs serving as the material of experiment. They experimented first by taking water at various temperatures, finding out when it was scalding, simmering, and boiling hot, and ascertained the effect of the various degrees of temperature on the white of the egg. That worked out, they were prepared not simply to cook eggs, but to understand the principle involved in the cooking of eggs. I do not wish to lose sight of the universal in the particular incident. For the child to desire to cook an egg, and accordingly to drop it in water for three minutes, and take it out when he is told, is not educative. But for the child to realize his own impulse by recognising the facts, materials, and conditions involved, and then to regulate his impulse through that recognition, is educative. This is the difference upon which I wish to insist between exciting or indulging an interest and realizing it through its direction."

A suggestive and, to my mind, extremely interesting statement was made to me when visiting Chicago, viz., that, in practice, the work in Domestic Science, as carried on in the University Elementary School, has been found to be one of the many valuable means employed for bringing the home and school life of the child into closer relationship. Cooking, sewing, and the study of textiles are included under this head, special attention being given to correlating these with as many other lines of work in the school as possible. Science, history and art, for instance, are studied, not as isolated subjects, but as the natural outgrowth of dealing with every-day materials and processes, such as those with which a child is familiar in home life. In cooking, *e.g.*, connection is made with botany through the plants from which food materials are obtained ; with chemistry and physics, through the analytical work done with foods and through the innumerable phenomena which continually present themselves in the study of nature ; with physiology, by the action of food in the body and by practical work in the preparation of meat, through

TABLE XXI.

UNIVERSITY OF CHICAGO, ELEMENTARY SCHOOL. (AS EDUCATIONAL THROUGHOUT)

EXTRACTED AND TABULATED FROM "THE ELEMENTARY SCHOOL RECORD," 1900–1901. PUBLISHED BY "THE UNIVERSITY OF CHICAGO."

which some knowledge is gained of muscle form and bone (a) Elemen-
structure; with history, in the development from primitive tary School
to modern methods of obtaining and preparing food; with shop- —*continued.*
work, in the demand for various articles made in the shop and used
in the kitchen, such as towel-racks, rolling-pins, wooden spoons,
etc.; while number work plays an important part in the weights
and measures used. Sewing is connected with the Fine Arts in the
drawing and colouring of designs and in all colour combinations;
with history, in the making of clothing and other articles typical
of the various periods; with shopwork, in the making of shop
aprons in the sewing-room and of spool-racks and yarn-winders
in the shop; with cooking, in the making of aprons and holders,
the hemming of towels and other household articles; and with
number work, through the continual use of ruler and tape measure,
in calculating the amount and cost of materials needed, measuring,
and verifying bills of goods purchased. The textile work connects
with botany in the study of the producing plants; with geology,
in the study of soils with reference to the various productions;
with geography, in the locating of the plant and animal-raising
districts and the factories and mills; with history, in the development of the textile industry and its influence on the people; with
physics, in the various properties of the different materials and in
the implements and machines used in their production; with
chemistry, in the preparation and dyeing of the textiles; with
shopwork, in the construction of distaff, spindles, and looms; and
with sewing, in the work with the finished products.

The preparation of the class lunch at this school, whether by
children in the Kindergarten or in older "Groups," affords
practical illustration of the possibility of realising many of
Dr. Dewey's views without departing from methods accepted by
convention, yet lending to them an educational value and a vivid
interest too often absent from such homely items in the routine of
daily life. These simple luncheons are served each morning.
Each class takes it in turn to render this social service, the various
members preparing the food, setting the table, and then waiting on
their companions during the meal. Social links are by this means
forged between school and home interests; the bodily activities are
exercised. The work appeals to the limited and familiar experience of the young cooks and servers, and, while demanding thought,
is yet of sufficient simplicity to function in habitual or suitably
acquired actions. Efforts to acquire technique are stimulated by
the interest aroused; the suitable correlation with other school
work links life with learning, and gives dignity to manual exercise.
As the lunch frequently consists of some form of cereal served
with cream or fruit the children are interested in finding out as
much as possible about each kind of grain used. They plant seeds
and observe their mode of growth and development; they talk
about the harvesting of the ripe grain (specimens of which are
shown) and the development of the various methods from primitive

to modern ways, considerable attention being given to pictures and other representations of methods, implements, and machines employed. The uses of the various parts of the plants are then discussed, with the necessary processes through which they must pass before they are ready for market ; as the cleaning and rolling, cracking or grinding of wheat, which are usually learned by a visit to the mills. Then there is an examination of each kind of grain by means of the microscope, which shows its parts. To discover the nature of these parts and the effect on them of water, heat, etc., some simple experiments are used. For example, in wheat, the grain is crushed in a mortar and sifted through cheese-cloth, thus separating the coarse outer covering ; this is then examined, treated with cold water and with hot, and boiled, the effect being carefully noted in each case. The fine part of the grain, which passed through the sieve, is tested in the same way, and its action compared with that of starch similarly treated, from which the inference is drawn that starch is present in the grain. The work with this fine part of the grain shows the presence of a sticky, glue-like substance, which stretches and catches the air when in a moist state. The names *bran, starch,* and *gluten* are given to these parts ; pictures of the grain are drawn representing them ; and sentences are written which tell what has been found out with regard to them. The amount of water necessary in cooking one cereal is used as a standard ; and the amount required for the others is found by balancing them with this standard and using a proportionate amount of water. Thus, the children find out that in cooking flaked corn it is necessary to use equal amounts of cereal and water, while corn-meal is five times as heavy, and, therefore, requires five times as much water. In making out a table, as the children do, for use in the cooking of all cereals, the necessity arises for the continual use of the balance and weights, and of the measuring cup (divided into quarters and thirds), all of which give familiarity with weights and measures, and with fractional parts in their various combinations. In the simple cooking of cereals the children also learn the properties of water, its simmering and boiling points, the meaning and use of steam and of dry heat, with their varying applications to suit different materials and conditions. Familiarity with certain materials and conditions are thus acquired, the natural impulse of the child is exercised and utilised, while both knowledge and discipline result. Throughout the whole course the same general plan is followed ; the children find out *by experiment* the nature and composition of the materials used and the treatment to which they must be subjected to render them most nutritious and palatable. The work in the kitchen, being correlated with that of the other departments of the school, is supplemented and emphasized by directing the attention along the same lines in these departments. It is hoped in time to make a greater number of connections, and to improve

KINDERGARTEN	FIRST GRADE	SECOND GRADE	THIRD GRADE	FOURTH GRADE	FIFTH GRADE	SIXTH GRADE	SEVENTH GRADE	EIGHTH GRADE	NINTH GRADE	TENTH GRADE
AIM.—To make the Kindergarten another home for the children, to introduce them in an orderly way to larger life and civilized forms, to introduce them to an objective view of home activities and relations.	**HISTORY.**—	**HISTORY.**—	**HISTORY AND LITERATURE.**—	**GEOGRAPHY AND LITERATURE.**—	**HISTORY.**—	**HISTORY.**—Recall.	**HISTORY.**—	**HISTORY.**—	**HISTORY.**—Primitive culture.	**HISTORY.**—Roman life.
	LITERATURE.—	**LITERATURE.**—	**GEOGRAPHY.**—	**GEOGRAPHY.**—	**LITERATURE.**—In connection with History.	**LITERATURE.**—In connection with History.	**LITERATURE.**—In connection with History.	**LITERATURE.**—In connection with History.		**GEOGRAPHY.**—
	GEOGRAPHY.—	**GEOGRAPHY.**—	**NATURE STUDY.**—	**NATURE STUDY.**—	**GEOGRAPHY.**—	**GEOGRAPHY.**—	**GEOGRAPHY.**—	**GEOGRAPHY.**—	**GEOGRAPHY.**—	**PHYSIOLOGY.**—
	NATURE STUDY.—	**NATURE STUDY.**—	**CORRELATED NUMBER.**—	**ARITHMETIC.**—	**NATURE STUDY.**—	**ARITHMETIC AND MATHEMATICS.**—	**NATURE STUDY.**—	**NATURE STUDY.**—	**PHYSIOLOGY.**—	**ASTRONOMY.**—
NATURE STUDY.	**CORRELATED NUMBER.**—	**CORRELATED NUMBER.**—	**READING.**—	**READING.**—	**NATURE WORK.**—		**ARITHMETIC AND MATHEMATICS.**—	**ARITHMETIC AND MATHEMATICS.**—	**ASTRONOMY.**—	**MATHEMATICS.**—
Games.	**CLAY MODELLING.**	**READING.**—	**READING AND SPELLING.**—		**DRAWING.**—	**DRAWING. READING.**—	**DRAWING. READING.**—	**DRAWING. READING.**—	**MATHEMATICS.**—	**ART.**—
Rhythmic games (with ball).	**DRAWING.**	**WRITING AND SPELLING.**—	**ART.**—	**ART.**—	**ART AND CRAFTS.**—	**ART.**—	**SCHOOL ECONOMICS.**—	**SCHOOL ECONOMICS.**—	**ART.**—	**CHEMISTRY.**—
Songs.	**Drawing.**	**SCHOOL ECONOMICS.**—	**SCHOOL ECONOMICS.**—	**INDUSTRIAL ART AND MANUAL TRAINING.**—	**TEXTILE ART.**—	**ARTS AND CRAFTS AND MANUAL TRAINING.**—	**ART.**—	**ART.**—	**PHYSIOLOGY OF NUTRITION.**—	**LANGUAGES.**—
	Paper Cutting.	**ART.**—	**MANUAL TRAINING.**—	**MUSIC.**—	**MANUAL TRAINING.**—	**MUSIC.**—	**MUSIC.**—	**MUSIC.**—	**LANGUAGES.**—	
	Painting.	**INDUSTRIAL ART.**—	**DRAMATIC ART.**—	**DRAMATIC ART.**—	**MUSIC.**—	**MANUAL TRAINING.**—	**MANUAL TRAINING.**—	**MANUAL TRAINING.**—		
	Large Blocks (building).	**DRAMATIC ART.**—	**MUSIC.**—	**PHYSICAL TRAINING.**—	**PHYSICAL TRAINING.**—	**PHYSICAL TRAINING.**—	**PHYSICAL TRAINING.**—	**PHYSICAL TRAINING.**—		
	Sand Work (plans of garden, etc.).	**MUSIC.**—	**MANUAL TRAINING.**—		**FRENCH.**—	**LANGUAGES.**—	**LANGUAGES.**—			
		MANUAL TRAINING.—	**PHYSICAL TRAINING.**—							
		PHYSICAL TRAINING.—	**FRENCH.**—							

NOTE.—All the subjects are correlated throughout — Geography, Literature and Reading included in the History. Drawing and Manual Work, including springs, and Nature Study included under several headings. Art is exercised by the representation and dramatization of the subject matter of other lessons.

the work, which was still in the experimental stage at the time of my visit (May, 1901), in many details.

The second experimental school I visited where Domestic Science is linked with home and social interests is now known as the University of Chicago School of Education, at that time under the directorship of the late Colonel F. W. Parker. While Dr. John Dewey approaches 'this question of the right education of the young in the spirit of a philosopher, the late Colonel Parker arrived at his conclusions animated rather by the inspiration of a prophet. His whole nature was imbued to an unusual degree with so intense a love for and sympathy with child nature that, in the opinion of some careful and skilled observers, there existed a risk lest sentiment should be allowed to obscure or to replace reason in the translation of his theories into practice. His school programme was the tentative outcome of years of enthusiastic earnestness devoted to its evolution, in which he received the cordial co-operation of his " Faculty." Weekly meetings were the rule (lasting from two to three hours), in which some contribution was expected or permitted from each member of the staff towards the solution of problems forced upon their notice by their daily work in teaching and training. Character building (or citizenship) was to Colonel Parker the end and aim of education ; to gain this " everything must be brought in (to the curriculum) which will concentrate and expand ideas and develop right habits." Education he believed to be " the all-sided growth of the individual, physical, mental, and moral. Community life is the ideal of education, because it is the only ideal great enough to provide for this all-sided development of the individual." " The ideal school is the ideal community. . . . it is the education of complete living." " Community life is that state of society in which every individual member orders his conduct with reference to the good of the whole : the whole being so constituted as to necessitate the highest development of its members." Consequently " the citizen must know something of the world in which he lives, and this knowledge comes best from actual contact." This being his creed, Colonel Parker framed his school programme with the view of giving actual personal experience to each child of what has contributed to the existing phase of civilisation. This conception of the scope of school education really involves a never-ending correlated study of man, his environment, and his works. In practice Colonel Parker attached much importance to the observation of a selected subject in its entire environment, and took great exception to conventional isolation and classification. His whole scheme was further planned in deference to the requirements of body and brain at the various periods of growth, so far as at present known. To find and arrange subject matter for the mental nutrition of each pupil, and for all grades of pupils, was a problem still imperfectly solved at the time of his death, but good ground had been broken. Life in his school was organised on a basis of (1) work, doing things for which the pupils felt a social need ; *e.g.*,

(b) School of Education. Table XXII.

gardening, cooking, working in wood or metal, clay modelling, sewing, weaving, printing, etc. ; (2) a study of human activities in the outside world, to help the children to interpret their own experiences ; (3) the study of Nature. The domestic sciences and arts found a place in the Kindergarten course because home activities, the common life of the children, furnish opportunities for work and service suited to their years, and constitute a desirable addition to play and games. These subjects appeared in the Primary grades because Colonel Parker believed (a) in the value of the primitive industries and arts in the early education of children ; and (b) in the importance of simple work in school economics, sanitation and hygiene for the establishment of an ideal of the conditions essential to good health in a community. Home economics took its place in the Grammar grades as an integral part of the study of Nature, and of Man as its highest manifestation. In each case the subjects were found to lend themselves as a means for the employment of thought and reason, for the application of scientific principles, and for the culture of the social instincts. This method of introducing the study of economics deserves consideration, associating, as it does, the conception of the value of health and time, as well as of money, with the facts and duties of daily life.

'ossible .pplication f foregoing iethods in 'ngland.

It would be unjust to convey the impression that either of these educationalists believe themselves to have realised their ideal in practice ; it would be equally inaccurate to give the impression that I advocate the wholesale adoption of principles and methods so admittedly tentative and experimental as those just referred to ; but I am of opinion that these conceptions, wisely modified, could be introduced into the kindergarten and primary classes of many English schools. The educational attractions and advantages attached to the employment, as part of school work, of familiar, homely occupations for quite young children has been hitherto very generally overlooked ; their ethical, sociological and economic values for seniors when progressively developed is certainly not yet recognised. A careful study of these School Programmes will reveal that their contents are selected, handled, and developed so as to forge social links between school and home, while experience proves that they foster an intelligent participation in communal life ; two points where, admittedly, our educational methods have hitherto proved unsuccessful. Acquaintance with subjects bearing on domestic life is largely acquired through the exercise of the bodily activities ; these subjects appeal to the child's limited experience ; they demand thought and permit its expression in action ; it is also believed that they arouse an interest so strong that it will cheerfully overcome obstacles and perseveringly face drudgery and difficulties to achieve realisation ; wherein lies their strong claim as formers of character and factors in the growth of a true communal spirit. Essential to their profitable introduction are (1) space, as individual participation in each occupation is essential, for which reason classes must be small ; (2) time, otherwise informing by the teacher has to replace thought and reflection by the child ; (3) elasticity of syllabus and confidence in the teacher by those in authority, to permit of thoroughly intelligent "doing." In the future, when these advantages are secured in our schools, teachers can profitably devote some attention to these methods of providing for children what Froebel called " the education of complete living."

There are, relatively, few private Primary and Grammar Schools, though they are found in large cities, such as New York or Detroit, but I had no opportunity of studying their attitude towards the teaching of Domestic Science. Private educational enterprise or endowment more usually finds its outlet in the provision of institutions for higher education from the High School upwards. *Few Private Primary and Grammar Schools.*

B.—HIGH SCHOOLS.

Private High Schools exist mainly in wealthy localities, for considerable capital and a large clientèle are necessary to compete in equipment and efficiency of staff with those State-aided by Boards of Education. The growing prejudice in favour of class distinction is frequently compelled to give place to the superior advantages offered by the public High School or to the obstacle of a high scale of fees. It is of special interest to note the belief in Hygiene and Home Science as suitable studies in these private High Schools, where the curriculum is independent of all outside control, except that exercised by college entrance requirements or the whims of parents. This belief promotes the formation of an intelligent public opinion among the more wealthy members of the community ; for, although the first introduction of these subjects is stated to be often unpalatable to the parents, the result to their children is so speedily apparent as to invariably overcome previous objections. *Typical Domestic Science Courses*

Notable among the High Schools supported by endowment and fees is that attached to the Pratt Institute, Brooklyn, of which the superintendence is entrusted to Dr. Luther Gülick, whose views on education repay careful study, and so far stand well the tests of practice to which they are subjected by their author. Expressed in the briefest terms, Dr. Gülick considers that two of the fundamental conditions to be met by a secondary school are (1) the needs of the individual for the development of a fairly rounded character and personality ; (2) the demands of society upon the individual. " The individual must be developed as an individual with reference to his personality. He must also be so trained as to fit into the existing world, to take his place in the present social régime . . . Health, character, a strong, constructive, sympathetic view of life, and the ability to do something that the world wants done, these deserve prominence as objects in school life." These views and the methods by which they seek to find expression harmonise with the idea of the founder of the Institute, viz., that boys and girls *(a) Pratt Institute High School, Brooklyn, N.Y. Table XXIII.*

should be placed under conditions which favour all-round development, and that school education should consist in the patient,
systematic, and constant training of body and mind. To this end
manual and physical training, art training and laboratory work
are given equal rank and standing with the academic studies ;
health, power, and a wholesome, earnest attitude towards work
being essential to the realisation of the ideas of both founder and
director. A second aim is to help each pupil to discover his gifts
and to start him in their effective development ; while, with the
object of encouraging all who can to continue their work at college,
it is endeavoured to frame a scheme such as shall enable those who
desire to do so to meet college entrance requirements. The accompanying diagrammatic illustration of the studies and occupations
pursued during this four years High School course shows how these
requirements are met ; though naturally it is impossible to indicate
by means of any figure the atmosphere of social claims and interests
which surrounds the young people, or the methods employed to
temper, while seeking to develop, the individuality of each boy and
girl. The school is open to all children of fourteen, who, in Dr.
Gülick's judgment, are ready, physically, mentally, and morally,
to profit by the work, without interfering with the progress of
others. The greatest sympathy is felt for those in feeble health,
but the amount of work, both physical and mental, is planned for
the best development of the normal child, and would be excessive
for the delicate. A standard of normal height, weight, and health
must be therefore conformed to.

The school day is divided into six periods of fifty minutes each ;
one-half of the time is given to academic work in languages and
the humanities, in mathematics, and in science ; the other half
is devoted to music, art, and manual training, laboratory practice
and gymnastics. The manual training, to which six periods a week
are devoted throughout the curriculum, comprises, in the first year,
bench-work in wood and wood-carving for boys and girls alike ;
in the second year it consists, for boys, of wood-turning, pattern
making and moulding, ; for girls, of sewing, drafting, cutting and
making garments, some study of materials being also included.
In the third year, boys take forging and the elements of decorative
iron-work ; while the girls study form, line, colour, and texture,
and the outline and proportions of the human figure. They also
practice costume designing (sketching hats, draperies, and gowns,
half life size), and devote some time to millinery. In the fourth
year the boys attend the machine shop, learning bench-work and the
use of machine tools ; and the girls are instructed in domestic science,
which comprises cookery, emergencies and home nursing. No
pains are spared to teach accuracy, economy, patience, judgment,
and perseverance throughout the whole course. It is maintained
by Pratt Institute teachers that after a year's " drill " in wood-work,
needlework *may* be so taught as to veritably merit the designation
of manual training. Their system of instruction is framed " to

TABLE XXIII.
PRATT INSTITUTE HIGH SCHOOL
Four years' course showing proportion of total course given to each subject.

Gymnasium 6·3 %	Chemistry 3·1 %	Physics 3·1 %
Latin, German or French 12·7 %	Biology 1·6 %	Physiography 1·6 %
	Music (including Chapel) 8·6 %	
Drawing 12·7 %	Mathematics 6·3 %	
	Higher Mathematics or another language 6·3 %	
Manual Training. 18·9 % .Boys take woodwork, forging and machine shop.. Girls take woodwork, sewing, cutting, draughting, dressmaking, millinery, cookery	English 11·8 %	
	History 3·1 %	

train the eye to recognise, the hand to produce, correct lines and
angles, as in matching stripes, turning hems, sewing seams, slanting
stitches, cutting gores from an oblong, drafting and machine
sewing. In dressmaking comes the additional study of beautiful
form, colour, and texture in relation to clothing of the body and
some knowledge of the intimate connection between the laws of
beauty and the laws of health. Millinery methods are considered to
develop lightness of touch and skilful handling of materials, and may
be employed in training the imagination to picture the desired
result." So far as my observations extended, these aims are kept
very steadily in view during the two years occupied with the study
of plain needlework, dressmaking, and millinery; indeed, the
primarily educational purpose of the manual and art training in this
High School is very evident throughout. Dr. Gulick believes that
there should be no division between the work of the artist and that
of the artisan, therefore a close connection is maintained between
the studio, the "shop," and the sewing-room. The girls especially
are unquestionably much interested by this development of the
educative and culture side of a pursuit, often treated with contempt
at their age on account of its utilitarian aspect being over emphasised.

I was fortunate in securing very full particulars concerning the
year's training in Domestic Science; and the following details are
couched chiefly in the words of Mrs. Chambers, who was the director
of all the cooking classes and courses given in the Pratt Institute
at the time of my visit. An earnest student of the best educational
methods, she agrees with many other teachers in their belief that
the educational value of cooking as a school subject lies as much in
its mind as in its manual training properties. " In Pratt Institute
an attempt is made to teach cookery scientifically, the main object
of the course is the development of the student through the subject
taught. While constantly stimulated to apply her knowledge of
chemistry, physics and biology, the lesson is so planned that these
applications are suggested by the work, not by the instructor. For
instance, at the beginning of a lesson the student may perform
under direction certain simple experiments to illustrate the effect
of the addition of salt or of soda on the solvent properties of water,
or of an acid on cellulose, etc. She may then be asked to cook
various classes of vegetables, sweet juiced, strong juiced, etc., or the
problem of cooking a cabbage may be given, a vegetable with both
strong juices and tough cellulose, entire freedom in treatment
of the water being allowed; but each student must subsequently
support the method she has pursued by sound reasons, while results
are compared and conclusions deduced by the whole class." In the
course of an interesting article on her methods in the Pratt Institute
Monthly for March, 1900, Mrs. Chambers threw light on how she
stimulated her students' powers of reflection and association:—

> They are encouraged, for instance, " to trace the probable history
> of cooking, from broiling directly over the coals to the skilful applica-
> tion of heat in oven or braising pan; from the crude combination
> of meal and wetting of water and milk, as in ' johnny-cake,' to the

beating in of air, as in ' gems,' or the addition of egg, as in ' pop-over.' (a) Pratt
They are led on to observe the advantages which follow the substitu- Institute
tion of some leavening agent for the prolonged labour of beating, as High School
in griddle-cake or crumpet ; or the variety gained by the addition of —*continued.*
a little shortening, and the use of a utensil calculated to give a large
extent of crisp surface, as in ' waffles.' They are called upon to note
the well-defined relation which is traceable in all the various flour
mixtures, and are made observant of the dependence for successful
results upon the use of a definite proportion of wetting, dry material
and leaven. A student who has found the key to this can form her
own combinations by the exercise of thought, independently of the
cookery-book, confident that by uniting materials in right proportions,
and by exposing them for the right time to the right temperature,
something good and wholesome will result. Has too much flour been
added to the gem-batter ? Well, change it to waffles, to biscuit, to
raised muffins. When the subject is taught on this basis the student
is given the recipes for various batters and doughs, but not in order,
for she is to assort and classify them, and to discover the relation.
Then let her take the cookery-book and study some other branch, such
as soups, or sauces, or puddings, and trace the connection, the evolution
for herself. A white sauce, made of milk, thickened with flour and
enriched by butter, may be developed into a soufflé, which also is made
of milk, thickened with flour and enriched by butter, but is further
enriched by the yolks of eggs, and is flavoured and baked. White
sauce may, by other additions which are governed in character by the
result desired, lead to American ice-cream, thence to pistachio bisque,
or to a frozen plum-pudding. Each one is free to trace his own combinations, and each has the joy of the investigator, the discoverer, the
creator of order out of disorder." Mrs. Chambers encourages the
making of graphic representations to illustrate these relations and
proportions, a method found very stimulating to children. For instance, in the Cake lesson, in which the cup-cake can be used as a
suitable foundation, the several varieties made by subtraction, addition,
or substitution can be illustrated by a simple diagram. The accompanying illustration* is here reproduced by kind permission of Mrs.
Chambers. No. 1 represents the cup-cake, with the varieties made
by subtraction, resulting in plainer cakes of the same type ; No. 2
(raisin, currant, fig, date, citron, nut, chocolate, and spice cakes), the
varieties made by addition, resulting in richer cakes, more or less
divergent from the type ; and No. 3 (gold, silver, and coffee cake),
those made by substitution, which gives apparently totally different
types of cake, resembling neither one another nor the original batter,
yet possessing an easily traced relationship. The plan once mastered,
the children are called upon, as a " time exercise," to write out in
detail the ingredients needed for a nut-cake, or any other variety,
using for a basis a fraction, as three-eighths, of a cup of flour. If
correct they are allowed to make a small specimen. . . . " Out
of more than thirty children in the last Saturday (mixed) morning
class only two or three failed in the first attempt, and none in the
second. They may then be given a number of simple recipes, and
asked to make a graphic representation for themselves. Much
originality and ingenuity have been shown in this work."

In conjunction with this pupils are encouraged to note, from the
beginning, the properties of the various materials used ; whether
soluble or insoluble, how affected by heat, how by acids, etc. This
leads to a classification of foods, and eventually into the separation
of the five-food principles—protein, fat, carbo-hydrates, water and salt.
Instruction is given in the right proportion of nutrients to meet
the needs of the body, simple dietetic rules are formulated, and students

---

* See Fig. V.

FIG. V.
"CAKE" DIAGRAM.
Reproduced by kind permission from "The Pratt Institute Monthly."
March 1900.

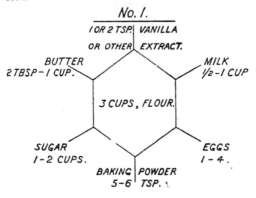

No. 1.

| 1 OR 2 TSP. | VANILLA |
OR OTHER | EXTRACT.

BUTTER
2 TBSP-1 CUP.

MILK
½-1 CUP

3 CUPS, FLOUR.

SUGAR
1-2 CUPS.

EGGS
1-4.

BAKING | POWDER
5-6 | TSP.

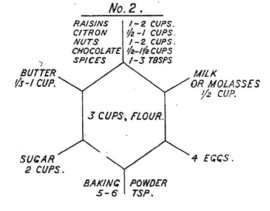

No. 2.

RAISINS	1-2 CUPS.
CITRON	½-1 CUPS.
NUTS	1-2 CUPS.
CHOCOLATE	½-1½ CUPS
SPICES	1-3 TBSPS

BUTTER
⅓-1 CUP.

MILK
OR MOLASSES
½ CUP.

3 CUPS, FLOUR.

SUGAR
2 CUPS.

4 EGGS.

BAKING | POWDER
5-6 | TSP.

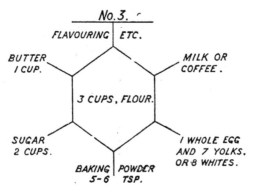

No. 3.

FLAVOURING | ETC.

BUTTER
1 CUP.

MILK OR
COFFEE.

3 CUPS, FLOUR.

SUGAR
2 CUPS.

1 WHOLE EGG
AND 7 YOLKS.
OR 8 WHITES.

BAKING | POWDER
5-6 | TSP.

are enabled to estimate correctly which food principle is in excess,
which is lacking, in each new recipe. and what other dishes should
be used with it in order to complete a well-balanced meal."

The High School girls have the advantage over the Saturday class,
to which the last part of the above extract refers, in that the cookery
they practise is based upon the knowledge they have previously
gained in elementary biology, physiology, physics and chemistry.
Miss Edith Greer, Directress of the Domestic Science Department,
and Mrs. Chambers told me that the girls are delighted with the
opportunities offered for the application of their other studies. The
scientific method of treatment first arouses " sheer amazement " by
the field of interest it opens up ; and this feeling is rapidly succeeded
by a satisfactory enthusiasm. " The High School girl finds a new
interest in both kitchen and laboratory when she applies her knowledge of the expansion of gases to the rising or falling of her cup-cake,
and when she is led to reason out the best way of cooking vegetables
from her knowledge of the degree of solubility of mineral salts."
The High School cooking classes consist of from twenty to thirty
girls ; last year (1901) they were conducted by Mrs. Chambers herself, without assistance ; she confessed that to superintend the
practical work of so large a class, which came to her without previous
training, taxed all her capacity No outside work was expected or
required of the pupils, but well kept, systematic note-books were
insisted upon, to assist in the development of methodical, scientific
habits. The arrangement of this High School course differs in some
respects from that in general use ; but the Directress was true to
her conviction that the allowance of time for somewhat experimental
work by the pupil, demanding observation and concentration of
attention, is more profitable than the rapid and correct execution
of a given number of dishes, so carefully superintended that
failure, with all the valuable lessons it covers, is impossible.

The course opened with the cooking of eggs in various
ways, so that the pupil might gain, through her own experience,
information as to the behaviour of albumen under a variety
of conditions, of which the final application was carried on,
without the teacher's assistance, in the manufacture of different
dishes. For example, a recipe was given for " water custard " ;
observation showed that the egg and water must be combined
in a definite proportion to ensure right consistency ; that
the use of sugar as a condiment to suit individual tastes must
be regulated with judgment ; that without care in the application
of heat at a certain temperature, failure was inevitable. The
next lesson, which included the making of egg lemonade, drew
attention to another characteristic of albumen, that it is
coagulated by acid as well as by heat. Subsequent lessons continued
the study somewhat as follows : No. 3, stuffed egg, seasoned and
pounded ; practical point, albumen is toughened by high temperatures ; No. 4, eggs cooked by pouring boiling water upon them and
allowing them to stand (*a*) 8 minutes, (*b*) 20 minutes. Examina-

tion showed that the yolk coagulated at a lower temperature than
the white. No. 5, the making of meringue ; observation demonstrated that the white of egg will hold air when beaten, whereas the
yolk will not become tenacious by this means. A series of experiments was subsequently introduced to ascertain more exactly the
solubility of albumen and the exact temperature at which the
various changes occur in the yolk and white ; after which the girls
were given some attractive recipes with eggs to carry out by themselves, which demanded intelligent application of the principles
just learned. Gelatine was next taken, studied by similar methods,
and the results compared with the knowledge of albumen gained
in previous lessons ; the double application derived from intimate
acquaintance with the properties of both substances was then
demanded, for example, in the cooking of fish. The girls would be
asked to solve the problem of boiling this successfully, knowing that
the albumen is soluble in cold water, the gelatinous fibres in hot.
Later on in the course they would be asked what substances are
needed to supply the nutrients lacking in fish, and required to
combine these substances in a soup, a sauce, or a pudding, to accompany the fish, adding condiments to enhance or to supplement
flavour. Thus as the work advanced the knowledge gained would be
constantly used for the purpose of acquiring further information,
always to be tested by practice, the pupils being encouraged to discuss
and to try various methods of procedure, after preliminary observations and experiments ; these being made in test tubes with very
small quantities of material. Space does not permit me to indicate in
detail the interesting and thorough manner in which the structure
and properties of meat were similarly studied. Carbohydrates were
subjected to the same method of observation, while in the case of
sugar the attention directed to how far cooking changes might be
carried, introduced the causes and control of fermentation. Lessons
on fats followed ; illustrations of the power of combination, emulsi-
fication, decomposition, under certain conditions, etc., being found
in dishes, such as velvet cream, clotted cream, toasted bacon, etc.
Water and its qualities were considered before vegetables and their
cooking, in order that advantage might be taken of the opportunities
offered in the cooking of vegetables to apply the lessons, learned
as to the effect of the use of hard or soft water in kitchen processes. Salts were left for the latter part of the course, because it
was considered that their intelligent study demanded some acquaintance with chemistry, and the girls, who had meanwhile been
continuing their general biology and chemistry courses, should
have become competent at this stage to detect the presence of
phosphates in wheat, potash in potatoes, etc., and were expected to
be intelligently interested in their preservation in the chief salt-
containing foods. A study of the general nutrition of the body
and its metabolism, and of well-balanced diets, was carried on
concurrently. so that the end of the year's work found these girls
of seventeen and eighteen intelligently trained and genuinely

interested in the food question, upon which the well-being of families so largely depends. Reports from mothers " are constantly received" expressing their surprise at the appetite created for practical work at home by this course in the High School. There seems to be a steadily increasing recognition on the part of the parents that the school can fitly provide a part of that education which used to be more generally furnished by home life ; and they readily admit that a decided impulse towards a higher estimate of household skill is given indirectly by their own increasing realisation of the value of these subjects as a profession, when properly studied. A wise emphasis is laid in this particular course upon nursery hygiene. The question of accommodation and equipment for this work presents no difficulties in this case, for though the High School is in a separate building from the Institute, the laboratories and workshops of the Technical Department are open to, and used by, the High School students.

An interesting departure was that initiated, some three years (*b*) Girls' ago, in the Girls' Classical School at Indianapolis, of which the prin- Classical cipal is Mrs. May Wright Sewall, president of the International School, Council of Women. In some respects this school is unique ; the apolis. courses of study are planned on somewhat broader and even more flexible lines than are usual in High Schools ; among the advantages are to be included opportunities for individual instruction consequent upon small classes, the intimate acquaintance formed by the principal with all her pupils, and the facilities offered to weak and backward students. Careful supervision and direction extends even to the uniform dress worn by the girls, which is suitably simple and thoroughly healthful. A commodious two-storey addition has been made to the building for the special accommodation of the Household Science Department, the organisation of which was entrusted to a graduate of the Drexel Institute, Philadelphia. Its establishment was entirely the result of Mrs. M. Wright Sewall's own initiative ; not at all in response to, indeed rather contrary to, existing public opinion. Her object in taking the step was to give to " well-born and well-bred girls, whose circumstances in life relieve them from the necessities of household work, a respect for labour, a comprehension of the skilled work demanded by domestic duties and an insight into the degree to which applied science may lighten daily household claims, turning drudgery into delight." Evidently the danger of a contempt arising on the part of the well-to-do for hand labour is not confined to one nation or to one hemisphere ; so, as her own pupils are drawn chiefly from wealthy homes, Mrs. Sewall wisely set herself to direct their attention to the hygienic, economic and æsthetic claims and possibilities of household science, in order effectually to counteract this regrettable tendency. Practice classes in cooking, one hour per week, are open to all school pupils, but the full course of study covers two years, and, in common with many other subjects, is " elective." This complete two-year course

(*b*) Girls'
Classical
School,
Indian-
apolis
—*continued.*
of study includes two lessons a week of one hour each, one of which
is devoted to theory and one to practice.' During the first two
years of its existence about twenty-five per cent. of those eligible to
elect the subject took the work; these pupils showed much enthusiasm and apparently real pleasure and profit were derived from
the course. The work of the department is carried on in the new,
admirably equipped kitchen and workrooms; it is related, so far as
is possible, with that of the other departments in the school, particularly with that carried on in physical culture, drawing and
natural science; the educational and disciplinary values are specially
emphasised. During the first year the work was limited to that of
the kitchen and dining room; the instruction covered the subjects
of foods, marketing, cooking, the cleansing and care of utensils,
and the serving of meals. Subsequently systematic instruction
was introduced in laundry work; in the care of bedrooms; in
house ventilation, heating and general sanitation; in the simple
principles of nursing; in the care of the sick and emergencies;
in plain sewing, dressmaking and millinery. Pupils are
required to carry out practically only that for which they have
already learnt good reason exists; and, under their teacher's
guidance, they endeavour to demonstrate the utility of the facts
and laws previously presented in theory. As has been stated, the
course is elective, but permission to elect it is regarded as a recognition of good standing in other classes and is esteemed a privilege. The charges to pupils in regular attendance are reduced
to the lowest amount that will cover the cost of the materials used
and of the expensive equipment provided for conducting the work,
viz., $10 (£2) per year.

An "applied science" course for students of Household
Economics is still in its infancy, but is reported to promise
well for the future. It covers two years; during the first
of these there is one three-hour lesson per week in cookery,
one hour's theoretical lecture, and three periods of laboratory
work in chemistry, physics, and physiology; in the second year
there are two lessons in theory and only two periods of laboratory
work in chemistry and physiology; this course entails really hard
work on its students. Mrs. Sewall tells me that, by its means,
she hopes to impress on her girls that "skill is important, but of
even more importance to them than skill, is a consciousness of the
fact that the principles inculcated in this work are fundamental;
and that their right comprehension materially affects the attitude
of the mind towards the work of women, and particularly towards
domestic interests."

To that proportion of the general public who may be interested
in household science, opportunity is also given to increase their
scientific knowledge of home subjects and their skill in housekeeping and home-making by means of adult classes. For these,
courses of lectures on physiology, hygiene, house sanitation, nursing,
emergencies, marketing, food values, table service, etc., are pro-

vided. Classes are organised, limited to ten students, for those who wish to supplement the theory thus obtained by practice in cooking; those who desire laboratory instruction may join the school classes in applied science. In general outline the subject matter presented to the regular school classes and to these classes of adults is identical, but the treatment is modified in detail, condensed or expanded, to suit the age, understanding, and present attainments of those in attendance.

In order to emphasise the evident tendency to direct the atten- (c) Home
tion of all social grades to this important subject of Household and Day
Science, I propose to refer, very briefly, to another excellent School,
illustration of the success which attends the introduction of Detroit.
the subject into schools where extra expense accompanies its pursuit. The Home and Day School at Detroit was opened in 1876 by
the Rev. James D. Liggett and his daughters; it is now installed in
an imposing building situated in the pleasantest part of the city,
and is attended by upwards of three hundred boys and girls of
varying ages. The school comprises four departments, Kindergarten, Primary, Intermediate, and Academic or High; the first
three are co-educational; about thirty girls find accommodation
as boarders. The new department of Domestic Science was opened
in September, 1900, when classes were organised in sewing and
cooking. Sewing is taught in four grades, which include the three
years in the Intermediate department and the first year in the
Academic. Two periods a week are given to the work, of which
the aim is to give manual training, and to set high standards for
fine work. The course in the first year covers simple stitches
carried out by hand; from these the girls pass on to machine work
and make underwear and blouses, for which they take their own
measurements and draft their own patterns. The objects of the
work done in the Domestic Science kitchen are threefold :—(1)
to acquire skill in preparation of foods; (2) to study the nutritive
value of food; (3) to study the chemical composition of foods. The
kitchen is a large, bright room, with complete equipment for sixteen
individual workers. The tables provide a drawer for each student,
containing all necessary utensils, and a gas-burner, over which
most of the cooking is done; a sink with hot and cold water is
fitted to each table; a coal range contains the oven which is used
in common by all; while a full dining-room equipment gives
opportunity for serving a dinner or luncheon at the end of each
term, to demonstrate the knowledge and skill acquired during
that time. The course is to extend through four years in the
Academic department, and is planned along good lines. Simple
cooking in the first year leads to food analysis, and later on to
chemical and bacteriological examination of foods. Students
throughout give two periods a week to the work, which is optional;
at the time of my visit it had been elected by one-third of the
girls. A very promising foundation for this course is laid by
previous studies; elementary science (chemistry, physics, geology,

meteorology, &c.) is introduced in connection with nature study (which enters largely into the time-table of the lower grades), and is subsequently differentiated into distinct subjects; all the studies included in the curriculum are entrusted to really competent teachers. I must not omit mention of a practice which also undoubtedly contributes to the efficiency of the teaching carried on in this school, namely, the frequent meetings held by the large staff of teachers, with the express object of maintaining an intelligent correlation between the subject or subjects for which each is responsible with other studies conducted by his or her colleagues.

(*d*) Boston High School. Appendix D.   I was interested to learn that useful work in the form of courses in lessons in Household Science is done in Boston High Schools by Miss S. Maria Elliott. These, though chiefly theoretical in character, in consequence of the conditions under which they are admitted to a place in the school programmes, have served a very good purpose; they have aroused interest among the pupils and their parents, they have attracted the attention of the authorities to a satisfactory extent, and have awakened a desire for more practical knowledge among the pupils. Miss Maria Elliott is herself well versed in both the theory and practice of her subject, and is further skilled in its presentation from the standpoint of experience. The syllabus of three of her courses is included to illustrate the scope and selection of subjects which her experience has shown her to be both serviceable and attractive, where but a limited time is allowed for such studies and where attendance is optional. Miss Elliott's pioneer efforts in this direction have throughout received substantial support from the Association of College Alumnæ, to whose initiative Boston owes so much of its educational and sanitary reform and progress; while they have so far assisted to form public opinion that the City Board of Education had under contemplation, at the time of my visit, the provision of a practical High School course in the subject of Household Economics. In this may be found a further example of the fact to which reference was made in the early pages of this Report, that private enterprise has almost invariably paved the way for the adoption of every branch of Domestic Science into the curriculum of State-aided schools.

Hygiene and Physiology Courses. Horace Mann School, New York City.   With reference to the teaching of hygiene and physiology in private schools, space will permit me to refer only to the excellent methods employed in the Horace Mann School. This can be done in part by extracts from the "Teachers College Record" for March, 1900, and January, 1901. This school is attached to Teachers College, Columbia University, N.Y., for the purposes of practice and observation. It comprises three departments. a kindergarten, an elementary and a secondary school, and is now housed in magnificent new buildings designed to be in all respects models of their kind. Hygiene and physiology are associated with nature study in the two lower departments and with biology in the High school. In describing the course in nature study, Professor Francis E. Lloyd writes as follows : " In general, we conclude, that the aim of nature study is to prepare the individual for life by training his mental power of observation and of generalisation, by deepening and rationalising his emotional life, and by increasing his social worth." . . . . . " Nature study at first must find its material in the immediate environment of the child, and as the mental grasp strengthens and the mental horizon broadens, new sources are made available. We believe that this is an important principle, for in this way the home and the school life can be woven together in the life of the child." . . . . . . After drawing attention to the special correlation with other studies emphasised in each grade, Prof. Lloyd concludes : " In the eighth grade a serious attempt has been made to introduce a course embodying the essentials of physiology, meaning thereby not merely the study of the human body, but strictly the essentials of both animal and plant physiology. This is done because we believe that such a course is of much more value educationally, bringing out, as it should do, the essential unity of animal and plant physiology than the usual course in physiology and hygiene. That idea of physiology which makes it for the most part the study of the two hundred odd bones in the human frame, leads us to believe that it is time to begin on a new tack. It must not be thought, however, that the course is not aiming at the human aspect of the study, for it is of profound importance that students should have accurate information concerning the workings of their own bodies. Furthermore, there could hardly be a better preparation for the work in biology, soon to follow in the High School, than the training given in such a course." . . .

I learnt on enquiry that the simplest principles of hygiene are introduced throughout the grades, not alone in connection with the study of animal and plant life, but successfully also in connection with elementary science ; for the elder children the principles of diffusion, solution and chemical change are directly applied in human physiology.

The " Teachers College Record " for January, 1901, discusses in detail the High School Course in Biology, which is made the medium for a more advanced study of physiology and hygiene. Again, a few extracts will best serve to indicate the general lines by which pupils are led on from the physiology of the lower to that of the higher forms of life. " The importance of interpreting the activities of the human body from the comparative standpoint seems sufficient reason for advocating the consideration of the fundamental principles of physiological action in connection with the study of elementary zoology. Experience has convinced the writers that there is no more profitable study for secondary pupils than the physiological side of animals. No other phase of zoological study arouses a deeper interest and appreciation or is more spontaneously applied by them in connection with their own life activities. It is scarcely necessary to offer a stronger reason for including such study in an elementary course." . . . "The principles of physiology should be introduced with the first animal which is studied morphologically, and each principle as introduced should receive concrete application. The study can easily and quickly be made comparative, as successive types of animals are taken up ; and, finally, such specific and comparative studies may be made to lead to a direct application of the principles of comparative physiology to the activities of the human body." . . .

Four periods a week, of forty-five minutes each, are given to this subject. The first half of the year is devoted to the zoological part of the course, followed by botany in the second half. It was desired to extend this time, and to do so would add materially to the value of the whole course. This interconnection of hygiene with nature study, chemistry, physics, and biology seems to me essentially the right method; the influence of heredity, environment and nutrition upon the highest as well as upon lower forms of life is emphasised; human physiology is robbed of any subjective aspect; concrete applications for the theories of science and art suggest themselves naturally; and while the time-table is impregnated with an atmosphere of hygiene it is not burdened with an additional, isolated subject. To those who are in agreement with me I strongly recommend a careful study of the two publications from which the above extracts are made, and from which I offer one more quotation before quitting the subject. Professor Lloyd has been detailing and supporting his outline scheme in botany ; he concludes his arguments as follows— "There is a further point of importance in that the very natural and essential facts about the subject of sexual reproduction may be made a part of the knowledge of young students. Such knowledge, it is believed, helps to lift them to a normal conception of a question which is in the young mind very frequently befogged and distorted to the pronounced detriment of the moral nature."

The above selection of examples of the adoption of Domestic Science and Hygiene as an integral part of their programme by private schools of high standing could be much increased ; but it will, I hope, suffice to show the strong conviction of the importance of the subject held by independent persons, and the possibility of finding time for the study where there is first " a willing mind."

C.—Institutions for Training Teachers in Domestic Science.

Training of Teachers in Household Science and Art.—
(a)The Oread Institute.
Table XXIV.

Teachers of Household Science obtain their training chiefly at Technical Institutes, which usually comprise many other departments, though at least one Normal course is offered at an institute devoted entirely to this subject. Considerable attention has been attracted to the Oread Institute, by its publications as well as by the generosity of its present owner. It was originally founded and built

TABLE XXIV.

THE OREAD NORMAL INSTITUTE OF DOMESTIC SCIENCE, WORCESTER, MASSACHUSETTS.

Institution and Course.	Entrance Requirements.	Scope of Course.	Methods.	Length of Course.	Fees and Finance.	Equipment.
Oread Normal Institute, Worcester, Mass. Domestic Science, Normal Course. Principal, Miss Harriet A. Higbee.	(1). Good health. (2). Maturity. Candidates from 23 to 35 years of age preferred. (3). Academic training, i.e., the full course in a good high school, or its equivalent. A knowledge of the following subjects is desirable:— Elementary Physics. Physiology. Chemistry. Mathematics. English and American History.	History of Foods, 9 lectures, 1 hour each. Cookery, 40 weeks, 3 hours daily. Sewing, 40 weeks, 2 hours per week. House Economics, 40 weeks, 2 hours per week. Marketing, 20 weeks, 4 hours per week. Laundry, 20 weeks, 1 hour per week. Sanitation, 40 weeks, 2 hours daily. Practical house work, 40 weeks, 3 hours per week. Chemistry, 40 weeks, 1 hour per week. Physics, 40 weeks, 1 hour per week. Physiology, 9 lectures, 1 hour each. History of Foods, 15 lectures, 1 hour each. Emergencies, 12 lectures, 1 hour each. Bacteriology, 12 lectures 1 hour per week. Feeding of Infants, 40 weeks, 2 hours per week. Elocution, 20 weeks, 2 hours per week. Pedagogy, 40 weeks, 1 hour per week. Psychology, English Composition, 40 weeks, 3 hours per week. Physical Training, Manual Training, Art and Nature Study } To be included this year (1902)	Much stress laid on individual work. Practice work in teaching is secured by extra classes for children and adults, as well as in outside schools. The scope of the work shows a desirable comprehensiveness, but the time is too limited to permit of thoroughness.	1 year of 10 months. Normal students work from 8.30a.m. to 5.45 p.m., and must also devote five evenings a week to study, from 7.30 to 9 p.m.	$200. (about £40.) Free scholarships were given by the chief promoter of the Institute, Mr. Henry D. Perky, to 29 out of the 40 students who took the course last year.	All modern apparatus for gymnasium, laboratory, and experimental work; illustrations for lectures and general instruction in all branches of household economy. The kitchen laboratory, science laboratory, and gymnasium are situated above each other on the three floors of a large circular tower, 40 feet in diameter.

at Worcester by Hon. Eli Thayer, a graduate of Brown University,
and was opened by him in 1848 as the first institution of higher
education for women in Massachusetts ; it was continued as a
school until the early eighties. The property was subsequently
bought by Mr. Henry D. Perky, the philanthropic manufacturer
of the " Shredded Wheat " preparations, who converted it into
the existing Oread Institute of Domestic Science. Of the forty
students who took the course during the past year twenty-nine
had the advantage of free scholarships ; the fee to those who pay
for their training is $200 (£40) ; the number of applicants for
the course was stated to be 600. The building has been thoroughly
remodelled, and is now supplied with the latest systems of drainage
and water supply. It is heated by steam, lit by electricity, and is
furnished with all modern apparatus for gymnastic, laboratory,
and experimental work, as well as for general instruction in all
branches of household economy. No expense has been spared in
the provision of equipment ; the great kitchen laboratory, science
laboratory, and gymnasium are situated above each other on the
three floors of one of the two circular towers, 40 feet in diameter,
which form a distinctive feature of the building. The kitchen is
open to visitors, a special gallery being provided for their accommodation, in order that the students may not be conscious of interrup-
tion. As the attempt is made to cover in one year the course of
study usually spread over at least two, more generally three, it is
essential that the students be in a condition to acquire a considerable
body of knowledge under pressure. In view of this necessity, the
requirements for admission to the school lay stress on—(1) good
health, to enable the student to stand a *régime* of industrious
application and very hard work ; (2) maturity, which is so largely
an individual matter that a minimum age limit is not rigidly fixed,
but in general candidates between twenty-two and thirty-five
years of age are preferred ; (3) academic training. The full course
in a High School, or its equivalent, is deemed an adequate academic
preparation ; the faculty, however, judge each application on its
merits, not according to an arbitrary standard. Some acquaintance
with the following subjects is held desirable : elementary physics,
chemistry and physiology ; mathematics, including arithmetic,
geometry, and algebra ; English and American history. The
regular school year consists of two terms of twenty weeks each.
Two training courses are offered—the Domestic Course and the
Normal Course—each extending over a similar period of time. The
first includes general care of the house, general cooking, laundry
work, a short course on marketing and lectures on the history and
chemistry of foods, infants' and invalid cookery and emergency
work, but omits the science and special lecture work included in
the second.

The Normal students are at work from 8.30 a.m. to 5.45 p.m.,
and are further required to devote five evenings a week to study—
from 7.30 to 9 p.m. In addition to this, each girl is responsible

for the arrangement of her own bedroom, and groups of girls are appointed to attend to the service of meals. Only three-quarters of an hour are allotted to air and exercise, though each student must, in addition, spend a quarter of an hour in the open air before going to bed. It is reported that the practical house-work, as well as that in the kitchen and laundry, are better carried out than the laboratory practice, though this is much appreciated. Much stress is laid on individual work in all studies. Practice work in teaching is obtained by means of the special classes offered to adults and children, as well as by those given in the schools of Worcester. Each student has also to give a specimen lecture and a practical lesson in each science before her companions, her subject being assigned to her.

The comprehensive syllabus shows a just appreciation of the scope of training desirable; but, in spite of the long hours devoted by the students to their studies, the crowded curriculum must nullify its own object, too much being demanded in the limited time. The Principal is so much interested in the organisation of this work, of which she desires to promote the practical utility, that it is to be hoped the period of Normal training, at least, will shortly be doubled in length. The physical and mental strain to which the young women are subjected, and to which their appearance, to my eyes, bore witness, is not the only matter for regret. To lower the prestige of a subject by entrusting it to insufficiently-equipped teachers is a matter of real moment where public opinion is still in process of formation. It is in this connection that I foresee that the desirable time extension will be made, for the exceedingly high standard attained by the graduates in Household Science at Teachers College, Columbia University, or at the Pratt and Drexel Institutes, necessitates that other Normal courses, in the interests of their future diplomées, must follow in the steps of those at these prominent institutions.

The work of the Oread Institute is not confined to its two groups of resident students; special classes for clubs, teachers, house-keepers, domestics and cooks, are offered in afternoons or evenings as most convenient; twelve weekly lessons in classes of fifteen each being given for fees of $5 (£1) and $3 (12s. 6d.) respectively. A kindergarten department has also been formed in connection with the Institute, where mothers may send their children from four years of age " to be instructed in the A B C of proper food while they are also learning the A B C of language." The children are taught, through games, to set and clear a table, wash dishes, sweep a room, make a bed, &c.; a weekly fee of 75 cents (about 3s.) is charged. A class for older children, from 10 to 12, is given on Saturdays, at a fee of 25 cents (about 1s.) per lesson. Courses for private individuals are also offered in sewing and home dressmaking.

The Normal course at the Boston Cooking School, which extends from the first Monday in January to the last Friday in June (a six-months' course of two sessions daily, even Saturday afternoon (*b*) Boston Cooking School.

(b) Boston Cooking School— *continued.*

being occasionally claimed) is another illustration of a short training, though it is by no means so ambitious as that just described at the Oread Institute, practice being confined to the kitchen and laundry. The course includes instruction in all branches of cookery and laundry work, with lectures and examinations in marketing, the physiology of digestion, hygiene, chemistry, bacteriology, psychology, and pedagogy. Special attention is given to the arrangement of lessons in cookery adapted to public school and hospital work, which include plans for kitchen equipment and the purchase of utensils and supplies. The Normal students are admitted to all demonstrations, and lectures given at the School, and when sufficiently advanced are required to give demonstrations before their companions, who subsequently test and criticise the dishes. Diplomas are awarded to those who pass the required examinations and satisfactorily meet the requirements of the course. A High school education is the essential qualification for admission, though more advanced studies are advantageous, especially previous attendance at a Normal School. I was told that several college graduates were taking the course in 1901. There is a steadily increasing demand, at good salaries, for qualified women, and graduates are helped to secure positions at hospitals and institutions, either for teaching or for supervision, in Grade schools and elsewhere. Grade school teachers follow this course occasionally to take a diploma in cooking. The Principal also told me that, owing to the number of good openings offered, several women previously engaged in office work have saved enough money to support themselves while they took the course, with subsequent satisfactory pecuniary results. The tuition fees are $125 (about £26), payable one half in advance, the balance at the middle of the term. Board and lodging may be obtained near the school at the Y.W.C.A., the boarding-house for students, or in private families, at rates varying from $5 (£1) to $9 (£1 15s.) per week, according to accommodation. Each pupil must be provided with light washing dresses, full-belted white aprons, sleeves and caps to be worn at the school. The number in the class is limited, and averages thirty, sub-divided into three divisions, each under a teacher; the students are drawn from all parts of the States and Canada. There is no laboratory for chemistry or bacteriology; the demonstrator in cooking brings her own microscope when required for the study of food stuffs. Each student has twenty practice lessons in Public School work, and the examinations are conducted by outside examiners. The premises are large and airy, three kitchens being provided for the accommodation of the normal students and of the ladies who attend private classes. The whole organisation is the outgrowth of Miss Maria Parloa's energy and enterprise; but its well-wishers now desire to see the course extended and the accommodation amplified to meet the modern requirements in this class of training.

An interesting four years' normal course in Household Economics is that provided at the Lake Erie College for Women, which is situated at Painesville, thirty miles east of Cleveland and three miles south of Lake Erie. Founded some forty years ago by private enterprise, most of the contributions to its funds have come from citizens of Painesville and Northern Ohio; the College buildings are beautifully situated in well-wooded grounds of over twenty acres. Frequent additions to the original accommodation have proved necessary, and Science Hall, in which are located the lecture rooms and laboratories for physics, chemistry, biology, botany, and physiology, dates only from 1897. The College offers three parallel courses which lead to the degrees of Bachelor of Arts, Bachelor of Science, and Bachelor of Literature. Each of these extends through four college years of thirty-five weeks each, and consists of specified studies for the first two years, with certain required studies and a definite amount of elective work in the last two. Entering students may present, in place of examinations. certificates from accredited schools, with the understanding that scholarship after entrance must be satisfactory; to this end the work of the first term is probationary. The charge for board, room, and tuition for the College year is $250 (about £50), The tuition fee of $75 (£15) must always be paid in advance. and is not subject to return or deduction; no deduction is made for board either, except in case of serious illness or other necessity; there are small extra charges made for use of laboratories, coaching, laundry work, and extra cleaning of students' rooms. The fact that the College is worked on what is known as the Mount Holyoke* plan is probably answerable in part for the moderate fees, as the institution is by no means wealthy.

(c) Lake Erie College for Women. Table XXV.

The original idea has been considerably modified at Mount Holyoke, but Lake Erie College holds true to its standard. All students are required to do a certain amount of daily domestic work, for, with the exception of certain rough kitchen processes, no service is provided. Each girl must attend to her own bedroom, and the other household duties are shared, each student taking thirty-five minutes daily for twelve weeks at a time. The service of the three daily meals devolves upon the girls; breakfast is at 6.45, lunch at 11.30, and dinner at 5.30. (I confess the question presented itself to my mind whether hygienic requirements were being

---

*The Mount Holyoke plan, referred to above, recognises the cultural as well as the economical value of housework, and is so designated because the Women's College at Mount Holyoke was founded with the object of its illustration. The students were called upon to participate in the daily domestic work, except cooking and scrubbing, in order that, while deriving the intellectual stimulus, and the broad scholarship, which tradition associates with men's collegiate studies, a high ideal of home life should be developed and maintained with its mutual helpfulness and its self restraint. The conception attempted to combine in practice the home ideal of dignified and systematic household service with the life of a scholar.

TABLE XXV.

LAKE ERIE COLLEGE, PAINESVILLE, OHIO.— SCHEDULE OF NORMAL COURSE IN HOME ECONOMICS.

Institution and Course.	Entrance Requirements.	Scope of Course.	Methods.	Length of Course.	Fees and Finance.	Equipment.
Lake Erie College for Women, Painesville, Ohio. President, Mary Evans, A.M., Litt. D.D. Normal Course in Home Economics leading to Degree of B.Sc. and ... Diploma.	The first term only. English, History, ..., Mathematics, as for other College Courses. German, French, Latin; two years' study of two languages. Physics, (one year Chemistry, of each Biology, six months.	Obligatory Subjects for all Students— Hygiene, Voice Culture, Physical Training, Short Course in Home Economics. First Year. Home Economics, German or French, Mathematics, English, Bible, Hygiene, Physiology, Botany.	The teaching is specially to provide ... with a scientific training to ... than to fulfil their responsibilities with regard to the ... and to the ... The ... course is taught ... and ... under pro-fessors. The ... service of ... for this large ..., to-gether with a large part of the house-hold ..., is so or-ganised as to pro-vide the students with practice in Domestic Economy.	Four college years of 35 weeks each.	$250 a year (about £50), an endow-ment of over $60,000, but one hundred thousand dollars still needed.	Large Science Hall with wings, containing labo-ratories for Phy-sics, Chemistry, ..., Botany, Physiology, and ...; also a ... but valuable ...
Professor of Physiology, Luetta P. Bentley. Professor of Home Economics, Chemistry, Bio-logy, Edna D. Day.		Second Year. ... or German, Art, Design and Decoration, Biology (including Bacteriology), Physiology, Chem-istry, Home Economics. Third Year. Home ..., Chemistry, His-tory, Bible, Psychology, Logic, Economics.				A large and rich ... of charts, medals, specimens and prepared sub-... arranged by the ... ... for illustrating the ... of Food. A good depart-mental library, ... the most recent ... and periodicals.
Professor of Household Art, Mary Keffer.		Fourth Year. Home Economics, Industrial His-tory, Sociology, Ethics, Pedagogy.				

considered when I learned that no refreshment of any description (c) Lake Erie College— *continued.* was provided for these young people between this early evening meal and the next morning's breakfast, although study for two or three hours was carried on before retiring to bed.) The setting of the tables and washing up of all utensils used for 130 people at each meal entails no small labour, but is carried on in most systematic fashion. Ten girls are appointed weekly to lay the tables for meals and to serve the food, which is brought to the dining hall by lifts. Another ten wash up, working in pairs ; the silver, glass, and small china are collected on each table, then little wagons, mounted on wheels, are run from one to another, carrying bowls of soapy water, cloths, etc., and the washing up is done on the spot. The residue of bread and butter, broken meat, etc., is also collected on to wheeled wagons and sorted ; those portions suitable for subsequent use being set aside in a convenient pantry. Batches of students are told off in regular order to attend to the sitting rooms, corridors, and staircases, which are very extensive. The Principal, Miss Evans, considers that the active interest maintained in these daily life processes conduces to the development of the social spirit, and prevents the girls acquiring a contempt for household duties, while it affords excellent training in methodical habits and in ready adaptability to circumstances. A strong religious atmosphere pervades the college. The average number of students is somewhat over a hundred, who, with their twenty-three professors, are all resident. Systematic work in physical training is carried on under a specially trained teacher (unless students are excused upon examination), who most wisely includes base-ball, basket ball, and tennis under this designation ; and conducts all her classes in the open air whenever the weather permits.

In the four years Normal course in Home Economics*, students entered for the degree of Bachelor of Science take prescribed courses as "electives" in this and related subjects, and receive at their graduation, in addition to their degree, a Teacher's Diploma in Home Economics ; thus they combine the liberal training of a college course with special training along one line. Their first year's chemistry deals with non-metals, and includes a certain amount of qualitative analysis, to which three laboratory periods of two hours each and one lecture period weekly are devoted. An introduction to organic chemistry follows in the first quarter of the second year ; the remaining twenty-four weeks are devoted to special work, of which the distinguishing feature is applications to food and physiology ; this course also includes a study of air, water and food principles from the standpoint of sanitary and physiological chemistry. A course in general bacteriology, in which cell structure is carefully studied, forms an introduction to botany, which in this instance consists of a laboratory study of typical forms, beginning with rusts, moulds and mosses, leading on to flowering plants. The laboratories in the new Science building give every opportunity for

* See Table XXV.

the pursuit of both these studies ; further assistance being afforded
by the excellent departmental reference library, the large collection
of slides for microscope and lantern, the herbarium, rich in local
species, and the fresh material for study easily available in adjacent
woods.   General biology and a short course on anthropology are
also open to seniors.

The immediate study of Home Economics comprises the following
courses :—

(1) *Household Sanitation.*—(The house, its location, construction
and care ; to be preceded or accompanied by courses in physics, chemistry, bacteriology and art.)   Time required, four hours a week for
twelve weeks.

(2) *Chemistry of Foods and Cooking.*—(Qualitative and quantitative analysis of foods ; detection of food adulterations, principles of
cooking illustrated by laboratory work.   To be preceded by general
chemistry and physiology.)   Time required, six hours a week for
twenty-four weeks.

(3) *Dietaries, Theoretical and Practical.*—(Planning of meals for
the college family with careful estimate of cost.)

(4) *Supervision of Domestic Work.*

(5) *Home Economics.*—(A review and unifying of all previous work
relating to the home, expenditure, values, the relation of the home
to society.)   To be preceded by a course in Economics.

(6) *Methods of Teaching Home Economics.*—To be preceded by a
course of Pedagogy.

The equipment for the practice of cookery was somewhat limited
at the time of my visit, though the kitchen had been well fitted up
and supplied with sets of the Pratt Institute Food Analyses, charts,
and sets of block models.   From the first a certain number of
students had shown great interest in this course, and it was anticipated that considerable impetus would be given to the practical work
in this department by the new teacher of cooking, to whose charge
it was to be entrusted that autumn.

A short course in Elementary Home Economics is arranged for
general students.   This is confined to an introduction to the study of
sanitation, food, principles of cooking, and dietaries ; no preparation
in the sciences is required, and only so much of the scientific basis
is given as is necessary for the understanding of practical methods.
The course is not included in college work, but is sufficiently in
request to show that, to an increasing degree, educated women
desire to gain an insight into the subjects upon which the right
ordering of daily life is based.

All students *must* attend the lectures upon hygiene and the
classes in voice culture.   The science work required of all also includes physiology and one year's work in physics or chemistry
for the classical and scientific courses ; physiology and six months'
work in physics or chemistry for the literary course.   The obligatory courses in hygiene and physiology are conducted by Miss
Luetta Bentley, who is profoundly and unusually interested in
her subjects.   The elementary courses deal with the principal

bodily functions and care of the health ; they are illustrated by dissections of an Auzoux dissectible mannikin, and by models of the eye, ear, heart, larynx and head ; four hours a week for twelve weeks are required in each year ; no practical work is carried out by the students. The course in advanced physiology is elective ; it is devoted to a microscopic study of the tissues and to detailed study of the special functions in relation to health and disease ; it covers the same length of time as the elementary. The fourth year course in hygiene and physiology is again obligatory on all graduating students ; this is concerned with embryology, the subject being gradually developed from plants, through fishes, birds, and mammals to human beings. With the assistance of a collection of special models and specimens, prepared and voluntarily contributed by leading medical men in Cleveland, Miss Bentley is enabled to introduce the young women in her class to a right understanding of the responsibilities of motherhood and the wise care of infant life. The results of her tactful, discreet, and sound methods of handling this subject during the past few years are stated to be already perceptible beyond the college walls ; meanwhile she is the recipient of many grateful letters from graduates who have subsequently married and who realise their deep obligations to her teaching. It is largely owing to Miss Bentley's enthusiasm and energy that the general equipment of this department has reached its present complete condition ; valuable charts and engravings, skeletons and anatomical preparations and histological specimens constitute a small museum. The wide-reaching influences for good of such a course, conducted on such a method, are incalculable, though, worthy as it is of imitation, one is compelled to recognise that few individuals combine the technical knowledge, enthusiasm, discretion and skill which distinguish Miss Bentley; and contribute to her admirable success. It is her ideal that all the science work carried on in the college shall be brought to bear in its application on the study of hygiene ; and she is fortunate in having as a colleague Miss Edna Day (a graduate of Michigan University, the recently appointed professor of chemistry, biology, and home economics in Lake Erie College), whose interest and training well qualify her to further develop the Normal Household Science course.

When writing in Part I. of the hygiene and physical culture courses obligatory in most colleges, no reference was made to the sources from which the professors of these subjects are drawn. This Report would be incomplete were no allusion made to one of the most prominent of these—the Boston Normal School of Gymnastics Mrs. Hemenway, in addition to her pioneer work in the establishment of the first public school kitchen in the United States and the inauguration of the first Normal school for teachers of Household Arts, also, in 1889, founded the Boston Normal School of Gymnastics. The promotion of true womanliness was her life-long object, and she looked for its attainment by two means—*i.e.*, by the

Training of Teachers in Physical Culture and Hygiene.— Boston Normal School of Gymnastics. TableXXVI.

Boston
Normal
School of
Gymnastics
—*continued.*

intelligent study of the household arts, and the perfect development of physique by a well-planned course in physical training,
based upon the knowledge and practice of hygiene. Mrs. Hemenway
was aided in her work by Miss Homans, at present Principal of
this Normal School of Physical Training, who has been its prime
organiser for a quarter of a century. Opportunities are here
offered to men and women to prepare themselves to conduct
gymnasia or to direct physical training according to sound methods.
To this end thorough instruction is provided, not only in gymnastics, games and dancing, but also in those principles of physiology, psychology, and the hygiene of the human body, upon
which physical training must always depend. A High School
certificate or its equivalent is required of entering students, as
well as proof of a sound elementary acquaintance with physics and
chemistry. The courses of instruction include a pursuance of
both these subjects, in addition to practical physiology and
histology ; the theory of gymnastics ; corrective gymnastics and
massage ; gymnastic games ; dancing, swimming, emergency work ;
psychology, educational theory, and practice lessons with Grammar
School and High School children, as well as with private classes and
instruction to shop women in the evening. The names of the
instructors answer for the admirable character of the training ;
they are drawn chiefly from the professors at Harvard University
and the Massachusetts Institute of Technology. The courses in
physics and chemistry are given in the ample laboratories of the
latter building ; the work in both branches of study has special
reference to preparation for the study of physiology and gymnastics. Instruction in histology and physiology is given by
means of lectures, recitations, demonstrations, and, in histology,
by laboratory work on the part of the student. The course is
planned so as to give a clear conception of the methods and results
of physiological investigation, and is made to bear directly upon
the subject of personal hygiene in its widest sense. To this end,
thirty hours are devoted to conferences, in which there is the
fullest possible discussion, on the part of students and instructor,
of the conditions of healthy life. Among the topics considered
in this part of the work are the relations of heredity and environment to health ; the effects of use and disuse of organs ; the physiological effects of muscular exercises ; clothing, bathing, and the
prevention of colds and other inflammatory processes ; feeding,
fatigue, rest, and sleep. During the entire period the amount
of didactic teaching is reduced to the minimum ; and the students
are, above all, encouraged to work out for themselves the applications of physiology to the healthy life of the organism.

Much thought has been devoted by Dr. Theodore Hough (Massachusetts Institute of Technology) to this eminently practical course
in physiology and hygiene; he considers it advisable to include a little
elementary bacteriology; to this only from fifteen to twenty hours
can be given, but it is very carefully done, great pains being taken
with the drawings and microscopic work; by this means the cellular

TABLE XXVI.

BOSTON NORMAL SCHOOL OF GYMNASTICS.

Two Years' Course of Instruction for Normal Students.

Physics with demonstrations - - - - - -	30 hours
Chemistry with laboratory work - - - - - -	45 hours
Histology and Physiology and Hygiene with laboratory work	195 hours
Kinesiology and Theory of Gymnastics - - -	100 hours
Descriptive and topographical Anatomy - - - -	86 hours
Symptomatology - - - - - - - - -	25 hours
Theory of Gymnastics and Art of Teaching - -	70 hours
Psychology and Pedagogy - - - - - - -	40 hours
Pedagogy and Art of Education - - - - - -	30 hours
Lectures on spinal curvature - - - - - -	12 hours
Lectures and practical exercises in Applied Anthropometry (in sections)	
Corrective gymnastics and massage - - - - -	95 hours
Instruction in gymnastic games - - -	30 hours
Instruction in dancing - - - - - - -	30 hours
Æsthetic dancing - - - - - - -	30 hours
Swimming (in sections) - - - - - - -	12 hours
Athletics (lectures and illustrations) - - - -	10 hours
Instruction in fencing (elective) - - - - -	
Emergencies, with practical instruction in bandaging - -	15 hours
Daily instruction in gymnastics - - - - -	
Daily review in gymnastics and instruction in teaching -	
Teaching classes of children - - - - - -	85 hours

M

structure of the simple tissues of the body can be more intelligently studied (epithelium, connective tissue, muscle and nerve- cells) ; embryology he approaches from the general philosophical stand-point, which he believes to have real pedagogical value. In his opinion not less than five hours a week for a year must be devoted to the study of anatomy, physiology and hygiene, practical and theo-retical, if the student is to teach the subject subsequently in Grammar and High Schools. Like many other scientific men, he deplores the limitations hitherto imposed by the state legislation as to the teaching of these subjects, one regrettable result of which has been the un-willingness of experts to write text books, which the law requires to be submitted to a lay committee prior to acceptance ; but his con-sciousness of the loss to the rising generation which results from this attitude has prompted him and his colleague, Professor Sedgwick, to consider the preparation of a manual, which should be at once reliable and acceptable ; there is evidence also of a movement to secure desir-able modification of existing legislation on the teaching of hygiene and physiology.

Much attention is directed in this course to the science of move-ments and to corrective gymnastics, the object of which is to impress the avoidance of harmful exercises and the use of pre-ventive measures. The etiology, development, and pathology of lateral curvature of the spine are dealt with so far as is necessary to a practical understanding of the subject ; special stress is laid upon the examination and detection of this condition as found in children of school age, with illustrations of the practical methods of recording such changes. The question of treatment is taken up through a consideration of the principles underlying the conditions which demand attention and of the range of application of the different means which may be employed. In the clinics of the Children's Hospital, and in the school itself, the students acquire considerable experience in the gymnastic treatment of various deformities, as well as in the practical application of massage. The brief course in Symptomatology is intended to convey to the minds of the students an estimate of the general appearance of the more common diseases. Two reasons are advanced in support of such instruction, first, that it enables the students in their future work as teachers to detect conditions of doubtful health in applicants for gymnastic training, and to warn them to consult a physician before undertaking the work ; second, that it fits them to comprehend more intelligently the information given by phy-sicians regarding patients whom they may advise to take gymnastic training.

A most careful physical examination is always made previous to the admission of candidates ; expert advice is at once taken on any doubtful point, free of expense to the would-be student. The physical training is undoubtedly severe, but great consideration is shown, while students are expected to co-operate with their instructors by the exercise of discretion and by the conduct of their daily life along healthy lines. The æsthetic dancing which enters into the curriculum of the second year is a form of applied gym-nastics, in which the power of co-ordination and the sense of rhythm áre especially trained. The movements are more complicated, less localised, less sharply defined than are formal gymnastics; they are continuous, rhythmical, of constantly varying character, and involve blended but partial action of a great number of joints and muscles, rather than powerful, complete action of a few. The practical results obtained are grace and ease of movement and bearing, together with a considerable amount of endurance. It seemed to me that they constitute a valuable addition to the more ordinary course of training, for they develop a graceful control of muscular power, charming to the beholder and refining to the possessor.

Boston Normal School of Gymnastics —*continued.*

The school itself contains rooms of unusual proportions. In addition to the gymnasium proper, which has an area of 4,000 square feet, there are lecture-rooms, an anthropometric-room, a library, a gymnasium for corrective work, etc. Shower baths and ample dressing-room accommodation are provided, while, thanks to the well-selected aspect, all the rooms are well lighted and flooded with sunshine. The equipment of the school includes forty microscopes, mounted and disarticulated skeletons, preparations of joints, a life-size Auzoux model of the human body, and a large number of anatomical charts, etc., besides a complete set of anthropometric instruments. The library contains about 1,000 volumes, brought chiefly from Europe; these are largely professional in character and include, in addition to the purely technical matter, standard works on psychology, metaphysics, sociology, natural science, and education.

The personal interest taken by the staff in their work for this school impressed me to a marked degree; no pains seemed spared to adequately prepare the students for their work, and the thoroughness of the training struck me forcibly. Miss Homans does not consider the experimental stage of the training to be yet passed; she would like the two years to become a four years' course, though compelled to await the realisation of her ambitious ideal until subsequent remuneration is calculated upon a scale which would compensate for the investment this prolongation would involve. She quotes insufficient opportunity for practice in teaching and the difficulty of raising the standard of admission, as the existing prominent defects, together with the pressure of study which necessitates a great deal of home work. The individual development and mental growth of each student is carefully studied; Miss Homans deals personally in a private interview with any pupil with whom she, or any member of the staff, has cause to be dissatisfied. Students are required to be careful of their personal appearance, and at all times to be neat in their dress, in the belief that professionals cannot be too careful on these points. Black serge is used for the gymnastic costume, a red tie distinguishes the junior class, while the seniors wear orange. One hundred graduates are now earning from $800 (about £160) to $2,000 (about £400) a year, and only those who for family reasons, such as marriage, do not desire to make use of their certificate remain unemployed. All applications

pass through Miss Homans' hands, and she has devised a system
of promotion, which gives advancement to experience, backed by
sound knowledge. All graduates can, indeed are advised to, return
periodically for further exercise and study—and they avail themselves fully of the privilege ; they are in such demand, that unusual
advantages are in most cases afforded them to visit Boston for
this purpose. The male students are generally members of the
medical profession, who have made a speciality of bodily deformity.
The cost of training is about £170, inclusive of board and lodging.
The tuition fees and incidentals average £18 to £20 a year.

D.—Technical Institutes.

There is no more striking illustration of the growing national
faith in the importance of affording to young people adequate
opportunities for industrial as well as for purely intellectual training than is found in the Technical Institutes of the United States.
This faith is certainly known by its works : from east to west,
from north to south, it has found expression in the erection
and endowment of numberless such schools. Of these, the intention is invariably excellent ; and of the greater number it may
be also truthfully said that they are handsome specimens of
architecture, usually the pride of the city to which they belong.
Their spacious lecture halls and laboratories are equipped with
the latest and best appliances ; the staff of professors is selected
from the most highly qualified and experienced teachers available
for the funds at the disposal of the Committee ; and their students
are imbued with an *esprit de corps* which at the same time
stimulates study by the desire it fosters to maintain the prestige
of the institute, and develops a healthy spirit of corporate life.

Typical Courses in Domestic Science (General and Normal Courses) and in Hygiene.
It is hard to resist the temptation to enlarge upon the good
work carried on in the teaching of Household Science
(General and Normal courses) and Hygiene in a considerable
number of these Institutes. The increased attention which
hygiene claims is clearly observable in the emphasis laid on
a study of the sanitary aspects and applications of such subjects
as architecture, engineering, bacteriology, and physiology— the
last two are frequently obligatory—upon all science students ; and
I was surprised to find courses on sanitation and personal hygiene
required even of those who had selected classical or literary studies.

(a) Bradley Institute, Peoria.
For instance, at the well-known Bradley Institute at Peoria, Illinois,
courses in physiology, bacteriology, and hygiene, based upon
biology, chemistry, or physics, are taken by the science group in
its fifth year ; while sanitation, food work, or dietary studies,
based upon the same fundamental sciences, are required of the
classics, literature, and general groups in their sixth year.

It appears to be quite usual to arrange courses of study in these
Institutes so that a student may enter at the end of a Grade School
course and continue in attendance for six years. This ensures
time for the acquirement, first, of a broad and practical general

education, corresponding to a general High School course ; and
subsequently of the special preparation essential to the selected
trade or profession. A limited amount of specialisation is allowed
in the third and fourth year, but it is in the last two that the
special work is carried forward with energy, usually with a considerable amount of freedom. Thus it comes about that the
students' courses in the subjects of this Report become annually
more prolonged and thorough.   A further illustration in this
connection may be drawn from the Bradley Institute. The required
study of physiology comprehends not only the structure and
functions of the body, but time is afforded for a careful microscopic
study of the tissues, as well as for carrying out some of the more
simple physiological experiments. The course in bacteriology and
hygiene is sufficiently prolonged to carry the student on from a
general introduction to these subjects, through the cultivation
and systematic study of the common non-pathogenic organisms
and their effects, to the more distinctively hygienic aspects of
bacteriology, such as the examination of water, air, soil, milk ; in
conclusion, some problems of public health are discussed. Again,
the sanitary science course includes, besides personal and general
domestic hygiene, a study of the details of sanitary house construction, of building materials and of house decoration ; practical
treatment is pursued in this course as far as possible, extending
even to visits to furniture stores, and to the selection of suitable
articles.

Typical examples of Technical Institutes which offer General and
Normal courses in Domestic Science may be found in the Pratt
Institute, Brooklyn, N.Y. ; the Drexel Institute, Philadelphia ;
and the Mechanics' Institute, Rochester. Perhaps in respect of
equipment, the Eastman building, at the latter school, might take
first place, though its Normal courses have not been conducted for
a sufficient time, or under such conditions, as to place its graduates
as yet in the front rank attained so justly by those of Pratt and
Drexel.

The handsome technological school opened in 1900, at *(b)* Eastman
Rochester, New York, is the outcome of the munificence of Mechanics'
Mr.   George   Eastman,   who   gave $200,000   for   the Institute,
purpose, supplemented by princely donations from Mrs. N.Y.
Henry Bevier and others.   The Institute previously carried
on its educational work in detached buildings, poorly adapted for
the purpose. Space, light, ventilation, and heat have now been
provided without stint ; the large rooms, wide halls, and abundant
provision of apartments for officers, teachers, and caretakers,
covering a large area. As far as practicable, the building has been
divided between industrial and fine arts and domestic science, the
latter department having been established in the south end. On
the first floor, for the Department of Domestic Science, is found a
large demonstration room used for lectures and instruction to large
audiences. Close to this demonstration room is the first group

(*b*) Eastman Mechanics' Institute, Rochester, N.Y.— *continued.* of Domestic Science rooms, those devoted to cookery; a small dining-room and butler's pantry which belong to this suite are used by Normal students for planning and serving the luncheons and dinners required as part of their training. Beyond the group of Normal class-rooms are three large kitchens, each with pantry and other adjuncts, used for day and evening classes. These constitute one of the most interesting series of rooms to be found in the building. The second floor is arranged on a similar plan. On the south side is a series of six large rooms used by the Department of Dressmaking; they are exceptionally well arranged, and have abundance of light both from the side and from skylights in the roof. A very attractive room is devoted to the study of art history; and an office for the head of the Department completes the suite. Close at hand are the millinery class-room and teachers' room, while continuing around to the rear are the first, second, and third grade sewing rooms in the order named. The laundry is placed in the basement; the equipment includes nine porcelain tubs, an immense boiler, a dryer, and other essentials.*

The branches of study offered in these departments of Domestic Science and Art are cookery, home science, laundry work, a housekeeper's course, a course in general and household chemistry, drawing, sewing, dressmaking, millinery, and physical culture. These are arranged to meet the requirements of several classes of pupils.

(1) *General Courses,* which afford practical instruction in all the subjects that pertain to the daily routine of home work. A pupil may enter for a single term or for a year, taking up for special study one or more subjects in which she is particularly interested. There are three terms of three months each in day and evening classes. The first, second, or third grade work in any subject may be taken up at the beginning of either autumn, winter, or spring term.

(2) *Certificate Courses,* i.e., separate courses in cookery, home science, laundry work, needlework or dressmaking, so carefully systematised and graded that a student may specialise in a particular branch and become fitted to take it up as a means of livelihood. Courses of twelve lessons each in advanced, invalid and fancy cooking are also offered to meet the needs of professional students, such as physicians and nurses, or confectioners, respectively. Certificates are granted to those who complete any of these courses satisfactorily and pass the required examinations.

(3) *Normal Courses,* which give such special training as shall fit young women to become teachers of the various branches included in the domestic arts and sciences. For admission, at least a High School education or its equivalent is required. The course may be completed in two years of five days a week. To those who satisfactorily complete the full Normal course of two years the diploma of the Institute is awarded. The Board of Education is

---

* See Fig. VI.

(i) Eastman
Mechanics
Institute,
Rochester,
N.Y.
continued.

of Domestic Science rooms, those ... belong to this suite are used
dining-room and butler's pantry which belong to this suite are used
by Normal students for planning and serving the luncheons and
dinners required as part of their training. Beyond the group of
Normal class-rooms are three large kitchens, each with pantry
and other adjuncts, used for day and evening classes. These con-

interesting series of rooms to be found in the
door is arranged on a similar plan. On the
six large rooms used by the Department of
are exceptionally well arranged, and have
th from the side and from skylights in the
a room is devoted to the study of art history;
of the Department completes the suite.
illinery class-room and teachers' room, while
are the first, second, and third grade
named. The laundry is placed in the
includes nine porcelain tubs, an immense
essentials.*

offered in these departments of Domestic
home science, laundry work, a house-
in general and household chemistry,
millinery, and physical culture.
the requirements of several classes of

which afford practical instruction in all
to the daily routine of home work. A
term or for a year, taking up for special
in which she is particularly interested.
three months each in day and evening
or third grade work in any subject may
ning of either autumn, winter, or spring

i.e., separate courses in cookery, home
needlework or dressmaking, so carefully
that a student may specialise in a particular
to take it up as a means of livelihood.
each in advanced, invalid and fancy
cooking are also offered to meet the needs of professional students,
uch as physicians and nurses, or confectioners, respectively. Certificates are granted to those who complete any of these courses
satisfactorily and pass the required examinations.

(3) *Normal Courses*, which give such special training as shall
fit young women to become teachers of the various branches included in the domestic arts and sciences. For admission, at least
a High School education or its equivalent is required. The course
may be completed in two years of five days a week. To those who
satisfactorily complete the full Normal course of two years the
diploma of the Institute is awarded. The Board of Education is

* See Fig. VI.

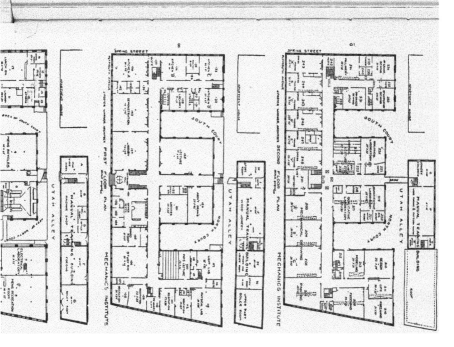

authorised to employ graduates of this Normal course to teach
domestic science and art in the city schools ; for which reason it
is satisfactory to add that it includes an excellent course in public
hygiene. This deals with contagious diseases, disinfection, food
inspection and protection, and last, but by no means least, school
hygiene. In the Normal training in Domestic Art special attention is given to the theory of colour, colour combinations, and a
study of colour schemes from textiles and natural objects ; study of
light and shade from drapery ; and of line and pose from the
works of great masters. House furnishing and house sanitation
are included in this course, while physiology, hygiene, and physical
culture must be studied by students of either group of Domestic
subjects.

The tuition fees vary from $3 to $27 per term, according to the
course ; in all cases they are reduced for evening classes.

I have selected as a detailed example of a six years' Technical (c) Lewis
Institute course in Domestic Economy for general students that Institute,
carried on under Miss L. C. Hunt at the Lewis Institute, Chicago. Table
The Institute owes its existence to the late Allen C. Lewis, who XXVII.
left a large part of his estate ($550,000) for its support
and provided for its organisation. The estate was so efficiently
managed, that when handed over to trustees in 1895, eighteen years
after Mr. Lewis's death, it amounted to $1,000,000 (£200,000).

> The work of the Department of Science and Literature is arranged
> in three divisions :—(1) Preparatory ; covering what is usually done in
> the first two years in a High School. (2) Academic ; covering the work
> of the last two High School years. (3) Collegiate ; corresponding
> to the first two years of a college course. Each candidate for admission
> is required to furnish a testimonial of honourable dismissal from the
> school last attended ; he must also refer to two persons, preferably
> his teachers or employers, from whom information about him may be
> obtained. Candidates from Chicago Grammar Schools and other
> schools of equal rank, who have completed satisfactorily the work of
> the eighth grade, may be admitted without examination, upon recom-
> mendation of the principal of the school from which they come. The
> uniform cost of instruction for full regular work is $20 (£4) a
> quarter of twelve weeks ; a reduction is made for a single course of
> instruction and for evening classes. In the Preparatory division
> most of the lessons are prepared under the direction of the teacher
> for whom the work is being done, for which purpose the
> students meet their teacher in his class room, library, laboratory,
> or workshop ; these are equipped with such appliances, in
> the way of books, apparatus, or tools, as will enable him
> to make his teaching most effective, and to furnish his students
> with whatever they need for the successful preparation of their
> lessons. In all divisions classes are limited in number to twenty-
> five, so that each student may receive such individual instruction
> as he needs, and be tested each day as to the conscientiousness with
> which he has prepared the work assigned. In the Preparatory Division,
> a " credit " signifies the successful completion of a twelve weeks'
> course of instruction, requiring from ten to twelve hours a week,
> counting time of preparation and recitation. To obtain the Prepara-
> tory certificate the student must secure twenty-one credits, of which
> sixteen are prescribed as follows :—English, three credits ; Algebra

and Geometry, four ; Latin, four ; Science, two ; Drawing, Shop-work or Domestic Economy, three. To follow four of the essential courses at a time means nine to twelve hours' work a day. More advanced students are trained in methods of greater self-dependence, though, thanks to the large and efficient staff secured by means of Mr. Lewis' liberal endowment, all studies are conducted under desirable supervision. Examinations are conducted by the staff, except in the case of students who are subsequently appointed under the Chicago Board of Education, when they are subjected to a further examination by that body.

The course in Domestic Economy carried on under Miss L. C. Hunt at the Lewis Institute, Chicago, covers six years. It includes the chemistry of daily life, cooking, sewing, home sanitation (this at present taught largely theoretically), and physiology. Biology, chemistry, and physics are still " elective " subjects ; for the Normal course, to be shortly initiated, they will be pre-requisites ; but even now they are frequently elected, as, by pursuing them, in addition to other courses in this department, a student can qualify for the B.Sc. degree, while she also prepares herself to teach domestic economy, or lays the foundation for the future professional study of medicine or nursing. The average age of the students is seven-teen ; about 100 were following the course at the time of my visit. In general terms, it may be stated that ten hours a week are given for one year respectively to cooking, sewing, housekeeping, and domestic economy (which includes house sanitation, and is incul-cated to a large extent by " field work "). A year's work in physics and three or four years' work in chemistry are required of those who elect these subjects ; the latter embraces general chemistry, qualitative and quantitative analysis and some organic chemistry ; general biology absorbs a year, to which the courses in animal physiology and hygiene form a con-tinuation; these, again, cover three terms of ten hours' work a week. In general biology each student studies the gross and microscopic anatomy of at least one representative of each of the chief groups into which plants and animals are divided, and assists in the preparation of material for microscopic study. In hygiene atten-tion is concentrated on a study of those factors in man's structural environment which chiefly affect his physical well-being, such as disease germs, household and public sanitation, exercise, clothing, etc. Practical histology enters into the physiology course ; no text-book is employed, but many reference books are at the disposal of the students, *e.g.*, Schaffer's " Histology," and Howell's " Dis-section of the Dog," which is followed in the dissection of rabbits. The results from the study of biology and physiology are con-sidered most successful ; students never before interested become almost invariably genuinely absorbed in these subjects, the scope of which promotes, in addition, general culture. Sixteen is the average number in the housekeepers' or cooking course. Judging by the lessons I was able to attend, the students are called upon to do their own thinking, and it did not surprise me that they should be recorded as developing intelligence under the process.

In addition to school practice, they are required to carry out at home processes learnt by demonstration in cookery, these demonstrations being given by Miss Hunt, or her assistant, once or twice daily. The practical work is chiefly individual, though, in the case of a searching lesson on the testing of milk for colouring matters and preservatives, for the specific gravity of whey, etc., the students were divided into groups of two.

Two hours a day for three quarters, each consisting of twelve weeks, is devoted to needlework under Miss Watson, who is a good example of the transfusion of perseverance and enthusiasm from teacher to taught. Her scheme of work emphasises colour matching, beauty of form and line, grace and fitness and the evolution of textile fabrics in addition to mere stitchery in which, however, her students attain to a high degree of proficiency. It seemed almost incredible that the excellent needlework displayed upon specimen knickerbockers, aprons, night-dresses, corset covers and petticoats, each crisp, dainty and elaborate, could be the unaided performance of pupils, who, a year before, did not know how to thread a needle. Their introduction to the art began with the usual technical series of specimen stitch samplers which are preserved in books, with written descriptions appended. Among the "fine art" points which specially attracted my attention in the work of Miss Watson's students were the perfection of the button holes and gussets, and the joining of lace or embroideries so accurately that detection was literally impossible. The happy energy of the students and the artistic arrangement of the room left a vivid and pleasant impression.

The whole building is light, airy, and admirably planned for its purposes, though the Domestic Economy department needs enlargement; under its able principal, Dr. George Carman, there is every prospect of increasing utility arising from its further development. Meanwhile, it is doing excellent work by evening classes for the general public, as well as by the more complete course above detailed; the former are confined chiefly to cooking and dressmaking and are well attended by working girls and women.

An active interest in Domestic Science and Hygiene has been aroused and maintained in Brooklyn among adults by means of courses at the Institute of Arts and Sciences, which for many years has been an important factor in the social, literary, scientific, and educational life of the city. A new era in its history was inaugurated in 1887, when it was decided to make its work broader and more comprehensive by providing for its sub-division into departments representing various branches of science and art. The membership increased in proportion to the new departments formed, reaching upwards of 6,000 in 1900, when the departments numbered twenty-eight; of these Domestic Science formed one. The presidents of each department form a Council, and meet monthly. Associate members pay $5 a year; each ticket admits one person to a day and two to an evening lecture. The Domestic

(d) Institute of Arts and Sciences, Brooklyn, N.Y.

TABLE XXVII.

TECHNICAL INSTITUTE, LEWIS INSTITUTE, CHICAGO.

SCHEDULE OF COURSES IN DOMESTIC SCIENCE AND DOMESTIC ART.

Institution and Course.	Entrance Requirements.	Scope of Courses.	Methods.	Length of Course.	Fees and Finance.	Equipment.
L wis Institute, Chicago. D tic Economy ..., Miss C. L. Hunt.	A testimonial of honourable dismissal from the school last attended, and two good personal references.	Chemistry—General, Qualitative, Quantitative, ... Biology. ..., Zoology, El: Bacteriology). Physiology, including practical histology. Hygiene (... is laid on ele-mentary bacteriology, personal, ..., and public sanitation). Cooking—Demonstration and practice. Chemistry of daily life. Sewing (Colour matching—Beauty of form and line—Evolution of textile fabrics). The "Field Work" includes visits to shops, factories, institutions. Day and Evening Classes. Sh ... Courses in Cooking and Sewing (free or six months) are given to outside ... ts of all ages.	The Lab tory method of teaching is applied to all subjects of study. No text obks are employed in most subjects, but nume-rous reference books are at the disposal of the students. Students are un-doubtedly ... upon to do their own thinking, and the intelligence de-veloped is emphati-cally ... They are required to carry out at home some of the processes in ... taught by ...	Six years. 9—12 hours work daily, ... four ... es at a ... Work of Schools of Science and Literature is arranged in three divisions,— 1. Preparatory, 2. Acad mic, 3. Collegiate. (The Pra-tory Course corresponds to 4 years in High School.) Full course qualifies for B.Sc. Degree.	$20 a quar-ter of 12 ... ... magnifi-cently en-...	The building is light, airy, and well ... for its purposes, but the resources of the Domestic Economy De-partment have been much ... owing to the large num-ber of students. The ... Physics, Biology, and Physiology courses are followed with the general students in the Science Laboratories, where the equipment is all that can be desired for individual work. This is the rule also in the Domestic Economy Department

Science Department was organised in 1893 with forty-two members, who increased in seven years to 170. Mrs. John Dunn has been president of the department since its formation, and is the only woman holding such a position in the Institute. Much attention is given to the study of practical problems in domestic science, and standing Committees have been appointed on the following subjects :—The sanitary and economic construction of dwellings ; the general principles of house furnishing ; the composition and value of foods ; labour-saving methods and utensils ; and sanitation and economy in clothing and domestic service. At present, the results to be observed among the members are improved common-sense and a feeling of responsibility for family welfare. By request of the Child Study department a special course on the feeding of children was organised in the Domestic Science Department last winter,—the first recognition by members of these two departments of the mutual assistance each can render the other by experience gained through their respective studies and enquiries. Such observational enquiries are of undoubted value, though, from the circumstances of the case, they are conducted along less fundamental lines than can be defined for more youthful students still engaged in preparation for their future callings.

The Massachusetts Institute of Technology, at Boston, affords a first-rate example of the favourable opportunities now offered to students of both sexes in the United States for studying the sanitary aspects of various professions. Facilities of an unusual character are here afforded for advanced or special work in hygiene or sanitary science. The departments which give the principal instruction in these subjects are the biological, chemical, physical, architectural, and that of sanitary engineering. In the department of biology the whole system of laboratories is well organised for work directed chiefly towards the hygienic and industrial sides of the subject. These laboratories are frequented by those who desire to fit themselves for teaching or for medical study, as well as by those whose future professions demand that their training should comprise some practical work in the biological sciences, including comparative physiology, zoology, bacteriology, and industrial and sanitary biology. Science teachers in secondary schools or Normal Colleges derive great assistance from the extensive course of laboratory work carried on in connection with the courses in comparative anatomy and embryology, as well as in comparative physiology ; while among those engaged in some branches of sanitary engineering or in food-preserving industries, the course in sanitary bacteriology and fermentation is in request, owing to the facility acquired in the examination of air, ice, and water, or to the insight gained into industrial applications. Graduates or special students, *e.g.*, physicians, inspectors under Boards of Health, or superintendents of water or sewage works, are, if qualified to pursue such work with

(e) Massachusetts Institute of Technology, Boston.

advantage, also admitted to such subjects as they select in this department, every opportunity being afforded them to equip themselves for their professional callings. The instruction in water, air, and food analysis in the chemical department consists mainly of laboratory work, supplemented by occasional lectures ; special laboratories have been assigned to these courses. The usual scheme of work includes practice in the methods commonly employed in the chemical examination of air and water, of milk, and of butter. For those who wish to take a more extended course, opportunity is provided for the critical study of methods of analysis and for the investigation of a variety of sanitary problems in which chemical questions are involved. The hygienic aspects of heating and ventilation are thoroughly handled by Professor Wood-bridge in the department of physics, while the architectural course includes a technical study of the same subjects in its third year, illustrated by the study of important public buildings in the city. Enumerated among the studies required of students in the sanitary engineering course are, in addition to the general, special, and sanitary biology courses referred to above, those in the principles of public health, municipal sanitation, and on air analysis. The specified object is to qualify engineers to deal intelligently with questions relating to the health of individuals and communities, and to plan intelligently works of sewerage and drainage. Frequent opportunities are given for the inspection of actual examples of sanitary engineering ; the work in the class-room is also supplemented by exercises in designing, and the students attend lectures and demonstrations in sanitary science.

It will be observed that in all departments the method pursued is to supplement lectures and recitations by practical work in the field, the laboratories, and the drawing rooms ; indeed, high value is set upon the educational effect of this practical work, which intentionally forms the foundation of each of the thirteen courses. Text-books are used in some subjects, but not in all. In many branches the instruction given varies considerably in available text-books ; in such cases notes on the lectures and laboratory work have been printed, either privately or by the Institute, and are furnished to the students at cost price. Both oral and written examinations take place from time to time. The general examinations are held near the close of the months of January and May ; after these the standing of the student in each distinct subject is reported to his parent or guardian, though these reports are based to a very large extent upon the quality of daily class work ; they constitute also the grounds for admonition or advice from the Faculty in the case of the students who are not profiting sufficiently by their connection with the Institute. The degree of Bachelor of Science in the course pursued is given for the satisfactory completion of any of the regular courses of study. To be entitled to a degree the student must have attended the Institute for not less than one year next preceding the taking of a degree, must have completed the prescribed studies and practical work of the four years, and must, in addition, pass final examinations, if required, on subjects relating particularly to his course. He must, moreover, prepare a dissertation on some subject included in his course of study, or give an account of some research made by himself, or present either an original report upon some machine, work of engineering, industrial works, mine or mineral survey, or an original design accompanied by an explanatory memoir; either thesis or design must be approved by the Faculty.

So numerous and comprehensive are the courses in Domestic Science and Domestic Art carried on in the departments for these subjects attached to the great Technical Institutes at Brooklyn, New York, and at Philadelphia, that an effort to detail them accurately could scarcely be rewarded with success, and would probably prove wearisome to the reader. The allusions throughout this Report, however, to the prestige which attaches to the graduates from the Normal courses at these two Institutes demand that the grounds should be stated upon which they are based. This I will endeavour to do; though, in justice to those who are responsible for the gradual evolution of these courses, it must be clearly understood that they recognise no finality in the existing phases of development. The curriculum of each is in a transitional, tentative stage, to be studied as offering valuable suggestion based upon experience, not criticised as a model held up as typical of perfection by its formulators. Some introductory words as to the origin and purpose of these two prominent institutes will prove of interest, and will serve as a useful explanation of their independent position in the educational world. *Pratt Institute, Brooklyn, N.Y.*

Pratt Institute was established in 1887, after many years of educational investigation on the part of its founder, Mr. Charles Pratt, of Brooklyn. Its objects are to promote manual and industrial education, to promote cultivation in literature, science, and art, and to foster all that makes for right living and good citizenship. Facilities are provided by which persons who wish to engage in educational, artistic, scientific, domestic, commercial, mechanical, or allied employments may lay the foundation of a thorough knowledge, theoretical and practical, or may perfect themselves in those occupations in which they are already engaged. Instruction is based upon an appreciation of the dignity as well as the value of intelligent handicraft and skilled manual labour; efforts are made to establish a system of instruction whereby habits of thrift may be inculcated, to develop those qualities which produce a spirit of self-reliance, and to teach that personal character is of greater consequence than material productions. While fees are required, there is an endeavour to make possible, by some means consistent with self-helpfulness and self-respect, the admission of every worthy applicant.

The courses have four distinct aims in view :—(1) Educational, pure and simple, as in the work of the High school ; (2) Normal, such training being given in four departments, those of fine arts, domestic art, domestic science, and kindergarten ; (3) Technical, *i.e.*, special training to secure practical skill in the arts, handicrafts, applied sciences, and mechanical trades ; (4) Supplementary and Special, intended for the benefit of those who wish to add to school or college training special subjects conducing to the more intelligent development of domestic, social, or other interests. The endowment is so liberal that not only can the best talent and facilities for the accomplishment of its aims be secured, but the charges for tuition can be and are most moderate. The buildings are six in number ; the departments of Domestic Art and Science are situated in the main building. The rooms are old-fashioned and not always convenient, the cause being an outcome of American caution. Mr. Pratt was somewhat uncertain as to the success of his original venture ; he therefore had the building designed to play the double part of technical institute or of textile factory, so that, were the first a failure, the second could redeem the disaster. Fortunately, his fears were not realised ; but, unfortunately, the light, air, and space so desirable for his students have been curtailed. Some considerable rebuilding is contemplated in the near future. The Institute is under the control of a Board of Trustees, with a secretary as executive officer ; the heads of each department constitute the faculty ; both sexes are admitted on equal footing to all classes.

The requirements for admission differ in the several departments ; those for applicants to the Normal course may best be quoted from the handbook. " All applicants for normal courses for the training of teachers should be at least eighteen years of age, and should have good health, a good voice, a mature and thoughtful mind, a love for teaching as a profession, and a good general education equivalent to a four-year course in a high school of good standing." Diplomas and certificates are granted for the quality of the work done, and not for the number of years spent in study. That progress in all courses depends upon individual ability and application was again and again impressed upon me. The Diploma of the Institute is given to those students who successfully complete one of the following courses of study :—High School course, Normal Art course, Normal Domestic Science course, Normal Domestic Art course, Normal Kindergarten course. The Certificate attests the successful completion of any one of the following Day courses, which represent from one to four years' work :—

  Fine Arts.—Regular art course, architecture, design, modelling, wood-carving, art metal.
  Domestic Art.—Sewing, full-time course ; dress-making, full-time course ; millinery, full-time course ; art needlework, basketry and weaving.

Science and Technology.—Steam and machine design, applied electricity.

Kindergarten.—Mothers' course.

General course in Domestic Science

Food Economics,

Library Science.

The Department of Domestic Art is under the direction of Miss Harriet S. Sackett; it offers a large choice of General and Technical courses in sewing, dress-making, and millinery, as well as the Normal course. Less familiar to English minds is the inclusion also of a course in Costume Design (which embraces an art course of two years, a study of the outlines and proportion of the human form, and of historic costume; the sketching of dresses and hats in water colour, etc.). There are also courses in art needlework (freehand drawing, design, colour, artistic needlework); in basketry and weaving; in physical training, which comprises Swedish educational gymnastics, carefully graded exercises with stationary and hand apparatus, and games. Indeed, this department includes comprehensive courses of study in those branches of the various arts which are related to healthful development and to household decoration, as well as to appropriate clothing of the body. All these courses are developed progressively, and are arranged to give either professional training, or to prepare teachers, or for use in the home. They vary in length from one term of plain sewing to two years in dress-making, or to three years in costume design, etc. The number of pupils in each class is limited, so that all may have opportunity for practical work under the direction of the teacher, in addition to the instruction given by means of lectures and recitations.

(a) Domestic Art Courses (General, Normal, Technical).

Table XXVIII.

The rooms of this department occupy the third floor of the main building, and are fully equipped with essential apparatus. Casts of the best examples of sculpture, photographs, coloured plates of costume, and many specimens of textile fabrics, both ancient and modern, afford excellent material for study. The Library is also an important factor in Miss Sackett's schemes of training. Books treating of domestic art and science are constantly added; material on class topics is secured for the pupils' use, and an almost unique collection of plates illustrating the historical development of costume has been made. The methods of instruction aim to instil the artistic and scientific principles underlying all good work, and to impress upon the students the value of economy, order, and accuracy. Instruction in freehand drawing, water-colour, and elementary design forms a part of all dressmaking and millinery courses, with a view to cultivate taste in dress, to impart skill in the harmonious combination of colours and textiles, and to foster selection of costumes in keeping with the individuality of the wearer. Eyes and hands are thus trained to see objects in their true proportions, and to sketch them in line

(a) Domestic Art Courses — *continued.* simple light and shade and water-colour. It will be easily realisable that a considerable amount of home practice is necessarily required. In the technical dress-making course lectures upon hygienic, artistic, and historic dress are given, pupils being expected to further inform themselves upon these subjects by the use of the library. Those who wish to become practical dressmakers have an opportunity in this class to make dresses for others in order to gain experience, and, if necessary, to defray a part of their expenses.

In the costume design course students are trained to become illustrators or designers of costume, and I learned that the fashion plates in one of the most popular women's journals have really been influenced for good through a graduate from this course having become a member of the staff. The first year is spent entirely in the Department of Fine Arts ; the second and third year are divided between this and the Department of Domestic Art. The instruction embraces cast drawing from ornament and the antique, freehand, perspective, colour, life and portrait drawing, sketching from the figure, composition, design, and the history of art. Normal students are required to devote a part of their second year, and the whole of the third year of their training to special study of costume design. The system of art training employed is derived from the French, and the designs and drapery studies are alike beautiful in colour and graceful in form. Textures and patterns of various materials are copied in water-colour, while advanced students are required to design and carry out dresses which exemplify the tints, position, and relative proportion of colours found in a selected flower, moth, or butterfly. The result seemed to me to embody the quotation appearing on the walls, " Grace of form and beauty of vesture." Careful studies in crayon and water-colour of hats (full size) are insisted upon before execution in the millinery course, and appear in considerable numbers on blackboards or easels. The fact that so many of the graduates enter into trade and professional life has led to the gradual evolution of this exhaustive method of training. Eight hundred students passed through the Domestic Art Department in 1900.

The following synopsis of some of the courses affords material for comparison with those pursued in the Technical classes in this country :

I. THE FULL DAY ONE-YEAR COURSE IN SEWING is organised in September only. It is arranged for those who can devote their whole time to the work. The first half of the year is devoted to practice in the various kinds of hand and machine sewing ; to learning the principles of draughting, cutting, and fitting undergarments ; and to children's dress. When a student can make this range of garments satisfactorily she may take orders for work, and thus put into practice the principles already learned. By this means an increased amount of accuracy, judgment and self-reliance is gained ; so that at the end of the year competent pupils may become seamstresses, work in shops, or find themselves fitted to be more useful in the home. This course is considered necessary as a preparation for the training in dress-making by those who have had but little experience in hand sewing or the making of simple garments.

(a) Domestic Art Courses —*continued.*

Course of Study.—Models in housework afterward applied on bed linen and table linen, aprons, patching and mending and simple repairing, draughting and making drawers, under-bodices, skirts blouses and nightdresses, children's dresses, undergarments and baby clothes.

Work in the gymnasium is required in connection with this course ; and a course in drawing runs concurrently, which assists the student to develop her own ideas in design and colour. A certificate is granted for the satisfactory completion of the whole. Applicants must be over fifteen years of age, and are required to present for entrance examination some article showing their hand-sewing. The fees are $15 per term (about £3 3s.).

II. THE SPECIAL COURSE FOR HOME USE WHICH MEETS TWICE A WEEK FOR ONE YEAR.—This course is arranged to meet the needs of those who wish to learn hand and machine sewing and the various kinds of mending merely for home use. In learning to make garments the pupils measure and fit each other. They furnish their own materials. The course of study is as follows :—

First grade.—Exercises in basting, stitching, overcasting, hemming, gathering, and buttonholing ; draughting drawers ; exercises in machine sewing, cutting, and making drawers.

Second grade.—Exercises in darning on stockingette and cashmere ; patching ; draughting ; cutting and making white petticoat ; exercises in feather stitching, and making underbodice from pattern.

Third grade.—The making of dainty lingerie, including fancy muslin and flannel petticoats, bodices, nightdresses and dressing jackets.

For mothers who desire to make their children's clothes, or seamstresses who wish to become more proficient, a course is offered in the making of infants' clothes, including knitting and crocheting, children's underclothes, guimpes, and dresses. The fee is $5 a term (about £1.).

Children's classes meet from nine to eleven o'clock on Saturday mornings, and are open to children between the ages of six and fifteen years. They cover a period of several school years, and include simple work with cord and raffia, weaving, hand-sewing, making of doll's garments, and elementary machine sewing. Such training, satisfactorily completed, prepares the student to enter the classes meeting twice a week. Tuition fees $2 per term (about 8s.).

III. THE FULL-DAY COURSE OF TWO YEARS IN DRESSMAKING* is arranged to give a thorough training in the principles of dressmaking, with as much practice in their application as the time will allow. It meets daily, except Saturdays, from 9 to 4.30 o'clock. This class is organised in September only, and continues through two school years. The mornings are given entirely to dressmaking ; three afternoons a week are devoted to costume design, methods of keeping accounts, and physical training. Students also attend lectures upon the history of costume, and a further course of lectures on the history of art, by the Director of the Department of Fine Arts, is open to them. The literature of hygienic and artistic costume is brought to their notice ; and they are expected to inform themselves upon these subjects, using the library of the Institute. The first year is devoted to plain dressmaking ; orders may be taken after each student has made a dress for herself ; in this way the students are able to defray part of their expenses.

Course of Study.—First Year.—Draughting, cutting, fitting and making unlined blouses and skirts ; draughting blouses with chart ; exercises with practice materials in cutting, fitting, and designing

---

* For Course in Home Dressmaking, see Appendix E.

skirts and lined bodices ; and in making dress trimmings and finish·
ings ; bow making ; study of colour, form, line and texture ; house
and street dresses not too elaborate in style.

Drawing, water-colour, elementary design : Practice in the use of
the pencil and of water-colour. Appearance of objects, bows, gowns
and drapery. Outline and proportion of the human form. Study
of gowns becoming to different types of figure, and also of historic
costume. Practice in designing gowns for street, home and evening
wear.

Second Year.—Draughting and making princesse gowns and negli-
gées ; study of contour and poise of the body ; making evening gowns ;
study of woollen textiles ; draughting, cutting and making tailor-
made jackets and skirts.

Applicants must be over seventeen years of age, and bring for examination a dress made by themselves from a pattern ; they must also
prove their ability to do good hand and machine sewing. A written
examination is given upon the method of making a simple dress.

Women who have had previous experience in dressmaking may be
admitted to advanced work upon passing an examination which will
prove their fitness to enter the second year class. Orders received in
this class furnish the materials to carry out the schedule of work.
A certificate is granted for the satisfactory completion of this course.
Tuition fees, $25 per term (about £5).

IV. The Full-Day Course in Millinery—two terms of two months
each. The first part of the course is planned to develop lightness of
touch in the making of bows, trimmings, and facings, and leads up
gradually to the later work of designing and making an entire hat.
The student provides her own materials, and is at liberty to bring
from home any materials which can be utilised. This class, completes the full course in four months ; it is organised in September and
February, and has been arranged for those who wish to prepare to
become milliners.   It meets daily, except on Saturday, from 9 to
12.30 and from 1.30 to 4 o'clock.   Two afternoons a week are devoted
to the course in design.   There are also lectures upon hygienic, artistic,
and historic dress, and instruction is given in methods of keeping
accounts.

Course of Study.—Facing and finishing hat-brims, making bows,
trimming hats, study of form, line, colour and textiles ; designing,
draughting, and making frames ; making and trimming covered
hats and bonnets ; making velvet hats and bonnets ; toques and evening bonnets ; making wire frames and straw hats ; lace and shirred
hats and bonnets ; children's hats.

Drawing, water-colour, elementary design ; practice in the use of
the pencil and of water-colour ; appearance of objects, drapery,
bows, hats ; outline and proportion of the head ; study of historic
costume ; designing of hats becoming to different types of face.

Applicants must bring for inspection a hat showing some skill in
the trimming and making ; and they must be able to work rapidly,
since the time devoted to the training is short. The class organised in
September prepares students to take positions at the opening of the
spring season, while the class which begins in February fits them for
the autumn season. They must be over sixteen years of age and able
to do good hand-sewing. Familiarity with the use of the tape measure
and ability to cut accurately are requisites. Only students who prove
themselves satisfactory workers are recommended to positions in
work-rooms. A certificate is granted for the satisfactory completion
of this course. Fees, $25 per term of two months (about £5).

· There is also a special course in millinery for home use, which
extends over four terms of three months each. While not all the

details of the mechanical side of millinery are taken up in this and other abridged classes, those points are selected which will be the most helpful in the home. In order to awaken an appreciation of good form and colour as related to dress, instruction in freehand drawing, water-colour, and design as related to millinery is given as outlined above. There are also classes without drawing for those who are unable to devote so much time to the course. *(a)* Domestic Art Courses —*continued.*

Course of Study.—First grade: practice in foundation work; making bows; making and trimming hats adapted to styles in vogue.

Second grade: designing, draughting and making frames; making and trimming covered hats.

Third and fourth grades, winter season: making draped toque, evening hat, street bonnet and velvet hat. Spring season, making hat and toque of fancy straw braid over frame, also lace and chiffon hats. Children's hats may be made in any grade. Fees, $10 per term (£2).

V. BASKETRY.—This course consists of one lesson a week for three months and teaches the methods of making baskets of various weaves and shapes in raffia, splint, reed, grasses, and other materials. The weaving and shaping are done by the eye; which is considered to give an opportunity for expression to the worker's feeling for form and design. Originality in design on the part of the student is thus encouraged, a slight difference in manipulation producing a variety in form and pattern, this lends especial charm and interest to the work and at the same time stimulates appreciation of good form. The art is practised for its value as manual training, as well as for the pleasure derived from the useful and decorative results. The fees are $5 per term (£1). There is also a series of children's classes in simple basketry in raffia and reed; experience shows that these materials are well adapted to interest children, while they teach firmness of touch and dexterity in handling. These classes consist of children from nine to fifteen years of age, and meet on Saturday mornings from nine to eleven o'clock. Fees, $2 per term (about 8s.).

Considerable rearrangement of the Normal Courses has taken place at the Pratt Institute since my visit in April, 1901. Experience has shown that the present professional opportunities open to women of special training usually require of them a command of more than one subject when they first undertake professional work. For instance, out of ninety-nine positions filled to-day, by women who chose Domestic Science as a major subject and Domestic Art as a minor in their training, in seventy they are required to teach both cookery and sewing, in twenty-five cookery only, and in four sewing. It is therefore considered advisable that the Normal course in Domestic Art* should consistently include work in Domestic Science, so that graduates may be efficiently prepared to teach elementary Domestic Science, in addition to being experts in Domestic Art. Consequently from the autumn of 1901 the work of the first year for Normal students in both subjects became identical, and is carried on entirely in the Domestic Science Department. At the end of this time, students are given an opportunity, if their work has been satisfactory, to choose whether they will devote their time in the second year to advanced work in Domestic Art or in Domestic Science. Those who desire and can give evidence of the necessary qualifications are then admitted to the Normal Domestic Art

---

* See Table XXVIII.

course. This includes normal methods, practice teaching, physical training, advanced sewing, basketry and weaving, dressmaking, millinery, art needlework, and costume design. Students are also required to write a thesis upon a subject relating to domestic art, showing a clear and thoughtful consideration of the selected subject.

(b) Domestic Science Courses (General, Normal, Technical) Table XXIX.

In the Department of Domestic Science the courses of study for adults are also Normal, Technical, and General, while others are provided for children of various ages.

The following are the outlines for the General and Special courses, the latter being planned for women who can devote but a few hours a week to such work ; to further meet their convenience they are subdivided upon entering into three groups, (a) those who can give six hours, (b) four hours, or (c) only one hour a week, for one year.

GENERAL COURSE (five days a week for one year).—Chemistry, bacteriology, physiology and hygiene, sanitation, household economics ; cookery, dietetics, marketing and accounts ; serving, sewing, laundry work, house construction. Fee, £6 a term.

SPECIAL COURSES.—(1) Cookery and dietetics ; (2) bacteriology, hygiene, marketing and accounts ; (3) serving, laundry work, household economics, sanitation and construction. Fees, £2 to £3 a term.

There are also day and evening courses designed for mothers or for women engaged in domestic service, which deal with the preparation, composition and purchase of foods ; these consist of two classes a week for two terms of three months. Cooks' courses ; Sick Nursing courses ; Saturday morning school girls' classes ; lectures on marketing, and private lessons are also given as desired. A course for waitresses and one in laundry work are provided, and a special one-year course is given in Food Economics, intended for women already qualified for responsible positions by character and practical experience. It is the result of a demand for trained persons as managers or housekeepers for public institutions, hospitals and schools, etc., and embraces the following topics : the selection of food material with regard to quality and cost and the principles of cookery. Methods of preparation in large quantities. Physiology, hygiene, sanitation. Chemistry, bacteriology. Dietetics, household economics, accounts. Marketing and serving, including general dining-room economy.

This course affords training along all the fundamental lines of practical housework ; and, so far as the time will permit, in the underlying natural sciences ; only mature women of fair general training with executive ability, experience in life, skill in practical house-work and possessed of physical strength and endurance are advised to take it. Six months are devoted to student work in the department and three to probationary professional service. The Institute kitchen and lunch room, serving daily between two and three hundred guests, provide necessary facilities. Dinners and luncheons are planned, prepared and served by students ; hospitals, orphanages, day nurseries and school lunch-rooms are visited ; and expeditions are made to public kitchens and to manufactories of kitchen and hotel furnishings.

Miss Edith Greer is director of this whole Department ; and brings a trained intelligence and much enthusiasm to bear upon her responsible duties. The Department itself occupies the sixth floor of the Institute ; it has large recently-remodelled and well-equipped chemical, physiological, and bacteriological laboratories and school kitchens planned for individual work ; rooms thoroughly equipped for handwork and sewing ; a collection of food products and a departmental library (Fig. VII.).

TABLE XXVIII.

TECHNICAL INSTITUTE. THE PRATT INSTITUTE, BROOKLYN N.Y.

NORMAL COURSE IN DOMESTIC ART AND SCIENCE.

Institution and Course.	Entrance Requirements.	Scope of Course.	Methods.	Length of Course.	Fees and Finance.	Equipment.
Pratt Institute, Brooklyn, N.Y.	At least 18 years of age. Proof of education equivalent to a four years' course in a high school of good standing, and ability to pass examinations in Physiology and Sewing.	Nature Study, 2; Chemistry, 3; Physiology, 3; Bacteriology, 1; Cookery, 3; Psychology, 3; History of Education, 1 (1st yr.); Normal Methods, 3 (2nd year); Observation and practice teaching, 2nd year.	The aim is to … sense of … in and design. The work of … year is …	Full … Leads to … Examination …	Private endowment.	Fully equipped rooms.
Domestic Art Normal Course.		Lectures on the History of Art, … on Historic … Design, … Drawing (… and design), weaving	… regular …		Fees, $25 per term (about £5).	The … sewing … irons, etc., …
Director, Miss Harriet S. Sackett.	… as is laid on …	… ketry, Methods of Sewing—B-sewing, … sewing, drafting, garment … dy of te … Dressmaking, … Art, … Physical Training,	The … ing is … French.	… as well as Domestic …	3 terms a year.	
The two year "General" Course, closely conforms to this schedule.	For fuller … course in Domestic Science and … Table XXIX.	A third year may be spent in special elective work, chiefly costume design, which qualifies graduates to become illustrators or designers of costumes.	Careful crayon or water colour studies are required for all articles of millinery, or specimens of dressmaking; the former half life size: previous to this, textures and patterns of various materials are copied in water colour. … is—Education (Psychology), nl Practical Teaching),7			A valuable … the fine … being constantly …

(*b*) Domestic Science Courses —*continued.*   The Normal students in Domestic Science* are prepared primarily to teach the group of subjects included under this title ; and secondarily to teach elementary sewing and handwork. They must be at least eighteen years of age, and must have satisfactorily completed a High School course of four years or its equivalent. Applicants must pass the general Institute examinations, and must also give evidence of having formed good mental habits, and of being able to use with facility their knowledge of arithmetic (especially percentage and the metric system), algebra, plane geometry, elementary physiology, physics, and English. Some knowledge of sewing and cooking is expected. They are accepted only on probation, which continues until they have shown the ability and the desire to develop into cultured women of character.

> The following extracts from "The Pratt Institute Monthly" for March, 1902, give in the words of its organiser a brief resumé of the objects and methods of the course : "The lines of work now embodied in the normal course are : Education for the training of the professional teacher ; Science, with the natural sciences as basal to a true conception of their application in such practical work as cookery, for the training of the special teacher of domestic science ; Art, including its expression in handwork, such as sewing and basketry, for the training of the special teacher of domestic art ; Physical training for the physical well-being of the teacher that is to be ; and for conscious development of interaction between her mind and the medium for expression, her body. . . . ."

The course requires two years for its completion. The student-work consists of an average of twenty-five fifty-minute periods of class work for five days a week, sixteen hours of preparation, and two hours of physical training throughout the course. Thus the student spends seven and a half hours a day for five days a week, and one and a half hours on Saturday, in class work and preparation for the same. The proportional distribution of the time is as follows :—For all Normal students approximately seven hours a week for two years to education (psychology, normal methods, practice teaching, etc.), and two hours to physical training ; for Domestic Science students, twenty hours to science and ten to hand work ; for Domestic Art students, twenty hours to domestic art and ten to domestic science. Until the second year there is neither evening nor Saturday class work. The schedule is so arranged that approximately three subjects are assigned for each day. The sequence maintained in the daily work is recitation, laboratory or practical work, and field work alternating with physical training. The character of the demand made upon the student by the type of work determines the time of day and the order of rotation for each subject or phase of a subject. In the first year the educational aspect of the work is emphasised ; in the second, the professional. The curriculum is strictly confined to the subjects essential for an intelligent understanding and free expression of the subjects to be used professionally by the graduates. Though the students are not introduced to many branches of knowledge with

---

* See Table XXIX.

FIG. VII.

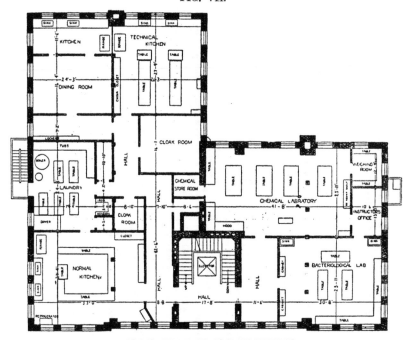

PLAN OF THE SIXTH FLOOR OF PRATT INSTITUTE

The offices and the Sewing, Hand-work and Lecture rooms of the Department are located on the first floor of the Main Building

Pratt Institute, Brooklyn, N.Y., Plan of Domestic Science Department.

TABLE XXIX.

TECHNICAL INSTITUTE.   THE PRATT INSTITUTE, BROOKLYN, N.Y.

NORMAL COURSE IN DOMESTIC SCIENCE AND ART.

Institution and Course.	Entrance Requirements.	Scope of Course.	Methods.	Length of Course.	Fees and Finance.	Equipment.
Pratt Institute, Brooklyn, N.Y. Domestic Science and Art Normal Course. Director, Miss Edith Greer. The two year "General" Course embodies the practical work of the Normal Course, but the Natural Sciences are condensed.	At 18 years of age. Proof of … School of … In addition to special … in … department for admission to normal classes are required to … test of general intelligence and … of cooking … sewing is ex … Graduates of Normal training schools … teachers, who in addition to a high school … three years of … are … tions … the special … which they seek to …	Nature …, 2 terms, 1st year. Physiology, 3 terms, 1st year. Bacteriology, 1 …, 2d year. Heat, 1 term, 2d year. … 6 … a week … 2 years. … 4 hours a week … 2 years. Marketing, 1 …, 2d year. Serving, 1 term, 2d year. … 1 term, 2nd year. Home Economics, 1 term, 2d year. Plumbing and Heating, … Construction, 1 term, 2d year. … and Design, 4 terms, 1st and 2d years. Kindergarten …, 2 terms, year. Sewing, 4 terms, 1st and 2nd years. …, 3 terms, 1st and 2d years. Physical Training, 2 hours a week for 2 years. Psychology, 2 terms, 1st year. History of …, 1 …, 1st year. …, 2 terms. …, 3 …, year.	In the first year the … of the work is … professional. The curriculum is to be strictly … or an … professionally by the … The … object of this course is to … carefully, … logically. All … chemistry … … includes:— (a) … (b) … analysis. The Course in … is essentially the lower … changes in which they are … to their … The … work consists of an … five days a … hours of class work … two … hours of physical … the … bution of time … … per week … two years. … 20 … per week … two years. Handwork 10 hours per week … two years.	Two years of hard … with the … of a third to consist of broad elective work in Dom … An … … … … in this train …	Liberal Endowment. Fees. $25 per term (about £5.) Three terms a year. $10 to $20 (£2 to £4) should purchase all text books, and materials required, as well as pay laboratory fees for an average amount of breakage.	… for saving … vices are … as they … on the market, and … also … … at a small outlay … Each … it is required to wear … the print … with … pur … … and in … and … provide herself with a … lation … my … and well … chemical, … … school … … dent … and di … chen … dining-room … cooking … serving in … quantities; a collection of … … thor- … and … library.

which they are entirely unfamiliar, a new point of view and more (*b*) Domestic
intelligent and personal responsibility for the quality of the work Science
are exacted by the nature of the normal training." Students find Courses—
a third year of work frequently advisable to gain the diploma. *continued*.
The lines of elective work suggested for them during this period
are as follows :—" The continuation of any subject pursued in the
earlier part of the course ; manual training if not already taken ;
the evening class for nurses and teachers in kindergarten
methods and the use of kindergarten materials, the ' Education
of Man ' ; drawing, composition, and design ; sewing, dressmaking, and millinery ; or Latin, French, and German in the
High School classes. The special subjects specified are given
under the auspices of the departments in the Institute which deal
with them primarily. In being thus given, apart from allied subjects, they afford general and not normal training, and are to be
taken for their value to the individual and not to be used professionally."

The general chemistry in the Normal course includes (*a*) qualitative analysis, (*b*) quantitative analysis (three experiments being
performed, one of which is gravimetric and one volumetric),
(*c*) organic chemistry. In physiology, one hour's lecture with
demonstrations is given by a physician once a week in the first
year ; in the second year the lecture is followed by two hours' laboratory work. This is ideally good, but I learned that its success
depends wholly on the personality of the professor. The only
branch of physics dealt with directly in the course is Heat.
The bacteriology comprises a study of lower forms of life and
their influence ; the changes in which they are agents ; and the
conditions necessary to their development. Four hours a week
for four months is devoted to its study, mostly under direct
supervision, though students do some outside work. The course
is essentially non-pathogenic, modelled on that for general
students at the University of Chicago ; it has been given along
the same lines for three years, and is considered fairly satisfactory ;
the class is usually limited to six or eight. Leitz's microscopes
with objectives 3 and 7 are those used ; and the equipment both
individual and general is essentially moderate, though sufficient.
The nature study course consists at first largely of field lessons ;
subsequently timbers are studied, and students are called upon
to apply their knowledge to furniture and house-fittings ; so
far their powers of observation are reported to be defective and
to demand much training. The course in psychology includes an
introduction to logic ; the professor in charge is well fitted for
this work, and has great sympathy with his students.

The History of Education and Educational Methods appears
in the syllabus ; but a weak point recorded in its present treatment is absence of sufficiently close study of child nature and the
child mind.

Household economics are studied under three heads :—(1.) house
construction, the instructors being an architect and an artist ;

(b) Domestic Science Courses —continued. (2.) house plumbing, taught by a master plumber; (3.) house furnishing; which includes care of furniture; methods of house ventilation, etc., etc.; disposal of garbage and waste; purchase of supplies, coal, wood, outside food stuffs, etc.

The laundry work is planned to demand a knowledge of applied chemistry and applied bacteriology.

> It is customary to require each normal student to prepare a set of bottles illustrating the percentage composition of twelve typical foods. These graphically represent the food principles present in some of the commonest articles of daily diet—meat, eggs, milk, butter, wheat, rice, apples, potatoes, etc.; the analyses are carried out with scientific accuracy, and are in request by schools and colleges where Domestic Science is taught. Their sale is a source of small profit to the Institute ; ·but, though such work has its value, it is objected that the amount of time demanded by the preparation of twelve such analyses is a heavy tax on the time of the students.

The number in the Normal classes for cooking has varied from thirty-four to twenty ; though it is considered that twenty should be the limit. At the time of my visit the kitchen was low and not very light, but thoroughly well equipped; it has since been re-modelled. The cooking table forms three sides of a square ; although this form in some ways minimises the steps of the teacher, it is not entirely approved. Each student has her own equipment in a numbered drawer, and all the work is individual. As has been already described, the director of these courses has thought out the fundamental principles of the art of cooking, and has a great idea of stimulating thought and application by presenting problems which demand the illustration of the underlying principles by her students. She is eminently mindful of the possibilities of cookery as a point of correlation with chemistry, physics, botany, physiology and hygiene. Knowledge acquired is, as usual in the United States, tested by members of the staff. For instance, in the cooking course, each student periodically draws a slip from a packet containing the names of different dishes ; then cooks that which she draws and submits it to criticism. Again, each senior student is required to supply three questions weekly ; and it has been Mrs. Chambers' habit to select three of these groups from the whole number submitted ; each student must then choose one group to answer and work out during the following week ; this plan is found to constitute a most satisfactory method of testing and promoting progress. The Normal students get into touch with social problems through their practice teaching in settlements, or in mission-halls connected with religious and philanthropic organisations, which increasingly demand such assistance. Here they have to face very practical difficulties in their environment, and gain useful experience along many lines. Students are not accepted for a shorter period than two years, unless so exceptionally well prepared for the work that they can satisfy very stringent conditions, which include the passing of both theoretical and practical examinations and the presentation of note books recording the mental work which accompanied the past practice. Such students are not expected to use professionally the knowledge they acquire unless they remain to complete the Normal course ; the opinion being wisely and strongly held that a partial course cannot prepare for intelligent and effective work.

(*b*) Domestic Science Courses —*continued.*

The following analysis of the subjects of this Normal course (Pratt Institute Monthly, March, 1902), is added in order to furnish as accurate and comprehensive a view as possible of its details.

Education :—

> Psychology: its principles and their application to education.
> Principles of education, the laws underlying development and their expression in educational practice.
> History of education, its relation to history as an expression of the social life and development of the race.
> Normal methods, the principles obtaining in the school-room whereby a wholesome atmosphere, self-activity of the pupil, and greatest efficiency in the special work are attained.
> Kindergarten methods and use of materials ; comprehensive survey of different phases of kindergarten work (the "Mother play," stories, occupations, and games), to give insight into the life of the child.
> Practice-teaching (under supervision) in Domestic Science and Art.

Science (Natural) :—

> General chemistry, qualitative and quantitative analysis, organic and physiological chemistry, and chemistry of foods.
> Physiology, function and structure of the body under normal conditions of life, with special emphasis upon digestion and the organs of the special senses ; hygiene (personal and public) ; emergencies and home nursing.
> Bacteriology : its principles, their significance and their application to life.
> Heat : its principles, and their significance and use in Domestic Science.
> Nature study : its principles and the methods of study involved as basal to correct scientific observation and inference.

Science (Applied) :—

> Cookery : its general principles in practice, their modification in the preparation of food for infants, invalids, and adults living under widely varying conditions.
> Dietetics : composition of the body, its waste and repair ; need of food ; kinds and proportions required ; composition of various food materials ; use of each in the body ; digestibility of each ; desirable combinations ; best methods of cooking in order to secure greatest nutritive value at least cost ; modes of meeting the needs of the individual ; calculation of dietaries ; comparison of the dietaries for persons of different ages and engaged in different occupations, and of those for different races ; and, so far as the present state of science will permit, the solution of special dietetic problems arising in the home.
> Serving : the principles and practices underlying wholesomeness and attractiveness.
> Marketing : economical purchase and preservation of food.
> Household economics : care of the house and its furnishings ; plumbing ; scientific principles involved and practices conducive to the maintenance of healthful conditions.

Construction : the sanitary and artistic expression of the
principles embodied.
Art :—
   Drawing : a comprehensive study of line, light and shade ;
      colour ; nature study ; hand-work and sewing affording
      material for design and blackboard illustration ; draughting
      in connection with sewing and construction for mechanical
      drawing.
Art (Applied) :—.
   Hand-work : braiding, knotting, netting, knitting, weaving,
      and basketry embodying the artistic and mechanical
      principles of good manual work.
   Sewing : hand sewing, draughting, and machine sewing, in-
      cluding undergarments and an unlined dress ; principles
      of construction and execution and their appropriate
      expression.

A student is expected to recognise her knowledge as the fund
upon which she is to draw for subject matter in her professional
work, but she must acquire skill in its adaptation (in accordance
with the principles instilled by her normal work, normal methods
and practice teaching) to the subjects and conditions under
which she finds herself at work. Evidence of power to do this,
as well as to work skilfully, economically, and harmoniously
under any conditions which may exist of necessity, is held to
be an essential qualification for the satisfactory completion of this
Normal course. In addition a thesis on a subject relating to
Domestic Science, showing research and original work, is required
of all Normal students before the diploma is awarded. Nevertheless, though the course is planned to develop the Normal
student, and to train her along special lines of domestic science
and art through wise stimulation and development, it also
embodies all the principles and most of the specific exercises in
general form which are adapted to other classes of students.

After the training has been completed satisfactorily, the Department interests itself in the future of those whom it has trained,
but naturally it does not assume the responsibility of undertaking
to procure positions for such as desire to enter professional life.
However, since applications are constantly received for candidates
qualified to render good service along the various lines of domestic
science and art, there is usually no difficulty in placing graduates.
The demand from manual training and private schools, from
agricultural colleges, hospitals, institutions, and university settlements is an ever increasing one.

Six instructors are in charge of this department, and give concentrated attention to their work and its problems. Upon them,
together with the director, devolve the general guidance and
thought for the well-being of the students, and from them, in the
main, emanate the good influences which mould their personalities.
They publicly make known their desire " to permeate the lives
of their students with consciousness of the fact that a choice is
the expression of a "moral motive" ; that action is impelled
by thought and is a test of it, and that it is in action that

possibilities are discovered and realised. Thus all encouragement Domestic Science Courses,— c^ntinu'd. is given to direction from within, and as far as possible suggestion is substituted for that from without. It is gratifying to learn how soon students begin to appreciate that they are, in the main, capable of being what they choose to be; that they gain power to see their work in the light of what it might be ; for it is thus that they are led to realise more fully their potentialities, and to grow in power, in freedom, and in helpfulness." Each student comes in contact with these six instructors within the department, with at least six Institute instructors in other departments, and with one or two lecturers from other institutions or engaged in other walks in life. It is believed that in this way the best intellectual, personal and technical results are attained.

The only significant change in the faculty of the department during the past year, *i.e.*, the appointment of a supervisor of practice-teaching, has proved even more beneficial than was anticipated. The wide experience of this lady brings in an invaluable element to the young teacher, confronted by many unexpected conditions in the public schools of the large cities and rural districts where she will work. Miss Snow was for eleven years superintendent of schools and director of the City Training School for Teachers, of Bangor, Maine, where her work attracted the attention of the educational institutions and associations of New England ; indeed the University of Maine, in recognition of her service to the State, conferred upon her the degree of Master of Philosophy. The Association of Superintendents of New England elected her to its presidency in 1899, as did also the Pedagogical Society of Maine ; the appointment in each instance being the first tribute of the kind shown to the work of a woman by either Association. Miss Snow teaches not only normal methods, but some physiology as well, in order that she may come in touch with the students in a study which is vitally connected with their future professional work. Since the missions in which they practice are widely scattered, and the work is in progress at all hours, on all days, among all kinds of people, and under extremely varying types of management, only a woman of exceptional abilities, experience, and broad sympathies could superintend it successfully. In the practice-classes the conditions are in many respects unfavourable ; they are irregular and ungraded. As a phase of Domestic Science work they possess a certain value, but in time it is hoped that this type of work may be supplemented by experience more nearly akin to that which the student will meet in professional life. The practice-classes in sewing greatly outnumber those in cookery ; it seems that some mothers find it troublesome to have a child cooking at home, while sewing can be turned to good account without serious inconvenience. Possibly the thought that sewing, as such, leads to a more acceptable professional career than cookery may not be without its influence. About 400 women and children are being instructed in these mission classes, nearly double the number taught by the Department during the previous year, as the size of the second

year Normal class made it possible to undertake more work of this
kind. That there should now be a long waiting list for teachers
seems marvellous to those who remember with what difficulty
such work was secured a few years since for even a small number
of Normal students. In this practice work, " the student is expected to study the class and its environment, and to aim to meet
the students where they are ; to direct and to stimulate them
to desire and strive for what will nourish best both body and mind.
This requires the exercise of insight, discrimination, mental flexi-
bility, and a genuine desire to help where help is needed."

Health and personality are considered such influential factors
in the life and success of a teacher, that much stress is laid upon
them in the selection of Normal students. Otherwise inadequately
prepared candidates, if promising in the above respects, are
encouraged to complete the necessary preliminary training ;
general direction of such student work is always offered, invariably
welcomed, and usually followed ; as a result from eight to twelve
students are each year conscientiously preparing themselves elsewhere
for the Normal course offered in this Department. Meanwhile,
no effort is spared to discourage girls from specialising in science
and handwork in the High School, with the intention of subsequently offering such work as the equivalent of that of a similar
nature in the Normal course. The feeling is strong that, though
early manual training and an elementary knowledge of science
are excellent and useful, they do not afford adequate professional
preparation for teachers of Domestic Science ; and when over
emphasised prematurely, at the expense of a firm foundation in
general knowledge and breadth of culture, a real loss results
instead of the anticipated gain.

Each year the Department prepares what are called " food
museums," for schools, consisting of blocks representing the composition of the body, and of others shewing the daily outgoing and
income, in addition to the set of bottles, before described, which illustrate the percentage composition of twelve typical foods. This year
the demand for the " museum " has been such, that orders
could only be taken on the condition that delivery could
be delayed from one to two months. This is interpreted to
mean that Domestic Science is more widely taught, and that its
place is becoming so assured that expensive equipment is
obtained for it. To many schools the Department has sent, by
request, suggestions relative to equipment and the subject matter
to be taught in Domestic Science and Art courses. It cordially
receives visitors who are interested in these subjects ; and turns such
visits to useful account by deriving from these sources fuller
information as to the needs which Domestic Science workers may
assist to meet. During the past ten years the curriculum for the
Normal students of Domestic Science has been materially modified.
Though some subjects have appeared in the course only to be
crowded out by others with still more urgent claims for recognition,
the effort of late years has been one of " simplification, not through

rejection, but through harmony." " It is not the intention to remain satisfied with the progress already made ; therefore, there will be changes; but with continuity of life and unity in purpose underlying them." In these concluding words are to be found evidence of that spirit of earnest self-criticism, and broad-minded openness to suggestion, which appeared to me to characterise the leaders of thought and practice in Household Economics in the United States.

A quotation from a letter recently received from the Director of the Pratt Institute Course throws light upon past results and indicates probable modifications in the near future :—" For several years," she writes, " some of our plans have been very tentative, because of the transition state of education in general ; but now that it is evident that such work as we are doing has entered the school system as an integral part, we feel that we should expand our work somewhat, as we propose doing next year. We are trying a new presentation of cookery with a group of ten normal students, which bids fair to be more effective in the training of teachers than any method which we have used in the past. It has always been discouragingly difficult to train a woman scientifically, and at the same time imbue her with a spirit which would make her desirous to teach cookery in conformity with science, instead of simply science through cookery. . . . It is with difficulty and through strenuous effort that we make teaching a child through the concrete interesting to the normal student." It may be anticipated, therefore, that actual cooking practice will now receive a larger measure of attention than hitherto in the Pratt Institute Normal course. The following extract from Miss Edith Greer's account of the Normal course in Domestic Science from the " Pratt Institute Monthly" for March, 1901, explains her reasons for the relatively limited time devoted up till now to this branch of Domestic Science. " Before speaking of cookery, its place and presentation in a normal course in Domestic Science, perchance it may preclude misunderstanding if the ever present question, ' Are the normal students taught to be skilful cooks ? ' be answered tentatively. It is the duty of the school, if it fulfil its mission, to train ' intelligent not skilful workers.' Skill, in mechanical manipulation especially, can come through repetition only and repetition does not to any great extent enforce conscious mental activity. When the hand has carried out the mandate of the head and thereby strengthened the mental impression, the act may be repeated almost automatically until muscular co-ordination becoming perfected results in skill. But inasmuch as ' he who is never given anything more to do than he can do, will never learn to do what he can,' so the mind when it has nothing further to learn from a special act, and thus is freed and strengthened for something new and more difficult, is defrauded and for ever impoverished if it be not taxed anew. Cookery, therefore, in the Normal course is, as will be surmised, considered primarily from the scientific point of view ; not theoretically, however, for practical work in the school kitchen for four hours each week for two years exacts of the student material expression of the training obtained. Familiarity with processes and sufficient skill therein to ensure with experience excellent results as to the quality and flavour of cooked food, are requisites of acceptable work."

Another example of courses in the same subjects, organised under directors as zealous as Miss Greer and Miss Sackett, are those carried on at the Drexel Institute, Philadelphia, founded by Anthony J. Drexel in 1891, for the promotion of education in art, science,

Drexel Institute, Philadelphia.

Drexel Insti-
tute, Phila-
delphia
—*continued*.
and industry. The chief object of the Institute is the extension
and improvement of industrial education as a means of opening
wider and better avenues of employment to young men and women.
In accordance with the founder's desire, however, the plan of organisation has been made comprehensive ; liberal means of culture
for the public are also provided by means of evening classes, free
lectures and concerts, the library and the museum. Mr. Drexel's
gifts to the Institution amount in all to three million dollars.
There are eighteen departments in Art, Science, Commerce, and
Domestic Subjects, both Normal and Technical courses being
available in most subjects. The exterior and much of the
interior of the building are handsome and impressive ; but the
general plan is inconvenient, so that considerable sums of money
are now compulsorily expended on re-arrangements and additions.
The main entrance hall is of magnificent proportions, and sump-
tuous in its lavish decoration of fine marble staircases, pillars, and
galleries. It is pleasant to note, on the authority of the President
of the Institute, that in spite of the daily use of this handsome hall
by thousands of students, no single instance has occurred of damage
to its beauty. The control of the Institute is entrusted to a Board
of Trustees, assisted by an Advisory Board of women, whose numbers
are well represented on the various committees. The general
courses are open to both sexes, on equal terms and conditions.

Mr. Drexel handed over the organisation of his great scheme at
an early stage to Dr. MacAlister, the present President of the
Institute, to whom much credit is due for the speedy introduction
of a successful Domestic Science course. From the first, the
diplomées secured excellent positions as teachers, managers of
large institutions and so forth, the demand continuing to
exceed the supply. This Department was soon reinforced by
one in Domestic Art, which is admirably equipped, and is
situated in spacious, airy, and well-lit rooms, artistic in their
decoration, and well suited to their purpose. The same may be
said of the Department of Domestic Science ; kitchens, laundry,
laboratories, dining-room, class-rooms, all give the impression of
convenience and space. Under Miss Caroline Hall and Miss Burgess
in the one, and under the directorship of Miss Helen Spring in the
other, skilled organisation fosters the growth of sound work among
the students. The Institute Library contains a large section
devoted to Art subjects, and includes a collection of books on
costume, ancient, mediæval, oriental, professional and hygienic ;
also a wide range of costly publications dealing with art needlework,
tapestry, colour, textiles, dyeing and weaving. Students can secure
a printed reference list containing the bibliography of these subjects
admirably classified, which also offers suggestions to those
anxious to follow a systematic course of reading in the various
branches (*e.g.*, references are furnished to certain books of travel
which contain good, brief descriptions and illustrations of the dress
of different nations)

A study of the schedules of the Normal courses in the Domestic Arts and Sciences at both the Pratt and Drexel Institutes reveals a general similarity, flavoured with the diversity to be anticipated where each is free to plan and practice as seems best in the light of experience and the needs of the community it serves. The scope of all the courses is wide ; for the reason that those responsible for them share the prevalent conviction that technical work of the highest, most intelligent order is impossible unless founded upon a firm basis of theoretical principles ; therefore, they maintain, the fundamental sciences and arts must find a place. Manual and physical training, in addition to the scientific methods and skilled manipulation gained in the chemical and biological laboratories, are included from the belief that the necessary co-ordination of hand, eye and brain can be more profitably acquired through suited variety of exercise than by the constant repetition of one class of operation. Obligatory attention to literature is required in order to develop a quick sympathy with varied temperaments, and a mind, not alone well balanced, because exercised in many directions, but broadened also by contact with the wise sayings of great philosophers and poets ; in addition, the necessary command of a good vocabulary is another result anticipated from wide reading of classics in several languages. As such culture studies are too often overlooked in the press of daily work, especially when this is of an essentially practical nature, English literature, composition and elementary psychology are compulsory, not "elective" subjects. Experience has shown that the same need for obligation exists in the case of physical training, which is, therefore, required of all students throughout their courses ; young and eager girls are prone to forget that a healthy body and a good carriage are indispensable to satisfactory study as well as to success as a teacher. The care for physical needs is further evidenced in the daily provision at these Institutes of inexpensive, nutritious and appetising lunches for students.

A comparison in detail of the Normal courses in Domestic Art* affords further illustration of this general similarity, though somewhat more prominence is given to artistic training at the Pratt Institute, while a recognition of the assistance to be derived from acquaintance with business methods and the keeping of accurate accounts is evident in the Drexel scheme. It also appeared to me that a more practical knowledge of the chemistry of dyeing and cleaning enters into the latter course, in which the study of human physiology is rather more prolonged ; in other respects the resemblance in scope, methods, and time periods allotted is such that I do not propose to detail the Normal course in Domestic Art at the Drexel Institute, though further particulars are supplied in Appendix F.† (See also Table XXX.).

---

* See Tables XXVIII. and XXX.
† Further reference to the work of the Domestic Art Department is made on p. 215.

TABLE XXX.

DREXEL TECHNICAL INSTITUTE, PHILADELPHIA.

NORMAL COURSE IN DOMESTIC ARTS.

Institution and Course.	Entrance Requirements.	Scope of Course.	Methods.	Length of Course.	Fees and Finance.	Equipment.
Drexel Institute, Philadelphia. Domestic Arts. Normal Course. Directors— Miss Caroline A. M. Hall. Miss Caroline L. T. Burgess.	Lowest age limit, 18 years. High School education or its equivalent. Diploma of approved institution accepted instead of examination. Previous knowledge of hand and machine sewing.	Sewing, Dressmaking, Millinery. { 4 hrs. per week. 1st and { 4 hrs. per week (1st yr.) 2nd yrs. { 6 hrs. per week (2nd yr.) 4 hrs. per week. Drawing. 1st and 2nd yrs. 4 hrs. per week. History of Costume. 2nd yr., 6 lectures of 1½ hrs. each. Chemistry of Textiles, Dyeing and Cleaning. 6 lectures of 1 hr. each. 2nd yr., 4 hrs. each week practice. Human Physiology and Hygiene. 1st yr. and half } 2 hrs. per week. of 2nd yr. } Emergencies. 2nd half yr. } 1 hr. per week. Observation and Practice in Teaching. 2nd yr. 6 hrs. per week. English Language and Literature. 2nd yr. — } 2 hrs. per week. first half yr. } Business Training. 1st yr. 2 hrs. per week. Physical Training. 2 hrs. per week.	Lectures on the Chemistry of Textiles are included for the purpose of teaching the hygienic properties of colours. Lessons are given in language, literature and business methods to enable students to use the technical knowledge they have gained in everyday life. The course is specially designed for teachers. Parallel studies are made of the art of making garments, of the requirements of the human body and of the best methods of adapting materials and fashions to the requirements of healthy clothing.	Two years of 34 weeks each, four hours for five days a week Diploma for full course.	$40 (£8) per term : two terms a year. Rich endowment by founder.	All necessary appliances and conveniences in spacious, handsome work-rooms. Specimens of fine designs of many kinds of needle-work, embroideries, lace, etc There is also a collection of historical costumes. A large department in the library is devoted to books bearing on the practice and history of the Domestic Arts, to which students are encouraged to resort, and in the systematic study of which they are guided.

Turning to the Domestic Science course, it will be seen that at the Drexel Institute human physiology is supplemented by a short course in biology and bacteriology, whereas at the Pratt Institute students of both Domestic Science and Art gain this desirable introduction to physiology through their preceding nature study; they have the advantage also of a short study of that branch of physics which is concerned with heat; dexterity with their hands is developed by a definite course in manual training, while sewing also finds a place, in order, as has been said, that graduates may be competent to conduct an elementary course in a grade school should it be desired. Speaking broadly, I gained the impression that, while substantially the same in conception and scope, manual training is somewhat more emphasised at the Pratt and chemical practice at the Drexel Institute. A comparison can be also instituted as to the number of hours spent on the different subjects by the students following the respectives courses at the two Institutes; for instance, at Pratt 330 hours are devoted to nature study, bacteriology and physiology, and 470 to physics (heat) and chemistry, while at Drexel 200 hours are given to biology, bacteriology, and physiology, and 500 to chemistry. The Pratt course gives 280 hours to actual cooking practice—little more than half the time expended on it at Drexel—in most other subjects the courses are of almost equal length.

Thanks to the ready courtesy of the Directors of these important Departments in both Institutes, many details have been furnished to me with which my too short visits prevented me from acquainting myself personally. Among these must be specially mentioned the series of syllabuses from the Drexel Institute included in the Appendix E., which cannot fail to interest those responsible for similar courses in Great Britain. In the Domestic Science Normal course* at the Drexel Institute the general chemistry extends through one year; and is followed by the practice of qualitative and quantitative analysis, with two lectures and two laboratory periods a week. The course in quantitative analysis is devoted to food analysis; the laboratory work is of such a character as to furnish data for the calculation of food values as well as to detect adulterations. I learned that the following indicates the general scope of this quantitative work, to which one year is devoted:—analysis of chemically pure soils, of potable water, of milk, of butter, of cereals, of tea and baking powder. Some study of organic chemistry follows, the method employed in both courses being (a) a lecture covering the ground of the week's work; (b) immediate practice, carried on under supervision where necessary. It is evident that Miss Spring and Professor Henwood attach very considerable importance to the chemistry of foods and to dietary studies; lectures on these subjects form a course in the last term; and problems, theoretical and practical, are furnished for solution to the students. Professor Henwood has worked out and carried

Marginal notes: (a) Domestic Science Courses. (General, Normal, Technical). Table XXXI

---

* See Table XXXI.

on a scheme in this subject for six years, three of which have now
been on the lines he finds to result in the accomplishment of good
work ; graduates attend these classes as well as the Normal students.
The class of sixteen works in groups of twos and threes.

During the junior year the course in anatomy and physiology
covers a general study of the body and its various systems ; the
laboratory demonstrations have reference to the lecture topics,
which embrace the subjects of physical development, physical
training, personal and domestic hygiene.

Each Normal student goes through practically eight courses in
cookery. Of these, however, three consist in repetitions of the
first three in general cookery, to ensure a thorough grasp of
principles and facility in practice. The course in advanced cookery
is then taken, as well as that in invalid cookery, followed by a
"lunch room" course, through which experience is gained in
providing for large numbers. Individual work with small quantities is usually followed by group work in which food is prepared
in sufficient amounts for a family of six or eight persons. The
"lunch room" is open for the use of all students who attend the
Institute. A handsomely decorated hall, resembling a high-class
restaurant, was approaching completion, at the time of my visit,
to replace the hitherto cramped and unsatisfactory quarters.
Each portion of food must represent a certain nutritive value, and
is sold at remarkably low prices ; it appears to be appetising and
varied. No special study is made of infant feeding in this course,
in consequence of the wide divergence of opinion and practice
which prevails, as well as of the increasing custom among physicians
to write prescriptions for individual cases. Students are throughout
referred to an excellent library of books of reference containing
not only the standard works, but all the newest and best as they
appear ; the invaluable Food Bulletins of the United States Department of Agriculture being also available for their use.

The Laundry course comprises only twelve lessons ; it appears,
so far as it goes, practical, and based on scientific principles ; as a
subject it does not as yet rank high in the curriculum of such
training courses, though here, as at the Pratt Institute and
Teachers College, great stress is laid upon its importance in household training. The plan and building of a house is at present
treated only theoretically ; this course of lectures is open to students
in several other departments besides those in the Normal and
Housekeepers' courses ; the synopsis of lectures appears well planned,
and the appended bibliography, which includes books on house
sanitation and hygiene, sites and environment, and the historical
development of the dwelling, is very complete and suggestive.
The course is given by Professor Prescott Hopkins of the Architectural Department of the Institute. Home nursing is practised
in a well-furnished bedroom, but, unfortunately, is not taught by
a trained nurse. The fees for the Normal courses are $40
(about £8) per term ; text books and stationery average $10

TABLE XXXI.

DREXEL TECHNICAL INSTITUTE, PHILADELPHIA.

NORMAL COURSE IN DOMESTIC SCIENCE.

Institution and Course.	Entrance Requirements.	Scope of Course.	Methods.	Length of course.	Fees and Finance.	Equipment.
Drexel Institute, Philadelphia. Domestic Science Normal Course. Director, Miss Helen M. Spring.	High School education or its equivalent. Diploma of approved institution accepted instead of examination.	Chemistry. General Principles **** Qualitative Analysis **** **** } Lectures, 3 hrs. per week. 1st yr., Laboratory, 3 hrs. per week. Organic Chemistry of Food and Dietetics } 2nd yr. { 3 hrs. per week for 16 weeks. 7 hrs. per week for 16 weeks. Food Analyses } 1 hr. per week for 12 weeks. Anatomy and Physiology, } 9 hrs. per week for 16 weeks. including **** use in Hygiene and Emergencies. } 1st yr., **** hrs, 3 hrs. per week. By and Physiological Chemistry. } 2nd yr. 1½ hrs, per week. Household **** **ce. } 2nd yr., 5 hrs. per week. Cookery. { 1st and { 8 hrs. per week (1st yr. } Waiting. 2nd. par., { 6 **. per week { 2nd yr. } Laundry Course. 1st { 2 **. per week for 16 weeks. Marketing. year. { 2 hrs. per week for 16 weeks. Food Economics. { Several **s. Luncheon Room Cookery. { 2 hrs. per week. Demonstrations. 2nd { 2 hrs. per week for 16 weeks. Home Nursing. year. { 2 hrs. per week for 16 weeks. Computing of Dietaries { 2 hrs. per week for 16 weeks. Physical ****g, } 1st and 2nd yrs., 2 hrs. per week. Business Forms and Accounts, } 1st yr., 1 hr. per week. English Language and } 1st yr., 1 hr. per week for 6 weeks. Literature. Domestic **ce, } 2nd yr., 1 hr. per week for 16 weeks. Teaching— **n of Public } 1st yr., 2 hrs. per week for 16 weeks. Scool Classes. Practice Class— } 1st and 2nd yr., 2 hrs. per week for 12 Teaching. } or 20 weeks. History and Institutes } 2nd yr., 1 hr. per week for 9 weeks. of Education. Lectures. Several demonstrations in Waitress Course, Laundry Course, Invalid Cookery, under Critic Teacher, 2nd year.	**** and practical; the bearing of the subject upon domestic and social improvement is daily kept in view. Every subject begins with a practical study of its principles, progresses by well adjusted instruction of the **** and with the object of securing so thorough a grasp of the **** as will **** of application in daily ****.	2 years of 2 sessions, 5 days a week Diploma for full course.	$40 per term (about £8) Deposit of $5 (£1) to cover breakages. Endowment of $3,000,000.	Exellent chemical and **** laboratories supplied with all **** apparatus; two large school kitchens furnished with every convenience, **s, cells by arrangement; dining-room ****. A large laundry with every **** **ent **e.

(a) Domestic (about £2 2s.) ; board may be had near the Institute at prices
Science   ranging from $5 to $8 (about £1 to £1 12s. 6d.) a week. A
Courses.   students' boarding-house has been organised in connection with
the department, the inclusive terms being $5 (£1) a week, board
only $3.50 (14s.) ; the accommodation, however, is limited, and
the long waiting-list shows how inadequate it is to the demand.
In the kitchen washing-dresses are not required, white blouses
and black skirts with the usual apron, sleeves, and cap being the
selected costume. The demand for the normal students on
graduation is at present larger than can be met; the training
received having a very high character throughout the United
States. The normal practice work is obtained by means of classes
for guilds, church schools, children's Saturday classes, etc., held
in various quarters of the city.

In addition to the Normal courses in cookery, ten alternative
courses are offered in this and other subjects connected with the
household ; each course occupies one term and is complete in itself.
Of these, three are confined to general cookery ; they are consecutive and must be taken up in regular order.

The First Course consists of instruction in the composition and
dietetic value of food materials. The lessons are arranged in logical
order, and each principle is illustrated by the preparation of simple
dishes. The teaching is largely individual, each student preparing
an entire dish ; the object of the course is the preparation of food in
the most digestible and appetising forms.

In the Second Course instruction and practice are given in the preparation of more complicated dishes and menus than are included in
the first course.

The Third Course includes the preparation of still more elaborate
and expensive dishes ; lessons in marketing and carving ; and practical
demonstration in the cutting of meat. In each course one lesson of
three hours is given weekly.

The course in Invalid Cookery is intended for professional nurses
and other persons desirous of acquiring a practical knowledge
of cookery suitable for the sick room. It extends throughout
one term, with one lesson of two and a-half hours each week.
Similar classes are arranged for medical students either in the
afternoon or evening to suit their convenience. The Housekeepers'
course is offered in the belief that greater skill and intelligence
are needed in the management of the home, and for the purpose
of providing thorough training for women who possess the requisite qualifications to fit themselves for positions as housekeepers
or as matrons of public institutions. It is analogous to that on
Food Economics at the Pratt Institute, and occupies a year.

It includes the general courses in cookery, courses in invalid and
lunch-room cookery ; a course for waitresses ; laundry work ;
marketing ; lectures on physiology and hygiene ; home nursing ;
familiar talks on food materials and other matters relating to the
household together with a study of business forms and accounts.
At present the number who attend it is very limited ; applicants must
be twenty-five years of age and must give evidence of a good education.

Courses are also organised in Home Nursing, Laundry work and
for Waitresses (six lessons of two hours each) ; there is a good

lecture course on Home Construction, as well as children's Saturday classes and evening classes in General Cookery ; there is also a " Chafing-dish " course for men ; all are open to the public ; occasionally boys are included among the Waitress course students.

The syllabus of the first course in the Evening Cooking Classes is included in Appendix B (p. 312), also one in Household Science ; they will be seen closely to resemble those employed for corresponding classes in this country. One lesson a week is usual in the above courses for one or two sessions ; the fees charged vary from twelve shillings to £1. 5s. All materials in the cookery classes are provided by the Institute. Good reports are given of the attendance at the greater number of these numerous classes.

The General Course of Instruction in Dressmaking consists of four grades, each occupying one term or half the academic year ; two lessons of two hours each being given weekly. All materials must be furnished by the students, except those supplied in the third and fourth grades for order work, when, for further practice, students are allowed to receive and execute orders. All work cut and planned in the class room must be finished at home. Instruction is also provided in accounts, business forms, and correspondence, two lessons of one hour each being given weekly during the second term. A course of lectures in the Chemistry of textiles, dyeing, and cleansing is given during the second term of each year. Throughout the Domestic Art Department, similar stress is laid upon the study of line, form, the proportions of the human figure, etc., as in the Pratt Institute ; one and a-half hours a week must be devoted to such instruction and practice in the General, as well as the Technical and Normal dressmaking and millinery classes. The two terms begin in September and February respectively ; students enter for one term at a time. The fees are £3 for the first grade, and £4 for each of the more advanced.

(b) Domestic Art Courses. (General, Normal,[*] Technical).

The Technical courses in Sewing, Dressmaking, and Millinery are arranged to meet the need of those who desire to train as professionals. The dressmaking students are expected to attend lectures in physiology and in hygiene with reference to dress, in addition to those in the chemistry of textiles, dyeing and cleansing, no additional fee being required; they also have the privilege of physical training in the gymnasium without extra payment. They must be at least eighteen years of age on admission, have a good knowledge of hand and machine sewing, and must present for inspection a dress made personally from patterns. Applicants are admitted only in September in each year ; certificates are granted to satisfactory students who have followed the entire course. The fees are $30 (£6) per term. In the evening classes instruction is given in hand and machine sewing, in the first, second, and third grades of the general course in dressmaking, and in millinery. The session extends through six months, from the beginning of

---

* With reference to the Normal Course in Domestic Art, see above page 209.

October to the end of March ; in each grade two lessons of two
hours each are given weekly ; the fees are 12s. 6d. for the first
course, and from £1 to £1. 12s. 6d. for the more advanced.

(c) Junior Course in Domestic Science and Art.

Brief mention must be made of the junior course in Domestic
Science and Art which is a non-professional course of prescribed
studies for girls ; it covers two years, and is designed to supply that
training for the duties and responsibilities of home life which the
ordinary academic education fails to give, and also to lay a broad and
solid foundation for the technical work involved in direct preparation for a profession or a skilled occupation. The course is based
upon the recognition of the fact that training for the practical
business of life should have its due place in the education of the
individual during the plastic period of life, and experience is constantly showing the soundness of this position. Of the pupils who
have thus far graduated, more than three-fourths have developed
aptitudes for some domestic art or science ; these have subsequently
taken advanced courses in chemistry, physiology and hygiene,
domestic science, millinery, or dressmaking, with a view in each
case to following the pursuit as a profession. " As a result of
this preparatory training in a well-arranged and soundly-correlated
course of study, these pupils have the advantage of entering
upon the pursuit of their technical courses with good habits of
thought and study, and with the ability to feel an intelligent
delight in their work." The course is divided broadly into scientific work, academic work, and technical work—about one-third
of the time being given to each of these branches.

The complete list of studies is as follows :—language and
literature, general history, civics, current events, mathematics,
elementary chemistry, physiology and hygiene, domestic science
and arts (including household economics), cookery (practical instruction in the school kitchen, talks on foods), sewing, millinery ;
the planning, decoration, and furnishing of a house ; business
customs and accounts ; drawing and physical training.

E.—Women's Colleges.

Courses in Hygiene and Household Economics.
(a) Vassar College.

A course in physiology and hygiene is given at Vassar College
for Women by Professor Thalberg, which is obligatory for all
freshmen during their first term. It comprises lectures, recitations, and practical investigation of the principles of house
sanitation ; drawings and models are provided for this study. An
elective course is also offered in advanced hygiene, which is open
to juniors and seniors ; this comprises, in addition to text-book
work, the microscopic study of tissues, experiments in physiological
chemistry and frequent dissections. Certain courses in biology
are recommended as a good introduction to these advanced
courses. In chemistry, the analysis of food is open to those who
have studied quantitative analysis and organic chemistry ; while
in the department of economics and sociology Professor Mills, in his
course on Charities and Corrections, treats of the physical and
physiological, as well as of other causes of abnormality.

A course in the Elements of Hygiene, conducted by Miss E. B. (*b*) Wellesley
Sherrard, resident health officer, is also required of all freshmen College.
at Wellesley College for Women, and counts towards the degree of
B.A. Miss Hazard, the President, believes that this course provides for health in the present and in the future by awakening
and helping to educate a " physical conscience." The part of the
subject presented is concerned chiefly with the proper care of the
body. The course is designed to give a practical knowledge of its
structure and an understanding of some of the chief causes which
lead to deterioration of health and to needless loss of life. A useful
outline is also given of the general principles of public hygiene.
The courses in zoology and animal physiology afford opportunity
for further study to any specially interested student. Instruction
in domestic science, including the theory of diet and cookery, was
given for some time ; the resignation of the instructor, on her
appointment to work in another college, brought this to a close.
Since then occasional lectures on this subject have been given, and
have invariably been received with much interest, but no regular
course has been organised.

In the other colleges for women—Bryn Mawr and Smith, for
instance—attention is devoted to physical culture, and a general
supervision is exercised over the health of the girls ; though
Wellesley College is still the exception in the excellent work
carried on by its resident health officers. These medical women
endeavour perseveringly to train students to judicious care of
themselves, chiefly by the adoption of a set of commonsense
rules for healthful living. The results to their well-being, physical
and mental, are first-rate.

Considerable interest has been aroused at Boston, and indeed (*c*) Simmons
over a much wider area, by the founding and endowment of the Female
Simmons Female College, several million dollars having been College,
bequeathed for the purpose by the late John Simmons. The Boston.
college is established as an institution in which the instruction
given is such as will best enable women to earn an independent
livelihood. The trustees believe that the purpose and plan will
interest and attract students who desire to fit themselves to become
superintendents or matrons of institutions, heads of college houses,
or of social settlements, private secretaries, librarians, and
teachers of household arts and sciences. Provision will be made
for those who desire to prepare themselves for the study of medicine
and nursing, and for others who wish to become more proficient
in a calling already adopted, or who need to add general training
to practical skill. Thus, college graduates who wish to secure
technical or professional training will have special opportunities for
doing so, while encouragement will be given to that large class
of women interested in educational problems, who feel not only
that constructive work should accompany academic studies, but
that no woman is well educated until she is thoroughly prepared
to obtain an independent livelihood, whether choice or necessity
may demand such self-maintenance. The plan of instruction

(c) Simmons Female College, Boston.— *continued.* provides for three classes of students. It offers a complete course of four years for such students as are able to give the requisite time for the college training, while shorter technical courses are to be provided for those who have had adequate preliminary preparation elsewhere, whether in college, or normal school, or in practical life. Properly qualified students will also be received for a partial course. There are to be Saturday and evening classes for students unable to attend the regular classes, with regard to which detailed announcements are not yet published.

The following courses in the departments of Household Economics, Secretarial work, Library training, and Science will be begun in the year 1902-3. The Corporation expects to open the department of Applied Art in the year 1903-4, and other departments in subsequent years.

 A. *Household Economics.*
  1. Regular course of four years in preparation for professional housekeeping and for teaching.
  2. Advanced course of one or more years for college graduates and others of sufficient training.
  3. Elementary course of one year.
  4. Special or partial courses.
 B. *Secretarial Courses.*
  1. Regular course of four years preparing for professional positions and for teaching.
  2. Advanced course of one or more years for college graduates.
  3. Special or partial courses.
 C. *Library Courses.*
  1. Regular course of four years.
  2. Special or partial courses.
 D. *Scientific Courses.*
  1. Collegiate course of four years in preparation for science teaching.
  2. Advanced course of one or more years for students with previous college or normal school training.
  3. Course of four years in preparation for the study of medicine.
  4. Courses of one, two, or three years in preparation for admission to training schools for nurses.
  5. Special or partial courses.

The regular course in Household Economics is designed for women who wish to prepare themselves for taking charge of institutions or social settlements, or for teaching the subjects of household arts and sciences. Students preparing to teach will be expected to take the theory and practice of teaching in their last year. Four years will be required for the course, unless students have had a satisfactory preparation subsequent to their High school training, such as two years in college study, a course in a Normal school, or sufficient experience in teaching, in which cases they may be admitted directly to the advanced course. The Elementary course is offered for those who desire to understand the principles underlying elementary Household Economics or to become proficient in the management of the home.

 The following tentative programme indicates the number of periods a week allotted to each subject in this elementary course ; the labo-

ratory and practice periods will occupy two or three hours each
lectures and recitations one hour each. Unless otherwise specified
electives may be chosen from all the subjects taught in the college,
which are not included in the prescribed portion of the programme.

Periods per week.

Cookery - - - - - - - - - 4
Marketing and accounts - - - - - - 2
Physiology and hygiene - - - - - - 1
House construction, decoration and equipment - - 2
Household administration and sanitation - - - 2
Conferences - - - - - - - - 1
Sewing and materials or elective subjects - - - 3

Special and partial courses may consist of a portion of the regular
course combined with any other studies offered by the college.
In the Science Department are found courses preparatory to
the study of medicine or of nursing; it is interesting to note
that mathematics, physics, chemistry, biology and physiology,
bacteriology, sanitation and cooking find a place in each of
these. In fact, a series of lessons in cookery, laundry work,
and household accounts will be provided for all students in this
Department. Arrangements have been made with the Boston
Normal School of Gymnastics whereby competent instruction
in gymnastics will be given to the college students in the gymnasium of that school. Two periods of physical culture will
be expected of all students each week unless excused for satisfactory reasons; in October and May outdoor exercises at the
Riverside Recreation Grounds, Newton, may be substituted for the
gymnasium practice; each student will be advised with regard to
her physical welfare by an experienced physician, and the gymnastic
training will be adapted to her needs.

The college year will be divided into two terms—October to
February, February to June—each term will close with examinations in all departments. The general admission requirements
are such as may be secured by a four years' course in a good High
School, but the advanced work in Household Economics is open to
college graduates without examination, and to others who show
that they have had the requisite training. A limited number of
scholarships have been established by the trustees, who have
also provided other means of affording pecuniary assistance to
those who are unable to meet the college charges. The fee for all
regular courses is $100 (£20) a year, payable in two instalments.
For special students and for evening and Saturday courses special
and reduced charges are made. The diploma of the college will be
granted only to those students who have completed the full requirements of one of the regular courses. Certificates may be issued to
other students, showing the list of studies successfully completed
and the grades attained in each. Suitable boarding accommodation can be secured for about $7 (£1 10s.) a week; a
college " dormitory " is also provided for sixty-six students. The
rooms are arranged in separate suites, each suite is intended for
two students, and consists of a study, a bedroom, and a bath-room.

Under certain conditions one student will be allowed to occupy à suite ; there are also a few single rooms. Ample and convenient dining-rooms are included in the " dormitory," so that students not in residence may secure table board. The cost of residence, in- cluding board, is from $275 (£55) to $300 (£60) per year, accord- ing to the position of the suite ; this must be paid in advance, one-half at the beginning of each term. The suites are lighted with both gas and electricity, which are furnished at the expense of the student ; service is not included. The " dormitory " is under the supervision of the Dean ; and one or more members of the Faculty will reside in the building. At the present time a part of the instruction is given in the buildings hitherto occupied by the School of Housekeeping ; while the remainder, including the larger part of the classes in the sciences and languages, is given by special arrangement in the Massachusetts Institute of Technology.

The School of House- keeping, Boston.

This School of Housekeeping was founded a few years since by the Women's Educational and Industrial Union of Boston. Its aim, of which there has been good promise of realisation, is a scientific study of home life, the object being " to save what is of permanent good, to discard what is useless, and to bring the whole into line with present industrial tendencies and scientific facts— social and physical. This study is not to the end that the homes of any one class may be bettered, but that the standard of living and life may be raised in all homes, in the belief that this would make for better citizenship, for a greater country, and for a healthier race." The course was first offered as one step in the re-organisation of the home on this broader social and scientific basis, and as a tangible recognition of the fact that housekeeping is a profession which demands scientific training. It was designed to meet the needs of young college women and others who wished to fit themselves to manage a household on the best economic and hygienic bases. The course consisted at first in the application of known principles and facts, scientific and economic, to the maintenance of a healthful well-ordered home ; besides which it included a study of the management of the household and expenditure of the income according to business methods. The movement received the cordial support of the professors of Harvard University and the Massa- chusetts Institute of Technology ; on its teaching staff were found the professors of sociology and physiology at Harvard (Dr. Ed. Cummings and Dr. Geo. W. Fitz) and the professors of biology and sanitary chemistry at the Institute (Dr. Wm. T. Sedgwick and Mrs. Ellen H. Richards). It is anticipated that yet greater success will attend the incorporation of the course as a department of the Simmons College. Hitherto it has covered the following general topics : (1) The home in relation to society ; the home in relation to public health ; the house—its construction, furnishing, manage- ment, and care. (2) The health of the individual (which embraced an exhaustive study of foods and dietaries, the hygiene of childhood and home nursing).* Original investigation was also undertaken

---

* See Appendix G.

to increase the body of exact information on household subjects, and to stimulate the thought and interest of the housekeeper.

As an illustration of the practical methods, based upon scientific principles, adopted at this school, I may mention that, at the date of my visit, each member of a class of eight or ten had been called upon to plan a dietary for one week, suitable for the students in residence. This, while required to be seasonable, varied and appetising, must not exceed in cost a certain sum per head, and must contain the nutrient principles in their right proportions to meet the body's needs. A selection was made from those submitted, and each compiler, in turn, was called upon to superintend the employment of her dietary for one week, in the residence attached to the school ; she became at once responsible for the purchase, cooking, service, etc., of all the articles which entered into her menu. The students meanwhile freely criticised these experimental dietaries, expressing their views as to the extent to which the various meals, etc., fulfilled the requirements; the questions raised were discussed with the professor in class ; and each purveyor was expected to offer sound reasons for the faith which was in her and which had found expression in the planning of food for her companions.

F.—UNIVERSITIES.

The belief that all living should be governed by hygienic, ethical, and economic principles, which is the root idea in the Simmons College Household Economic course, is evidently founded on a sociological basis. This belief has also constituted the standpoint of those responsible for the courses in Household Technology and related subjects at the Chicago University, for which a place is found in the Department of Sociology and Anthropology. It will be remembered that the University of Chicago owes its existence chiefly to Mr. John D. Rockefeller, whose generous gifts for its endowment date from 1888, and amount to several million dollars. The new University opened its doors to students in October, 1892, few of its many handsome buildings being then ready for use. It includes five divisions—the Schools, College and Academies ; the University Extension ; the University libraries, laboratories, and museums ; the University Press ; the University affiliations. *University of Chicago. Courses in Household Technology and related subjects. Table XXXII.*

Provision is made for the admission of students at the beginning of a junior college course, or at any further stage of advancement. In addition to students in regular standing, provision is made for the admission of certain classes of undergraduate students not seeking degrees—such are known as "unclassified." Those who have completed at least one year's work in a college or university of high rank may also be admitted to the College of the University under certain definite conditions. Students are admitted to a Senior College either after receiving the Junior College certificate from the University, or upon the completion of a corresponding amount of work in another institution. A Bachelor's degree is granted at the conclusion of the required amount of Junior College work.

The ordinary tuition fee is $40 (£8) a quarter, though it is somewhat influenced by the subject selected ; incidental expenses also vary from the same cause. Eight "dormitories" have been thus far erected in the quadrangle, and it is calculated that $300 (£60) might, by the exercise of great care, cover board and tuition, with all sundries, for thirty-six weeks of annual residence ; though $400 (£80) is nearer the average.

TABLE XXXII.
CHICAGO UNIVERSITY.

SCHEDULE OF SANITARY SCIENCE COURSES (HOUSEHOLD TECHNOLOGY AND RELATED SUBJECTS).

Institution and Course.	Entrance Requirements.	Scope of Course.	Methods.	Length of Course.	Fees and Finance.	Equipment.
University of Chicago. Department of Sociology and Anthropology. Sanitary Science, Professor Marion Talbot. Sociology, Professors Geo. E. Vincent, Chas. R. Henderson. Chemistry of Foods, &c., Professor Alice P. Norton. General Bacteriology, Professor E. O. Jordan. Physiological Chemistry, Prof. Albert P. Mathews.	Pre-requisites. Physiography and Geology, Physics, Chemistry, Botany (General), Biology (Sanitary) Physiology, Political Economy, English, German } Reading French } knowledge. These courses may be taken by special students who have had preparation at least to a good High School course, and, with a few exceptions, by candidates for degrees.	House Sanitation. Food Supplies and Dietaries. The Economy of Living. Food. The Principles of Cookery. Chemistry of Foods. Evolution of the House. General Bacteriology. Household Bacteriology. Public Hygiene. Physiological Chemistry. Contemporary Society in the United States. American Cities. The Family. The Group of Industrials. Rural Communities. Urban Communities. Sanitary Science. (This work is designed only for students capable of carrying on independent investigations. The topics assigned are chemical, physiological, bacteriological, economic, or sociological according to the preferences and training of the individual students). Seminar in Sanitary Science.	The work in Sanitary Science is planned to be in correlation with the aims and methods of social philosophy. The trend of the courses is not altogether technical, but their aim is to serve as a foundation for future duties and interests as householders, owners and agents of tenements, students of social reform, administrators of schools, hospitals, prisons and kindred institutions, and practical philanthropists. Students showing requisite capacity are encouraged to pursue investigations along purely scientific lines.	Each of the six courses occupies three months, four or five classes being held weekly. An "elective" subject for M.A. degree. The length of time which may be profitably devoted to these studies depends upon the preliminary training and on the object the student has in view.	$40 a quarter (about £8.) Largely endowed by Mr. Rockefeller.	The liberal endowment of this University enables every facility for practical work to be provided; the fine buildings having all been erected within the last ten years are replete with every modern convenience and improvement.

The special courses described as "Household Technology" are offered to meet the needs of the day and the demands of the students for some training in sanitary science. The instruction is intended to give men and women a general view of the place of the household in society, to train both sexes for the rational and scientific administration of the home as a social unit, and to prepare teachers in the subject. Supplementary courses in physics, chemistry, physiology, bacteriology, political economy, and the Study of Society are provided and required. Of course, these subjects are all elective, but they are attended by a fair and increasing number of students of both sexes. Three months is usually devoted to each sub-division, four, or perhaps five, classes a week being held. The tabulated particulars supply certain details, but a concise *resumé* of the topics included is desirable to indicate the scope assigned to the subject. Courses on Home Sanitation, Food Supplies and Dietaries, the Economy of living, and a "seminar" in Sanitary Science (designed for students capable of carrying on independent investigation) are conducted by Professor Marion Talbot, Dean of Women, at the University. The subject of Food, a practical course in the principles of Cookery, laboratory courses in the Chemistry of Foods and Household Bacteriology, and a theoretical course on the evolution of the house are entrusted to Professor Alice P. Norton. Professor Edwin O. Jordan undertakes courses in General Bacteriology and in Public Hygiene, studied from the standpoint of the bacteriologist; Physical Chemistry is under the charge of Professor A. P. Matthews. The sociological aspect of the subject is strongly emphasised throughout. Professor Charles R. Henderson himself takes charge of the courses on "The Family," the "Group of Industrials," and "Rural and Urban Communities"; while those on "Contemporary Society in the United States" and on "American Cities" are conducted by Professor Geo. E. Vincent. In the opinion of Professor Henderson, a knowledge of health principles is essential for everyone, and is required by him from all his students, many of whom are engaged in post-graduate work. The attention of these mature students is directed to the special study of such questions as the influence upon health of home and school, and kindred topics. In the seminar in Sanitary Science, for instance, each student is required to carry on some selected investigation, and to report upon their work. Such subjects as the use of food preservatives, the division of income in household expenses, or the comparative plumbing regulations in New York or Chicago are undertaken. The problem of domestic service is entered into fully in the "Economy of Living." The admirable conditions planned for the staff of servants in the Women's Hall of the University by Mrs. Ellen H. Richards of Boston, and Miss Sarah Wentworth, so long ago as 1893, offer an object lesson in the possibility of an eight hours' day for servants, at least in institutional life.

Professor Jordan's course in Public Hygiene proves both attractive and valuable. It deals with the application of bacteriology to the

Courses in Household Technology and related subjects— *continued.*

University of Chicago. Courses in Household Technology and related subjects — continued.

water supply, food supply, and sewage disposal of a city. The treatment has hitherto been by lecture and demonstration ; but last autumn he proposed to include practical work, bacteriological, chemical, and microscopic, for his students. In their company he visits model farms and dairies, reservoirs, sewage works, and so forth. These expeditions arouse very marked interest among his students of both sexes.

Some prominence is assigned to hygiene in the Department of Pedagogy at this University, where the attention of students is consistently directed to related courses in biology, physiology, neurology, and social science. Dr. Dewey's lectures on the " General principles of elementary education," and Miss Camp's on the " Science of elementary education," require a previous elementary knowledge of general biology, physics, and chemistry. Miss Harmer, Director of Domestic Arts in the University Elementary School, gives two courses on the " Educational value and uses of the Domestic Arts," in which she indicates the claims and place of such work in education and their hygienic influence in the home ; while Professor Locke deals with " School hygiene, sanitation, and construction." His students are referred to schools in Chicago and elsewhere for the practical solution of certain problems in heating, ventilation, and lighting ; economic problems of fatigue, school diseases, faults of posture, etc., also receive practical as well as theoretical attention.

In the Department of Political Economy, Dr. Hatfield's course on Social Economics is also useful in the emphasis it lays upon the results of hygienic ignorance on the economic conditions of working men. Chicago and its vicinity afford abundant materials for the practical observation demanded of his students. This recognition of the almost imperative necsssity for scientific training on the part of those who assume responsible positions, whether such positions be held as employers, paid officials, or as philanthropic and honorary workers, has been instrumental in the introduction of other classes in sociology by Professors Henderson and Vincent. In each of these the fundamental principles of hygiene are brought forward and their importance is affirmed.

I cannot resist mentioning in this connection the valuable Outline of Studies for Officers of Correctional Institutions drawn up by Professor Henderson, in fulfilment of a promise made at the National Prison Association meeting at Cleveland in 1900. The suggested course includes the elements of physiology and sanitation ; a study of hygienic foods and clothing and a suitable introduction to sociology, psychology and pedagogy. It is proposed that such a curriculum should constitute a part of the training of all officials employed as prison warders, superintendents, assistants, and school teachers in reformatories and industrial schools. The outline contains an excellent bibliography arranged for each of the subjects suggested, all of which have not been enumerated above, but all of which would contribute towards approaching the inmates of such institutions in a spirit of true philanthropy, based upon a study of the human mind and body, as influenced by heredity, environment, and temperament.

In the Correspondence Study Department of the University Extension division, sanitary science also finds a place. Courses in Foods and in House Sanitation are conducted by Miss Talbot and Mrs. Raycroft, which have been turned to account by students scattered throughout the States. These are elementary in character, but they serve to assist members of Women's Clubs and others who have no opportunity, or who cannot devote time, to attend a definite college course.

The last courses of study with which I propose to deal possess an unusual interest, for they find an honoured place at Teachers College, Columbia University, an institution of so unique a character that its history and aims must be briefly recorded before I pass on to my more immediate subject. Teachers College is the professional school of Columbia University for the study of education and the training of teachers. It is neither a Normal school nor a University Department of Pedagogy, but ranks as a professional school for teachers. It maintains University standards, aiming at the development of the four qualities held by its Dean to be pre-eminently desirable in a teacher; *i.e.*, general culture, professional knowledge, special knowledge and skill in teaching. Students may be of either sex, and may be engaged in, or preparing for, work in elementary, secondary, and normal schools. Opportunities for advanced study are available for specialists in various branches of school work, as well as for principals, supervisors, and superintendents of schools. The college was founded in 1888, and was the practical outcome of a noticeable discussion on "Education as a subject of University study," contained in President Barnard's reports; but it only became part of the educational system of Columbia University in 1898, when it was transferred to its present locality. It now takes academic rank with the Schools of Law, Medicine, and Applied Science. The donations towards its development have been most generous, amounting to at least $1,250,000. In the early days of the college there was only one course, followed by every regular student; but the work offered in the several departments soon increased beyond the capacity of one individual, and sub-divisions became necessary. No department, however, undertakes work that is done adequately in other faculties of the University. This original course of study occupied two years; and from the outset a school of observation and practice was an integral part of the plan. Teachers College now offers forty-six courses in Education, among which may be mentioned those on the history and principles of education, educational administration, genetic psychology and child study, and others on the theory and practice of teaching biology, domestic art, domestic science, English, fine arts, languages, manual training, and physical training. Qualified students of Teachers College are allowed to pursue University courses in history, language and literature, natural science, mathematics, philosophy, psychology, ethics, anthropology, music, economics, and social science. Two Schools of Observation and Practice are maintained, one the Horace Mann

(marginal note: Teachers College, Columbia University, New York.*)*

School, the other but just inaugurated, known as the Experimental School. The Horace Mann School, with its three departments, has been already mentioned. The Experimental School consists of a kindergarten and elementary school, also of special classes in sewing, cooking, and manual training.

The requirements for admission to Teachers College are as follows : to the two years' collegiate course—completion of a High school course ; if this be followed by a two years' professional course it leads to the degree of Bachelor of Science. To the two years' courses which lead to diplomas in elementary and kindergarten teaching, domestic art and domestic science, the fine arts, manual training, &c., completion of the collegiate course is the qualification for admission, or its equivalent in an approved college, or graduation from an approved normal school, or two years of technical training, or experience in teaching. To the graduate courses, college graduation, or its equivalent, qualifies for entrance. The fees for the graduate courses average $150 (£30) ; in other courses $100 (£20). The Faculty annually awards five fellowships of $650 each, and seventeen scholarships of varying amounts.

The Dean of Teachers College fully maintains the convictions of its founders in his statement that a university " is true to itself when it undertakes the professional training of teachers ; for the interests of public education are as urgent and important as the interests of law, medicine or engineering." Dean Russell has also drawn desirable attention to the relation of other university studies to education. First, those " which contribute directly to the science of education, such as biology, which is concerned with vital processes ; psychology, which discloses the nature of the mind ; sociology, which deals with the inter-relations of individuals in society ; and ethics, which seeks to establish the principles of right action. Second, all studies, regardless of their immediate bearing on the science of education, may be considered as a means to inform and to develop the minds of the young."

It is the policy of Teachers College to afford every opportunity for specialisation ; but the faculty insists that the true basis of specialisation in education lies in liberal culture, accurate scholarship, and that professional knowledge which characterises the intelligent teacher. The chief problem in the educational administration of Teachers College, since it became a part of the University system, has been to devise and conduct courses of study suited to the needs of advanced students. The first step was to provide graduate courses for students who were capable of undertaking research and investigation in one special field ; to this end the course leading to the higher diploma was planned for graduate students whose interests were chiefly professional. It is intended to fit teachers of superior ability and of special academic attainments for the work of training teachers in colleges and normal schools, and for positions in the public school service requiring a high degree of professional insight and technical skill. Candidates for the higher diploma must be graduates of an approved institution of learning—a college, engineering school, a normal school, or the equivalent of one of these—and must present satisfactory evidence of a high degree of professional ability as a result of the study of education or experience in teaching. The real test of fitness, however, is the ability of the candidate to undertake research and investigation in one major and two minor subjects. The minimum period of residence is fixed at one year, but the necessity for completing some special task in line with the major subject, and of putting the results in form for publication make it difficult for the average student to secure the diploma in the minimum time.

The Faculty is constantly engaged in the modification of courses, the raising of standards and the revision of curricula. Each year increases the confidence that progress is being made in the right direction, though it is realised with equal force that the end is not yet in sight ; a sentiment keenly experienced by Mrs. Woolman and Miss Kinné, who are respectively in charge of the Departments of Domestic Art and Domestic Science.

The courses of study pursued in these departments present many points of interest ; year by year they are developed and modified in the light of experience gained. Probably considerable changes in detail have taken place since my visit ; but the broad lines are the same, and I venture to hope that the necessarily imperfect notes I present in these pages may nevertheless serve to stimulate my readers to secure from headquarters fuller and further information on courses of such value and importance. The wide scope and sociological import of the groups of subjects described as Domestic Art or Domestic Science is evidently realised by those responsible for their selection and treatment. That this point of view receives the full support of the entire staff is again evident from the fact that students in Domestic Art are required to correlate their studies either with Domestic Science, with Fine Arts, or with Manual Training, while students in Domestic Science are advised to correlate their studies with Domestic Art or with Manual Training. The details I furnish differ apparently but little from those already supplied in regard to Technical School or certain College Courses, but in the spirit and methods is recognisable the end in view ; not the development of manual facility or even of hygienic habits, but " the meaning of the physical, social, moral, æsthetic and spiritual conditions of the home to the individual, and to society at large. The courses may be described as applied science and art, they do not offer technical training. It is felt that in a University these applied courses must have the same standing as pure science, and on these lines they are formulated, and from this point of view the Schedule of the two courses should be studied. For instance, the students of Domestic *(a)* Course in Art are required to practise, early in their training, advanced Domestic basketry and raffia work, as well as to construct a systematic Art. Table series of models to cover the ground of plain needlework, not so XXXIII. much with the view of acquiring manual dexterity, as with the aim of thoroughly comprehending how, by such means, to draw out and build up a child's ideas ; how to substitute broad, free movements in place of fine stitching for young pupils, how to convert the subject into a general means of self-expression for all. Students are trained to observe and consider the interests, capacities and instincts of the child, and to adapt their instruction to these at various ages. In support of her methods, Mrs. Woolman points out that " early nations used the needle in many ways adapted to the use of children, in coarse weaving, in

basketry, in which rigid material was sewed together
with softer fibres, such as wool and twisted bark; in mats,
hats and baskets of the raffia palm fibre, in braiding, knotting,
twining, netting, etc. All of these early steps in domestic art
make an excellent foundation for sewing, and may be used to great
advantage in the primary grades, where the awakening power of
the child demands work in rapid construction and large adjust-
ments. The articles should be simple in construction—of a character to appeal to the child's interests—and worth doing." Their
practice work in the Horace Mann School affords the necessary
opportunity to the students for testing their own command of this
method, and for observing its influence on children. The remainder of the practical work in the Domestic Art Course follows
accepted lines in the teaching of drafting and cutting of materials,
dressmaking—elementary and advanced (the Vienna dressmaking
system is that adopted), and millinery. At Teachers College, as in
the Technical Institute courses, infinite pains are expended in the
effort to cultivate a sense of what is appropriate and beautiful in
design and colour and in developing the power to express this in
execution. Certain Art courses are obligatory, while the Department itself provides one in Household Art and Design.* Of this the
aim is to apply general rules of art to the home, in order to foster
good taste and appreciation of beauty in every-day life. It includes
some consideration of healthful living and dressing; the colour
effects and uses of textiles; and the principles of home decoration;
training in facility to sketch and design with accuracy and rapidity;
and the use of the needle in applying these principles to articles of
home and ceremonial use. To further strengthen students in
what seems to be fundamental to their speciality, they are advised
to continue their studies along lines calculated to aid in understanding the scope and meaning of art; the result is evident in the
bold and frequently artistic sketches made when they are engaged in
the final stages of dressmaking and millinery. Domestic science is
not ignored in this Domestic Art course; the study of foods and the
processes of their production, manufacture, and cooking are obligatory subjects, while students are strongly advised to follow
the course in Household Chemistry under Dr. Vulté. Practice
lessons in sewing are given under supervision in the Experimental
School. Here, from the first grade upwards, children are guided
progressively from the practice of primitive methods of weaving
and basketry, through varied phases of hand and needlework,
until this evolutionary method brings them, in the High school,
to a study of the existing manufacturing system and its
social influences. Mrs. Woolman's interest in these sociological and
industrial aspects of her subject becomes very apparent in
her lectures on Textiles. This course covers a study of fabrics;
the processes of their manufacture; the development of these
processes, and their effect on social conditions, with the object of
giving students not merely a knowledge of textiles, but of affording

---

* See Appendix H.

TABLE XXXIII.

TEACHERS COLLEGE, COLUMBIA UNIVERSITY, NEW YORK CITY.

SCHEDULE OF DOMESTIC ART COURSE.

Institution and Course.	Entrance Requirements.	Scope of Course.	Methods.	Length of Course.	Fees and Finance.	Equipment.
Teachers College, Columbia University. (The professional school of the University for the training of teachers.) Domestic Art Course. Directress, Professor Mary S. Woolman.	Evidence of completion of a satisfactory course in a secondary school, followed by at least 2 years' college study; or technical training; or experience in teaching.	Domestic Art. Needlework. Textiles, study of. Drafting and making Garments. Principles of Dressmaking. } 1 year, 6 hours a week. Household Art and Design. } 1 year, 3 hours a week. Foods. 1 year, 4 hours a week. Manual Training, Hand work } 1 year, 3 hours a week. Fine Arts (Design) 1 year, 1 hour a week. Psychology (Elements) 1 year, 1½ hours a week. Education. Application of Psychology Principles and Methods } 1 year, 3 hours a week. History of Education. Theory and Practice of Teaching } 1 year, 5 hours a week. Domestic Art. Students are also recommended to take the following Courses. Advanced Course in Drafting, Dressmaking, and Millinery. Advanced Design and Art Interpretation in the General Course. Food Production and Household Chemistry. Theory and Practice of Teaching of Domestic Science.	The course aims at being both academic and technical. It is intended to present the methods of teaching Domestic Art in schools of all grades.	Two years. Leads to Domestic Art Diploma, which is the equivalent of three years' University work.	Graduates $150(£30) Undergraduates $100(£20) Books, etc. $15 - $30 (£3 - £6) Total living expenses, $300-$500 (£60-£100). Income derived from legacies and gifts administered by a Board of Trustees.	The most complete modern apparatus and appliances are provided throughout the spacious workrooms and studios. A splendid library is at the service of students; with 18 special rooms to be used for study by advanced students only.

them suggestions for methods of presentation in connection with their lessons in sewing. " The way things are made is of intense interest to children," writes Mrs. Woolman, " and the skilled teacher can easily make their history and manufacture a part of geography, school lessons in history, mathematics, etc." Through the right presentation of the whole subject, she anticipates also a revival of sympathy with and respect for manual labour.

In connection with this course on Textiles and that on Household Art, visits are paid to the mills, furniture stores, and museums. Lectures on the educational aspects of Domestic Art are preceded by a course in elementary psychology, given by Professor Thorndike, which includes the elements of the science, as well as the general principles which control successful teaching, so far as these can be derived from psychological laws, or from the study of school practice. Its aim is to prepare students for subsequent courses in the methods of teaching separate subjects. Professor Monroe takes the history of education, which is supplemented by Professor Woolman's course on the Theory and Practice of Teaching Domestic Art. Here the relationship of Domestic Art is considered (1) to the aims and means of education ; (2) to the best methods of teaching it in public and other schools ; and (3) to its correlation with other grade work. The planning and cost of courses of instruction are also considered. Students are constantly reminded that the personality of a teacher is one of the most important factors in her work ; " her physical, mental, and moral influence is ever moulding her pupils, even without her effort ; her teaching must, therefore, be grounded on culture ; she should thoroughly understand the problems of modern education. . . . she should be inspired by a high ethical aim . . . to make the children efficient for good in the world, she must study their characteristics and interests ; she must see, too, that the child's own will power is at work, and that he thinks out for himself every step in connection with the article in hand." Bearing this ideal in mind, a study of even the condensed outline of the course (Table XXXIII.) will have its own interest in showing by what means its realisation is attempted.

Miss Helen Kinné, the professor of Domestic Science, is imbued with the same true educational spirit as Mrs. Woolman, and (*h*) Course in both ladies receive an increasing amount of encouraging co-Science. operation from other members of the faculty. The course in Table Domestic Science, as defined in the college " Announcement," XXXIV. is even more comprehensive in its allied studies than that in Domestic Art. The introductory courses in psychology and education are similar to those in the Domestic Art course, as is also the " recommended " course in the Economic and Social History of the United States. This last deals with those special topics and phases of economic and social history which have direct and practical bearing upon the work of students in the departments of Manual Training, Domestic Science, and Domestic Art. It gives an idea of the nature and purpose of industrial growth ; considers in detail the various economic and industrial conditions and problems of the various sections of the United States at the present time ; (*b*) Course in Domestic Science— *continued.* and the relation of economic and industrial forces to contemporary social conditions. A partial study is made of the economic and industrial condition of Europe in the sixteenth and seventeenth centuries, as based upon the mercantile system. The outcome of these conditions is traced in exploration and colonisation, and in the growth of economic industry in the American colonies, which culminated in the American Revolution. Attention is also directed to the industrial problems of the nation ; and the contemporary social condition and problems are noted as outgrowths of economic development.

Another course common to students of either Domestic Art or Domestic Science is that given by Dr. Vulté in Household Chemistry. To this he has given much thought, and through his courtesy I am enabled to include its synopsis.* It is designed to include the study of the principal food products, such as sugars, starches, proteids, animal and vegetable fats, water and mineral salts. Special attention is given to the changes which take place during the operation of cooking, to the analytical tests applied to them, as well as to the chemical aspects of fermentation and putrefaction, and their prevention by chemical means, and sterilisation. The corrosive action of food constituents, acids, &c., on utensils is dealt with, as well as saponification, the action of detergents, hard and soft water, testing of milk, butter, cheese, water, &c.; the chemistry of fuels and of illuminants is also studied. Dr. Vulté does not lay stress upon expression of results in chemical equations, but aims rather that the subject should be approached and dealt with from the point of view of daily life requirements. He gives the theory in his lectures, and leaves the carrying out of experiments, in the form of problems, to his students, who work under his personal supervision. He also conducts an advanced course in the same subject ; here original research is undertaken in the working out of problems which arise in the preparation of food, the use of fuels and cooking apparatus, and in laundering and other cleansing processes. It is intended only for advanced students who have a sound knowledge of elementary and organic chemistry.

The subject of Foods is taken up exhaustively in the Domestic Science course, and is studied in three courses. The first is designed to give a thorough knowledge of theory and practice in cooking, and to aid the student in arranging matter for teaching; it deals with the composition and nutritive value of foods, the fundamental principles and processes of cookery, and a comparative study of fuels and of cooking apparatus. Special attention is given to scientific methods in kitchen laboratory work, and to the adaptation of such methods to schools. The second is concerned with the production of food materials, such as dairy products, manufacture of flours, cereals, spices, &c.,

* See Appendix H.

TABLE XXXIV.

TEACHERS COLLEGE, COLUMBIA UNIVERSITY, NEW YORK CITY.

SCHEDULE OF COURSE IN DOMESTIC SCIENCE.

Institution and Course.	Entrance Requirements.	Scope of Course.	Methods.	Length of Course.	Fees and Finance.	Equipment.
Teachers College, Columbia University, N.Y. Domestic Science Course. Directress, Miss Helen Kinné.	Evidence of completion of a satisfactory course in a secondary school, followed by at least two years collegiate study, or technical training, or experience in teaching.	Domestic Science. Foods, 2 years, 4 hours a week. Food production and manufacture, 1 year, 2 hours a week. House Sanitation and Economics, 1 year, 2 hours a week. Chemistry — General, Household, 2 years, 2 hours a week. Biology, Physiology, Personal Hygiene (this includes Occupation, Recreation, Physical Culture), 1 year, 2 hours a week. Psychology, 1 year, 1½ hours a week. Education—Application of Psychology, History of Education, 1 year, 3 hours a week. Theory and Practice of teaching Domestic Science, 1 year, 4 hours a week. Students are recommended to take as "electives":—Bacteriology, Household Chemistry (advanced course), Laundry work, Home Nursing and First Aid, The Teaching of Domestic Art, Sewing and Making Garments, Critic Teaching, Hand Work, Economic and Social History of the United States.	The practical work includes practice in the kitchen, chemical and bacteriological laboratories, observation, assistance and teaching in school classes, the planning of laboratory equipment, and assistance in the management of the departmental housekeeping. The theoretical work includes the consideration of courses of study and the planning of lessons. The course is intended to present the methods of teaching Domestic Science in schools of all grades.	2 years. Leads to Science Diploma.	Per annum Graduates, $150 (£30). Under-graduates, $100 (£20). Books, etc., $15-$30 (£3-£6). Total living expenses, $300-$500. (£60-£100). Income derived from legacies and gifts administered by a Board of Trustees.	Very complete laboratories, biological, chemical and for special Domestic Science work; all equipped for individual work.

as well as with food adulterations and other processes in the preparation of food materials. The third takes up advanced cookery, the preservation of food, cookery for invalids and children, food values and dietaries, the planning, cooking, and serving of meals, a waitresses' course, and marketing. The cookery practice is made as experimental as it can be, in order to enforce and to illustrate fundamental principles. Students are set problems from which to gain their own experience, and are trained not to rely on that of others as recorded in cookery books. No stereotyped set of recipes is worked through; laboratory rather than ordinary kitchen methods are enforced, and such variety of problems presented as to demand practical individual solution from each member of the class. A tabulated method of record is usually employed, by which the effects of heat, of varying proportions of materials, &c., are set out graphically.

(*b*) Course in Domestic Science— *continued.*

Botany and zoology, under Professors Lloyd and Bigelow, are studied in the form of lectures, laboratory work, recitations, excursions for field work, and collateral reading. These courses are obligatory on Domestic Science students, and must be taken before the course in physiology and hygiene, in which the same professors adopt similar methods. This latter course covers a laboratory study of the structure of cells, tissues, and organs in various organisms, both plant and animal, including man, and of the fundamental principles of hygiene, personal and domestic. Individual hygiene is also studied from the standpoint of occupation and recreation, the claims of physical culture receiving attention. Home sanitation and economics find a place in the second year of study. The course embraces the following subjects: situation and structure of the house, water supply, disposal of waste, heating and ventilation, lighting, healthful furnishing, cleansing of the house, development and organisation of the home and its adaptation to modern conditions, systematic methods of housekeeping, the cost of living and household accounts, domestic service. The lectures on bacteriology are optional; they are associated with practical laboratory work, in illustration of the theoretical teaching which deals with the nature of bacteria, with methods of isolation and recognition of species, the part which bacteria play in nature, the industrial uses to which they are put; the bacteria of air, water, ice, milk, and foods generally; the methods of sterilisation and disinfection; the relation of bacteria to disease, and, in connection with this, certain phases of hygiene and household sanitation, extending to the care of the sick. This and the courses in Home Nursing and Emergencies are so usually elected that they enter into the training of the majority of students. These last-mentioned subjects consist of lectures, with practical illustrations and experiments on the part of the students, and are considered to afford sufficient training to enable teachers to present the subjects in the schools. Both are conducted by a trained nurse. The course in Laundry-work includes both theory and practice. No

(*b*) Course in
Domestic
Science—
continued.
laundry is provided, but the practical work is carried out in the large kitchen laboratory by means of portable equipment, upon which much thought has been expended. That this has been to good effect is shown by the success which has attended its employment not only for the college students, but for public school work in poor districts where no " centres " are yet organised. This subject is of recent introduction, and has by no means reached its final development.

Another course described as " Supervision and Critic Teaching in Domestic Science " consists of conferences and practical work under Professor Kinné. It affords opportunity for practical investigations of conditions and problems in Domestic Science teaching in schools, colleges, universities, clubs, and social settlements; it also includes a study of the development and present status of domestic science at home and abroad ; the organisation and management of departments; supervision in city schools; and critic teaching in normal schools.

The enrolment in both departments is progressing steadily in number. During last year 114 students, all women, were under instruction in the department of Domestic Science, while sixty-six, of whom four were men, were found in that of Domestic Art. Miss Kinné and her colleague, Mrs. Woolman, have in view a scheme to combine the two-years courses in each of these two subjects into one three-years course, especially for the training of inspectors; but, among other difficulties, they are confronted with the fact that the students who select the one or the other of these courses of study are usually of temperaments and types of mind so different that for one individual to gain intelligent command of all that would be involved in such a combined course would be a relatively rare attainment.

A perusal of the preceding pages cannot fail to have impressed on the mind of the reader the valuable impetus given to educational progress by the work carried on in the independent institutions of all grades to which this part of the Report refers. It is evident that official coercion is not needed to stimulate the zeal which finds an honourable outlet in thus promoting studies framed to advance the efficiency of the nation. It is true that much still remains to be done in the development, multiplication and organisation of these courses, nevertheless, each year's work is more full of promise for the future, while at least a decade must elapse before its fruition can reasonably be anticipated.

PART III.

SOCIAL AGENCIES FOR THE PROMOTION OF DOMESTIC SCIENCE TEACHING.

That the educational institutions of a country reflect the public opinion of its people is an assured, though relatively somewhat recently recognised fact. Its acceptance will direct the attention of thoughtful observers to a study of the forces active in the formation of current national beliefs. Of these, there are two distinct classes: the one, by its progressive spirit, moulding the conception of the few wise or far-sighted into the ideals of the many; the other retarding advisable developments, because the issues at stake are allowed to be obscured by the prejudices it fosters. These dual factors are constantly at work, and always important, whether in the sphere of sociology and philanthropy, or in the scholastic, commercial and professional worlds; most particularly so when the subject presented to the public for consideration is closely linked with daily life. Therefore, this Report on " The Teaching of Hygiene and Household Science in the United States of America " would be incomplete without a reference, however brief, to the social, as well as to the educational, agencies which are responsible, to a greater or less degree, for the promising activity of interest in these subjects observable in the schools and colleges of the country. The provision of a more healthy, happy, intelligent, and economical home life is rightly considered to be a national problem; its solution is not relegated to one profession, or confined to one state; the movement in favour of sanitary reform is increasingly general, and I could not fail to be impressed with the unfeigned interest expressed in it by both sexes in many different centres. In the case of men, this seemed stimulated chiefly by their desire for national supremacy; in the case of women, it was more often the domestic side which appealed to their sympathies. It also appeared to me that there exists a small percentage of professional and commercial men, who sincerely deplore the melancholy corruption which is so serious a blight on the country's municipal life. Their hopes for sweeping and immediate reform are not great; but they look for a gradual transmutation of the base ore of self-seeking into the refined metal of zeal for social progress by a succeeding generation, which shall be trained in the best traditions of citizenship during early and impressionable years. Professor Adams has said that " the requisite of a citizen is that he should be able to appreciate and feel and understand those forces that touch his life " ; he must be able to grasp something of the import of heredity, and of the powerful influences of environment. Apart from sanitary science based upon biology, how is this appreciation or understanding to be fully gained ? Testimony that a study of hygiene furnishes one necessary foundation to good citizenship

Introductory.

is afforded by the fact that in Chicago University, the State University of Michigan, and elsewhere, the courses offered are the direct outcome of the male students' sense of need ; a sensation of sufficient strength to embolden men in some other universities to follow Household Science Courses, hitherto confined to female students, until provision is made for courses better suited to masculine requirements.

Sociology and Economics are subjects much discussed just now in the States ; increasing attention, for example, is devoted to their study in High Schools ; and it would seem to good purpose, if a more general demand for and interest in the study of public health be the enduring fruit. The mere making of man into a better animal is the argument which it must be admitted carries weight with the majority in the business world. That Boston merchant is by no means unique, who supported the introduction of Physical Culture (to include a knowledge of Hygiene) into the curriculum of both boys and girls in the High School of Brookline, on the grounds that the clerk who knows how to keep himself mentally and physically at high-water mark has his financial worth to his employer materially increased. Thus, though the motives, when analysed, may be very mixed, and not always of a high ethical standard, their outcome bodes well for the efficiency of the nation.

A.—Women's Clubs.

Their organisation and methods.

This awakening to the importance of intelligent civic administration is, however, not confined to men. The records of many cities testify to the vivid interest taken in " municipal housekeeping " by women, and to their achievements in that sphere. The influence they exercise upon public life in the United States is due, among other causes, to the strength derived from co-operation. The social life of the nation is woven into one great web by a network of women's clubs. These are federated into large organizations, which knit together those units separated by apparent distance, and facilitate the concentration of an almost irresistible force upon any selected subject. The significance of the term " club " differs from that attached to it in this country ; any community of interest which links a few women together for some common object—for example, the study of art, or of history, or a foreign language, or some measure of social reform, or some political alarm, results in the formation of a " club," or perhaps of a special branch of one already in existence. The clubs of a district, town, or city are usually federated under a President, who, while supreme in her district, is subservient to the County or State President ; the whole organisation finds its focus in the National President, elected at definite intervals from among the State Presidents. Great independence is characteristic of these clubs ; there may be activity or indolence, concentration of interest or diffusion of energy, ideals confined to vague theories, or demanding instant realisation in practice ; but there is one fact assured, and that is that women have it in their power, by this means, to mould public opinion to an extent inconceivable in Great Britain. Signs are not wanting of the realisation that the responsibility thus involved must be lived up to and prepared for; among these may be mentioned the growing demand for assistance from University Extension lectures, and increased attendance at the Summer Schools.

In addition to periodical congresses, at which the attendance of experts gives worth and vitality to the proceedings, it is the custom among these women's clubs to meet at frequent intervals, to pursue the study of some selected subject. A yearly programme is drawn up; for instance, in the Domestic Science Club, the topics chosen range over the whole wide field of personal, domestic, educational and municipal hygiene:—House Construction; Plumbing; Ice Supply; the Problem of Domestic Service; what constitutes a good Menu; Household Accounts; Art in the Household; Recreations; School Sanitation; these are a few culled at random from a last year's list. A subject is assigned to each member, who is required to study and present a paper upon it at a given date; free discussion follows the reading of this essay. I heard repeatedly of the beneficial results which follow this amateur work; not the least of which is the growing interest among mothers as to the teaching of Domestic Science in High and Grammar schools. Material assistance in home and club study is afforded by the system of Travelling Libraries, loaned, for six months or longer, to any registered club by the Public Library Division of several State Libraries.

In illustration of the good missionary work possible of performance by a local branch of one Women's Club, I may mention the Illinois Association of Domestic Science, though examples could be easily multiplied. The objects of this Association are "to stimulate interest in all that pertains to home-making; to instigate the organisation of domestic science associations in order to co-ordinate the work; and to secure the introduction of the study of domestic science into the educational system." The President and her Committee were animated in the first instance by a desire to introduce better methods, based upon sound reasons, into the conduct of their own home life; then they desired to interest those whose existence is usually hampered by unintelligent "rule of thumb" habits, and who are hard to reach in consequence of their often isolated dwellings. Stimulated by enthusiasm, these women took advantage of the presence of a large number of club members on the occasion of the annual meeting of the Illinois Farmers' Institute, held at Champaign in February, 1898; they called a meeting, at which attention was directed to the advantage of organising a State Domestic Science Association. In this instance, the intention was more particularly to reach the farmers' wives; that is to say, to initiate a movement which should provide for them what these Institutes do for the farmers, *i.e.*, a recurring opportunity for the discussion of professional questions, and for the securing of new light or reliable information upon doubtful points. The support afforded by the men was so cordial that, from the start, the Association was looked upon as a legitimate

Specimen organisations for promoting Domestic Science Teaching. (a) Illinois Association of Domestic Science.

part of the Farmers' Institute's work; and, soon after the first annual meeting, the Institution Board passed a formal resolution by which the Illinois Association of Domestic Science was recog- .nised as an organisation affiliated to the Illinois Farmers' Institute, while a committee of the directors was appointed to look after its interests. That the women worked to some purpose is evident from the endowment three years later of scholarships for girls in Household Economics, tenable at the Illinois State University, of the same number (two to each county of the State) and on the same terms as those in Agriculture, appropriated some years previously to young men.

b) Sanitary Science Club of the Association of College lumnæ.

Foremost in the earnest, intelligent, public service rendered by women has been the Sanitary Science Club of the Association of College Alumnæ, which is itself composed of graduates from certain selected women's colleges of high standing This depart- ment of the Association was organised in Boston twenty years ago, when there were as yet few college graduates in the country, and fewer still at the head of homes of their own. Its object was the promotion of home sanitation, and for the first two years of the Club's existence, its members devoted their time to general study of the subject and to research into methods, either in the homes of the club members, or in those opened for this purpose by friends. Such positive help and satisfactory material resulted from this work that two of the members were appointed to edit the notes made. The resulting publication, issued in 1887 and brought up to date by subsequent new editions, retains its position as an acknowledged text-book, and has influenced large numbers for good. With the advantage of that increased knowledge, which results from accumulated and sifted experience, this Sanitary Science Club has directed its attention to the betterment of homes of all classes; to the securing of necessary reforms in school and muni- cipal sanitation; and to the introduction of suitable opportunities for a study of the subject of Home Economics into High Schools and Colleges. For some years several of the most prominent Club members have been engaged in teaching Sanitary Science at the University of Chicago, the Massachusetts Institute of Tech- nology, and other important educational centres. It is regrettable that the interesting exhibit of "The Work of College Women for the Home" was not more generally observed at the Paris Exhi- bition of 1900, for it constituted an instructive record of good work done. Plans and descriptions of houses were included, as well as specimen details of administrative work carried on by these women, and a bibliography of their published writings. A recent exhibit in the cause of Home Economics at Boston illustrated in seven sections their practical services to the community; these con- sisted of: (i.) Bibliography; (ii.) Home Economics applied to children; (iii.) applied to Shelter and Furnishings; (iv.) applied to Food; (v.) applied to Clothing; (vi.) applied to Household Management; (vii.) suggested applications of the subjects to Public School instruction. The exhibits included useful models, notably one of the New England Kitchen at Boston ; a clever portable device for the division of an ordinary schoolroom into four rooms for housewifery lessons ; examples of hygienic clothing for children ; laundry and food exhibits ; dietaries calculated at various figures, and some of Mrs. Ellen H. Richards' useful aids to intelligent and wholesome housekeeping. Indeed, it may be justly said, to their honour, that the college women of the United States were among the first to see the importance to the home of healthful management and environment, and to take practical means to secure such conditions. To them is due the credit for directing attention also to the true significance of Domestic Economy, viz., that it embraces economy of time, of method, and of strength, as well as of pounds, shillings, and pence.

The work and publications of the Sanitary Science Club of the College Alumnæ are undoubtedly largely responsible for the inception of another social organisation, the National Household Economic Association. This was actually formed as the direct result of a congress held at the Chicago Exhibition, 1893 ; it now embraces a large membership in thirty of the States and in Canada. Its work lies chiefly among the well-to-do classes, though its members assist in the training of women in very poor districts. Both sexes are eligible for membership. The Annual Congress, held for three or four days in some important centre, serves to stimulate its own supporters, while it arouses interest among those previously indifferent to its objects. To awaken the middle class to a sense of the dignity, interest, and importance of Household Economics has been very uphill work. But the President can now report hopeful signs of ground securely gained among a class often difficult to influence, hedged in as it is by social convention and the possession of homes, which, because they bear the hall-marks of comfort or wealth, are presupposed to possess the sign manual of health. However, the Committee are spurred on to persevering efforts by the conviction that the formation of an intelligent public opinion on the right conduct of home life among these educated members of the community is an indispensable factor in its general study ; while, incidentally, they anticipate that one outcome may be some promising solution of that most vexed problem, the future of domestic service. The Association endeavours to work through existing organisations ; consequently, it puts itself in touch with the Women's Clubs throughout the country, and has successfully secured the inauguration of many a department in this subject, as well as organising local committees for the conduct of specific lines of study. These local committees are urged, in their turn, to influence the Farmers' Institutes, School Managers, Factory Girls' Clubs, indeed all industrial, sociological and educational organisations ; as a result, more attention is given annually to the essentials of successful housekeeping, to the right care of children, and to the making of attractive and healthy homes.

(c) The National Household Economic Association.

(d) The Women's Institute, Yonkers, N.Y.

The Women's Institute, Yonkers, New York, offers an excellent example of somewhat similar work, carried on among another section of society, in which also the Young Women's Christian Association is satisfactorily active. This Institute was founded in 1880, and owes its existence to Miss Mary Marshall Butler ; its membership is largely composed of those employed in the factories and mills in the neighbourhood. Club membership entitles to the use of a lunch-room, where excellent hot food, tea, coffee, and fruit are served daily to upwards of eighty or a hundred of these factory workers. Evening classes in cooking, sewing, millinery, and dressmaking, etc., are provided at very low fees, usually two shillings for ten lessons. Special classes for married women are provided in the same subjects ; also courses in invalid cooking for nurses from the local hospital, and Saturday classes for school children.

(e) The Civic League.

But the departure to which I now desire to draw attention was the foundation, in 1895, of the Civic League, which can already show a good record of practical results, attained through the active co-operation existing between the members and the public authorities. Lectures have been given on " The Hygienic Care of Milk," " Improved Housing," " The Consumers' League," " Our Public Schools," " Children's Playgrounds," and other kindred topics, which have not only stimulated interest but borne fruit. The appointment of a woman Sanitary Inspector in 1900 is the direct outcome of tactful action taken by this League. The approval by the Board of Education of the appointment of a School Visiting Committee is another tangible result of its work. This committee visits the schools regularly, confers with the teachers, and reports concerning hygienic and sanitary matters. Not only do problems of ventilation and cleanliness receive their attention, but care is given to the physical condition of children in need of fresh air, of improved food, or of warm clothing. The teachers eminently appreciate the interest displayed by this committee in the teaching of civics, of nature work, and of physiology, as well as in the suitable decoration of schoolrooms and in the organisation of boys' and girls' clubs. Among other hygienic achievements may be enumerated the introduction of Cooking into the Evening Schools, and the initiation of Kindergartens during the three months' summer vacations.

(f) Women's Educational and Industrial Union.

The last of these numerous social, as distinguished from philanthropic, organisations which I will mention is the Women's Educational and Industrial Union. This Union has branches in numerous cities, with committees on Domestic Science, Hygiene, Physical Culture, and " Kitchen Garden" work for children, as well as on its other numerous interests. The activity of these branches is probably a variable quantity ; but annual reports testify to new ground broken and fresh seed sown. Reference has already been made in Part II. to the special outgrowth of this Union, the School of Housekeeping, now a department of the Simmons College for Women at Boston.

B.—Philanthropic Agencies.

Before I touch upon the numerous philanthropic agencies which play a valuable part in the formation of an intelligent public opinion upon Household and Sanitary Science, it may be well to remind my readers of the influence exercised on the public school curriculum by private individuals and by voluntary organisations.* These agencies, when convinced of the social advantage to be derived from certain subjects, initiate them at first on a modest scale, in the form of free Saturday, evening, or vacation classes ; when satisfied that the instruction meets a distinct want and is worthy of public recognition, they exert all their influence to secure its adoption by the official school authorities. Instances are not far to seek of this zeal attaining such proportions that private individuals even undertake to defray all expenses for a time after the subject has been introduced into the public schools.

Such pioneer work, along many lines, has been carried on with success in Indianapolis for some years past ; indeed, the free Kindergarten movement in that city dates back to 1875, and its superintendent reports continuous and encouraging developments. It would seem that honest efforts are made, even at the early age of Kindergarten children, to judiciously prepare the little ones for home and school life and for future citizenship, as well as to provide for them conditions of wholesome growth. And so it comes about that five and six-year-old children are admitted to what is described as the " Kitchen Garden," or the " Little Housekeepers' School," where the miniature furniture, dishes, brooms, and buckets are arranged with special consideration for their capacity and strength. Every phase of home work, except cooking and laundrying, is taught in these classes. That pleasure and profit is derived from this weekly instruction is apparent from the demand for promotion to the regular Domestic Training School as soon as the age limit is attained. This is from eight to seventeen years, although coloured students up to twenty have gladly availed themselves of the opportunity for securing the training in Domestic Science afforded by this means. The children of all ages attend at the various centres each Saturday at 9.30 a.m. ; that particular hour is fixed to give both boys and girls time to assist previously in regular home duties, and thus to impress upon them the priority of home claims. The training is thoroughly practical in all lines of domestic work ; the children are asked to practise these weekly lessons at home, and the mothers can themselves have the methods taught to their children explained in special classes should they so desire. The Domestic Science Course is arranged as follows :—Cooking, seven lessons ; practical dining-room and table-setting classes, six lessons ; hall and stair-cleaning classes, four lessons ; parlour classes, three lessons ; bedroom classes, four lessons ; sewing classes, twelve lessons ; laundry, three lessons ; cellar, three lessons ; elementary Sloyd and woodwork, nine lessons ; whitewashing, one lesson.

---

* See Introduction to Report.

(a) India-
napolis
Kinder-
garten and
Domestic
Training
Schools—
centinued.

The food cooked is, so far as possible, that which the children could
afford to have at home; they are taught how to choose and use it
economically and to prepare it wholesomely. They keep their
own recipe-books, but are required to know their contents sufficiently well to cook from memory; incidentally they learn the care
of the kitchen, pantry, and closets. Right methods of daily,
weekly, and yearly cleaning are slowly and carefully inculcated,
by theory and in practice; while the practical dining-room work
includes, besides table-setting and serving, the proprieties of personal behaviour and the care at table of a baby or of little children.
The sewing course has six divisions; in the first the different stitches
are learnt, to be applied in the doll-dressing department; there
is a crochet class (for which the mothers asked) and another for
the mending of garments and the darning of stockings; the fifth
is ambitiously described as the Dressmaking School, in which the
use of the sewing machine is acquired; and, finally, satisfactory
results are quoted from the hat and bonnet trimming class, which
forms the sixth department. The superintendent, Mrs. Eliza A.
Blaker, reported to me that the result of this training is readily
apparent in many homes of the districts from which the children
attend; and from other sources I learnt what excellent results
follow the instruction. It seems as if the aims held in view were
actually attained. Mrs. Blaker states her objects to be the
brightening of the homes of to-day; the removal of drudgery from
home work; the formation of industrious habits; the inculcation
of the great value of personal cleanliness, courtesy, neatness,
method, clean houses, and well cooked food to others besides the
individual learner. Attendance is purely voluntary; it amounts
to 2,000 annually; the young pupils flock to the classes because
they really enjoy the work. The first of these Indianapolis
Domestic Training Schools was established in 1888, and the number
of centres has apparently increased at the rate of one a year. The
students at the Normal School at once volunteered their services
as helpers, whereupon an unforeseen result followed. In 1894
practical work in Domestic Training became the regular exercise
on Friday afternoon in the Normal School, where hitherto the
students had gained their information by theory only. Each
pupil has, since that date, rehearsed in practice the work she will
teach to, and require of, the children the following morning.
No materials were purchased with which to begin the teaching—
" Had we not rooms to sweep, chairs to be dusted, floors to be
scrubbed, woodwork to be cleansed?" Sewing, cooking, table-
setting, were introduced as occasion offered, and the majority of
necessary and desirable articles have been given by degrees.

The organisation of this Indianapolis Society is far-reaching,
for in this Domestic Science Department alone, in addition to the
work being carried on for children, fourteen Mothers' Classes on
Cooking and on the Training of Children are conducted in different
sections of the city, and the same subjects are dealt with in the
Young Women's Evening Clubs.

The School of Domestic Science attached to the Boston Branch of the Young Women's Christian Association provides a series of lessons in Domestic Science for primary school children, described as 'the " Kitchen Garden.''' Here again the course of ten hours' is devoted to lessons in cooking and to the practice of household occupations, by the use of toys and by means of songs and games. (*b*) Y.W.C.A. School of Domestic Science, Boston.

Another most interesting pioneer course exists at the Louisa M. Alcott Club, started in one of the poorest neighbourhoods of Boston by Miss Isabel F. Hyams, as a result of observing on all sides the ignorance of how to manage a home. She felt that to enter each house with a view to training its inmates would be, if not impossible, yet a great waste of power, and concluded that the young citizen should rather be trained in the principles of home-making through a system of " play in earnest," continued through several years of life, until the methods learnt would have become habitual. She therefore took a house in one of the most unpromising streets, furnished it brightly yet simply, and opened its doors to the children of the neighbourhood. The upper rooms are devoted to Kindergarten; the well-lit basement is reserved for these domestic classes. The utensils provided are of such a size and so arranged in the cupboards that they are within the reach of the smallest child, and each is entirely responsible for her own. They are taught to wash the dishes, set the table, sweep and dust; small brooms, dustpans, etc., being provided. As the lessons usually succeed the ordinary school day, they are rightly limited to one hour in length. This frequently necessitates previous preparation of some part of the work, as all the processes cannot be carried through in so short a time. For instance, if the lesson be on the service and clearing up of a meal, the food required must be prepared before the class assembles. The first year's experiment was but a qualified success; too much was attempted, and the character of the work proved unsatisfactory. The second year's experience was much more encouraging; provision was made for individual, not group, work, evidently indispensable to obtain the desired results. The average age of the youngest class is eight years. The kitchen is kept as near the home ideal as possible. Miss Hyams hopes eventually to furnish a living-room and bedroom in the same way. It must be remembered that the work is carried on in what we should describe as a slum district, where ignorance and often poverty prevail. No one in the neighbourhood occupies a whole house; many families live in dark rooms, with air-shafts only to ventilate the inside bedrooms; and the children are entirely unconscious of any other possible conditions; so the first lessons are given to thoughts about what constitutes a home. The rooms of a house are talked about in turn and their uses considered; then the children think out and decide the names and uses of the simple kitchen utensils provided. Next, they fill their own linen chest, a famous incentive to conquer the use of the needle. A start is made with cheese-cloth dusters, after which towels, napkins, and table-cloths are hemmed, each (*c*) The Louisa M. Alcott Club, Boston.

article being on a scale proportioned to its maker. This introduces the need for laundry work, to which the children take very kindly. The subject of cooking is approached through the consideration of some seasonable, familiar, and simple food, *e.g.*, the potato ; few of the children can at first trace its origin further back than the shop ; so a sprouting potato is examined, compared with other plants, and planted, to be finally compared with a picture. By this and other means their eyes are gradually opened to the realisation of the many agencies needed to provide the boiled potato which forms so common an article of daily diet. All the lessons and their subjects are taken up in this way ; a method which Miss Hyams feels to be best in this instance, as it widens the children's horizons and exercises their imagination and observation, while it guides them into more wholesome and intelligent habits The whole object of this particular club is to better the home conditions of a very poor neighbourhood, to further which a class for elder girls in cooking is also carried on. At first the preparation of a whole meal was tried with them, but time limits obliged this to be too hurried ; so at last the existing plan was devised. The lady in charge supervises the preparation of and gives the recipe for the dish selected at one lesson, while on the next occasion the girls are required to come in, set about and carry on the entire process alone, though their instructor remains in the room and assists where help proves necessary. This method, while making no serious demand on the children, leads to the exercise of attention, forethought, and good method.

Much care and ingenuity have been devoted to the equipment of this children's kitchen, which impressed me particularly by its practical completeness, compact arrangement, and the advantages it offers for the acquirement of orderly habits and a desirable sense of personal ownership. Three wooden shelves are fixed below the windows, right across one end of the room. These are sub-divided by partitions into ten cupboards, each two feet high by one foot wide ; in these are kept, respectively, a half-pint saucepan, bowl, baking-dish, tin plate, vegetable knife, fork, spoon, and other small ware. On the long shelf which forms the top of the series of cupboards, and on the wall above, are placed the articles less frequently used, such as scales, spice boxes, meat chopper, etc. The children have also an extension table for cooking and little chairs of the right height for meals, a refrigerator, a chest of drawers to hold table and kitchen linen, a china closet and gas range, etc., all small, but perfect in detail. The means for washing and ironing have also been provided ; tubs, trestle tables, irons, ironing boards, and so forth ; bare necessaries, no luxuries, but everything bears the impress of being used and kept decently and in order.

(*d*) Free Lectures.　The educational value of all this private enterprise in good habit training, with its eventual influence on public health, is not lost upon the Boards of Education in the cities where it is at work ; while its social worth is recognised, though as yet vaguely, by

TABLE XXXV.

CHAUTAUQUA (SUMMER) SCHOOL OF DOMESTIC SCIENCE.

INSTITUTION AND COURSE.	ENTRANCE REQUIREMENTS.	SCOPE OF COURSE.	LENGTH OF COURSE.	FEES.
Chautauqua School of Domestic Science. Normal Course in Domestic Science. Directress: Mrs. Alice Peloubet Norton.	(1) A High School Diploma or its equivalent. (2) Actual teaching experience.	*First Year.* General Chemistry. 8 hours a week: (Lectures and laboratory.) Physics. 5 ohrs a week: Energy in its forms : Air. Mr. Wells. Heat. Electricity. Physiology. 3 hrs a week : Chemical elements : Tissues and organs of human body ; circulation, respiration, and digestion. Botany of Food Plants. 5 hrs a week. (Lectures and microscope work.) Domestic Science. 5 ohrs a week : Food materials : Their composition, cost, and digestibility. Home Sanitation : Its planning, furnishing and care ; plumbing and drainage; physics and physiology of ventilation ; heating and lighting; the chemistry of combustion ; chemistry and bacteriology of cleaning. Cookery. 5 ohrs a week : Practice work. Food principles and laws of cooking. Animal, vegetable and cereal foods. Making of dough ; simple daily menus ; invalid cooking. *Second Year.* Applied Chemistry. 5 ohrs a week : (Laboratory work and lectures.) Qualitative tests of food materials. Study of proteids, starch, sugar. Physiology. 2 hrs a week : Animal functions. Muscular physiology. Digestion. (Illustrated with fresh specimens and mannikin.) Bacteriology. 5 ohrs per week : (Lectures and laboratory work.) Description and life history of bacteria. Methods of culture. Bacteria in dust, water, and milk, etc. Administration of Households. 5 ohrs a week. (Small and Large.) Household expenditure. Food as an economic factor. Diet and dietaries (schools and institutions.) Methods of keeping accounts. Housekeeping equipment. Helpers, their training, duties, hours, and wages. Economic buying and storing of food. Planning of menus with balanced ration. Simplest ways of serving meals. Experimental Cooking. 5 ohrs a week : Existing methods of preparing food judged by scientific standards. Pedagogy. 5 hrs a week : Principles of pedagogy as applied to the teaching of domestic science. Planning of courses. Sewing.—(Special fees with extra fee.)	2 years. 6 weeks a year.	First year, $40 (£8). Second year, $45 (£9). Single lectures, 35 cents (1s. 6d.).

many of the community at large. Some city Boards of Education have Saturday Morning Classes in Cooking and Sewing for girls, while these and Evening Classes for girls and adults are offered by practically all the Technical Institutes and in some Manual Training High Schools. The subjects of Physiology and Hygiene being obligatory in schools do not depend for their introduction upon outside agencies, but that an interest in them is manifesting itself among adults is evident from the fact that courses of instruction in them are becoming more general in the published schedules of Free Lectures; especially has this been the case in the boroughs of Manhattan and the Bronx, New York City. The Superintendent of the " Free Lectures to the People," Dr. H. M. Leipzinger, brought forward some interesting facts in this connection in his last Report. After drawing attention to the large and steady attendance at most of the centres, and to the discomfort frequently but cheerfully suffered by the crowded audiences (old men and women, after climbing sixty-five steps, obliged to sit on benches meant for children, etc.), he enumerates in order the subjects which excite this thirst to learn, and which, in one season, held the attention and awakened permanent interest among more than half a million middle-aged people. Physiology and Hygiene head the list; Civics appear in company with History and Geography, while Sociology closes the roll of first favourites, following after Music and Art. By means of illustrations, where possible by experiments and lantern views, the eye, ear and brain are stimulated and trained; so that he feels it to be now justifiable to plan a four-years' course in several lines of study, of which Hygiene is to be one. Those who wish to pursue a definite course will thus be enabled to get a general and well-defined outline of their subject; at the conclusion of the period they will be entitled to receive a certificate, which shall possess a genuine value.

(*e*) People's University Extension Society, N.Y.C.

(*f*) University Settlements.

Hygiene teaching on simple lines is undertaken by the People's University Extension Society of New York; while similar educational lectures are given by competent teachers at many University Settlements, among which special mention should be made of those at Hull House, Chicago. I must not omit to mention that domestic subjects are also included in the classes offered to boys and girls in most of the social settlements in New York City, Chicago, Cleveland, O., Columbus, O., and elsewhere. These, with many other branches of manual work, prove, exclusive of the excursions, the most popular features at the various schools carried on by voluntary agencies, in an increasing number of cities, during a part of the three months' summer vacation. It

(*g*) Vacation Schools.

would be beside the mark to dwell at length upon these Vacation Schools, with their ideas, methods and influences; though it has quite recently been proved in London, that the short holidays usual in England among the class of children they are designed to benefit, does not prevent the possibility of their successful introduction into this country.

C.—SUMMER SCHOOLS.

The case of Summer Schools for adults is somewhat different. These are also held during the long cessation of school work, rendered desirable by the intense heat of a climate very diverse from the English. They are attended by a great number of teachers of all subjects, so that the scholastic element is well represented ; but a large body of their students is furnished by members of other professions and by the leisured classes. Mothers of families will speak in a matter-of-fact way of the number of consecutive summers which have found them at one or other such school, in pursuit of knowledge either to equip themselves better for their household duties, for their social position, or to make them more intelligently companionable to their sons and daughters. These Summer Schools correspond somewhat to the University Extension Meetings held at Oxford and Cambridge, but are on a much larger scale ; their programmes offer a considerable range of practical courses in the arts and sciences ; while a feature is made of opportunities for consecutive study. These schools are attached to the greater number of Universities and Colleges, as well as occupying an independent position, as, for instance, the world-renowned Chautauqua. Professor Herbert B. Adams has given a vivid and exhaustive exposition of the popular enthusiasm for this class of education in his monograph for the Department of Education at the Paris Exhibition. (Monographs on Education in the United States, No. 16, " Summer Schools and University Extension".) The courses average six weeks in length, and, by judicious arrangement and selection, very real work can be accomplished. This possibility is illustrated by the comprehensive practical course in Household Science at Chautauqua.*

To illustrate that the civic side also is kept in view in these courses, I may mention those available for summer students at Chicago University. The Department of Sociology heads its list of Summer School lectures with the " Citizen as Householder " (the house as a factor in public health, the control of the householder by the State, his duties in relation to sanitation and food supplies) ; while the second course is on " Food Supplies and Dietaries " under the same professor, Dean Marion Talbot. Eight alternate courses are detailed, of which four are largely concerned with sanitary science, viz., the two just enumerated and two more, of which the titles are " The Elements and Structure of Society " (a study of the economic, physiological, social, æsthetic, intellectual and moral elements in American Society), and " Municipal Sociology."

The School of Education attached to the University also has classes in Home Economics and Art, and in Applied Art in its Summer School. These are, however, practically Normal, not general classes. Their end is the illustration of educational principles in connection with the subjects selected for study, with special reference to the needs of those who are already engaged in teaching ; the subject matter of the classes falls, therefore,

Side notes:

Typical Domestic Science Courses.—

(a) Chautauqua School of Domestic Science. Table XXXV.

(b) Chicago University.

(c) Chicago University School of Education. Table XXXVI.

---

* See Appendix J.

TABLE XXXVI.

CHICAGO UNIVERSITY SCHOOL OF EDUCATION.—SUMMER SCHOOL.

COURSE OF INSTRUCTION.	ENTRANCE REQUIREMENTS.	LENGTH OF COURSE.	FEES AND FINANCE.	SCOPE OF COURSES.
Summer Term of the School of Education. President:— Will. Rainey H a r p e r, Ph.D., D.D., LL.D.	Open to all, but intended especially for teachers and teachers elect.	Six weeks, divided into two terms.	$10 a term. $20 the full course. Average amount of expenses for six weeks (including tuition fees) $69 (about £14).	Education: Philosophy of education. Training and supervision of teachers. Applied pedagogy. Kindergarten: Introductory Course (for primary teachers). Advanced course (for experienced Kindergartners). Work with the Kindergarten children. Natural Science: Pedagogics of Nature Study. General Chemistry. Elementary Biology. Museum: Arrangement and preservation of collections suitable for public schools. Home Economics: Lectures and laboratory work in Applied Chemistry. History and Literature: History and Literature for the elementary schools. History and Literature for the primary grades. Geography: General Geography. French: Pedagogy of the teaching of the French language. Beginners in French. Mathematics: Mathematics of the High School. Arithmetic for the Intermediate and Grammar Grades. Applied Mathematics. Speech and Oral Reading: Speech, reading and dramatic art. Art: Nature Study, Drawing and Painting; illustrations of history, etc. Chalk and clay modelling. Applied Art: Textiles, woodwork, book-binding. Manual Training: Course in woodwork. Course for Primary Grades. Physical Training: Educational Gymnastics. The basis of Gymnastic Development. Corrective work (bas-d upon anatomy and the science of nutrition.) Dancing and Gymnastic Dancing. Primary games adapted to the school-room. Library: Library economy. Music: Psychology and Pedagogy of Music.

NOTE.—The regular work for a summer student is three courses; any of those on the list may be selected except Art, Applied Art, Library and Museum work (which are always extras); each course takes five hours a week. A charge of $7.50 is made for each extra subject taken in addition to the regular work.

within the fields of elementary and secondary education, treated from the point of view of philosophy and pedagogy. The course in Home Economics consists of lectures and laboratory work in Applied Chemistry, the Study of Food Principles, the Chemistry of Food Fermentation, Detection of Food Adulterants and Preservatives, etc. Cooking and Sewing, as introduced into the primary grades, are discussed also in another course on Applied Pedagogy.

So widespread is this system of Summer Schools that it is quite impossible to do more than thus concisely indicate the attention their organisers devote to the study of Domestic Science and Art, an attention rendered necessary by the demand, not among members of the teaching profession only, but among the public in general, who find in them a useful and feasible means of acquiring information and practical experience. The fees, naturally somewhat variable in amount, are distinctly reasonable; the teaching staff is, as a rule, chosen with care, and of a high quality.

D.—University Extension.

The University Extension system of instruction in these subjects is also successful, and has developments of detail in the several States to meet local and particular needs. It acts in more ways than one as a support and a stimulus to the Women's Clubs, the Farmers' Institutes, and to similar organisations for self and communal improvement. When employed, as is habitual in this country, its lectures furnish the expert's standpoint, desirable in the study of any subject, but especially so where the students are drawn from those whose sphere and experience are somewhat limited and along similar lines. When active chiefly by means of its Travelling Libraries it brings the written views of leading authorities into the homes of those who, owing to narrow means or to home claims, are unable otherwise to come in touch with this suggestive material. If this agency for education be " extended " into a reading course, controlled by some department of the University with which it is connected, correspondents are guided in their studies, encouraged to submit practical problems to their directors, and to persevere in one line of work until a degree of thoroughness has been attained. The Travelling Library method is specially well organised in New York State, under the leadership of Mr. Melvil Dewey, State Librarian of the New York Library at Albany. Compliance with the rules he has framed requires, for instance, that one subject must be studied for at least ten weeks; continuity to this extent is insisted upon. Excellent printed outlines of the topics included in the selected subjects are prepared by experts, and are supplied at nominal fees. Members are expected to submit occasional written exercises for criticism, and occasional conferences with qualified lecturers are advised. The admirable syllabus on " Home Economics " is reproduced by kind permission in Appendix L., and gives an insight into the care and skill lavished upon these publications,

Illustrations of System of Instruction in Domestic Science Subjects.

(a) New York State Travelling Library.

(b) Cornell University Reading Courses for Farmers' Wives.

Cornell University has also organised Reading Courses, in which it is customary to send short especially prepared lessons to the students, followed after a brief interval by a paper of questions. Each subject is under the charge of a professor of wide practical experience. For example, the general supervision of reading courses for farmers' wives is entrusted to Miss Martha Van Rensselaer, who, as a result of her sympathetic work, has a large and constant correspondence among her flock; this enables her to give individual advice on questions which arise out of their perusal of the "Reading Lessons," and opens her mind to the needs, aspirations, and limitations of her correspondents, a source of valuable guidance in the preparation of her quarterly "Bulletin." Each quarter also sees a useful Supplement, issued gratuitously to the 6,000 members, on some home question, sanitary, economic, etc., freely illustrated, absolutely practical, eminently suggestive. That for January, 1900, was entitled, "Saving Steps." It is so full of useful hints that it is hard to resist the temptation to reproduce it in its entirety. The text taken is, "All household improvements which can be provided to conserve a woman's strength will add to her power and efficiency." The exposition suggests a hundred feasible ways for the attainment of this end, while the illustrations graphically depict their practical application in kitchen and parlour. Similar in tone and value is "Home Sanitation," issued in April, 1901; not the least interesting part of which is, "What our correspondents say"—an appendix consisting of the comments, suggestions and criticisms elicited by the previous number. It would be tedious to enumerate further the subjects and methods of treatment in these Bulletins; that they meet a need is evident, that they are doing valuable work in the formation of an intelligent public opinion is unquestionable. They awaken the minds of farmers and their wives to the usually unrecognised fact that housekeeping is a fine art, and that women possess the ability to change much that is passively permitted to prejudice the health and happiness of a family. They direct thought and attention to modes of healthful living, and teach that to minister to the bodily, intellectual, and spiritual needs of humanity is the highest type of world's work. They show that to accomplish this it is unnecessary to sacrifice either woman's health or comfort; for by intelligent thought and skilled practice mountains of tacitly existing difficulties and prejudices may be surmounted or removed. The circular of suggestions for initiating such Reading Courses in new districts is worthy of attention from those who recognise the opening which exists for similar work in this country.*

E.—The Domestic Service Problem.

With the energy characteristic of their nation, the women of the Eastern States have set themselves seriously to study that acute problem, the Domestic Service question; fortunately for the cause in which they are interested they are animated by a spirit of dogged determination which remains undaunted by the discourage-

---

* See Appendix K.

ments which attend their investigations. That the complexities which are encountered should be intricate and well-nigh innumerable appears inevitable in the conduct of an inquiry where social, economic, professional, and domestic interests are all concerned ; that the difficulties are very real is recognisable, when the conditions incidental to the collection of accurate information on so delicate a subject are taken into account. To grumble and remain quiescent is an old-world monopoly ; to grumble and find therein a spur to action of some sort appears to be instinctive among the members of a younger race. As the activity, in this instance, first arose amongst the most highly educated women it assumed a sound form. Careful observations of existing conditions, under which domestic service becomes increasingly unpopular, were succeeded by a series of carefully-conducted investigations, upon which reliable statistics might be based, and certain assertions and conclusions tested. The Massachusetts Labour Bureau has prepared and published three studies of considerable interest upon this subject, consisting of information collected by the Women's Educational and Industrial Union of Boston and the School of Housekeeping. Of these the first was issued in 1898, entitled, "The Hours of Labour in Domestic Service" ; the second appeared in 1900, under the title of "Social Conditions of Domestic Service ; " the third was made public in 1901, and deals with some "Social Statistics of Working Women." The inquiries were in each case hampered by the very personal relations of mistress to maid, which lead the former usually to resent requests for explicit information ; the result of this attitude is that deductions have to be made from relatively small numbers. The first bulletin, for instance, embodies the analysis of returns from 184 different families in which 289 persons were employed ; though few in number, these were found to be decidedly representative of the general conditions obtaining in Boston. It appears that the average length of a day's work for all branches of domestic service somewhat exceeded twelve hours ; that, although the employees nominally had a "day out," the full amount of business time on that day amounted to but three hours less than the daily average for the entire week ; and on Saturdays about four hours less ; and that restrictions existed as to the employment of "free time" (reception of visitors ; meals not to be served to friends ; stated hour of return usually 10 p.m.). All these facts substantiate some of the invariable objections raised to this occupation, viz., the difference between the number of hours required in domestic service and the amount and character of free time afforded, as compared with conditions which obtain in factories and some kinds of mercantile employment, plus the indefiniteness of the hours, which many consider to be an insuperable drawback. In the 1900 bulletin, attention is directed to the unfortunate "social stigma" which attaches to domestic servants.

Massachusetts Labour Bureau Bulletins, showing existing conditions.

"No criticism is intended, either direct or implied, of either mistress or servant. The fragmentary character of the data, and the comparatively

limited field covered by the inquiries may be at once admitted. It is,
however, beyond question that while certain social opportunities are enjoyed
by those who are employed in the factory or the shop, due, in a measure,
to unity of action on the part of the workers, and to generally accepted
customs growing out of the employment, in domestic service there is
neither uniformity of privilege nor recognised social status. There is
neither clear recognition of mutual responsibility and reciprocal rights
and duties which marked the old relation of mistress and servant, nor
the equally well defined relations which in industrial or mercantile employment exist between employer and employee. The domestic has ceased
to be a servant as that term was formerly used ; she has not yet become
an employee as that term is now used in industrial occupations."

Inquiries addressed to 181 families included the following
topics :—" What church is attended, and to what extent does it
play a part in the social life of your servants ? What opportunities
do you offer for intellectual improvement ? What is the character
of the reading they affect—is the servant allowed access to the
library, or given newspapers ? When not on duty, what opportunities for enjoyment are open to her (playing on a musical instru-
ment, attendance at a choral class, etc.), is she permitted to entertain visitors ? Is she afforded opportunity to do her personal
sewing ? Is she given facilities to attend lectures, entertain-
ments, or classes for self-improvement ?" The data collected
exemplified every possible variety of treatment of, and interest in,
the welfare of the servant concerned ; to tabulate or work out
percentages is impossible, but it would seem that the words used by
Professor Mary Roberts Smith in a recent number of the " Forum "
might be considered to their advantage by many employers.
" Whatever is done for manners or morals must be done, as for
other working girls, by establishing friendly relations with them,
and by winning them to more refined conceptions of life. The
want of rational social pleasures and of opportunities for self-
education is the result of all the conditions just discussed, to
which must be added the one most fatal of all, namely, the want
of aspiration. With the improvement of other conditions, this will
remedy itself. But the desire for some social and intellectual recreation may be stimulated through clubs, books, and amusements.
To all these the mistress can at least contribute the stimulus of her
own culture and friendly interest."

The following conclusion, quoted from the last published investigation, suggests that in some respects at least, the conditions of
domestic service in England and the United States have a good
deal in common : " The social and economic conditions prevailing
in domestic service place it quite apart from other groups. It
appears that *houseworkers* have less free time and fewer vacation
privileges than the women in other groups ; that these employees
are generally foreign born ; and that they have had fewer educational opportunities than the others. The conditions of their
employment, especially when but one employee is engaged in a
family, often isolate them from other workers and tend to a
narrower point of view. Their home surroundings, and, to a
large extent, their social environment, must vary greatly, since

these are dependent on the conditions prevailing in the families in which they are employed and are largely governed by the will of the employer, and their content of life must be correspondingly affected. On the other hand, housework has a decided advantage from the standpoint of healthfulness; and the food and general surroundings of the employees in housework are frequently somewhat better than in other employments. Making due allowance for board and lodging, the wages of the houseworkers appear to be better also; at any rate, they seem to have a larger surplus. A fairly skilled houseworker is in little danger of being out of employment for any length of time. The consideration which more than anything else leads women to prefer factory, shop, or restaurant work to housework, appears to be the greater independence enjoyed in these employments."

The next point considered has been the possible sources of relief for the tension which now exists. What are the remedies proposed by our neighbours? It seemed to me they are broadly divisible into three groups:— *Proposed Remedie.*

I. Those which are directed to the organisation of domestic service as a profession or skilled trade.

II. Those which would dignify domestic service, as a necessity coincident with the growing desire to elevate home life in all departments. The supporters of this view would not confine training in household occupations to one section of its members; their scheme requires the intelligent co-operation of all.

III. Those which, seeing in the discontent of the servant class a part of the evolutionary process going on throughout the world, and viewing it as a process of preparation for new developments (incidentally disagreeable, because society is not yet wholly ripe for the change), recommend intelligent adjustment to new conditions.

The supporters of the first opinion point out that the old relation of master and servant has passed away, and that of employers and employee must be established. *(a) Household Service as a Profession.*

Miss Haggenbotham has usefully summarised what this involves in a paper she read at the semi-annual meeting of the Housekeeper's Alliance at Philadelphia, May 30th, 1900. She said:—"Women must frankly accept this situation and strive to understand what mutual obligations this relation (of employer and employee) imposes; and what changes must be made to meet the new conditions. The new relation cannot be at once established—it must be a growth—an evolution from present conditions—not a revolution. No movement can be made to-day that will to-morrow lift household service at a bound to the plane of other forms of labour. Much progress may be made, however, if women, everywhere united into some such association as the Housekeepers' Alliance, will agree upon certain principles and certain general measures in the conduct of the household, which may be advocated as advantageous to the relations between the housekeeper and her domestic labourers. A few suggestions are offered in the hope that they may provoke discussion and form the basis of a movement towards establishing household service on business principles so far as is consistent with the very large personal element that enters into it.

(a) House-
hold Service
as a
Profession
—continued.

" 1. *We claim that the employer should offer fair conditions for efficient
and faithful service; and that the employee on his or her part
should recognise that efficient and faithful service should be
rendered for fair wages and just conditions.*

" Some standard should be fixed. It rests with the employer, being
presumably the better educated and equipped of the two, to prove that
the interests of employer and employee are the same, and to lead the way
in reasonable, business-like action. Let the employers consider what may
be regarded as 'fair conditions,' and frankly state them and agree to
hold to them even at the cost of some personal inconvenience. Let them
then invite the consideration of these conditions by the employees, and
also in return let them consider what rights and privileges they (the employees) have to ask for themselves. Everywhere, except in the household,
mutual interests are drawing together 'for consultation, for economy
of forces and resources, those engaged in the same activities.'

" 2. *A standard of work and wages should be established.*

" Here again the employer must lead and stand firm. So long as the
unskilled worker can command as much as the skilled worker, so long
will employees be indifferent to the advantages for improvement offered
by the Schools of Housekeeping. There should be a discrimination in
wages paid, according to the length of time for which the employee is to
serve. Much unreason exists on the part of both employer and employee
on this point. A domestic whose work is worth say \$3.50 per week,
may, through the desperation of some employer, obtain a place at \$5.
Of course she loses the place as soon as a more competent person can be
found to replace her. But for ever after the \$3.50 person will contend
for \$5—declaring 'that is what I have had '—and for days and weeks
she will lose all wages until she has consumed many times the difference
between her real value and the fictitious one. Employers, on the other
hand, will frequently refuse to pay for those whom they know they shall
need for only eight or ten months in the year, more than others are paid
who have employment all the year round. This is not paralleled by the
custom in any other field of labour. The man who has permanent work
of any kind does not expect to receive the same pay as one who is employed
only temporarily, or for a fraction of a year.

" 3 *A fair amount of time should be allowed for rest and recreation.
Stated times of absolute freedom should be agreed upon and the
privilege should be accorded, within due limits, of receiving
and entertaining friends.*

" There are still many 'mistresses' who object to the 'afternoon out'
and to the visitor, forgetting that change and recreation are absolutely necessary to the preservation of normal conditions in the human being ; and
forgetting that servants are mentally and socially constituted very much as
their masters and mistresses are. The best domestic economy in the world
would dictate the wisdom of ample provisions for change and recreation.
It is unfortunate that most houses are so constructed that there is no convenient place for the servant to receive her friends outside of the kitchen.
If, however, public sentiment recognises the need of such provision, future
architectural schemes will take it into account.

" 4. *Everything reasonable should be done to lessen the 'drudgery'
in housework.*

" In proportion as intelligence and skill are offered on the part of the
employee, employers should provide labour saving machines and all appur-
tenances that will lessen the irritation and nervous strain of striving to
make bricks without straw—in other words, of striving to perform the
work of the household without the proper equipment.

"5. *As steps towards lessening the disadvantages of household services, employers should give their attention to the subject | bakeries and laundries.*

" It is an enormous waste of strength and of money to carry on a hundred family washes with a hundred separate fires, yet the lawlessness of laundries is a serious menace to health ; and the conscientious housewife rightly hesitates about patronising them. The same may be said of bakeries in general. These institutions should be established under sanitary regulations, and placed with dairies and food supply institutions under restriction of the law. Household employers should see that these things are done.

" 6. As a further aid in raising the standard of household service and making it a business, it is suggested—

" *To abolish private employment agencies and intelligence offices, and substitute either Government employment bureaus or reputable business institutions, like the employment bureau of the Housekeepers' Alliance, which shall be conducted with intelligent regard for the office they assume to fill.*

"The ordinary intelligence office is responsible for a large part of the degradation of household service."

These ideas underlie the experiments being now, I believe, made at Chicago and Boston ; they consist in an undertaking to supply servants from a central bureau for days of eight hours, the bureau holding itself responsible for the uninterrupted service of its clients on strictly business lines. At present English home life could not easily adapt itself to such a method of service ; the more active part taken by the mistress and family in the domestic duties of the average American household renders possible, if not desirable, what would be at present impossible here. Nevertheless, the conception of domestic service as a profession, and the reasonable proposals of Miss Haggenbotham merit full consideration.

With reference to the second point of view I enumerated (the restoration of dignity to domestic work), the writer just quoted comments upon " the aversion to household labour, both inside and outside of the home, as a marked characteristic of the present generation. Children are reared to despise the arts of the household, and to treat with scant respect those who practise them. Wage earners who can find any other avenue of employment shun that of household service, though it offers moral and material advantages that belong to no other employment. Young people enter upon married life not only ignorant of the necessary work of the household, but without any clear conception of the ethical relations involved in the family community, and without the faintest idea as to how the family income ought to be spent—what percentage may be paid for rent, food, clothing, etc. The man does not manage his business that way, but it never seems to occur to him that his housekeeping is a business ; or, if it does, he concludes that it is his wife's special domain ; and his only duty is to look with indulgent eye upon her ignorance and failures . . . .
It has been justly said that 'a very large part of the wealth produced in the world is consumed in the household, yet neither those who produce nor those who consume know on what principle it is done.' . . . .
" Public sentiment does not yet demand the preparation of the woman for what is commonly claimed to be her ' heaven-appointed ' mission—the wife and the homemaker. It is vaguely believed that when the necessity arises, some domestic instinct will quicken in her, and enable her to administer the duties of her office without previous thought or training. This is an anomaly that exists in no other walk in life. But a household cannot be run on the inspiration plan any more than can a factory, a

(*b*) Restoration of Dignity to Domestic Work.

(*b*) Restora-
tion of
Dignity to
Domestic
Work —
continued.
steel plant, or a department store. Household service can never become
a business (or trade) and command the same respect as other forms of
labour, until there is a better general conception of household affairs from
an ethical, sociological and economic standpoint. With this conception
will come a greater respect for the household and those who work in it ;
and then will come also a demand for the better equipment of the *employer
and the employee,* and for the application of the scientific and business principles needful for the organisation of the modern household." . . . .
" This conception can be attained only by the greater prevalence of education in the true sense of the word. In addition to the mental training
which the so-called ' higher ' education is striving to give, there must
be, for all classes, from the lowest to the highest, for the poor
equally with the rich, an education in the true standards of living, in
what constitutes better homes, more comfortable conditions ; and in a
clearer perception of those tendencies towards mere imitation and luxury
which lead to the degeneration of mind and body." . . . . " Social
training in ethical ideals, and the inculcation of the belief that home-
making must be the woman's profession, for which she requires a power-
giving knowledge, must become accepted factors in the education of every
woman, rich or poor." . . . . " Women are especially responsible
for the promotion of this better education through which alone can be
accomplished a readjustment in household organisation in accordance
with modern conditions."

I quote Miss Haggenbotham's words because the patience of my
readers must have been taxed by the frequent presentation of the
same idea, in my own language, throughout this Report. Let the
thought but once permeate the people that all which conduces to
the fullest development of the human being is honourable in the
highest degree ; that the knowledge necessary to this right care
demands the exercise of the best intellectual faculties and is no mere
illiterate " rule of thumb " drudgery ; and a different complexion is
placed upon domestic service. But with its removal from the
ranks of unskilled labour comes the question of pay. Will those
who desire assistance pay for skilled work ? Will they combine to
demand it, and be courageous in the endurance of inevitable
difficulties during the period that this changed attitude on their
part is being realised by a class, whose capacity for duties assumed
has not been hitherto tested by any defined standard ; whose
members, indeed, from the pressing need of employers have in
most cases been accepted at their own valuation ? Miss Haggenbotham refers to the " ethical, sociological, and economic " aspects
of household service as being yet but imperfectly apprehended by
either employers or employees ; and I think with justice. Considered from the ethical standpoint, the mistress owes a duty to her
maid, the maid to her mistress ; in thousands of instances this is
fulfilled in a measure ; in thousands it is ignored. Suitable and
wholesome conditions and opportunities for self-improvement are
the due of each member of a household. Conscientious performance of duties undertaken is the return rightly demanded for
wages paid ; damage to food or furniture resulting from ignorant
assumption of positions for which no qualifications have been
acquired, slovenly evasions of routine work agreed to at the time
of engagement, are acts of dishonesty ; they constitute a breach of

ethical duty. The sociological standpoint I shall refer to under the opinion of Group III. The economic standpoint is as yet dimly grasped by either party concerned in a calling which has not progressed in company with almost all other means of livelihood in the industrial and commercial worlds. There are members of the directing classes who refuse to recognise that a trained worker must be worth more than an untrained; who deplore " education " as the undoing of domestic service; who do not anticipate the day with any satisfaction when training will be insisted upon, and rate of pay regulated by other rules than the needs of a large family or the pressing inconveniences which often lead to the overpayment of the undeserving. To develop a comprehension of the economic point of view employers should have a more than theoretical acquaintance with the work in question; they should know the time necessarily absorbed in some processes; the immense saving of time to be effected in others through skill, or the use of labour-saving appliances, or the thoughtful rearrangement of kitchen and pantry. They must be trained to appreciate the better class of work which coincides with judicious recreation and suited diversity of interest; and they should study the history of combination and the advantages to be derived from co-operation, if employees are to be guided into the right conception of their relation to employers. The simpler social life in the United States undoubtedly facilitates this self-discipline of housekeepers, while the larger proportion of highly educated women has already led to a modicum of recognition of the imperative claims of these ethical and economic considerations. Not that the period of discomfort incidental to a stage of transition is passed; the present pangs are sharper than with us, but a few tentative efforts are being made to gain relief, based on scientific observation of the past and intelligent adaptation of the knowledge so acquired to the needs of to-day. A few mistresses are submitting themselves to courses of training; unremitting efforts are being made by a small number of thoughtful women to induce girls *to* train and employers to make it worth their while to do so. In an annually increasing number of schools, colleges and institutes, the dignity of ministering with intelligence to the needs of the body is impressed upon the young people. Nevertheless, some years must necessarily elapse even in that country of mercurial activity before it will be possible to gauge results of these tentative reforms with any degree of accuracy.

My report of the opinions held by Group III. must be very concise; the grounds upon which they are based are detailed with some elaboration in an article by Miss A. S. Vrooman on the " Servant Question," published in the " Arena " for June, 1901. This lady points out that the acute stage of her subject, from which society is suffering, is in reality the effect of a great force, actively contributing towards the preparation of humanity for a full co-operative life. The process she admits is far from agreeable. Those who share her views maintain that the home of to-day presents in

(c) Reconstruction of Domestic Life.

miniature a picture of " society in its strife, its unequal division of labour and enjoyments, its suppression of some for the luxurious self-indulgence of others." The process of home destruction evident to some eyes in the rapid growth (in New York City and elsewhere) of the " apartment house " is antecedent in her opinion only to construction on sounder lines. The " apartment house " in its present form is but a milestone on the road of domestic evolution ; in its methods may be seen the crude beginnings of a new system, that of co-operative housekeeping.

Miss Vrooman writes very helpfully upon one point, namely, the somewhat unwise use made of their liberty by domestic servants when all restrictions are removed from the employment of their leisure hours. The latitude they permit themselves is a favourite argument with employers against the granting of periods of recreation. " First effects of emancipation usually appear as an argument against it ; a fact familiar to the student of sociology ; therefore patient forbearance needs to be exercised with the servant class ; only after long emancipation from restraint is the sense of personal responsibility and self-control developed ; yet both a sense of responsibility and the power of self-control are essential qualities to honest intelligent service."

Miss Salmon on Domestic Service. *Miss Salmon has rendered a real service to the cause of Domestic Service by the scholarly methods in which she presents it. In the first instance she draws attention to the omission of domestic service from previous theoretical, statistical and historical discussions of economic problems, for which she accounts mainly because (1) the occupation does not involve the investment of a large amount of capital on the part of the individual employer or employee ; (2) no combinations have yet been found among employers or employees ; (3) the products of domestic service are more transient than are the results of other forms of labour. After an interesting enumeration of various subsidiary explanations of the failure to consider domestic service in connection with these other forms of labour, Miss Salmon concludes that these are all in reality but different phases of one fundamental reason—the isolation that has always attended household service and household employments. Though the facts revealed in her historical sketch of Domestic Employments in the United States are not identical with those which a similar study would bring to light in this country, they deserve our attention and point to conclusions to which analogous inquiries in Great Britain would probably lead, viz., that the question is one of preparing for the next step in the process of evolution, not of retrograding towards a condition impossible to restore. Domestic service is not only amenable to some of the general economic laws and conditions which affect other occupations,

---

*A most valuable epitome of her scientific and thorough study of this servant question is found in her book on " Domestic Service," by Miss Lucy M. Salmon, Professor of History at Vassar College. In this volume she approaches her subject as part of the general labour problem ; the first real attempt to treat it from the historical and economic, rather than from the personal standpoint. Her comments suggest that in the recognition of the professional aspect of the problem lies its solution.
The book is published by Macmillan & Co.

but is also governed by economic laws developed within itself. " The difficulties that meet the employer of domestic labour both in America and Europe are the difficulties that arise from the attempt to harmonise an ancient, patriarchal industrial system with the conditions of modern life. Everywhere the employer closes his eyes to the incongruities of the attempt and lays the blame of failure, not to a defective system, but to the natural weaknesses in the character of the unfortunate persons obliged to carry it out. The difficulties in the path of both employer and employee will not only never be removed but will increase until the subject of domestic service is regarded as a part of the great labour question of the day and given the same serious consideration.' (Chapter VI.) Miss Salmon devotes some space to the consideration of the advantages of domestic service, which, though patent, are unequal to counter-balancing the industrial and social disadvantages which she discusses. More to my immediate purpose is her enumeration of the popularly prescribed remedial measures which she truthfully describes as " doubtful," and of which she disposes one by one, for the good reasons that they do not touch the economic, educational, and industrial difficulties, or that they run at right angles to general economic, educational and industrial progress.

They include the application of intelligence by the employer ; the reception of the employee into the family of the employer ; increased employment of negro or Chinese labour ; the licensing of domestic employees by municipal corporations ; the system of German service books ; the abolition of public schools above the primary grade, on the ground that girls are educated above their station ; the introduction of housework into all public schools, a proposition which ignores the fact that it is the function of the public school to educate, not to supply information on technical subjects ; and the establishment of training schools for servants, a plan which Miss Salmon considers in opposition to present political and social tendencies ; lastly, co-operative housekeeping.

She points out that relief from present difficulties must be sought in accordance with certain social and economic tendencies ; among which she mentions the concentration of capital and labour in large industrial enterprises ; specialisation in every department of labour, and the training this necessitates ; the association for mutual benefit of persons interested in special lines of work ; the growth of productive and distributive co-operation ; greater industrial independence on the part of women ; finally, " that result of the systematic study of social conditions which aims at the amelioration of some of the conditions under which work is performed, not at the cessation of the work itself. The application of these principles has led to wiser charities, to the Chautauqua movement, to University Extension, to working girls' clubs, to enlarged opportunities everywhere for every class, . . . " they mean that ultimately the position in society of every person is to depend not on his occupation, but on the use he has made of these increasing opportunities for self help and self improvement ; they mean that in time all social stigma will be removed from every occupation, and work will be judged by its quality rather than its

nature; that in time, for example, a first-class cook will receive
more honour than a second-class china decorator or a third-class
teacher."

Miss Salmon concludes this portion of her book as follows :—
" The general remedies must include a wider prevalence of education in the true sense of the word, not its counterfeit, information ;
that mental education which results in habits of accuracy, precision and observation, in the exercise of reason, judgment and
self-control ; and that education of character which results in the
ability constantly to put one's self in the place of another. There
must be scientific training and investigation in economic theory,
history, and statistics, especially in their application to the household, and an increased popular knowledge of all scientific subjects
concerning the home. . . . The educational forces must ' pull
from the top ' and draw domestic service into the general current
of industrial development." (Chap. XI.) Miss Salmon looks with
hopeful anticipation for the future to improvement in the social
condition of employees ; to specialisation of household employments so far as possible ; and to education in household affairs, *i.e.*,
the careful, systematic education of housekeepers, through the
study of art, chemistry, economics, physiology, psychology, and
history. " Housekeeping must advance," she maintains, and must
become " on its own part an active creative force." She also traces
the prevalent inactivity in all household affairs to three causes,
(1) the belief that a knowledge of all things pertaining to the house,
home, and family, " unlike anything else, comes by instinct " ;
(2) the assumption that household affairs concern women only,
whereas, " when the fact is everywhere recognised that both men
and women have a vital concern in the affairs of the house, the
relation between the different parts of the household will become an
organic one, and its highest development reached "; (3) the erroneous
conviction that " all women have a natural taste for household affairs,
which without cultivation grows into positive genius for carrying
them on." Systematic and scientific training in, and professional
investigation of, all matters appertaining to the household, this is a
concise summary of Miss Salmon's Recommendations, each of which
she considers to be essential to lift the subject " out of the domain
of sentiment and to transfer it to a realm where reason and judgment have control." The chapter entitled " Conclusion " is too
condensed to be further summarised ; in the space of ten pages the
problem and its solution are compressed into the proverbial nutshell.
Space is also found to touch upon several complications which
obtain in this country as in hers ; for instance, the growing wealth
of the nation and increased luxury in living ; the natural con-
servatism of many women ; the desire of both employers and
employees to get everything for nothing—" the largest expenditure
of woman for the smallest expenditure of money " ; the many
elements of uncertainty which enter into a woman's life. Miss
Salmon claims no novelty or originality for her remedial proposals,

but we are indebted to her for a clear statement of a complicated
case, wherein lies my excuse for detailing somewhat *in extenso* views,
which, after all, can only be adequately digested by their study in
her own pages. One strong conviction, which she reiterates, has
so close a connection with the subject of this Report that its
proper introduction would alone justify this lengthy presentation
of her views :—" One thing, and only one thing, will turn the household into the channel where every other occupation has made
advancement. This is the establishment of a great professional
school, amply equipped for the investigation of all matters pertaining
to the household, and open only to graduates of the leading colleges
and universities of the country. . . . Professional training and
investigation must supplement home and collegiate instruction in
the case of the housekeeper, as the professional school supplements
private and collegiate instruction for the physician, the lawyer and
the clergyman." Indications are not wanting that this desired
opportunity will be presently afforded in the United States ; times
in England are not perhaps yet ripe for such a movement, even
were funds and other essentials available for the purpose ; but,
meanwhile, we can profit by the inquiries, experiences and investigations of a less conservative people. At least we can begin to
set our own ideas in order, and endeavour by judicious methods,
at school, at technical institute, and at college, to open the minds
of all classes to the economic, social, hygienic, and industrial principles, upon a due recognition of which depends any feasible
solution of the domestic service problem.

While fully alive to the fact that the diverse sociological conditions which exist in the two countries demand diverse treatment
of a difficulty which confronts both, I still believe that a thoughtful
study of the writings of our American sisters upon the subject will
prove instructive and suggestive to those called upon to grapple
with its complexities ; and I confidently look to a measure of
success being attained here as there by the same means ; viz.,
the suitable training in their duties of both parties to these engage-
ments ; a more extended and intelligent study of the economic
side of housekeeping (economy of time, labour, strength, and
money) ; and a consistent and sustained national effort to dignify
home life and all the term comprehends. The college women of
the States are foremost in this movement of reform. They pride
themselves upon their skill in the performance of daily domestic
duties equally with their achievements in literature and history,
or in their selected branches of science. It behoves the " educated "
women of England to bring their skilled minds and trained bodies
also to the aid of their less intelligent or capable sisters, in order
that the period of unrest and waste of energy may be shortened
and the necessary adjustment made to the changes consequent upon
social evolution. To attempt to remedy the increasing troubles,
the whole situation must be studied from the bottom ; the same
patient and scientific method must be used as in the interpretation

of an obscure fact in natural history, or in the decision upon a vexed question in the history of nations.   Trained minds must be brought to bear on the subject, intelligent heads and willing hands must all work together.   The responsibilities of all concerned must be recognised ; rank does not release from obligation, neither does the possession of exceptional mental ability or of abundant means relieve from liability.   Were the efforts to solve the domestic service problem now being made in England accorded the intelligent and active support furnished to similar movements in the United States, the outlook would assume a brighter aspect than is at present apparent to an interested observer.

SUMMARY OF ENQUIRY.

Prior to my visit to the United States, in 1901, I was provided for my guidance with certain " Suggested Heads of Enquiry," intended to cover, more or less, the scope of my commission.   A brief résumé of the resultant Report, reproduced in the order of these instructions, suggests itself as a suitable form of conclusion ; for while it should serve to gauge the thoroughness with which I executed the commission entrusted to me, it will, at the same time, focus the main points to which reference has been made in the preceding pages.

Scope of Enquiry.

The first of these " Suggestions " detailed the subjects into the position and teaching of which I was to enquire, all of these being included in this country under the title of Domestic Science, viz :— Cookery, Laundry Work, Housewifery, including learning to purchase commodities, the Elements of Domestic and Personal Hygiene, Needlework, Dressmaking, Millinery, Care of the Nursery, and of Children.   The general practice in the United States is to divide the above subjects into three groups :—(1) Cookery (which always includes some practical Housewifery), Laundry-work, and the Care of Children, which are all comprehended under Domestic, or Home, or Household Science, as it is variously described ; (2) Needlework, Dressmaking and Millinery, which are classified as Domestic Arts ; (3) Personal and Domestic Hygiene, which is invariably based upon Physiology, and forms a part of the ordinary State school curriculum ; as such being studied co-educationally by all children, boys and girls alike.   In many Elementary Schools, and in some Secondary, cookery and needlework appear under the designation of Manual Training, being used with that intention for girls, while boys are engaged in wood or iron work.   " Household Economics " is a term much favoured when the broadest aspect of the whole subject is intended ; that is to say, when technical skill in the domestic applications is based upon a sound knowledge of the fundamental sciences and arts, supplemented by a comprehension of the ethical and economic principles involved in their intelligent employment.

The second " Suggestion " dealt with the classification of the differ-

ent grades and types of institution in which these subjects, under Classifi-
whatever designation, are taught, *e.g.*, Primary Day Schools, cation and
Evening Continuation Schools for pupils from thirteen to sixteen Character of
years of age or older, Secondary Day Schools, Technical Institutes, Institutions.
Training Colleges for Teachers in the above various types of schools
and Universities.

The fact is familiar that English methods of school nomenclature
vary from those adopted in the States; Elementary Day Schools
are there habitually described as Grade Schools (Grades I. to VIII.
or IX.); and this term I have usually employed. It includes
certain sub-divisions—as a rule, but two—Primary and Grammar;
but occasionally there are three departments—Primary, Intermediate, and Grammar. The expression "Evening Continuation
School" is not in use, but Evening Schools are connected with
Grade and High Schools in most, if not in all, cities. No restrictions,
so far as I could learn, are placed upon the age of pupils. High
Schools of various types and for both sexes do not exactly correspond
with our "Secondary" Schools; they are a sequence to the Grade
Schools, the entering age is fourteen, and no fees exist. Certain
departments of State Agricultural Colleges, and of the great Technical Institutes endowed by private citizens, permit of classification
under the one head of Technical Schools; in these teachers of
Domestic Science and Art most usually receive their training,
though half of the State Universities and one or two Normal Colleges
also offer Household Science courses. Columbia, Chicago, Leland
Stanford, Michigan, and one or two more Universities of the first
rank have initiated courses in Sanitary or Household Science; some
of a special character, as at Teachers College, Columbia University,
but more usually open to all students.

Cooking and Sewing may be described as now generally taught in Extent of
Grade Schools; these subjects have been introduced in a still limited Domestic
but steadily increasing, amount in High Schools; they are studied Science and
to a very considerable extent, on exhaustive and elaborate lines, in Teaching.
Technical Institutes as well as more simply in Evening and Saturday
classes. This latter type of instruction is also provided by such
agencies as the Young Women's Christian Association and Girls'
Clubs. Laundry-work is almost unknown as a subject in Grade
Schools, but is usually included in Domestic Science as taught in
High Schools, while it finds a place in the courses at Technical Institutes and Normal Colleges. Dressmaking and Millinery are
popular subjects in Manual Training High Schools, Technical
Institutes and in Evening Classes. With few exceptions, definite
artistic training in design, form, colour and the use of brush and
pencil constitute an important feature in these latter courses. Personal, Domestic, and Civic Hygiene appears, though to a variable
extent, in the programmes of all schools, colleges and Technical Institutes. It is at present, in conjunction with physiology, an obligatory
subject in the Grade Schools of nearly all the States; in the High
Schools it is usually optional; but it is again practically obligatory

in the majority of colleges, for it constitutes the theoretical study required to accompany, and to give intelligent impetus to, the Physical Culture Courses required of all students. The peculiar educational advantages it offers, especially as the outcome of Nature Study and Biology, to which much attention is now paid, leads to its voluntary inclusion in the curricula of both High Schools and Colleges. The Care of Children is specifically taught in relatively few schools, but incidentally the subject receives attention in the study of hygiene. The case is different in institutions for higher education; in these Child Study, Psychology, Ethics and Sociology all serve to bring the question of child hygiene before students.

The "commencing age" in Grade Schools for instruction in any of these subjects, except Hygiene, varies from ten to thirteen years; twelve may be taken as the average age for Cooking classes; nine or ten for Sewing. I think the age selected for the cooking classes is especially influenced by the consideration that increased physical capacity (*i.e.*, muscular strength and height) and intelligence (*i.c.*, the power to use the reasoning faculty) are secured by placing it as late as possible in the curriculum. Where, as is now very often the case, girls receive equally with boys actual manual training in wood or chip carving and in clay modelling, dexterity of manipulation is acquired previously; this is found materially to influence the amount of good gained during the subsequent course in cooking; observation, accuracy in detail, and so forth, having become to a greater or less degree habitual. The average age for city children to leave school is certainly later than in England; most girls remain until fully thirteen; a growing number stay till they are fourteen, and then pass on to the High School for at least two years more; so that a large proportion receive the benefit of this instruction, even where thirteen is the commencing age. These facts are taken into account in planning most Domestic Science Courses. In cities where industrial conditions and economic considerations shorten school life, I found that the age for attendance at cooking classes was earlier—eleven years, or even ten, being fixed in some instances. Domestic Science is not taught in rural schools; these serve, as a rule, very scattered districts, and are usually somewhat under-staffed; consequently, much division into separate classes is not possible, especially as the co-educational system requires, under such circumstances, that the instruction shall be adapted throughout for mixed classes.

Sewing, where taught, almost without exception precedes Cooking. There is a marked divergence from English methods in this connection; one or two years is the usual length of time apportioned to weekly or bi-weekly lessons in needlework, either in Grade or High Schools—a great contrast to the five or six years devoted to its practice in our elementary schools. This may be attributed to several causes; for instance, it has proved difficult to break down public prejudice against devoting precious school hours to so "homely" a subject; consequently, short courses could only be introduced tentatively, almost apologetically, though this is a fast-vanishing stage. There is also a strong and prevalent objection to wearying children with the constant and often monotonous repetition of very similar processes, or to requiring fine muscular movements and concentration of sight upon near objects for too long a period. I was frequently assured, and I confess my eyes substantiated the assertion, that if this subject be but presented at the right time in a child's development, it will be rapidly and more satisfactorily acquired than when attempted prematurely. In children whose eyes and hands have been systematically trained from Kindergarten upwards, two years of needlework practice produces very promising results. As a whole, I considered these to hold their own with those attained by the longer practice common in England; but accurate comparisons are almost impossible, because the United States Grade Schools are frequented by children of all social grades, so that the general standards of intelligence, nutrition and energy should be, and are, higher than in our English Elementary Schools. It would, however, be interesting to test by experiment here a method which seems well worthy of consideration and fair trial from the results gained in that country; among other advantages claimed are the wider variety of interest and occupation afforded to the children, and the development of a larger number of muscles in the practice of the diverse manual exercises for which time thus becomes available. Sewing, too, is so commonly classed as Manual Training that it readily falls into rank with the other exercises included under that title. The great interest in and rapid progress made by High School girls in needlework, both elementary and advanced, bodes well for the future housewifery of the country. The subject is held in special esteem educationally at the High School age, on account of the valuable training it affords in method, neatness, cleanliness, discretion, good taste, and economy; while it lends itself admirably to home application.

Domestic Science subjects are taught to deaf and blind children of both sexes at New York, Boston, Providence, and elsewhere, with reported excellent results. The one school I was able to visit (Horace Mann School, Boston) amply confirmed the testimony I received; deaf lads, of fifteen and upwards, as well as girls, become in some cases so thoroughly proficient with their needles and such really good cooks that they are fit for wage-earning situations. The number of feeble-minded children is very small; special provision is made for their training in most States, but time did not permit me to secure information from personal observation.

The High School courses in Household Science and Art have only this in common, that they are all conducted along very practical lines; they vary in length from ten months to four years; they may be correlated with work in the laboratory or studio, or may be complete in themselves. With rare exceptions, no branch of Domestic Science is taught to boys in Grade Schools, but attendance at courses on House Sanitation is occasionally optional in

High Schools. Physiology and Hygiene are studied co-educationally throughout school and college life. A marked interest in these subjects is evinced by school boys; while the demand for a knowledge of Sanitary Science on the part of a small proportion of male students at some colleges and universities has warranted the introduction of courses to meet it.

The "General Courses" in Household Economics at High Schools, Technical Institutes and at half the total number of State Universities serve as admirable schools for training young women as home-makers; a very considerable number make use of these opportunities before marriage. The Summer School and Technical Institute courses serve a similar purpose for those who do not realise till after marriage the need of such preparation for, or assistance in, their domestic duties. It is also now the object of University Extension organisers and of Women's Clubs to secure suitable instruction, though necessarily of a more limited character, for farmers' wives and others whose place of residence or home-claims prevent their attendance at a prolonged course of study.

Position of Domestic Science in School and College Curricula.

I was further desired to give special attention as to the present position of Domestic Science teaching in school and college curricula; and was also invited to make observations as to the methods employed, the equipment provided, and other essential details. This "Suggestion" necessarily implied a study of other important points, viz., to what extent are teachers allowed a free hand in shaping the courses of instruction; must syllabuses be rigidly followed, and how far is Domestic Science correlated with other subjects in the time-table, *e.g.*, with Natural Science, Arithmetic, Reading and Drawing. The authorities I consulted were practically unanimous in their opinion that Domestic Science is now spontaneously assigned a much more important and honourable place in school and college curricula than was the case until quite recent years. Its claims to recognition on the grounds of its high educational, ethical, and sociological value are proved true, and each session sees its more general introduction, under one or other of its many titles, into Grade and High Schools, as well as into College courses. This Report contains a large number of specimen Tables, which illustrate how the necessary time is found for the various subjects; and I again desire emphatically to draw attention to the invaluable opportunities thus afforded for linking learning with life. That Teachers College, Columbia University, includes both Domestic Science and Domestic Art in the post-graduate courses bears high testimony to the estimation in which these subjects are held; the fact that the degree of B.Sc. is offered in Universities of good and recognised standing to graduates in Household Economics, equally with other sciences, is a valuable proof of the support accorded to its introduction by the respective faculties. The presence of highly-educated college women as students in these courses at the leading Technical Institutes attests to the intellectual as well as to the utilitarian attractions of Household Economics when efficiently organised. The growing demand for instruction in Sanitary Science among male students testifies both to the interest aroused by the elementary teaching in Physiology and Hygiene obligatory in Grade Schools, and to their own practical realisation that the possession of still more advanced information is an essential equipment for the student of economics, for the intelligent citizen or for the social reformer. The principals of several widely-separated High Schools told me that, from the purely educational standpoint, Physiology and Hygiene for both sexes, and Domestic Science and Art for girls, prove of high value—ethically, sociologically, scientifically, and as manual exercises ; and on these grounds an honourable place is assigned to them in their school programmes. Not that this opinion is as yet universal ; in some cities these subjects still receive scant and contemptuous consideration ; but those chiefly responsible for what has been accomplished are full of hope for the future, and are content with, even prefer, slow progress, if it be but sure and steady.

Many details of methods of teaching have been given in Parts I. and II. of this Report, so that I now merely propose to emphasise certain points which might be overlooked in the previous pages. The following remarks bear upon the teaching of Domestic Science and Hygiene in the Grade Schools. It will have been observed that instruction in these subjects is common to the children of all classes of society. It may still be said that there are no social distinctions in the national system of education. The children of the professional man, merchant, clerk, artisan and mill-hand sit side by side at the school desk, and no distinction is made in the curriculum they pursue. I was told the interest aroused in and desire to apply the knowledge gained in these studies were mutually strong ; while " good breeding " will often show itself in the voluntary assumption of the less pleasing duties in connection, for instance, with the cleansing of cooking utensils by the more delicately-nurtured child. It is hoped that this mutual training in home duties may eventually assist in the solution of the existing difficulties which have to be faced in domestic service and other industrial problems.

A study of these Grade School Household Science courses shows the sustained efforts to teach underlying principles for what is done ; this is as apparent in the Sewing as in the Cooking classes. Two characteristics of the American child, as I observed him, are an insatiable thirst to know the " reason why " for all he does, and an admirable (though not invariably an *apropos*) energy in the application of new knowledge. These characteristics facilitate the teacher's work to a great degree, but they also necessitate broad-minded, well-cultured instructors, to whom sufficient scope must be given for the legitimate satisfaction and direction of these qualities. Much confidence is usually reposed in his staff by a principal. It is rare to require the accomplishment of a definite amount of instruction in each lesson ; elasticity of method, if it promote the children's good, is freely permitted, and time for revision is accorded, even at

Marginal note: Methods of Teaching Domestic Science and Hygiene in Grade Schools.

Methods of
Teaching
Domestic
Science and
Hygiene in
Grade
Schools—
continued.

the sacrifice of a part of the syllabus, if considered necessary. It must not be assumed that irregularity and incompleteness rule in these schools. I saw no such tendency; but I did notice much intelligence among pupils, a good comprehension of the " reason why," and tangible examples of the results of the active interest aroused in the shape of excellent specimens of home practice.

In the teaching of cooking, our English system of alternate demonstration and practice is entirely disapproved, as is also our custom of defraying a part of the cost by the sale of the food prepared by a class. Against the first method it is argued that few girls of eleven or twelve are intellectually capable of profiting by prolonged observation unrelieved by active participation in the processes under demonstration. They may be interested, but to what extent are they informed ? Constant practice under supervision, immediately subsequent to, or, if necessary, interrupted by, a short demonstration, is the generally approved plan. With regard to the sale of the food cooked, rather than its consumption by those who had prepared it, the feeling was unanimously adverse ; without exception, all authorities on the subject maintained that the cause of failures, as in deficient beating of a cake, or the fact of possible improvement—as in the seasoning of a dish, for instance—cannot be realised by the inexperienced cook unless results be tasted when the whole process is complete. It is also held that the strength of interest can be hardly equal in the two cases ; the desire to improve is but poorly stimulated, and a practical difficulty will thrust itself into prominence, viz., that the tastes of possible purchasers may be occasionally consulted, rather than making the rigorous inculcation of principles by practice the first consideration. The use of printed recipes is advocated, on the plea of the valuable time thus saved ; these are preserved in books specially provided, which contain, in addition, directions, &c., dictated by the teacher when necessary, or made by the child herself. As a whole, these special teachers are well trained and of a high stamp ; most usually I found them to be interested in the correlation of both cooking and needlework with other school work. One of their chief difficulties in this respect is met with in the common custom of " centres," by which children are taught these subjects by teachers not in touch with their ordinary work. In the case of one school used as a "centre," I found the special teacher overcame this difficulty by conferences with her fellows : but this could not be managed for the majority of her pupils when these numbered several hundred and were drawn from perhaps nine separate schools.

In respect of sewing I would like to remind my readers of the good results which have followed, in a few cities, this teaching to boys, as well as to girls, from the age of nine to ten or eleven years. In addition to its practical and educational values it is said to promote community of interest, while small boys take to it most kindly and apply it readily. Great diversity of opinion prevails as to the use of the " specimen " system of teaching needlework ; I should say unhesitatingly that the best results I observed were attained where it was not in force, or only to a modified degree ; for instance, where the specimens of stitches for preservation formed the conclusion of the whole course. The interest of the children is markedly greater where they learn to sew on some article for which they see an immediate purpose ; but in all my comments, it is necessary to bear in mind that my personal observations were necessarily limited.

In the Grade School teaching of Personal and Domestic Hygiene (Physiology and Hygiene, as it is invariably described) the best teachers lose no opportunity to inculcate ideas of duty to one's self, duty to one's neighbour, duty to one's country. They impress that the body is worthy of, and well repays, intelligent care ; that without this good work cannot be accomplished. Children are led to see that no one has a right to injure his neighbour by his slovenly, ignorant, or filthy habits ; and that the State demands that her children shall maintain her prestige by their efficiency and good health. Such practical physical morality comes within the daily observation of children ; it throws a new light on the daily bath, the orderly back yard, the decent habits ; it sets before them as an ideal the conduct of a self-respecting, self-controlled citizen.

The evidences of home application of Cookery, Housewifery, Sewing, and, last but not least, the practice of good habits are quite evident. Great stress is laid upon the encouragement of such applications, though it is reported to be usually spontaneous ; indeed, it appears to have been the means of breaking down much parental opposition to Domestic Science teaching, and has served, in some cases, to form the first connecting link between home and school life. What impressed me even more than the specimens of home productions brought for inspection at the cookery classes, were the corresponding examples of home needlework, especially where the making of a simple blouse and skirt forms part of the course. These spoke of sustained perseverance and of practical ability, as well as of lively interest. It would be wearisome to quote instances of the influence exercised on personal habits and family life by the instruction in Physiology and Hygiene ; but I must mention that this seemed to be very noticeable among boys, in whom, also, I was told, this teaching, when well conducted, serves the useful purpose of developing the latent sense of civic responsibility.

So far Domestic Science has had a somewhat difficult position to face in some cities. These difficulties are, however, described as diminishing, and are usually short-lived. It is habitual to entrust the organisation of manual training in city schools to an expert, and though this expert is not necessarily a woman, the interests of girls are not as a rule overlooked, the funds at a Superintendent's disposal for purposes of manual work (under which Cookery and Needlework are grouped) being equally distributed. In High Schools, so far as my observations extended, no financial problems have presented themselves. With regard to equipment, I have already said that the " centre " system is usual in the case of Grade Schools ; but institutions for higher education have each their own kitchen laboratories and work-rooms. The equipment, in respect to the provision of specially planned and fitted tables,* has been most carefully thought out, and presents certain definite advantages ; some of these have been dealt with in Part I. of this Report. Teachers are trained to be very resourceful in the matter of apparatus, though the cost of equipment does not usually present insurmountable obstacles, there is too much appreciation of the necessity to provide all that contributes to the efficiency of the schools. To trammel work, for want of financial support, in which the public has faith, is contrary to general American practice. Those responsible for the organisation of education continue their representations until private or public funds are found for the desired purpose. Nevertheless my informants emphasised the encouragement given to judicious simplicity and to the employment of " home made " apparatus. The use of text books is unusual in any course, in any grade of institution ; training in the right use of books of reference is the prevalent method ; and the teacher causes careful notes to be kept of the theory she supplies, which usually precedes practice. Only very rarely is adherence to an entire syllabus rigidly required, it is usual to repose confidence in the teacher's judgment, and no cases of abuse were reported. The teachers habitually consult upon this point with their principals or inspectors, and the plan is found to work well for all concerned. Much time and thought is evidently expended upon wise correlation of Domestic Science with other school subjects. The presentation of all knowledge in a form to permit of its speedy application is very present just now in the minds of school authorities, and the children seem so generally anxious to turn what they study to some immediate use, that their enthusiasm acts as a spur to the teacher, and introduces a very pleasant atmosphere into the schools.

Household Science and Hygiene in High Schools.

In High Schools all courses in these subjects are of a more comprehensive and scientific character than those in the lower grades. They usually include a fairly thorough treatment of cooking, housewifery, needlework, dressmaking and millinery ; laundry work also almost invariably finds a place. Where Household Science is taught, house sanitation is generally introduced, but hygiene in its personal aspects is reserved for the courses in Physiology. It is usual to accompany this training by a study of fundamental principles in laboratory and studio. There appear to be two weighty arguments in favour of adopting Household Science and Art into the curriculum, which counterbalance all the objections ; the one, that these subjects afford an unrivalled field for correlation with and application of other studies, literary, artistic, and scientific ; the other, that much advantage is gained from the variety of occupation incidental to the active practical work they necessitate, that better results are secured in these other studies, even though they

*See Fig. VIII.

Fig. VIII.

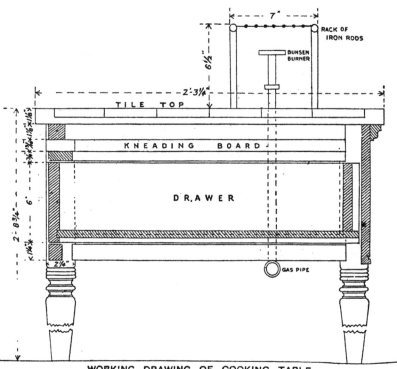

WORKING DRAWING OF COOKING TABLE,
School Kitchen, Pratt Institute, Brooklyn, New York.

Household   are pursued for shorter periods than are assumed to be desirable where
Science   Household Science is not in favour. In his article on High Schools
and Hygiene in the "Pratt Institute Monthly" for April, 1901, Dr. Luther Gülick
in High
Schools.   emphasises yet another argument in its favour, viz., that "in the
—*continued.* teens there is a great accession to the capacity for, and delight in,
reason. This fact is so generally recognised that it needs no particular discussion. The High School programme should be definitely related to the increasing capacity to reason. Facts should be
continually put into relation with one another. This is the time
for the laboratory method, which is well worked out in physics,
chemistry, physiography, and in certain respects in biology. It
needs to be, and can be worked out in history, mathematics and
art." Under his interested supervision the girls' High School
course in Household Science, pursued on lines consonant with
these developing faculties, has well justified its existence at the
Pratt Institute. To Dr. Gülick this term, "laboratory method,"
means that process by which "the pupil discovers his own facts;
comes to his own conclusions in regard to them, and formulates
for himself the laws that grow out of these facts"—a different
form of procedure from that which often goes under this designation.
Nevertheless, Professor Francis E. Lloyd, of Teachers College.
Columbia University, recognises the danger which accompanies
careless use of this laboratory method, and sounds a note of timely
warning when he points out that it is valuable, "just in proportion
as it trains in careful methods of observation, and cultivates a
scientific habit of mind. It succeeds when it trains a pupil in
inductive reasoning; it fails, at least in school life, when it becomes
an end in itself." To guard against this perversion of its worth,
and to stimulate the development of the reasoning faculties by its
judicious introduction, seemed to me the guiding principles of those
in charge of the best High School courses I observed in Household
Science. Thus on educational grounds alone the subject justifies
its introduction into the curriculum of Secondary Schools; but
there are other forcible arguments which appeal to those not
immediately concerned with the training of young people. There
are few who have not noted that it is at the High School age especially that girls' ideas of life are apt to be falsified; they become
discontented with their environment, and often ashamed of family
claims or relationships. Observation shows that a rational study
of Household Science helps to bind the girl to her home, to centre
her interest there, and to show her the worth and beauty of family
life. It has been well said that this subject, above all others,
forges the facts of science and art into practical tools, by whose
aid the home's efficiency in the production of health and character
is materially increased. It would seem, at least over a certain
area in the United States, as if this conception of domestic dignity
has a fascination for the growing girl, who appears to be also un-
expectedly alive to the communal and economic aspects of the
subject. Her mind receives ideas readily concerning the duty
of right living, and its effect upon the community. She is easily

aroused to realise the responsibilities of each individual home as a social unit, whose character inevitably assists to determine the composition of the whole mass. She is impressed by the thought that home and school together form the social workshop, in which are moulded the citizens of the future. The economics of consumption also exercise an attraction which was not anticipated. When the topic is judiciously introduced, girls exhibit eagerness and perseverance in learning the right use of energy, health, time, and money. Speaking generally, it seemed to me that the aspects of Household Science and Art most emphasised in High School courses are the sound theoretical and scientific bases which underlie household duties ; the opportunities for immediate application afforded in home life for artistic training ; the increased mental and physical efficiency which follows upon a wise economy of time and an intelligent expenditure of money ; and the claims of civics and patriotism upon those responsible for the rearing of the race. In Physiology and Hygiene, where the boys and girls work together, continued stress is laid upon the close relationship of living conditions to health and working power. Here, as in Domestic Science, the method employed is almost exclusively that of lectures, followed by periods of laboratory work. My observations, and the information I gained, convinced me that, under the best professors, the teaching is based upon the lines defined by Dr. W. Townsend Porter, of the Harvard Medical School, in an article entitled, " The Teaching of Physiology," published in the Philadelphia " Medical Journal," September 1st, 1900 :—" Deal as far as possible with the phenomena themselves, and not with the descriptions of them. Where the fundamental experiments cannot all be performed, fill the gap with the orginal protocols from the classical sources. Associate facts which the student can observe for himself with those which he cannot observe. Use as the basis of instruction, where practicable, the facts and methods to be used by the student in earning his living. Teach the elements by practical work. Let the student state his observations and results in a laboratory note-book. Control his progress, and remove his difficulties, by a daily written examination and a daily conference, in which the instructor shall discuss the observations made by the student, and supplement them from his own reading. Stimulate the student by personal intercourse in the laboratory, by glimpses of the researches in progress, and by constant reference to the original sources. From the beginning to the end of the instruction hold fast to concentration, sequence, and election."

Of an interest equal to these High School courses are those in the State Agricultural Colleges ; not alone those concerned with Household Economics, but the lectures on Hygiene associated with active physical culture, which enters compulsorily into the curriculum of students of both sexes. Mrs. Ellen H. Richards, of the Massachusetts Institute of Technology, has pointed out on more than one occasion that Household Economics rest on two

Household
Economics
and Hygiene
in Colleges.

chief corner stones—economy of health and economy of wealth.
Economy of wealth appeals with force, and receives implicit, if
not explicit, attention from students engaged in equipping themselves for their future callings in life. That their attention should
be directed with equal emphasis to the study of the economy of
health, in a country where the pursuit of money is considered
a national characteristic, augurs well for the race; it speaks
volumes also for the common sense attitude of a people whose point
of view is occasionally obstructed by the excitement and effervescence
incidental to the rapid progress of a new country. The claim
that these subjects have for a recognition from college authorities
is again based upon their comprehensive and educational character.
Household Economics and Hygiene are neither the one nor the other
separate sciences or arts to be taught by one person with a specialist
training; all departments of a University can and should contribute to their right presentation. Where the experiment has been
tried the results are most emphatically favourable. It is also
stated that in no other instances have such valuable and successful
efforts at co-operation been established between faculties. The
leaven is manifestly at work for the spread of this movement
in colleges. Some college presidents are standing with open minds,
waiting for a longer observation of existing courses before formulating a definite opinion; but all are apparently inquiring as to the
attitude of their confrères. Many professors show a disposition
to accept the subject under the plea that college teaching of Economics, Sociology, Pedagogy, History or Sanitary Science, must
include the relation of the family and the household to society;
and that distinct advantages accompany practical demonstration
of this truth by the work carried on in a department set apart
for the purpose. It is true that the accomplishments of women
in Chemistry, Physics, or Biology, have not yet inspired men with
full confidence in their power to successfully attack a new problem
in a consistently scientific spirit; but, though somewhat less
unanimous upon the definite adoption of Household Economics
as a distinct college subject, than upon its inclusion under some
branch of Sociology, college professors are as a whole favourable to
some place being assigned to it on the grounds of its great importance: so far women have justified any confidence reposed in them
in respect of the organisation of such advanced courses.

Domestic
Science as a
" Technical "
Subject.

A further point to which I was directed to give special attention
was the extent to which Domestic Science is regarded as an early
instalment of technical education, inserted in the Primary or
Secondary School curriculum. " How far is an attempt made
(and, if made, how far is it successful) to deal with the subject as
part of a liberal education—*i.e.* for its value as an educational
discipline as distinct from its practical utility? In practice, does
the aim in view affect the course of instruction, and has it been
found possible to combine the benefits of disciplining the intelligence
and the reasoning power with those of increased manual and prac-

tical skill ? " Such were my instructions. There seemed to me no tendency to introduce the subject into elementáry schools as a preliminary stage in technical education. To fit their charges for life, not for one means of earning a livelihood, is the aim of all the best superintendents and teachers at the present day. The leading idea, much emphasised by educationalists, is that the early periods of education should be essentially devoted to general culture and not to premature specialisation. The " poise " or well-balanced characters which it is desired to form by school education, can only be developed by an all-round training of the mind and body, and not by early concentration upon any one branch of study to the exclusion of others. I learnt that the early efforts made to introduce Domestic Science into schools were, more or less, leavened with the trade school idea, but the later realisation of the true scope of education and more enlightened methods of instruction have led to the virtual extinction of this misapprehension. It is true that inculcation of the principles, that is of the fundamental laws of matter and form, with enough practice to illustrate them, play an important part in the High School courses ; but there is no ulterior object of training children technically for domestic service or as juvenile dressmakers ; the idea is to bring the teaching of Domestic Science into harmony with the broad, scientific, and educational theories characteristic of the time.

In Manual Training High Schools, the technical, as distinct from the educational study of Household Science, is naturally brought into more prominence than in others. During the last two of a four year course, girls of sixteen have attained an age when specialisation is admissible ; and the fact that they have sought their education in a Manual Training rather than in an ordinary High School indicates that their intention is to select some form of occupation in the future in which the hands are to be as active as the head. But a study of the time-tables will make clear that the first two years of these courses are emphatically " general " in method ; indeed the necessity of supporting a special subject by means of coincident, systematic study of other branches of knowledge is clearly realised by those responsible for the schemes of technical training in Household Science and Art at all the Institutes and Colleges, as well as in Manual Training High Schools.

It would be superfluous for me to reiterate the success which has attended efforts to deal with these subjects as part of a liberal education. Indeed, it is on account of their peculiar value in this connection that they find favour in the eyes of some who otherwise would not countenance them as either school or college subjects. Their sociological, ethical, and economic as well as their industrial values are of quite recent appreciation ; but, as I have pointed out, now that students of these sciences clearly see the intimate relation of family life to the whole social and industrial order, they deem it right, not only to devote some of their precious hours to a study absolutely essential for intelligent life under twentieth-century

conditions, but desire that an early interest shall be awakened
in those who may be unable to pursue the subject at a later period
in their lives.

Training of
Teachers in
Domestic
Science.
Table
XXXVII.

A further request was made that I should give careful observation
to the methods of training and qualifications of teachers of Domestic
Science. Readers of this Report will have observed what stress
is laid upon the preparation of well-equipped teachers for this
subject, and what liberal opportunities are offered for their training. Definite qualifications are required of all teachers of Domestic
Science, and each year the standard of these is raised. The accompanying comparative Table sets forth in detail the subjects included
in what are recognised as among the best training courses now available in the United States, and the length of time devoted respectively
to the various studies. What, however, no tabulated statement
can show is the method upon which successful results depend.
However, it will be noted that the general scope of the courses is
somewhat broader in the United States than in this country;
that considerable time is devoted to the careful study of the
theory which underlies all practice; and that importance is attached
to a practical study of the scientific and artistic principles basal
to that technical skill, to the attainment of which the training is
directed. For these reasons the Domestic Sciences and Arts are
almost always studied in two distinct courses; time does not
permit of a command of both being acquired by the same student
in the three years she can invest in the special preparation for her
profession. There *is* a feeling, at least in one Institute, that the
scientific side of Household Science has been slightly over emphasised. Probably the fact that this is recognised and that already
definite efforts are being made for the more accurate adjustment
of values, indicates that if the danger exist it will soon be averted.
The weak points which would probably immediately present
themselves to an experienced eye, will be want of teaching practice
in some of the American Normal Courses, and the very short
time devoted to laundry training. It must, however, be borne
in mind that each year sees modifications of these courses, as
experience shows their strength or weakness. The ideal set forth
is very high. The directress of one of these departments said to
me that it is set so high they sometimes feel disheartened—it seems
beyond human attainment; yet, each year, the Lake Placid Conference of experts, men and women, spurs them on to renewed
exertions by reiterating from some new standpoint the enormous
importance to the individual and to the nation of this work of
home-making. Evidence of good preliminary preparation in
elementary science or art, in addition to a sound general education,
is demanded of all students. As a fact, college women are preferred
to those who have had only the advantage of a high school education, on account of the greater breadth of culture they will bring
to their class work. In all cases, general information and physical
well-being are not allowed to suffer during the special training.

TABLE XXXVII.
DOMESTIC SCIENCE.

NORMAL TRAINING COURSES, UNITED STATES OF AMERICA. | NORMAL TRAINING COURSES, ENGLAND.

STATE NORMAL SCHOOL, FRAMINGHAM.	DREXEL INSTITUTE, PHILADELPHIA.	PRATT INSTITUTE, BROOKLYN.	GLOUCESTERSHIRE SCHOOL OF DOMESTIC SCIENCE.			LEEDS SCHOOL OF COOKERY.			BATTERSEA POLYTECHNIC TRAINING SCHOOL OF DOMESTIC ECONOMY.		
			COOKERY.	LAUNDRY.	HOUSEWIFERY.	COOKERY.	LAUNDRY.	HOUSEWIFERY.	COOKERY.	LAUNDRY.	HOUSEWIFERY.

DOMESTIC ARTS.

STATE NORMAL SCHOOL, FRAMINGHAM.	DREXEL INSTITUTE, PHILADELPHIA.	PRATT INSTITUTE, BROOKLYN.	GLOUCESTERSHIRE SCHOOL OF DOMESTIC SCIENCE.	LEEDS SCHOOL OF COOKERY.	BATTERSEA POLYTECHNIC TRAINING SCHOOL OF DOMESTIC ECONOMY.		
					PLAIN NEEDLEWORK.	DRESSMAKING.	MILLINERY.

The type of woman attracted to the Normal Courses is distinctly good, and when qualified she takes rank with teachers or professors of any other subjects taught at school or college. The dignity which attaches to the teaching profession in the United States is also conducive to a selection of these subjects by independent and well-bred women, who do not thereby feel that they in any way diminish their social status. I found them resourceful, interested, and possessed usually of considerable enterprise and independence of thought. Many have had considerable difficulties to encounter in their work, as the prejudices of parents, and even of members of Boards of Education, have died hard; but enthusiasm is rarely lacking, and the excellent results observed from their exertions in each grade of educational institution serve apparently as a sufficient stimulus to continued efforts.

Very great account is taken of personal equation in all Normal students, and greater stress is laid upon the estimate formed of their daily work than upon the results of a final examination. The teaching staff meet periodically to discuss and to compare notes as to the students' dispositions, progress, and conduct in their various classes; this study of individual character is taken into careful account by the examiners. The fact that applications for training so far exceed available vacancies permits a careful sifting in the first instance. At present about a fifth or sixth only of those who seek training in the best Normal Courses can be admitted.

Diplomas are usually, if not invariably, given upon the successful completion of a whole course of training; they are not dependent upon the results of a final examination. As has been stated above, estimates of efficiency are based upon the general character and work; small importance is attached to a single examination, however practical, which demands chiefly presence of mind, a good memory, and manual dexterity. It is quite unusual for an outside examiner to conduct any tests. Periodical examinations are made at intervals by members of the staff, as, for instance, at Teachers College, Columbia University, where each professor examines his or her own students in theory and practice at various periods in the course, and considers the results in consultation with his colleagues. In some States there is a Central Examining Board, which conducts entrance examinations for teachers before admittance to its schools: this is the case in New York State, but the custom is not general. It will be thus realised that diplomas have different values. The prestige of a school or college is maintained by the work of its graduates; and it is considered that in this lies the guarantee for the maintenance of a high standard in its teaching. Were the students insufficiently trained or graduated unfairly their work would rapidly reveal the fact, and the whole institution would suffer. Probably it is the difficulty of attaining or maintaining the required standard which accounts for the gradual dying out of the short, pioneer, private

Training of
Teachers in
Domestic
Science —
continued.

Normal Courses in Domestic Science, now being superseded as unsatisfactory. Normal diplomas are not granted for separate subjects, but only for specified groups, under the comprehensive title of Domestic Science or of Domestic Art; the studies are carried on concurrently, and proficiency in the whole scheme is demanded. This is one of the broad distinctions in the United States between Normal and Technical courses; in Technical courses certificates are granted separately for each subject, a group of which constitute the complete Normal course. There is very little inspection of normal courses by outside experts; those conducted in primary or secondary schools are under the supervision of city or state inspectors; the general courses in Technical schools are practically independent of inspection, as these institutions are chiefly under the control of private bodies.

It has been found difficult, in some cases, to prevent teachers of the humanities, whose tastes are purely artistic and literary, from disparaging the important and intellectual attractions of Household Science; and, as I have mentioned, there is also a danger of specialist teachers treating it in so complex a manner as to dissociate it from daily life. Efforts to meet both tendencies are constantly at work; and I learned that the introduction of a Household Arts Department into institutions attended by teachers going through a literary or general course of study has had the result of converting those who previously depreciated Household Science into its interested supporters. Information to the same effect was furnished me by professors under more than one important Board of Education; general teachers disposed to look upon the study and practice of cooking and sewing unfavourably, because of the time so taken away from other studies, have become advocates of such work when pains have been taken to investigate its claims. The principal of one State College mentioned to me particularly that the male professors had become the warmest supporters of the Household Economic course.

There is a strong feeling among some superintendents in favour of removing these subjects from the hands of special teachers in Grade schools, owing to a tendency to lose the right sense of proportion in the lessons. They argue that a young specialist teacher has too narrow an experience of life to enable her to interpret her special knowledge in the light of common things, whereas it is most essential that it should be so presented to the children. This is used as a strong point by those who advocate the pursuit of all special training, normal or otherwise, in general colleges, where work is not confined to one special line and much assistance is available in attaining and maintaining a broad and open outlook. It seemed to me that the constant interchange of opinion and experience common in the school world of the United States is in any case favourable to the breaking down of prejudices and contributes to the maintenance of that sense of proportion hard to attain when working in an isolated position. Two good features in all its educational work, which balance some of the exaggerations to which the enthusiasms of the people are inclined to lead, are the ready recognition of mistakes made and an open mind towards suggested reforms. In these qualities lies the promise of strength, which bids fair to develop eventually the necessary sense of proportion and right values.

State or Municipal Boards of Education encourage Domestic Science by allotting to it a suitable proportion of the money voted for educational purposes in their respective districts. The same system supports the work in State Agricultural Colleges. The appropriation, granted by the State, is subdivided according to the needs of the different departments. *Financial Support accorded to Domestic Science.*

In conclusion it was suggested to me to collect information under the following heads :—" Is it felt to be necessary for schools to provide an increasing part of that education which used to be more generally furnished by home life ? Is there a feeling that there is a danger of an actual decline in household skill owing to the conditions of modern city life, or to the increasing employment of women in houses of·business ? Is it felt that the school should attempt to arrest this decline ? Are people at all concerned by any observed or suspected tendency in primary education, as now organised, to make girls wish to be typewriters, clerks, shop assistants, etc., rather than housekeepers or domestic servants ? " *Influence of Domestic Science on Social Conditions.*

The following remarks embody the result of the extended inquiries I made in fulfilment of this part of my commission :— (The changing social conditions which demand rearrangement of former expenditure of time and energy *are* recognised as a factor in the evident need to secure for young people in school that which a previous state of society permitted to be gained in the home. That the integrity and dignity of home life must be maintained as a coefficient of national prosperity is widely accepted ; that the power and interest necessary for the realisation of this ideal have been weakened has been slowly dawning upon the few for more than a quarter of a century. That this conception is now reaching the many seems evident from the great increase of attention devoted to the whole question during the last five or even ten years, credit for which is largely due to the Association of College Alumnæ and the Women's Clubs. I should place as the most powerful motive, held perhaps unconsciously but nevertheless tenaciously, by the majority of the population, the determination that the United States shall be foremost among the nations. This determination leads a people, instinctively interested in the study of cause and effect, to observe wherein lies their weakness and in what direction may be found their strength. The stress and strain of professional and commercial life soon test the vigour of the physical as well as of the mental constitution of those subjected to it, and thus turn the thoughts to the essentials of physical well-being. The constant inroads of immigrants, whose habits

Influence
of Domestic
Science on
Social condi-
tions—
continued.
and standard of existence are a menace to their neighbours, have
also stimulated many minds to a study of Sociology and Economics,
in neither of which can much progress be made without some
knowledge of Sanitary Science. / The trained intelligence of college
women has also been directed by circumstances too numerous to
detail to the economic effects of ignorance, carelessness, or indif-
ference in the conduct of homes or of cities. Among their sisters
whose minds are more immediately centred upon daily domestic
difficulties, interest in the subject is arising from the desire to do
something to make housekeeping easier ; their efforts being first
inspired by probably no higher motive than to secure alleviation
from the troubles which spring out of the present chaotic state of
domestic service. The expression given to their views by representatives amongst these different classes has exerted an influence
upon public opinion, which causes it now to demand that schools
shall provide for children such training in citizenship and home
making as shall raise up a strong race of well-nurtured people,
skilled not alone in the right conduct of their own lives, but impatient of the existence of any conditions unfavourable to the health
of the community. Among these conditions would rank decline
in household skill and a weakening of the maternal instincts,
both, when apparent, being traceable results of the increasing
employment of women outside their homes. The false sense of
shame associated with domestic service, impatience of the so-called
uneventful life of the young mother engaged in household or
family cares, are prevalent on both sides of the ocean ; but I am
able to report that in the United States determined efforts are
now being made to combat these erroneous sentiments. In many
directions, in the east and west, systematic efforts are evidently
and spontaneously active, directed to enhance the dignity of household service, to point out the beauty and intense responsibility of
motherhood, and to encourage all women to consider that their
education is incomplete unless they are practically acquainted
with household management, which must necessarily include
knowledge of child hygiene.

The reader of Part III. of this Report cannot fail to realise the
admirable spirit animating some among the leisured women of
the community to set personal example of the strength of their
convictions in respect of home dignity and worth. Direct acquaintance with, and practice of, domestic duties stimulates their minds
to consider and to introduce improved methods and labour-saving
appliances. Their sympathy with the difficulties dependent upon
dirt, inconvenient dwellings, and futile expenditure of time and
strength experienced by the less well-to-do, ceases to exist as
sentiment, but finds expression in urging on responsible authorities the absolute importance of housing and similar reforms.
Their perception of the bearing upon domestic processes and
national health of municipal regulations concerned with cleanliness of streets and markets, adulteration of food, provision of

safe supplies of water and of means for refuse disposal, has resulted in raising the level of public administration, as visitors to certain cities rapidly recognise.

Professor James L. Hughes, Superintendent of the Public Schools at Toronto, has well expressed the sentiment, now happily common to a considerable section of society, that the Home is the most comprehensive influence in deciding a child's qualification for sustained and effective work in adult life. " The child's whole life power, in its essential elements of physical, intellectual, and spiritual vitality, is influenced directly and indirectly in the home. If the best conditions of physical power, and the apperceptive centres of true and rich intellectual and spiritual development are not established in the home, no other agencies can raise the child to the richest and truest manhood or womanhood. A dwarfed or undeveloped childhood necessarily results in impaired power and defective life. (Every child has a right to the best conditions known for childhood by the highest civilisation. Full growth, physically, intellectually and spiritually, is possible only in the best conditions. | The ' lost waif ' will never cease to disgrace civilisation so long as homes are less efficient than they should be. (The improvement of homes does not demand greater expense so much as better training and more practical common sense.) The aims of progressive workers in securing improved home conditions are, not to spend more money, but to get greater returns for the money spent; not to increase labour, but to make labour more effective in promoting health, comfort, and happiness. The true home maker considers every element that influences the life of the family physically, intellectually, and spiritually. The physical conditions especially require careful attention from the most advanced scientific minds. The schools and some of the churches have recognised the fundamental fact that physical culture is a very important element in the development of human character. The quality of intellectual and spiritual power, and the capacity for sustained intellectual and spiritual effort depends to a large extent on the perfect growth of the body. The higher the character of the physical life the more completely it aids in the development and the expression of intellectual and spiritual energy. Rousseau taught the great truth that the more perfect the body the more readily it obeys the intellect and will; but the perfect body does more than respond to the mind and spirit; it contributes to their power and fuller growth. (It is, therefore, of vital importance to consider all subjects related to the proper construction and sanitation of the home, and the whole range of domestic science, including the correct choice and proper preparation of foods. Pure air, proper lighting, and sanitary cleanliness in the home are essential elements in promoting health, comfort, and happiness, and these are the conditions in which man's best nature develops most rapidly, most naturally, and most harmoniously. The highest success demands harmonious development. But even

Influence
of Domestic
Science on
Social
Conditions
—*continued.*

with these conditions in a high degree of efficiency we require the
most perfect possible nutrition in order that each individual may
be raised to, and sustained in, the best condition physically, intellectually, and spiritually for effective work without unnatural
and therefore destructive over-fatigue. The 'wear and tear' of
life results not from overwork, as is generally believed, but from
work under improper conditions. Most men and women work
at a rate under their capacity rather than over it. Men wear out
quickly because they are not properly nourished. They wear
out most quickly when they take unnatural stimulants to overcome the lack of energy resulting from imperfect nutrition, and
thus force their enfeebled bodies to do work under pressure beyond
the natural fatigue point. Under these conditions the 'wear
and tear' is inevitable, because work then is an unnatural strain
on the physical and intellectual power, and because work
done beyond the fatigue point destroys the reactive
tendency to rest that results from fatigue under normal conditions. The basis of intemperance is largely physical. The
nervous systems that are not kept in comfortable working
order crave something that for a time will bring exhilaration.
Unnatural exhilaration is always debilitating. Natural exhilaration, resulting in appropriate and well-cooked food
eaten in proper quantities and at proper times, is always
productive of greater power along life's broadest and highest
lines of effort. When school children become nervous and irritable,
and feeble, the schools are continually blamed for these evil conditions. Sometimes the schools have shared in the causes that lead
to such undesirable results by long hours and inadequate ventilation, by the substitution of pressure for natural interest, by continuous sitting, and by lack of play ; but the homes have done the
greater part of the wrong to childhood by failing to send children
to school in a proper condition for work. The true remedies for a
weak, nervous system are food suitable for nerve and brain building,
and physical exercise, especially free play. One of the fundamental
thoughts in Domestic Science is a new and higher ideal of the
higher meaning of digestion. Digestion should be regarded as
the transmutation of material things into physical, intellectual,
and spiritual energy. This function of elevating food into the
highest forms of human power is the true work of digestion, but
it has been almost universally degraded. The selection and preparation of foods has been regarded as one of the baser departments
of household economics. The systematic study of foods and their
scientific preparation for the table have been carefully conducted,
chiefly to provide gratification for unnatural appetite. (The true
study of foods and their scientific preparation should be conducted
in order to find what foods are best for all conditions and ages of
humanity—for sickness and health, for infancy, childhood, vigorous
adult and declining age ; for brain building, nerve strengthening,
muscle development, and bone growth ; for promoting or retarding

the storing of fat, and for aiding the functional work of all the vital organs, and preserving the harmonious balance of man's powers. This study is now recognised as a most important department of the science of human evolution. Domestic art is a necessary part of the study of scientific home-making. Our mental and spiritual conditions, and therefore our physical life, are directly influenced by the nature of our environment. Calmness or irritation, hopefulness or despondency, joyousness or moroseness, definiteness or carelessness, prospering ambition or lack of vital interest, may depend to a greater extent than is generally realised on the colour of the walls, the ceilings, and the carpets in our homes. The study of pictures and furniture, and furnishings, and gardens, and the beautifying of front yards, and especially of back yards, will lead to a true æsthetic culture, and promote the happiness and the broader and higher development of the race. The new century will elevate the character of household work, cleaning, cooking, and all departments of service, by making them more scientific and more systematic ; and with this elevation of the service will come a corresponding elevation in the qualification of servants, and in the greater recognition of their rights."

I employ this lengthy quotation as my conclusion, because it is the accurate embodiment by a British subject of the sentiments his prolonged personal acquaintance with the educational world of the United States has led him to recognise as inspiring its leaders. I have also selected it because it is the expressed opinion of a member of that sex, which, in England, is disposed to release itself from any direct responsibility in the promotion of a higher level in home comfort and family life. Only by co-operation of the sexes can the ideal standard be attained. It has been well said that co-operation for a common aim creates a spirit of mutual helpfulness. The common aim of all who are concerned with the affairs of men, personal, domestic, communal, or national, is the physical, moral, and intellectual development of each child born into the world. Upon women, properly and naturally, devolve the care of the young and the right conduct of the home for all whom it shelters. Upon men, as naturally, devolve the provision and maintenance of such conditions in connection with, though outside, the home as shall secure the means without which women's special duties are seriously hampered or even rendered impossible of fulfilment. To this end boys and girls should learn together as they do in the United States the essentials to a healthy existence, and be familiarised with the broad, general principles upon which life and its functions depend for their continuance. In subsequent years, or even concurrently, girls are introduced to the processes of home making, which are indispensable to domestic well-being and happiness ; while boys are encouraged to a study of the duties of citizenship, with all these mean to the welfare of the community. At college, as at school, opportunities for this wise preparation for their future lives are offered to the young men

and women ; it speaks well for the influence of the teaching profession that the numbers of those glad to seize these opportunities
show annual increase. Public (and parental) opinion is gradually
giving intelligent heed to the growth of a movement which promises,
if wisely controlled and intelligently fostered, to yield a harvest of
rich national results ; for, to quote Mrs. Browning's words—
the " multitude of leaves " will hold—

> "Loves filial, loves fraternal, neighbour-loves
> And civic—all fair petals, all good scents,
> All reddened, sweetened from one central Heart,"*

inspired with the belief that " man is made in God's image," and
as such must· be freed from all conditions which hinder the
expression of his inherent powers.

It now remains for me to express, though most inadequately,
my deep sense of gratitude to those whose generous response to
inquiries, ready sacrifice of valuable time for the promotion of my
object, and sympathetic interest in my commission are mainly
responsible for its execution. Their number is so large, the
evidences of their cordial co-operation so numerous, that individual
acknowledgment becomes impossible. The debt of gratitude which
stands in my name would be overwhelming in its extent were it
not rather a national than an individual liability. Not to the
Commissioner of small account, but to the old Mother Country,
was the gift of experience, experiment, theory and practice so
freely tendered. Though social and other diverse conditions
necessarily militate against any proposal to adopt or to imitate in this
country methods of proved worth in the United States, it is nevertheless of immense advantage to all concerned with the public
health and prosperity of Great Britain to become acquainted with
the measures designed to promote these objects in other thriving
communities. That this necessarily imperfect Report of the
educational means devoted to these ends in the United States
should achieve even a partial degree of success or of completeness,
is entirely the outcome of the stimulus and assistance received
from my generous friends in that country.

I have spared no pains in the effort to be impartial, accurate,
and consistent in the sifting and employment of the mass of material
I collected ; if, therefore, there be misrepresentation, exaggera-
tion or culpable omission in the preceding pages I would offer my
sincere apology to those whose cause I may thus most uninten-
tionally wrong. That some errors of observation and of comprehension should have occurred in the course of my compulsorily
short visits to a large number of centres in the Eastern and
Middle West States appears to me to be inevitable. In spite of
much concentrated effort on my part and of most valuable
assistance rendered me in the form of personal and written
explanations and of printed matter, it would be presumptuous

---

* "Aurora Leigh," IX., 884.   E. B. B.

to imagine I could grasp in a few hours all the points in courses of study, the evolutions which have constantly cost years of thought and experimental practice, and which are also adapted to social conditions diverse from our own. For all these reasons I have abstained from critical analysis, preferring to present my Report in a descriptive form, in which I hope it may, in spite of its many shortcomings, prove stimulating and suggestive.

Of all my readers I will ask for kindly forbearance and for lenient judgment on a work which has been fraught for me throughout with a lively sense of responsibility, not alone towards those by whom the commission was entrusted to me, but towards those whose aspirations and attainments were given into my hands to present, as well as to my fellow teachers whose methods in practice or whose estimate of another nation's educational standards may be influenced by the perusal of the preceding pages.

ALICE RAVENHILL.

May, 1903.

APPENDIX A.

EQUIPMENT FOR GRADE SCHOOL COOKERY COURSES.

The following exhaustive list of the equipment recommended for use in Cookery Courses is reproduced by kind permission from "The Economics of Manual Training" Teachers' College Record. Vol. II., No. 5. November, 1901. It is presented as a model; considerable modifications are compatible with efficiency, and discretion would dictate suitable selection according to the class and grade of school for which equipment is to be provided. The United States of America Coinage has been converted for convenience into English money.

COOKING.

KITCHEN EQUIPMENT.

	£	s.	d.
Table for 15 pupils, with drawers for provisions and materials: cupboard, closed with roll-front, sliding board, and tiled top made of quartered oak, about	100	0	0
Table for 15 pupils, with one drawer for each pupil, made of Georgia pine, white pine or stained white-wood, from £31 5s. 0d. to	52	1	8
Kitchen tables may be used where funds are extremely limited, but are not advisable, about	6	0	0
Individual stove equipment for tables £6 to	15	12	6
Coal or Gas ranges £3 to	6	13	4

UTENSILS.

(Two for each pupil.)

	£	s.	d.
Bowl, 1 pint, earthen or granite	0	0	3
Tea-spoon, nickel or aluminium	0	0	5½
Towel, 1 yard long, crash	0	0	8
	£0	1	4½

(One for each pupil.)

	£	s.	d.
Baking dish, 1 quart, earthen or granite	0	0	4
Bowl, 4 quarts, earthen or granite	0	0	10
Bread board, small wood	0	0	10
Dish cloth or mop	0	0	5
Egg beater, medium, wire or iron	0	0	5
Frying pan, small, iron	0	0	7½
Kitchen fork, steel, wood handle	0	0	2½
Kitchen knife, steel, wood handle	0	0	2½
Mat, 8 inches square, linoleum	0	0	2¼
Pepper shaker, glass	0	0	5
Plate, granite or tin	0	0	7½
Salt shaker, glass	0	0	5
Salt-spoon, bone	0	0	2½
Saucepan, with cover, granite	0	0	9
Table-spoon, nickle or aluminium	0	0	7½
Vegetable brush, small, wood back	0	0	2½
Vegetable knife, steel, wood handle	0	0	5
Measuring cup, ½ pint, block tin	0	0	5
	£0	8	2

(One for each two pupils.)

	£	s.	d.
Biscuit cutter, block tin	0	0	3
Bread pan, medium, block tin	0	0	8½
Colander, medium, block tin	0	1	4
Double boiler, 1 or ½ pint, block tin or granite	0	2	1

(One for each two pupils)—*continued.*

	£	s.	d.
Flour dredger, block tin - - - - - -	0	0	5
Flour sifter (revolving handle) block tin - - -	0	0	11
Grater, medium, block tin - - - - -	0	0	5
Nutmeg grater, block tin - - - - -	0	0	4
Potato-masher, wire, wood handle - - - -	0	0	4½
Rolling-pin, wood- - - - - - -	0	0	3
Scrubbing brush, large wood - - - - -	0	0	5
Skimmer, small, block tin - - - - -	0	0	4
Strainer, medium, block tin - - - - -	0	0	6
Teapot, 1 pint earthen (Japanese) - - - -	0	1	0½
Thermometer - - - - - - -	0	3	1½
	£0	**12**	**6**

(Three or four for class of twelve.)

	£	s.	d.
Apple-corer, block tin - - - - - -	0	0	2½
Chopping knife, steel - - - - - -	0	2	1½
Chopping tray, wood - - - - - -	0	1	8
Coffee pot, 1 quart, granite or tin - - -	0	1	5½
Japanned tray, medium - - - - -	0	1	10½
Mixing spoon, large, wood - - - - -	0	0	2½
Muffin pan, 12 in a pan, block tin - - -	0	0	7½
Pitcher, 1, 2 and 3 quarts, earthen - - -	0	1	6
	£0	**9**	**8**

(Two for a class of twelve.)

	£	s.	d.
Cake pan, medium, block tin - - - -	0	1	0½
Double boiler, 3 pints, granite - - - -	0	4	9
Griddle, medium, soapstone - - - -	0	4	8
Griddle cake turner, iron - - - - -	0	0	5
Kettle, 6 quarts, granite - - - - -	0	7	9
Lemon squeezer, glass - - - - - -	0	0	4½
Saucepan, 2 quarts, granite - - - - -	0	2	10½
Strainer, 3 pints, block tin - - - - -	0	1	0½
Toaster, wire - - - - - - -	0	0	5
	£1	**3**	**4**

(One for a class of twelve.)

	£	s.	d.
Bread knife - - - - - - - -	0	2	1
Can-opener - - - - - - - -	0	0	5
Coffee-mill - - - - - - - -	0	4	8
Corkscrew - - - - - - - -	0	0	5
Egg beater (Dover), large, iron - - - -	0	0	5
Fruit jars, 1 doz., 1 quart, glass - - - -	0	4	8
Fruit jars, 1 doz., 1 pint, glass - - - -	0	3	1½
Frying kettle, large, iron - - - - -	0	7	7
Funnel, medium, block tin - - - - -	0	0	7½
Ice cream freezer (Packer's standard), 3 quarts - -	0	9	4½
Jelly glasses, 1 doz. - - - - - -	0	2	1
Knife sharpener - - - - - - -	0	2	3½
Larding needle - - - - - - -	0	0	10
Measure, 1 quart, block tin - - - - -	0	0	10
Measure, 1 pint, block tin - - - - -	0	0	2½
Meat broiler, medium, iron - - - - -	0	2	1
Meat knife - - - - - - - -	0	0	10
Pot chain - - - - - - - -	0	0	3½
Pudding mould, 3 pints, block tin - - -	0	1	3
Scales, to 10 pounds - - - - - -	0	9	4
Skimmer, large, tin - - - - - -	0	0	5
Steamer, medium, block tin - - - -	0	2	3½
Tea-kettle, large, iron, granite or aluminium - -	0	2	1½
	£2	**18**	**3**

UTENSILS FOR HOUSEWORK.

	£	s.	d.
Blacking brush - - - - - - - -	0	0	2½
Broom - - - - - - - - -	0	1	0½
Cheese-cloth duster - - - - - -	0	0	5
Dust brush - - - - - - - -	0	0	5
Dust pan - - - - - - - -	0	0	7½
Floor brush - - - - - - - -	0	3	1½
Lamp cloths - - - - - - - -	0	0	5
Mop - - - - - - - - -	0	1	0½
Pail, indurated fibre - - - - - -	0	1	1½
Scrubbing brush - - - - - - -	0	1	0
Whisk broom - - - - - - - -	0	0	5
Window cloths etc. - - - - - -	0	0	5
	£0	10	3

STORE-ROOM EQUIPMENT.

	£	s.	d.
Bread cloths - - - - - - -	0	0	5
6 crocks, large, earthen - - - - -	0	10	5
6 crocks, medium - - - - - -	0	8	4
4 flour pails, wooden - - - - - -	0	8	4
Ice bag, 1 yard, duck - - - - -	0	0	3½
1 dozen jelly glasses, with covers - - -	0	1	3
6 2-quart Mason jars, for coffee, glass - -	0	5	0
Strainers, 5 yards, cheese-cloth - - -	0	1	0½
Strainers, 1 yard, flannel - - - -	0	0	10
Cupboards for provisions, utensils and dishes - - - - -	£4 3 4 to 10	8	4
Refrigerator, medium size - - -	£3 2 6 to 4	3	6
	£9 1 9 to £16	7	9

DINING-ROOM EQUIPMENT.

	£	s.	d.
Canton flannel cloth			
1 dining table and 6 chairs - - -	£4 3 6 to 6	13	4
2 table cloths and napkins - - -	- -	2 1	8
Enough dishes for setting table and serving a simple meal - - -	- -	2 1	8
Knives, forks, spoons, glasses, etc. -	- -	4 3	4
	£12 10 2 to £15	0	0

(If a sideboard is added, the cost would be about £5 16s. 8d. additional.)

SUMMARY OF COST OF EQUIPMENT TO ACCOMMODATE TWELVE PUPILS AT A TIME.

KITCHEN EQUIPMENT.

	£	s.	d.
Table with cupboards, etc., stools, stove, range and sink - - -	£113 15 0 to 135	8	4
Utensils, as per detailed statement -	- -	17 17	9½
Store-room equipment - - -	£9 1 9 to 16	7	9
Dining-room equipment - -	£12 10 2 to 15	0	0
	£153 4 8½ to £184 13	10½	

APPENDIX B.

STATE MANUAL TRAINING HIGH SCHOOL, PROVIDENCE, RHODE ISLAND.

The Year is nominally 40 Weeks, excluding Vacations 38 Weeks.

DOMESTIC SCIENCE COURSE.
First Year.

*Academic.	Domestic Science.	†Household Art and Manual Training.	‡Art.
Elementary rhetoric. English composition. American authors by Brander Mathews. 38 weeks.		Carpentry : — 60 hours. Elementary carpentry and joinery. Making of useful articles :— Model of hand loom.	Lettering. Geometrical figures, working drawings used in carpentry.
Algebra to quadratics. 38 weeks.		Basketry :—60 hours. Woven baskets of rattan, sewed baskets of raffia. (a) Plain. (b) Coloured.	Drawing from models. Historic ornaments, elementary design.
Physical geography, Laboratory work in physical character of minerals. 19 weeks.			Application in basketry.
Book - keeping. Sadler's system. Physics. Dynamics of liquids. Dynamics of gases. Sound, heat. 19 weeks. } Alternate.		Sewing : — 112½ hours. Hand-machine work, undergarments, cooking apron and cap, hygienic clothing, economics of buying, study of textiles, including study of fibres and methods of manufacture. Simple weaving on model loom, made in carpentry. Note book work supplements the English work. Millinery 52½ hours. Bows, rosettes, facings, shirred linings. Braid, sew and trim raffia hat after individual design.	
*Lessons are in 45 minute periods daily, unless otherwise indicated by a numeral to show number of days per week.		†Manual and household art classes are 1½ hour periods on alternate days.	‡Art work is in 45 minute periods daily during the four years.

6490.   T

T

APPENDIX B.—*continued.*

DOMESTIC SCIENCE COURSE.

Second Year.

Academic.	*Domestic Science.	†Household Art and Manual Training.	Art.
English composition, alternating with English history with especial reference to American institutions. 19 weeks. Ancient and Mediæval History alternating with German. 19 weeks. Geometry, plane. 38 weeks. Civil Government alternating with physics, dynamics of solids, work-energy, magnetism. 19 weeks. General chemistry alternating with science of cooking. 38 weeks.	Science of cooking. Application of laws of heat: water, fire. Application of chemistry to cookery of proteids, albuminoids, starches, sugars, fats. 38 weeks. Yeast and baking powder used in flour mixtures. Dietary standards, calculating daily dietary for a family of six. Cooking and serving of breakfast, luncheon, dinner, thus planned. Visit to the public market to see meats cut, and inspect vegetables. Note books in students' language and essays aid in English composition work. *Periods are 1½ hours alternate days for 38 weeks.	Millinery (winter hats). Alternating with sewing : — Cotton dress or blouse, and unlined skirt. 45 hours. Modelling in clay and wood from nature ; casts and designs. Brief study of the ornament of local buildings. †Time given per day the same as in first year.	Historic ornament used in wood carving designs. Values in light and shade. — Still life. Charcoal from casts. Pen and ink.

APPENDIX B.—*continued.*

DOMESTIC SCIENCE COURSE.

Third Year.

Academic.	Domestic Science.	Household Art and Manual Training.	Art.
English literature (as required for admission to American colleges.) (2) 38 weeks. German— (3) 38 weeks. Algebra—completed. 19 weeks. Geometry—solid, 19 weeks. Physics, light, electricity. 19 weeks. Botany — structural preparation of bacteriology: cultures from air, water, milk, clothing, hands.	Chemistry of foods and physiology of digestion. 19 weeks. Food for the sick. I. Water analysis. II. Proteid analysis. III. Albuminoid analysis. IV. Sugar analysis. V. Starch analysis. VI. Fat analysis. Analysis of milk, meat, some baby food VII. Digestion experiment. VIII. Practice in cookery for the sick. IX. Diet in special diseases.	Dressmaking. 19 weeks. Drafting, cutting, fitting, making lined bodice and lined skirt the sketch for which has been made in the Art department.	Water colour :— I. Still life. II. Design in wall paper, rugs, hangings. III. Sketching from nature. IV. Costume design. Design in embroidery stencil. Pyrography.

APPENDIX B.—*continued.*

DOMESTIC SCIENCE COURSE.

Fourth Year.

Academic.	Domestic Science.	Household Art and Manual Training.	Art.
English literature "College English." (2) 38 weeks. German. 38 weeks. Trigonometry. (3) 19 weeks. Analytical chemistry, Study of five groups. Analysis of minerals studied in first year. Analysis of unknown. 19 weeks. Psychology, in part experimental. 19 weeks. Electives for those who are to take the teacher's training. 19 weeks. Review arithmetic alternating with review English grammar (Elective) 19 weeks. Photographic science.	Sanitation. . 19 weeks. House : soil, foundation, floor plans, plumbing, finishings, heating and ventilating systems. Visits to house in process of erection to study details. Plan a house. Food supply :— Purity in foods. (a) Adulterations. (b) Plant life, bacteria, moulds. (c) Insects. Air Supply. Rate of entrance of fresh air ; bacterial cultures of air. Water. Disinfection (experiment on germ life.) Theory of disease. Home-nursing (visit to hospital). Cost of living.	Electives. 19 weeks. Advanced dressmaking. Wood carving, applied historic ornament. Advanced carpentry—design in furniture.	Charcoal from the antique. House plans :— floor plans drawn to scale. Theory of colour. Household decoration ; colour sketches of interiors. Illustrations, pen and ink. Book covers.

APPENDIX C.

COMPREHENSIVE EQUIPMENT FOR HIGH SCHOOL COURSE IN DRESSMAKING AND LAUNDRY WORK.

The following is reproduced by kind permission from "Teachers College Record." Vol. II., No. 5, November, 1901. "The Economics of Manual Training." (TheUnited States of America dollars have been converted for convenience into English coinage.)

(1.)—DRESSMAKING.

EQUIPMENT FOR CLASS OF FIFTEEN GIRLS.

(1) Drafting and dressmaking room.

		£.	s.	d.
8 tables		12	10	0
Mirror	£3. 2s. 6d. to	4	3	4
Pedestal		1	7	0
Screen -		1	13	4
1 gas stove, 3 burners -		1	0	10
Connections to stove		0	8	4
8 irons, 4 heavy, and 4 long narrow		0	8	4
Wardrobe	£5. 4s. 2d. to	8	6	8
15 chairs		6	5	0
15 high stools		1	11	3
Clothes tree		0	14	7
5 sewing machines	£31. 5s. 0d. to	57	5	10
4 ironing boards -		0	16	8
Board for curved seams		0	3	9
15 boxes for materials -		0	4	4
Paper roll holder -		1	0	10
18 yard sticks		0	17	10
18 tape measures -		0	3	5
18 scissors -		1	1	10
3 bust forms-		0	6	3
2 skirt forms		1	5	0

£71. 10s. 3d. to £101 14 5

(2) Sewing room, to accommodate thirty pupils.

		£.	s	.d
Roll front case for materials for 90 pupils -		10	8	4
Tables to accommodate 30 pupils	£6. 5s. 0d. to	16	13	6
30 chairs		12	10	0
30 footstools		12	10	0
36 boxes (6 large and 30 small) -		0	17	6
Demonstration frame -		0	8	4

£42. 19s. 2d. to £53 7 8

Total cost of equipment - - £114. 9s. 5d. to £155 2 1

CHEAPER EQUIPMENTS FOR FIFTEEN IN DRESSMAKING AND THIRTY IN SEWING.

Dressmaking and Sewing Room combined.

	£.	s.	d.
8 tables, 5 foot kitchen - - - - -	4	14	0

(An even less expensive table arrangement may be obtained of boards supported on saw-horses, when the two kinds of work are practised in the same room. A convenient plan for the dressmaking tables is to have these hinged to the wall, so as to drop down when not in use.)

	£.	s.	d.
30 chairs at £1 11s. 3d. per doz. - - - -	3	18	1
1 stove (3 burners) and tubing - - - -	0	15	7
6 irons - - - - - -	0	6	3
4 ironing boards - - - - - -	0	15	0
Wardrobe - - - - £1 0s. 10d. to	4	3	4
4 sewing machines - - - £25 0s. 0d. to	45	16	8
Screen - - - - - - -	0	12	6
18 yard sticks - - - - - -	0	17	4
33 scissors (3 of them buttonhole) - - -	1	19	2
6 large boxes at 1s. 5½d. - - - -	0	8	9
30 small boxes at 3½d. - - - - -	0	8	9
Total cost - - - - £40 16s. 3d. to £64	**15**	**5**	

Average cost of maintenance for the work in the High school, if the pupils furnish their own garment materials, is about 6d. per pupil.

(2.)—LAUNDRY EQUIPMENT.

Equipment for class of eight pupils.

	£.	s.	d.
Large fibre tub - - - - - -	0	3	5½
Double boiler for starch - - - -	0	4	3½
Tea-kettle - - - - - -	0	4	0½
12 small fibre tubs - - - - -	1	10	0
Small fibre pail - - - - - -	0	0	10
Granite soap cooker - - - - -	0	2	8½
Yellow earthen bowl, 1 quart - - - -	0	0	6
Yellow earthen bowl, 2 quarts - - - -	0	0	8
Yellow earthen bowl, 4 quarts - - - -	0	1	8½
8 yellow earthenware bowls, 1 quart - - -	0	1	8
2 tin measuring cups - - - - -	0	0	10
6 table-spoons - - - - - -	0	2	0
6 tea-spoons - - - - - -	0	1	3
Knife - - - - - - -	0	0	5
Wooden spoon - - - - - -	0	0	2½
Carried forward - - - £2	**14**	**7**	

	£	s.	d.
Brought forward - - - - - -	2	14	7
100 feet of clothes line - - - - - -	0	3	9
Clothes pins - - - - - - -	0	0	5
Towel roller - - - - - - -	0	0	5
Skirt board covers :			
10 yards unbleached cotton cloth - - - -	0	3	4
4 yards cotton felting, 54 inches - - - -	0	8	4
1 yard white flannel - - - - - - -	0	1	8
Safety pins - - - - - - - -	0	1	0½
3 roller towels (7½ in., linen-towelling) - -	0	3	8
Dish pan, 14 quarts - - - - - -	0	2	7½
Universal wringer, large - - - - -	0	17	8½
2 universal wringers, small - - - - -	1	0	10
Tin dipper - - - - - - - -	0	0	10
Oval clothes basket - - - - - -	0	5	2½
Oval boiler - - - - - - -	0	5	2½
6 4-foot benches - - - - - - -	1	2	6
8 4½-foot skirt boards, with adjustable supports - -	2	10	0
8 small wash boards, two-thirds usual size - -	0	12	6
2 clothes horses (4 feet high, 4 folds) - - -	0	7	4
Fringe brush - - - - - - -	0	2	7½
3 soft brushes - - - - - - -	0	4	9
3 whisk brooms, for sprinkling - - - -	0	2	3
4 flat irons, 7 pounds - - - - - -	0	9	2
8 flat irons, 5 pounds - - - - - -	0	10	8
8 flat irons, 4 pounds - - - - - -	0	13	4
4 flat irons, 3 pounds - - - - - -	0	5	10
(Cheaper irons may be had at twopence per pound.)			
8 Troy polishers - - - - - - -	0	15	0
8 iron stands - - - - - - -	0	1	8
8 iron holders (asbestos) - - - - - -	0	1	4
	£14	8	7

Maintenance.

	£.	s.	d.
3 dozen ivory soap - - - - - - -	0	6	3
Starch - - - - - - - - - -	0	1	3
Blueing - - - - - - - - -	0	1	0½
Beeswax - - - - - - - - -	0	1	8
Borax - - - - - - - - - -	0	0	10
Ammonia - - - - - - - - -	0	0	10
White wine vinegar - - - - - - -	0	0	5
Salt - - - - - - - - - -	0	0	2½
Cost per pupil 1s. 6½d. - - -	£0	12	6

APPENDIX D.

HOUSEHOLD SCIENCE COURSES IN BOSTON HIGH SCHOOLS.

A Course of Twenty Lectures for High School Students

Miss S. Maria Elliott, Boston, Mass.

I. Choice of a Home.

1. Requisites and conditions—air, light, situation, soil, etc.
2. Heating, ventilation, lighting—health, comfort, etc.
3. Drainage—purpose, dangers, etc.
4. House inspection—health, convenience, economy of energy.

II. Furnishing the House.

. Dust, a study of—the foundation for.
6. The Science of Cleanliness.
7. House furnishings—sanitary, artistic, economical.

III. Care of the House.

8. Removal of dust—sweeping, dusting.
9. Care of woodwork—cleanliness and preservation
10. Care of metallic, mineral surfaces and fabrics.
11. Special sanitation and disinfection.

IV. Food.

12. The five Food Principles.
13. Food materials.
14. Food combinations.
15. { Diet and dietaries
16. { applied to different ages and conditions.

V. Health and Hygiene.

17. Emergencies.
18. What to do for the invalid and sick.
19. School and public hygiene.
20. Disposal of refuse.

A Course of Twenty Lessons for High School Students.

1. Necessities of a house—location, soil, etc.
2. Building materials and general healthful construction.
3. Elements in house-building—arrangement, size, mechanics, etc.
4. Heating and ventilation.
5. Drainage systems. Water supply.
6. House inspection.
7. House furnishings—principles of sanitary, artistic, economical furnishings.
8. Study of dust and its dangers.
9. Construction and form applied to furnishings.
10. Colour.
11. Removal of dust.
12. Study of woodwork.
13. Care of woodwork.
14. Study of metals and mineral surfaces.
15. Care of metals and mineral surfaces
16. Study of fabrics.
17. Care of fabrics.
18. Principles of laundry-work.
19. Household insects.
20. Care of plumbing. Disposal of refuse.

The Evolution of the House.

A Course of Lessons for High School Student

Miss Maria Elliott, Boston, Mass.

Shelter—protection from animals and elements.
Privacy—safety of person and possessions.
Necessities of a house.
Luxuries of a house.
Care of necessities.
Care of luxuries.
Personal hygiene.
School hygiene.
Public hygiene.
Duty to self.
Duty to friends.
Duty to public at large.
Bacteriology.
Chemistry applied to food principles.
Chemistry applied to cleaning principles
Physics applied to food principles.
Physics applied to cleaning principles.
Physics of house building and care.

APPENDIX E.

COURSE IN HOME DRESSMAKING, PRATT INSTITUTE,
BROOKLYN, NEW YORK.

Two lessons a week ; five terms of three months each.

Entrance Requirements.—Students are required to be over sixteen years of age, to have a knowledge of hand and machine sewing, to be able to use the tape measure, and to make simple garments and cambric dresses as taught in the sewing classes.

COURSE OF STUDY.

First Grade.—Draughting skirts and bodices. Exercise with practice material in fitting and designing and in making dress trimmings and finishings. Study of colour, form, line and texture.

Second Grade.—Draughting and making walking skirt. Cutting fitting and making lined bodice. Study of the contour and poise of the body.

Third Grade.—Matching stripes and plaids. Draughting and making princess gown. Practice in designing : study of artistic principles.

Fourth Grade.—Draughting, cutting, and making jacket. Draughting child's dress and coat. Study of woollen textiles.

Fifth Grade.—Draughting and making evening gown. Practice in designing gowns for home and evening wear.

Drawing, Water-colour and Elementary Design—Practice in the use of the pencil and of water-colour. Appearance of objects, bows, gowns and drapery. Outline and proportion of the human form. Study of historic costumes : designing of gowns.

APPENDIX F,

COURSES OF DOMESTIC SCIENCE AND ART AT DREXEL INSTITUTE.

(Drexel Institute of Art, Science, and Industry, Philadelphia.)

I.—NORMAL COURSE OF DOMESTIC SCIENCE.

Applicants to enter the Normal Course in Domestic Science are requested to give the following information :—

Name (in full)..

Address..

Date of birth..

What is your general health ?..

Have you any noticeable defect of any kind as in sight, hearing, or any other defect ?..

From what school, or college, or courses of study have you been graduated ?..

Year of graduation ?..

Have you taught ?...

In what grades ?..

Where ?...

How long ?..

What year or years ?..

Have you any knowledge of cookery ?..

Do you intend taking this course to fit yourself as a director or instructor of Domestic Science ?..

Remarks...

Applicants to enter the Housekeepers' Course are requested to give the following information :—

Name (in full)..

Philadelphia address..

If not a resident of Philadelphia, also give home address..........................

Age...

From what school, or courses of study have you been graduated ?.....................

What has been your occupation ?..

Have you any knowledge of cookery ?..

Do you intend taking this course to fit yourself to take a position as housekeeper or matron ?..

DEPARTMENT OF DOMESTIC SCIENCE.
NORMAL COURSE.

The following additional information concerning the Normal Course in Domestic Science will answer a large number of the questions made by inquirers :—

Examinations.—No entrance examination is required. For admission at least a high-school education or its equivalent is necessary. Age, education, previous experience, personal fitness, etc., are considered in the selection of applicants.

Expenses.—There are no free scholarships. Tuition fee $80 (£16) per year, text-books and stationery, $10 (£2). Board may be had near the Institute at prices ranging from five to eight dollars per week.

The following articles are required for work—

FOR KITCHEN LABORATORY.

Black woollen skirt.

Four plain white blouses. Not a thin material and without tucks or insertion.

One dozen white linen collars.

Narrow tie of any colour.

Black belt.

Six aprons:—White cambric, 36 in. wide ; use one and a half widths, finish with a five-inch hem ; length three inches from the bottom of skirt. Band, one and a half inches, finished. Bib, eight inches by nine, finished, with a hem of half an inch. Straps, one and a quarter inches wide, finished ; fasten to upper corners of the bib, pass over shoulders, and button on waist button. May be bought at the Institute.

Six pairs of sleeves ; seven inches deep, finished ; one inch hem top and bottom. May be purchased at the Institute for ten cents a pair.

Caps : Must be purchased at the Institute as needed, 15 cents each.

Holders : Four thin holders with tape 27 inches long, with a loop to put on apron band.

Towels : Five towels made of glass towelling, 18 inches long, with a tape loop to put on apron band.

Gymnasium Suits.—Black serge, made into a simple blouse with a rolling collar and a divided skirt.

Length of skirt, from waist to ankle. Divided two inches above the knee and an eight-inch gusset inserted. It requires four widths of 42-inch material, two widths in each leg ; or three widths of 56-inch goods, with one and a half widths in each leg. Put elastic at the bottom of each leg. Skirt opens in front.

Blouse and skirt must be buttoned together by no less than six buttons.

Black tie.

Black stockings. Black rubber-soled shoes, bought at 25 North 13th Street, Philadelphia.

Positions.—The school does not guarantee positions to graduates, but assists them when it can. Salaries depend upon the kind of work done, the responsibility involved, the capabilities of the applicant, etc.

Outside Work.—Students have no time to engage in outside work, and cannot, therefore, earn any money while taking the course.

There are no summer, evening, or correspondence courses for Normal Students.

STUDENTS' HOUSE.

A Students House has been organized in connection with the work of the Department of Domestic Science. Board and room may be obtained at $.5 per week. Board alone $3.50 per week.

Applicants wishing to have a place in the house should send in their names and they will be put on the waiting list.

The three following Courses are taken by Normal students, House-keepers, and General Students.

The First Course is given by Normal students as Practice Classes to children.

FIRST COURSE IN COOKERY.

1. Combustion, building fire, scalloped oysters.

2. Food principles, water, tea coffee, chocolate.

3. Starch, white sauce, milk toast.

4. Vegetables in white sauce, celery, cabbage, carrots, stuffed potatoes.

5. Soups without meats, cream of potato, potato, croutons, crisp crackers

6. Cereals, sugar, steamed apples, apple sauce, avena, steamed and boiled rice, wheatena.

7. Fats and oils, caramel, beef drippings, fried oysters, cranberry jelly.

8. Fish balls, baked apples.

9. Proteids, eggs cooked in water, plain omelet, flour omelet, poached egg, soft cooked egg.

10. Milk, cup custard, floating island, pasteurized milk, rennet.

11. Cheese, soufflé, welsh rarebit, cheese straws.

12. Meats, cuts for broiling and roasting, roast, broiled chops, lemon jelly, Hamburg steaks.

13. Meats, cuts for soups and stews, soup stock, scalloped mutton, baking powder biscuits.

14. Corn beef hash, corn muffins.

15. Bread, large quantity.

16. Small loaves of bread, hash with gravy.

SECOND COURSE IN COOKERY.

1. Parker house rolls, bread sticks, buns, cinnamon buns.

2. Brown bread, fruit pudding, hard and lemon sauces, butter balls.

3. Plain griddle cakes, waffles, fricassees, oysters.

4. Fish, baked fish with stuffing, tomato sauce, Hollandaise sauce, steamed fish.

5. Poultry, draw a fowl, truss for roasting, cut for fricassee.

6. Cooking in deep fat, alternate rice and chicken croquettes, crumpets.

7. Soup lesson with white stock, cream and potato, clam purée, soup sticks, noodles.

8. Review meat, veal cutlets, noodles with cheese.

9. Pastry, apple and lemon pie.

10. Desserts, snow pudding, soft custard, coffee cream, sponge cake.

11. Cake, plain, cream almond frosting,

12. Cookies, strawberry shortcake.

13. Salads, potato, French dressing, cole slaw, boiled dressing, stuffed eggs.

14. Opening a lobster, Mayonnaise dressing.

15. Luncheon, served on desks.

16. Ice cream, chocolate cakes.

THIRD COURSE IN COOKERY.

1 Preserving, general rules, canned peaches, crab apple jelly, spiced pears.

2. Preserving continued, ketchup, quince preserve, grape juice, grape jam.

3. Reed birds, Bavarian cream, stuffed peppers, black bean soup.

4. Devilled crabs, chocolate cake, boiled frosting, chocolate filling.

5. Sweetbread patties, Swedish timbales, breaded mutton cutlets, Cuban sauce, potatoes for garnishing.

6. Caramel Charlotte, Charlotte Russe, bombe glacé, jumbles, macaroons.

7. Fillet of beef, mushroom sauce, mock turtle soup.

8. Lobster cutlets, sauce tartare, rolled wafers.

9. Candy, candied orange peel, peppermints, glacé, salted almonds, mint leaves.

10. Roast duck, potato stuffing, gravy, plum pudding.
11. Boned chicken, tomato salad, brandy sauce.
12. Puff paste, cream horns, condés, patties, tarts.
13. Terrapin, cream puffs.
14. Ginger ice cream, white sponge cake, meringues, grape frappé.
15. Nesselrode pudding, plain cake, ornamental frosting, sponge fingers.
16. Marketing.

Normal Domestic Science.—Work in Senior Year.
Advanced Cookery.

1. Veal croquettes.
   Creole soup.
   Buns.
   Molasses cookies.
   White corn cake.
   Clam chowder
   Smelts.
   Pop overs.
   Jelly roll.
   Chicken cutlets.
   Macaroni croquettes.

2. Calf's foot jelly.
   Duchess soup.
   Ox tail soup.
   Consommé.
   Boiled fish.
   Banbury tarts.
   Puff paste.
   Cannelon of beef.
   Yorkshire pudding.
   Queen fritters.
   Roast turkey.

3. Breakfast.   Cost $1.25.
   Oranges.
   Germea.   Sugar, cream.
   Halibut.   Potato balls.
   Waffles with syrup.
   . Butter balls.   Bread.
   Coffee.

Prepared by four members of the class and served to eight members of the class.

4. Oyster croquettes.
   Fish chowder.
   Guinea fowl.
   Veal loaf.
   Jumbles.
   Rabbit.
   Capon.
   Orange puffs.
   Chocolate Charlotte.
   Orange sauce.
   White mountain cake.
   Fig filling.

5. Braised tongue.
   Roast pork.
   Boiled leg of mutton.
   Caper sauce.
   Cream puffs.
   Ginger pudding.
   Molasses drop cake.
   Custard soufflé.
   Cranberry pudding.
   Sterling sauce.

6. Luncheon.   Cost $ 1.50 (about 6s.).
   Cream of tomato soup.
   Soup sticks.
   Salmon cutlets.
   Potato soufflé.   Corn pudding.
   Lettuce.
   Crackers.   Cheese.
   Grape frappé.
   Cake.   Coffee.
   Olives.

7. Sally Lunn.
   Chicken pie.
   Lemon pie.
   Mock terrapin.
   French rusks.
   Brown bread.
   Bavarian cream.
   White sponge cake.
   Cream puffs.
   Salmon croquettes.
   Peptonized beef broth.
   Squab in paper.
   Tomato jelly.

8. Aladdin cooker used for following dishes :—

Stewed chicken.	Baked potatoes.
Stewed tomatoes.	Chocolate bread pudding.
Rolled almond wafers.	Devilled scallops.
Chocolate wafers.	Meat cakes.
Coffee mousse.	Chestnut purée.

Loin of veal with vegetables.

9. Luncheon.   Cost $ 2.00.

Cranberry pie.	Peach short cake.
Coffee cake.	Coffee mousse.
Planked shad.	Spring chicken.
Spring lamb.	Lemon pie.
White corn cake.	Ice rice pudding.

Rice cream.

10. Dinner.   Cost $ 2.50.

Mock turtle soup.

Bread sticks.   Radishes.

Boiled trout.

Potato roses.

Baked chicken.

Brown gravy.   Asparagus.

Brain patties.

Lettuce salad.

French dressing.   Cheese.

Crackers.

Wafers.   Frozen strawberries.   Coffee.

COURSE OF DEMONSTRATIONS.—ONE TERM.

SENIOR CLASS.

SUBJECTS.	DEMONSTRATIONS.
1. - - - - - - - -	Instructor in Cookery
2. - - - - - - - -	„ „
3. - - - - - - - -	„
4. Eggs - - - - - - -	Student.
5. Milk - - - - - - -	„
6. Invalid Cookery - - - - - -	
7. Use of Chafing Dish - - - - - -	
8. Milk - - - - - - - -	
9. Meat - - - - - - - -	
10. Bread - - - - - - - -	
11. Invalid Cookery - - - - - -	
12. Soups - - - - - - - -	
13. Use of Chafing Dish - - - - - -	
14. Meat - - - - - - - -	
15. Baking - - - - - - - -	
16. Desserts - - - - - - - -	

NORMAL DOMESTIC SCIENCE.

SHORT COURSE IN HOME NURSING.

(Additional lectures given in the course in Physiology.)

Spring term.   Senior year.

1. Sick room.
2. Sick bed, changing bed and body clothing.
3. Baths, for cleanliness.
4. Baths, hot water, hot air, vapour.
5. Baths, cold ; poultices, fomentation.
6. Sleep. Method of inducing it, administration of medicine, feeding a patient.

Normal and Technical Classes.
Laundry Course.

1. General notes. Removal of stains.
2. Wash : table linen, tablecloths, napkins, doylies.;
 . Wash : bed linen, sheets, pillow cases. Iron : Table linen.
 . Wash : body linen, night dress, drawers. Iron : Bed linen.
 . Wash : body linen, white skirt, corset cover. Iron : Body linen.
 . Wash : shirt-waist ; collars. Iron : corset cover, skirts.
 . Wash : stockings. Starch : blouse, collars.
 8. Iron : blouse, collars.
 9. Wash : flannels and coloured clothes.
10. Iron : flannels and coloured clothes.
11. Wash : handkerchiefs, embroideries. Iron : embroideries, handkerchiefs.
12. Clean and wash black and coloured woollen goods. Wash, clear starch,
and iron sash curtains.
Theoretical instruction of the scientific principles involved in the various
processes is followed by practice.
 Soaps, washing fluids, bleaching powders, blueings, and starch, are
discussed in their scientific and practical relations to laundry work.

Normal and Technical Domestic Science Courses.
Waitresses' Course.

1. Appearance and dress of waitresses.
2. Washing dishes.
3. Care of pantry.
4. Care of dining-room.
5. Rules for serving.
6. Rules for making and serving chocolate, tea, black coffee, bread, butter
balls, sandwiches, salads, French dressing, mayonnaise dressing, potato
salad, soft cooked egg.
7. The keeping of table linen.
8. Early morning work in bedroom.
9. Later morning work in bedroom.
10. Evening work in bedroom.
11. General directions for bedroom.

Domestic Science Course for Normal and other Students.

Synopsis of Lectures on Planning and Building of a House.

 First Lecture.—The location and surroundings of the house, the placing of the house, topography, drawings of site, opportunities of situation
cost of houses and general method of figuring them.

 Second Lecture.—The house in detail, the rooms and their position in
the house, the basement, first floor, second floor, attic. The materials used
in their construction as they interest the housekeeper.

 Third Lecture.—The planning of suburban houses ; when a wooden
house is preferable, when a masonry house, stone or brick, style of architecture.

 Fourth Lecture.—The simple city house, fire limits, planning of the
city house as to economy of space and conveniences, the architectural
character of the front, architectural details of the interior.

 Fifth Lecture.—Sanitation of the house, heating and ventilation,
water supply and drainage, plumbing, lighting, the kitchen, importance of
sanitary arrangements of the house.
This is succeeded by a course in House Decoration and Furnishing,
illustrated by visits of observation to houses, shops, factories, etc.

HOUSEHOLD SCIENCE AND ECONOMICS.

Classification of Food Principles.
Food adjuncts.
Fermentation.
Preservation of food materials.
National and State laws regarding food adulteration and inspection.
Manufactured food materials.
Scientific kitchens (public, school, home).
Care of the house according to hygienic laws.
Water supply—filtration of water.
Heating and lighting. Care of lamps.
Care of rooms—dining-room, bath-room, bed-room.
The kitchen.
Disposal of waste.
Chemicals for household use. Care and cleaning of silver, nickel, iron, paints, copper, tin, marble, woodwork, brass, zinc, porcelain, glass.
Laundry of table linen, removal of stains.
Laundry of lace.

LECTURES TO DOMESTIC SCIENCE AND DOMESTIC ART STUDENTS.

By PRESIDENT MAC ALISTER.

HISTORY OF EDUCATION.

1. Education in ancient times.
2. Education in the Middle Ages, with special reference to monastic institutions.
3. The great reformers of education in modern times.
4. The beginnings of scientific, technical, and industrial education.
5. The fundamental principles of method in education. (2 lectures.)
6. Domestic Science Training in schools.
7. Domestic Arts Training in schools.
8. Domestic Science and Arts in their relations to some social problems.
9. The duties and responsibilities of the teacher.

CHEMISTRY.

Junior Year.

I—*General Chemistry—*
    Lectures illustrated by experiments, diagrams, specimens, etc.
    Laboratory work.
    The student is trained—
        (*a*) to deduce the more important facts of the science ;
        (*b*) to study comparative properties of substances ;
        (*c*) to acquire a scientific habit of thought

II. *Qualitative Analysis—*
    Common metals and their reactions.
    Analysis of solutions containing those metals.
    Acids and their reactions.
    Analysis of solutions containing bases and acids studied.
    General miscellaneous qualitative work, examination of powders, alloys, insoluble substances, as time permits.

Senior Year.

I—*Organic Chemistry—*
    Hydrocarbons and their derivatives.
    The students prepare and study a typical compound of each class.

II—*Quantitative Analysis—*
    Analysis of food materials.
    The following list indicates the general scope of the quantitative work.
    Chemically pure salts, potable water, common salt, bi-carbonate of sodium, flour or bread, baking powders, sugar or syrups, milk, butter, lard, cheese, tea, coffee, chocolate.

During the senior year, second term, a course of lectures in the Chemistry of Food and Dietetics is given, the lectures being supplemented by laboratory work.

Outline of Lecture Course on Food and Dietetics, 1901.

By Ernest A. Congdon, Professor of Chemistry.

I.—Introductory. Historical. Relation of chemistry to food and diet.

II.—Definition of a food. Uses of food in the human economy (repair tissues ; produce heat ; produce force).

III.—Chemical composition of the human body. (Elements present. Compounds present.)

IV.—Chemical composition of food materials. Proximate food principles : Proteids, fats, carbohydrates, water, mineral matter.

V.—Chemical analysis of food materials. (Analyses of American food materials—Atwater.)

VI.—Value of foods. Use of the "Calorie" (heat unit). Value of the nutrients (proteids, fats, carbohydrates) expressed in calories. The nutrient ratio, the ratio expressed in calories, between the nitrogenous and non-nitrogenous nutrients.

VII.—Metabolism, or the exchange of food materials in the animal economy. (Anabolism and Katabolism.) Metabolism divided . into—introduction, digestion, absorption, and assimilation of food.

VIII.—Study of diet. Standard for dietaries. Foreign and American. (Work of Voit, Atwater and others.)

IX.—Computation of amounts of foods necessary to conform to standard dietaries. Calculation of the value of various diets and of prepared foods.

X.—Chemical study of materials used as foods. Water (potable and mineral), common salt, starch foods, sugars, fats, oils, cereals ; dairy products—milk, butter, cheese, etc., eggs ; flesh foods—meat, fish, etc. ; fruits, vegetables, salads, beverages, food adjuncts.

XI.—Study of fermentation. Organized and unorganized ferments. Fermentative and putrefactive changes. Yeast. Work of Bacteria.

XII.—Preparation of food materials for consumption. Chemical study of changes that foods undergo in cooking processes. Food adulterations and their detection. Bibliography. Literature on foods and dietetics.

` Outline of Course on Food Analysis, 1901.

(Laboratory Work and Recitations.)

By A. Honwood, Instructor in Chemistry.

I. Analysis of crystallized barium chloride.—
    (*a*) Determination of barium.
    (*b*)   ,,   chloride.
    (*c*)   ,,   water.
II. Analysis of potable water :—
    (*a*) Total solids.
    (*b*) Chlorine.
    (*c*) Free ammonia.
    (*d*) Albuminoid ammonia

III. Analysis of milk.—
 (*a*) Specific gravity.
 (*b*) Water or total solids.
 (*c*) Fat (Feser lactoscope, lacto-butyrometer and Adam's
  method).
 (*d*) Casein (Kjeldahl method).
 (*e*) Ash.
 (*f*) Milk sugar (Soxhlet, gravimetric).
IV. Analysis of butter.-
 (*a*) Water.
 (*b*) Fat.
 (*c*) Curd
 (*d*) Salt.
 (*e*) Ash.
 (*f*) Volatile acids (distinction from oleomargarine.)
V. Analysis of cereal foods, bread, flour.—
 (*a*) Water.
 (*b*) Fat.
 (*c*) Proteid.
 (*d*) Carbohydrate (starch, sugar)
 (*e*) Fibre.
 (*f*) Ash.
VI. Analysis of tea.—
 (*a*) Moisture.
 (*b*) Tannin.
 (*c*) Extract.
 (*d*) Caffein
 (*e*) Ash.
VII. Analysis of baking powders.-—
 (*a*) Determination of class (phosphate, alum, etc.).
 (*b*) Total carbon dioxide.
 (*c*) Available carbon dioxide.

REFERENCES.

U. S. Government Bulletin, No. 46. Leffman and Beam, Water Analysis. Wanklyn, Water Analysis. Leffman and Beam, Milk and Butter. Gerber, Analysis of Milk.

NORMAL DOMESTIC SCIENCE AND DOMESTIC ART STUDENTS.
PHYSIOLOGY COURSE.

Junior Year.

1.—Introduction. Definitions. Plan of organization of the animal body. General dissection of an animal.

2.—Chemic composition of the human body. The carbo-hydrates and fats.

3.—Chemic composition of the human body. The proteids and inorganic compounds.

4.—The physiology of the cell. Its growth, movements, reproduction and general nutrition.

5.—Histology and physiology of the epithelial and connective tissues.

6.—Mechanism of the skeleton. Structure and function of the joints. The animal body as a machine for doing work.

7.—The general physiology of muscle tissue. The structure and chemic composition of muscle.

8.—The muscle contraction. The conditions influencing the contraction. The production of heat. The relation of food to heat and work. The special physiology of muscles

9.—The general physiology of nerve tissue. The general arrangement of the nervous system. The structure and function of the nerves.

10.—Reflex and voluntary actions.

11.—Foods. Dietetics. The necessity for foods. Phenomena of starvation. Classification of alimentary principles. The uses of foods in the body.

12.—The heat values of foods. The chemic composition of the animal. The vegetable and cereal foods.

13.—Digestion. The structure of the alimentary canal. Mastication.

14.—Insalivation. The physical and chemic action of saliva on the food and starch.

15.—Gastric digestion. The composition of gastric juice and its chemic action on the proteids. Influences affecting digestion.

16.—Intestinal digestion. The physiologic action of the pancreatic juice. The bile and intestinal juice. Their actions on foods.

17.—Absorption. The mechanism by which the digested products enter the blood.

18.—The blood. Its physical properties. Its chemic composition.

19.—The blood corpuscles, red and white. The relation of the blood to the tissues.

20.—The circulation of the blood. The general anatomy of the circulating apparatus. The structure and functions of the heart.

21.—The structure and functions of the arteries.

22.—The capillaries and veins.

23.—Respiration—the object of. The general structure of the respiratory apparatus. The movements of respiration. The amount of air breathed under different conditions. The composition of the air.

24.—The changes it undergoes at the time of breathing. The amount of oxygen absorbed and the amount of CO_2 discharged.

25.—Ventilation.

26.—Animal heat. Source and causes of heat production. The disposition of heat in the body. The manner in which the normal temperature is regulated.

27.—The skin. Its structure and functions.

28.—The kidneys. Their structure and functions. The urine and its chemical composition.

Senior Year.

The Physiological Chemistry of—
Starches and sugars ⎫
Fats ⎬ Three lectures.
Proteids ⎭

The Physiological Chemistry of Digestion—
Salivary digestion ⎫
Gastric digestion ⎬ Three lectures.
Intestinal digestion ⎭

Absorption of Foods—
Demonstration. One lecture.

The Fermentation of Foods—
Causes and conditions determining it. One lecture

The Putrefactive Changes in Foods—
The causes and the conditions determining ⎫ One lecture.
it and the products ⎭

BACTERIOLOGY—
Bacteria. Their nature, structure ⎫ One lecture.
Mode of activity and classification ⎭

The Parasites of Animal Foods. One lecture.

The Bacterial Infection of Foods. One lecture.

Ptomaines. Leucomaines—
Their influence in the production of disease.
The Thymus and Thyroid Glands. One lecture.

BIOLOGY—
> General dissection of animal forms.
> The structure of the fish, turtle, frog, chicken, rabbit, lobster, oyster and clam.
> Reproduction   Three lectures.

THE DISEASES CONNECTED WITH DISORDERED NUTRITION—
> Gout. Diabetes. Rickets. Rheumatism. Scurvy.

HYGIENE.

Physical development (details of).
Physical training (supplemented by practice).
Effects of diet.
Care of the skin.
Clothing suited for various ages.
Ventilation—Natural and Artificial.
Household sanitation.
Emergencies—First aid and accidents, etc., etc.

LECTURES ON BACTERIOLOGY.

1.—Place in Nature.
2.—Presence.
3.—Morphology.
> (a) Bacillus—grouping.
> (b) Micrococcus—grouping.
> (c) Spirillum.
4.—Size and numbers.
5.—Motility.
6.—Nutrition.
7.—Relation to air.
8.—Relation to temperature.
9.—Reproduction.
10.—Helpful and harmful.
> (a) Saprophytes.
> (b) Parasites.
11.—Relation to water supply.
12.—Relation to milk supply.
13.—Relation to butter and cheese making.
14.—Products of activity.
15.—Sterilization. Antiseptics. Disinfectants.
16.—Yeasts and Moulds..
17.—History.

LABORATORY WORK IN BACTERIOLOGY.

1.—Use of microscope.—Cover class preparations.
2.—Unicellular organisms.—Bacteria, infusoria, yeast.
3.—Washing, plugging, and sterilizing glassware.
4.—Preparation of media for pure cultures.—Bouillon, gelatin, agar-agar, potatoes, milk.
5.—Sterilizing media.
6.—Making air plate.
7.—Staining bacteria.
8.—Effect of light on bacteria.
9.—Quantitative analysis of—Tap water, Pasteur filtered water, ice.
10.—Testing Pasteur filter.
11.—Quantitative analysis of :—Walker-Gordon milk, lunch room milk.
12.—Examination and identification of bacteria.
13.—M. butyri aromafaciens.
14.—Tests of disinfectants and antiseptics.—Milk of lime, carbolic acid, boiling water, listerine.

BUSINESS CUSTOMS AND ACCOUNTS.

Lectures on—
  Money and its circulation.
  Banks and banking methods.
  Trust companies.
  Women as stockholders and bondholders.
  Capital and credit, failures. assignments, etc.
  Legal status of women.
  Business papers, cheques, promissory notes, etc.
  Practical work in drawing cheques, writing business letters.
  Book-keeping by double entry (cash book, day book, ledger).

II.—NORMAL COURSE OF DOMESTIC ART.

HAND AND MACHINE SEWING.

Junior Year.

First Grade.—History of implements used in hand sewing ; kinds and qualities of materials for undergarments ; proper position of the body in sewing ; methods of using thread and needles, thimble and tape-measure ; woven textiles ; different kinds of stitches ; combination of stitches ; seams, hems, tucks, button-holes ; making simple garments.

Second Grade.—Sewing machines ; measurements ; drafting drawers, underskirts and nightgowns ; making of garments ; cutting and making corset-covers from patterns ; cutting and making blouses.

Third Grade.—Drafting, cutting, making blouses, cotton dresses, and garments for infants.

DRESSMAKING.

First Grade.

I.—Implements and appliances used in dressmaking.

II.—Cotton staple, its various uses ; choice of materials ; textiles as to colour and application to dress.

III.—Taking measurements ; drafting foundation skirt ; drafting draperies and principles of same ; finishing skirt for trimming or draping ; making lined skirt.

IV.—Form, proportion and line relating to ornament in dress.

V.—Plans for completing skirts ; cutting blouses with seams from patterns drafted by students of the advanced grades, from measurements taken from different members of the class ; basting, fitting planning trimming ; general finish.

Senior Year.

Second Grade.

I.—Colour and textiles ; their various uses and relations to personal adornment ; growth of wool and silk ; manufacture of fabrics.

II.—Taking measurements ; drafting plain bodice from different measurements ; drafting bodice with extra seams for large figure ; cutting and matching striped, plaid, or figured material for bodice-making and trimming the same ; drafting and making dresses on the gown-form.

III.—Artistic dress in its relation to the body ; design in drapery.

IV.—Making dress on gown-form from the students' own designs.

Third Grade.

I.—Advanced drafting. Choice of materials for gowns of special character.

II.—Making dinner dress, evening dress; choice of materials for same. Handling of velvet.

III.—Making models of inexpensive materials to test the design.

IV.—The form and poise of the body in their relation to dress.

V.—Child's dress-materials, drafting, cutting and making the same.

Fourth Grade.

I.—Materials used in making coats, as staple and manufactured.

II.—Drafting jackets and coats of various styles; cutting, basting, fitting, pressing; practice in making pockets, applying same to garments; making button holes, sewing on buttons; lining and finish of coat; making collars.

III.—Principles applied to tailor-made dresses.

MILLINERY.

Junior Year.

First Grade.

I.—Colour and materials as related to the head dress.

II.—Wiring; folds; fitted facing; shirred facing; puffed edge.

III.—Bows and rosettes.

IV.—Study of line and form as applied to frame-making; buckram hat frames.

V.—Fitted hat made, lined and trimmed.

VI.—Manufactures of straw and felt hats, velvet, and ribbon explained.

Second Grade.

I.—Bonnet, with plain crown and with puffing, made, lined, and trimmed.

II.—Bonnet of more complex design.

III.—Toque made, lined, and trimmed.

IV.—Practical work, regulated by the season in which the grade is studied, and leading to a knowledge of the designing of bonnets and hats. At least four pieces of millinery must be made by each student.

Senior Year.

Third Grade.

I.—Crêpe bonnet.

II.—Silk bonnet or hat.

III.—Growth and manufacture of silk explained.

IV.—Wire frame-making.

V.—Large velvet hat.

VI.—Evening bonnet from student's own design

VII.—Shirred hat.

Designing of head-dresses.

DRAWING.

Junior Year.

Outline and light and shade drawing.

Colour studies.

Proportions of the human figure.

Draperies, bows, feathers and hat trimmings in black and white and in colour.

Colour values.

Senior Year.

Rendering of dresses and gowns in black and white and colour.
Designing of hats, bonnets and toques, in black and white and in colour.
Designing of costumes and head-dresses in colour.

Lectures on the Chemistry of Textiles—Dyeing and Cleansing.

Historical sketch { Use of textiles.
{ Art of dyeing.

Study of textiles. { Cotton.
{ Flax.
{ Ramie.
{ Wool.
{ Silk.

Microscopic and chemical methods of ascertaining organic structure.
Materials used in dyeing.
Operations preliminary to process.
Chemistry of —
      Washing.
      Cleansing.
      Bleaching.
      Dyeing.

Colouring matters { Natural.
{ Artificial.

Chemistry of coal-tar colours

III.—EVENING CLASSES IN HOUSEHOLD SCIENCE.

First Course in Cookery.

Lesson   I   Introductory talk and measurements.
      II. Build fire ; scalloped oysters.
      III. Food Principles ; Chocolate and whipped cream.
      IV. Water ; Boiled and filtered coffee.   Tea.
      V. Starch ; Baked potatoes, cornstarch pudding.
      VI. Starch ; Toast with white sauce.
      VII. Vegetables ; Vegetables with white sauce.
      VIII. Soups ; Cream of tomato, potato soup, croutons and crisped crackers.
      IX. Cereals, avena, wheatena ; boiled rice, steamed apples, steamed rice, stewed apples.
      X. Sugar ; Peanut candy, fish balls.
      XI. Fats ; Fried oysters, cranberry jelly.
      XII. Eggs ; Dropped eggs, omelet, eggs cooked in water.
      XIII. Milk ; Cup custard, rennet, floating island.
      XIV. Cheese ; Welsh rarebit, cheese soufflé, Pasteurized milk.
      XV. Meat ; broiled chops, Hamburg steaks, lemon jelly.
      XVI. Meat ; scalloped mutton, corn muffins.
      XVII. Meat ; casserole of rice, tomato sauce, baking powder biscuits.
      XVIII. Meat ; Browned hash, whole wheat muffins.
      XIX. Cake ; Gingerbread, lemon sauce.
      XX. Cake.
      XXI. Bread.
      XXII. Invalid Cookery ; Beef broth, beef juice, milk porridge, flour gruel.
      XXIII. Practical examination.
      XXIV. Apple snowballs ; lemon sauce.

IV.—JUNIOR DOMESTIC SCIENCE COURSE.

SPECIMEN HOUSEHOLD SCIENCE COURSE.

Senior Year.

1. Cellar : Plan and care.
2. Kitchen : Range, etc.
3. Care of pantry.
4. Clean dining-room.
5. Review and have a talk on serving meals.
6. Serving breakfast.
7. Serving luncheon.
8. Serving dinner.
9. Lighting and heating : Care of lamps.
10. Washing table linen.
11. Ironing table linen.
12. Washing and ironing embroideries.
13. Care of bedroom.
14. Spring cleaning : Daily care of a home.

APPENDIX G.

SCHOOL OF HOUSEKEEPING, BOSTON.
SYNOPSIS OF COURSE.

Term I.

1.—HOME SOCIOLOGY.

A study of the home in its sociological aspects. Evolution of the family. Its forms and functions. The standard of living among different races. Industrial changes in their reaction on the home. Tendencies of present industrial forces, and of city life. Economics of production in relation to the family. The home as the unit of consumption. Ethical relation of the home to society ; responsibility of the home as a factor in public health and education. (Eight lectures.)

2.—BACTERIOLOGY IN RELATION TO DAILY LIVING.

Bacteria, their nature and life-history. Conditions affecting growth. Helpful bacteria, with special emphasis on bacteria which are of use to the housekeeper. Bacteria harmful in household processes. Disease germs, with a brief discussion of the most common contagious diseases, and the means by which the intelligent housekeeper can prevent their spread. (Lectures, laboratory work and recitations.)

3.—HOUSE SANITATION.

Location of house, with discussion of soil and drainage of land. Building materials. Construction of cellar. Plumbing. Water supply. Heating, lighting, ventilation, furnishing, cleaning and disinfection. (Lectures, laboratory work and recitations.)

4.—CHEMISTRY OF FOOD-STUFFS.

Relation of food to health. Classes of food-stuffs ; definition, description, physical and chemical properties, decomposition products, occurrence in natural food materials. Effects on food-stuffs of heat, of acids, of alkalies. Typical foods. Composition, food value, money value, and principles of cooking of :—milk and milk products, eggs and meat, fish, cereals, breads, legumes, roots and tubers, fresh vegetables and fruits. (Lectures, laboratory work and recitations.)

5.—DIETARIES.

Aim—to find that combination of food-stuffs which will produce the most efficient individual, and to indicate how this may be done with the least expenditure of money. In planning a dietary there are to be considered : nutritive value, digestibility, palatability, complementary qualities and cost. The common foods are studied in various combinations as suited for children up to the age of fifteen. (Lectures and recitations.)

6.—HYGIENE OF CHILDHOOD.

These exercises will include ·lectures, reading and reports upon the development of the normal child. Special attention will be given to sleep. diet, clothing, exercise, and play. The course will be illustrated by diagrams, photographs and demonstrations of normal and abnormal conditions. (Six lectures.)

7.—HOME NURSING.

Bed-making for bed patients. Change of sheet and night dress. Lifting and moving helpless patients. Bandaging. Baths. (Five lectures, with demonstrations.)

8.—Emergencies.

Anatomy. Cause, symptoms and first treatment of hæmorrhages, burns and scalds, of sprains, dislocations and fractures, of unconscious conditions. (Five lectures, with demonstrations.)

9.—Journal Club.

A resumé of the most recent publications in current literature relating to the Household.

10.—Elementary Chemistry

Chemical and physical change. Constitution of matter. Valence. Laws of chemical actions. Acids, bases and salts. Writing of reactions. Chemistry of combustion, of water, of the atmosphere. Methods of preparation and uses of the more common acids, bases and salts. Chemistry of the common elements and their compounds. (Sixteen lectures and recitations.)

11.—Principles of Cooking.

Practical individual work, including both large and small quantities of material. Food value, cost, preparation and cooking of soup, meats, eggs, fish, poultry, cereals, vegetables, batters and doughs, including breads, sauces, salad dressings, jellies, frozen mixtures, pastry, puddings, and beverages.

12.—Practice Work in Cooking.

Resident pupils will be required to do practice work in cooking and serving on Wednesday afternoons.

Term II.

1.—Home Economics.

Purpose of the home. Its significance as a civilizing force. Its danger to-day. Ideals of living in relation to the home. Economics of living, of the house, of furniture and decoration, of purchase and of food, as controlled by standards of life. Women's responsibility for these standards. The home mother. The house worker. (Lectures and recitations.)

2.—Public Hygiene in Relation to the Housekeeper.

Points of contact between the housekeeper and the public in sanitary matters. Responsibility of the housekeeper. Water supply, ice supply, milk supply. Gas and electricity. House drainage. The disposal of sewage in city and country. Laws regulating the inspection of meat, milk, other foods and drugs. Pavements, street cleaning and disposal of garbage. The relation of the housekeeper to public health in quarantine, isolation notification and disinfection. School hygiene. The sanitation of bake-shops. The abatement of noises and of smoke. Public playgrounds, baths, gymnasia, open spaces. The disposal of arbage, ashes and combustible waste. (Lectures and recitations.)

3.—House Architecture.

Designed to supplement a woman's practical knowledge of the needs of the housekeeper, with a few of the fundamental principles of domestic architecture, in order to secure more intelligent co-operation between herself and the architect. Preparation of site. Construction of foundation, cellar, walls, floors, ceilings, roofs. House plans, with a discussion of what can be done for varying sums of money. Relation of plan to ideals of home life, and to work to be done in the house. (Eight lessons. Lectures, recitations, and field lessons.)

4.—Art in the Home.

Fundamental rules of Art. General principles of proportion, colour an construction. Treatment of walls, floors, ceiling. Selection and cost of furniture, floor coverings, hangings, pictures, chandeliers, lamps, and bric-a-brac. Present shop-standards ; house buyer's responsibility for these standards. Artistic clothing. (Eight lessons. Lectures, recitations, and field lessons.)

5.—Chemisty of Food Stuffs.

Energy giving power of foods. Bodily energy. Methods of food analysis. Study of food values. Effect of storage, of drying, of preservatives. Results of wrong combinations. The science of nutrition. (Lectures and recitations.)

6.—Dietaries.

Review of principles governing dietary standards. The balanced ration. Combinations of food suited for workers, for old persons, for invalids. Economic dietaries. Practice in providing acceptable food for from fifteen to sixty cents per person per day. (Lectures, recitations, and practical work.)

7.—Estimates of Household Expenditure.

To proportion incomes wisely; the real expense in heating, lighting, cleaning, laundry work; serving and preparing food, by various processes and with different materials must be known. No body of exact information on these lines exists. The aim of this course is to obtain such information and to give practice in the actual management of a family income and in the keeping of household accounts. (Recitations and practical work.)

8.—Household Buying.

Equipment required for a house. Qualities to be secured in buying equipment. Quality and money value of different grades in the market, with reference to the furnishing of—kitchen, laundry, dining-room, bedroom. Quality and cost of—cleaning supplies, furniture, carpets, rugs, curtains, etc. (Lectures, recitations, field and practice lessons.)

9.—Marketing.

Beef, anatomy and cuts, illustrated by charts and cutting up of fore and hind quarters of beef. Mutton, veal, pork, fish, poultry, game. Vegetables and their season. Buying of groceries, quantity and quality. Simple methods of detecting adulterations in foods. Canned goods. Practice in marketing and in cooking and comparing different cuts of meat, different grades of canned goods, etc. (Lectures, recitations, field and practice lessons.)

10.—Journal Club.

A continuation of course 9, first term.

11.—Principles of Housework.

Care of cellar, including vegetable cellar and storage room. Kitchen, involving care of refrigerator, pantries, sinks, and disposal of garbage. Cleaning and care of china, glass, silver and brasses. Laundry work. Care of bedroom, plumbing, floors, etc. (Practice lessons.)

12.—Principles of Cooking.

Preparation of breakfasts, luncheons, dinners. Salads and sandwiches Chafing-dish recipes. (Practice lessons.)

13.—Practice Work in Cooking.

Resident pupils will be required to do practice work in cooking and serving on Thursday afternoons.

APPENDIX H.

TEACHERS' COLLEGE, COLUMBIA UNIVERSITY, NEW YORK.

I.—OUTLINE OF COURSE IN HOUSEHOLD ART.

PROFESSOR WOOLMAN, Teachers College, Columbia University, New York

DOMESTIC ART DEPARTMENT.

I. ART IN GENERAL.

(I.) Place in civilization—
    1. Definition.
    2. As related to characteristics of a people.
    3. Value.
        Culture.
        Industry and economics.

(II.) Distinction between decorative art and pictorial art. (Suggested thoughts, purpose, relation of colour, material, etc.)

(III.) Leading Principles.
    1. Fine Arts (painting, music, poetry, architecture, sculpture).
    2. Decorative Arts.
    3. Art in everyday relations.
        (1) Gaining good taste and applying it
        (2) How to present the subject in schools.

(IV.) Historic Ornament.
    1. Important national variations and their distinctive features.
        (1) Egyptian, Grecian, Roman, Byzantine, Romanesque, Gothic, Renaissance and Modern, with comparative study of the architecture, ornament, dress, and furniture of each era.

II. WOMAN'S INFLUENCE.

(I.) Health.
    1. Mental and physical.
    2. Keeping in health—Exercise, food, baths, disposition, fresh air, care of person, complexion, hair, etc., posture, standing, walking, sitting.
    3. Injurious habits.
    4. Effect on classes.

(II.) Voice and manner.

(III.) Study of children.
    1. General condition, health, eyes, fatigue, posture, etc.,
    2. Diseases, understanding indications, care needed after disease.

(IV.) Dress.
    1. Purpose.
    2. Hygienic.
        (1) Warmth—Next body, in doors, out of doors, evening different seasons.
        (2) Weight.
        (3) Pressure.
    3 Artistic.
        (1) Applying laws of art to dress—use, simplicity, truth individuality, harmony, relation of colour, etc.
    4. Cost and purchase.
        (1) Choice of materials—Manufacture, properties of people value and durability. Ethics of shopping, economic standpoint, relation of consumer to manufacturer, etc.
        (2) Dress for varied purposes.
        (3) Care.

(V.) Home.
    1. Laws of art applied to architecture, furnishing and decoration ; economics ; ethics ; individuality, health, etc.

VI.) Business Life.

III. COLOUR.

(I.) Physics, physiology, psychology.
(II.) Terms in use.
(III.) Investigation of colour—Coloured paper and materials, standards, secondary, broken, scales, etc., contrast of colour, harmony of colour.
(IV.) Application to decoration, furnishing and dress.

II.—OUTLINE OF COURSE IN HOUSEHOLD CHEMISTRY.

DOMESTIC SCIENCE DEPARTMENT.

(To be preceded by a year's work in General Chemistry.)

PROFESSOR VULTÉ.

Carbon and Combustion.

Water.—Physical properties of.
　　　　Distillation of.
　　　　Qualitative examination of.
　　　　Tests for Ammonia in.
　　　　Tests for Nitrites.
　　　　Tests for Chlorine.
　　　　Estimation of hardness (Temporary).
　　　　　　　　　　　　　　　(Permanent).
The Atmosphere.—Presence of CO_2 and H_2S.
　　　　　　　　　Moisture.
　　　　　　　　　Dust and solid matter.
　　　　　　　　　Ferments.
Starch and sugar.　Examination of Dextrine.
　　　　　　　　　　　　　　　　Glucose.
　　　　　　　　　　　　　Fehling's Solution Test.
　　　　　　　　　　　　　Action of Unorganised Ferments.
　　　　　　　　　　　　　Polariscope or Saccharimeter Test.
Cellulose.　Examination of various forms.
Fats.　　Butter
　　　　Olive or cotton seed oil　} Specific Tests.
　　　　Tallow
Proteids.　Egg Albumen, examination of—
　　　　　　　　　　　　Millon's Test.
　　　　　　　　　　　　Precipitation Test.
　　　　　　　　　　　　Heller's Test.
　　　　　　　　　　　　Biuret Test.
　　　　　　　　　　　　Meta phosphoric Acid Test, etc.
　　　　Globulins, Nucleo Albumens.　Alkali and acid albuminates.
　　　　　　　　　　　　Tests for Albumose and Peptone.
　　　　Gelatine.　Examination of—
　　　　Tests on milk.
　　　　Bread and flour, examination of
　　　　Meat (muscle) examination of
　　　　Glycogen, examination of
Review work on the proteids.
Digestive fluids and their action (in detail).
Action of ferments and their prevention (in detail).
Antiseptics (in detail).
Action of alkalis and vegetable acids on metals or their oxides.
Baking powders.　Three general types.
Tests on bread, tea, coffee, etc.

APPENDIX J.

CHAUTAUQUA SCHOOL OF DOMESTIC SCIENCE.

GENERAL PURPOSE.

The School of Domestic Science is designed primarily for teachers who wish to compare their own methods with those of others, or who desire to supplement their training in this department ; but the work will also be of especial value to housekeepers, whether engaged in the administration of large institutions or in the direction of their own homes.

THE DEPARTMENT OF COOKERY.—This department offers the following lines of work : (a) Courses for teachers of Domestic Science ; (b) a series of thirty demonstration lectures on practical subjects, extending through six weeks ; (c) practice classes for young housekeepers ; (d) such private lessons as may be desired. The economic selection of materials, the wise choice of implements for each process, and the application of the right temperature to secure the best results, are points which receive careful attention in both lectures and practice lessons.

NORMAL COURSE IN DOMESTIC SCIENCE.—This embraces two years of work, and a certificate is given to those satisfactorily completing it. Young women without experience as teachers must present, for admission to this course, the equivalent of a High School diploma. The curriculum is as follows :—

FIRST YEAR.

1. GENERAL CHEMISTRY (Five hours a week).—Lectures and laboratory. The course will include a study of air, water, and their constituents, of acids, bases and salts, and of the various groups or elements with their more important compounds.

2. PHYSICS (Five hours a week).—The subjects discussed will be energy in all its forms, the air, physical properties of water, wells, springs, fountains, etc., with a full explanation of the instruments used in investigating problems in these subjects. Heat will be thoroughly discussed, since it occupies so important a place in these sciences, and the application of electricity in the arts will be fully explained and illustrated. Syllabus text (Gage's recommended).

3. PHYSIOLOGY (Three hours a week).—Chemical elements of human body. Cell life, illustrated by amœbæ, etc. Study of tissues. The anatomy, physiology and hygiene of the internal organs. Circulation of the blood, respiration, animal heat, general study of digestion.

4. BOTANY OF FOOD PLANTS (Five hours a week).—Lectures and laboratory work with the compound microscope ; the illustrative material, food plants ; as lettuce for leaves, potatoes for store rooms, and wheat for seeds. Emphasis will also be put on starch and vegetable proteids yeasts and moulds.

5. SANITATION (Five hours a week).—Principles of sanitation applied to the house—location, surroundings, plan, construction, furnishing, and care. Application of chemistry, physics, physiology, bacteriology, and kindred sciences, to water supply, drainage, and plumbing, disposal of wastes; lighting, heating, and ventilation. Care of woodwork, metallic and mineral surfaces and coloured fabrics. Laundry processes. Household pests. Problems of public hygiene discussed in relation to house sanitation.

6. COOKERY (Five hours a week).—Practice work. Food principles and the fundamental laws of cookery. Animal foods, vegetables, cereals, methods of making doughs light, menus for daily meals, and cooking for invalids will be discussed.

Second Year.

7. APPLIED CHEMISTRY (Five hours a week).—Laboratory work and lectures. Qualitative tests of food materials. Study of proteids, carbohydrates, fats, etc. Experiments with soda and baking powder. Detection of food adulterants and preservatives. Testing of various household supplies.

8. EXPERIMENTAL COOKERY (Five hours a week).—Existing methods of preparing food judged by scientific standards. Arrangement of lessons, the details of recipes and the order of work are planned in a way to help teachers.

9. PHYSIOLOGY (Two hours a week).—Animal functions, muscular physiology, digestion, with the study of the body fluids, and the nervous system. During the two years' course demonstrations with manikins and fresh specimens will be furnished. The course also deals especially and most practically with the digestion and nutritive value of food stuffs.

10. BACTERIOLOGY (Five hours a week).—Lectures and laboratory work. Description and life history of bacteria and other micro-organisms: Methods of culture. Bacteria in dust, water, milk, etc.

11. PEDAGOGY (Five hours a week).—Principles of pedagogy as applied to the teaching of Domestic Science. Schools of Cookery and Domestic Economy. Planning of courses.

12. ADMINISTRATION OF HOUSEHOLDS, SMALL AND LARGE (Five hours a week).—Household expenditure. Food as an economic factor. Diet and dietaries. Especially planned for matrons of schools and public institutions. Methods of keeping accounts. The best implements for housekeeping and the general equipment. The helpers, their training and advancement and the adjustment of duties, hours and wages. Economic buying and storing of food. The planning of menus, with due regard to a balanced ration; and the simplest way of serving meals.

13.*—Classes in sewing will be organized during the second term.

FEES.

	$		£	s.	d.
Full normal course (first year) . - - -	40.00	about	8	0	0
Full normal course (second year) - - - -	45.00	„	9	0	0
Cookery (six weeks) - - .- - - -	15.00	„	3	0	0
Cookery (three weeks) - - - - - -	9.00	„	1	15	0
Single courses (six weeks) - - - - -	12.00	„	2	10	0
Half courses (three weeks) - - - -	7.00	„	1	10	0
Cookery (Demonstration only) :—					
Six weeks - - - - - - -	5.00	„	1	0	0
Per week - - - - - - -	1.00	„		4	0
Single lectures - - - - - -	35	„		1	6

---

* Special fees will be charged for the classes in sewing.

APPENDIX K.,

CORNELL UNIVERSITY, COLLEGE OF AGRICULTURE.

BUREAU OF NATURE-STUDY AND FARMERS' READING-COURSE.

How to Organize a Farmers' Wives' Reading-Club.

At the present time there are three Correspondence courses conducted by the Farmers' Reading-course and Nature-study Bureau. These are (*a*) the Farmers' Reading-course, (*b*) the Farmers' Wives' Reading-course, and (*c*) the Home Nature-study course. These are especially adapted for study in clubs, and this circular suggests how women's clubs may be organized and conducted.

A club may consist of five or more members. An ideal number is twelve. Anyone interested in home work, directly or indirectly, is eligible to membership.

How to organize :—Some one must take the lead. Let this person (you) write us for information regarding the Reading-courses, distribute the circulars, and talk it over personally with as many women as possible. When interest has ripened, call a meeting at your own home, or some other convenient place, to consider organization. Then select a president and a secretary. She may be asked by the club to forward the answered quizzes in one consignment to this office. She should supply this office promptly with a list of the members and their addresses.

Select a suitable night for meeting. Each lesson will furnish subject matter for two meetings. One lesson is furnished each month, so that meetings may be held fortnightly. An excellent way is to meet at the house of the members of the club. Early in the season arrange a schedule giving places of meeting for some time ahead. Of course if a room in the grange, town hall, or school house is available and convenient, this may prove to be the most desirable arrangement. The club may apply for a charter from this Bureau, by adopting a name and reporting it to us with the first consignment of answered quizzes.

The sessions should not last over an hour and a half ; the discussion should be brisk, and it is better to adjourn early when interest is warm, than to wait till it cools and discussion lags. The meeting should begin promptly at 8 p.m., better still at 7.30.

When the meaning is not clear, or when new ideas occur to you, write us by all means. Let us labour together for the success of **your** club.

APPENDIX L.

UNIVERSITY OF THE STATE OF NEW YORK, ALBANY, N.Y.
HOME EDUCATION DEPARTMENT.

HOME ECONOMICS SYLLABUS.

Syllabus prepared by the Lake Placid Conference Committee on Home
Economics.

This syllabus, giving a suggestive outline of the present state of the subject,
is expanded from a course given in 1900 by Mrs. Ellen H. Richards, B.S.,
M.A., Instructor in Sanitary Chemistry, Massachusetts Institute of Tech-
nology, and Mrs. Alice Peloubet Norton, M.A., Home Economics Depart-
ment, Chicago Institute. Only a few of the best books are referred to, and
enough topics for papers given to provide for local conditions and needs.

LECTURE 1.

HOME AND FAMILY LIFE: IDEALS AND STANDARDS.

To keep the home a centre of moral and intellectual progress in the face
of the economic tendencies encroaching on its position the problem of the
day.

Family life is unselfish devotion inspired by self-sacrificing love. Co-
operation for a common aim creates a spirit of mutual helpfulness.

The significance of the family to the individuals composing it and to
the nation. The physical, moral, and intellectual development of its
members.

Its historical development: growth from reproductive and social institution in which wife and child were alike valued for their powers of
production, to a spiritual relationship in which each gives according to
his power and receives according to his need. Basis of choice in primitive
marriage; economic utility and physiological attraction ; modern basis,
personal relationship.

The growing individualism of all the members of the family ; the union
of all in the service of each.

Woman's past progress conditioned on the overcoming of men's passions
and her education ; her future progress dependent on the growth of her
self-respect and her work ; the result of knowledge.

Farther progress conditioned on evolution, not revolution ; the family
life, the development of ages, is to be spiritualised, not materialised.

The significance of a higher or more complicated adaptation is not reduced to the level of a lower or simpler one by showing that it has been
evolved from the latter.—*Griggs.*

The future of the race is bound up in the development of home ideals.
Standards of life come before standards of living. "There is little moral
consequence in the association of parents and children unless there are
ideas to communicate."—*Ross, Journal of Sociology*, Vol. 5, No. 5, 1900.

Home life distinguished from community life ; the home educational
rather than economic. Character building above price.

REFERENCES.

American Journal of Sociology, v. 1-6.
Bosanquet.—*Standard of Life.*
Demolins.—*Anglo-Saxon Superiority.*
Dewey.—*School and Society.*
Earle.—*Home Life in Colonial Days.*
Griggs.—*The New Humanism.*
Patten.—*The Development of English Thought.*
Richards.—*Cost of Living*, ch. 1-2.

Salmon.—*Domestic Service.*
Small and Vincent.—*Introduction to the Study of Society.*
Stetson.—*Women and Economics.*
Wright.—*Industrial Evolution of the United States.*

Topics for Papers.

1. How can the ideals of family life be maintained under present economic and social conditions?
2. Is it necessary to prepare and eat food and to make and launder clothing in the house in order to retain the essentials of the home?
3. The family as a unit of society.
4. The "living" wage; definition; rises according to standards of living. Show that comforts increase and luxuries decrease efficiency.
5. The woman in bondage to her neighbour's opinion; how may she be set free?
6. The inveterate shopper; how can her ideals be elevated?

Lecture 2.

The House Beautiful : Situation and Architecture.

Shelter the protection of home life. Maintains unity and privacy with sense of ownership.

The house beautiful: Location, plan, grounds. Soil must be clean, dry, porous. Influence of ground water and ground air. Sunshine and pure air essential ; scientific reasons for need of sunlight.

Plan of house according to needs of family ; both privacy and community of interests to be provided for ; individual rights respected. Labour saving in stairs, in proximity of certain rooms ; care in placing doors and windows for various reasons. Sun plan the most important requisite. "Sweetness and light" interpreted by the sanitary means sunshine and pure air.

The detached house needs its setting of grass or shrubs, or both, and flowers, if there is one to care for them ; sickly, straggling flower-beds are as distasteful as uncared-for children. Treatment of small grounds may relieve ugly architecture.

References.

Brown.—*Healthy Foundations for Houses.*
Clark.—*Building Superintendence.*
Gardner.—*The House that Jill Built.*
Grimshaw.—*Hints on House Building.*
Osborne.—*Notes on the Art of House Planning.*
Parsons.—*How to Plan the Home Grounds.*
Richards and Talbot.—*Home Sanitation. Ch. 2.*

Topics for Papers.

1. House architecture ; how to secure beautiful, comfortable homes.
2. The apartment house ; its advantages and disadvantages.
3. The lawn ; its treatment and care.
4. How to improve that eyesore, the small back yard.

Lecture 3.

The House Beautiful : Sanitation.

Æsthetic and sanitary requirements not opposed ; often identical. The poorly-built, ill-equipped house, neither healthful nor beautiful.

Ventilation and heating in close connection. Pure air not free in cold climates. Importance to health ; methods of providing ; tests.

Plumbing and drainage : General requirements are simplicity, accessibility ventilation of system. soundness of material, tightness of joints, thorough flushing.

REFERENCES.

Barré.—La Maison Salubre.
Billings.—Ventilation and Heating.
Corfield.—Dwelling Houses.
Currier.—Outlines of Practical Hygiene.
Egbert.—Manual of Hygiene and Sanitation.
Gerhard.—House Drainage and Sanitary Plumbing.
Plunkett.—Women, Plumbers and Doctors.
Putnam.—Lectures on Principles of House Drainage.
Richard and Talbot.—Home Sanitation. Ch. 3-6, 9.
Tracy.—Handbook of Sanitary Information.
Waring.—How to Drain a House.
——— *Principles and Practice of House Drainage.*
——— *Sanitary Condition of City and Country Dwelling Houses.*
——— *Sanitary Drainage of Houses and Towns.*

TOPICS FOR PAPERS.

1. The house plan with special reference to sanitary requirements.
2. An ideal system of ventilation for a modern house.
3. How to adapt modern principles to an old house.
4. Advantages and dangers of modern plumbing.

LECTURE 4.

THE HOUSE BEAUTIFUL : FURNISHING.

Adaptation to purpose and environment. Fitness as to form, colour, cleanliness, and durability. Truth a fundamental element of beauty.

Simplicity tends towards healthfulness and beauty. Overcrowding spoils effect of really good things. Furnishings should minister to comfort or pleasure ; should not make a slave of mistress or maid.

Knowledge of true values necessary.

REFERENCES.

Beauty in the Home.—20th Century Club Leaflets.
Church.—How to Furnish a Home.
Cook.—The House Beautiful.
Dewing.—Beauty in the Household.
Gardner.—Homes and All About Them.
Garrett.—Suggestions for House Decoration.
Loftie.—A Plea for Art in the House.
Lyon.—Colonial Furniture of New England.
Ormsbee.—The House Comfortable.
Salisbury.—Principles of Domestic Taste.
Watson.—Art of the House.
Wharton and Codman.—Decoration of Houses.
Wheeler.—Household Art.

TOPICS FOR PAPERS.

1. Hall and reception room : How to express hospitality without sacrificing family privacy and reserve.
2. The living room : Its furniture, decoration, schemes of colour.
3. The nursery : What it can do for the character of the child.
4. The dining room : Influence of surroundings on digestion ; special reference to cleanliness.
5. The sleeping room : Not a sitting room ; appropriate furnishing.

LECTURE 5.

THE HOUSE BEAUTIFUL: CLEANING AND CARE.

Cleanliness is next to godliness.

DUST, INDOORS AND OUT:
> Composed of inorganic and dead matter, and living organisms; danger chiefly from the latter. Of these "dust plants" the most important are bacteria.

BACTERIA:
> 1. Description and life history:
>> Simple one-celled plants; smallest of living things and perhaps most numerous. Classified according to shape as cocci, bacilli, spirilla. Reproduction by cell division.
> 2. Methods of culture. "Dust plant" gardens:
>> Bacteria too small to be thoroughly studied even under the microscope till methods of cultivating them were devised. Beef tea, specially prepared and stiffened with gelatin or agar-agar, serves as food and also as a prison. Bacteria planted in this grow and form "colonies" large enough to be seen and studied. A small particle of dust introduced into this medium may produce thousands of these colonies.

DUST AND DISEASE:
> 1. Disease germs:
>> Most bacteria harmless or even useful, but some foes to human existence. Some of these disease germs, notably those of tuberculosis, often conveyed in dust.
> 2. Protection of body against disease:
>> Ciliated cells of air passages; dust filters in lungs; phagocytes or wandering cells of body.

HOUSEHOLD APPLICATIONS:
> 1. Cleanliness of food:
>> Milk supply. Fruit and candy exposed on street for sale.
> 2. Care of house:
>> (a) House should be finished and furnished so as to provide as few dust traps as possible. Smooth finish, rounded corners, simple ornaments desirable. Carpets *v.* bare floors.
>> (b) Removal of dust. Sweeping and dusting should remove and destroy dust, not merely stir it up. Results of experiments with different methods.

MUNICIPAL HOUSEKEEPING:
> Clean streets and sidewalks; proper disposal of refuse; influence of clean houses and schoolhouses; moral effect of good housekeeping.

REFERENCES.

Abbott.—Principles of Bacteriology.
Conn.—Story of Germ Life.
Frankland.—Our Secret Friends and Foes.
Hüppe.—Principles of Bacteriology.
Prudden.—Dust and its Dangers.
———— *Story of the Bacteria.*
Tyndall.—Essays on Floating Matter of the Air.

TOPICS FOR PAPERS.

1. Dust as a means for carrying disease.
2. Plan for furnishing a house with special reference to avoidance of dust.
3. Housekeeping *v.* home making. Is the care necessary for exquisite cleanliness conducive to the happiest home?
4. Some devices in house building which would simplify housekeeping.

LECTURE 6.

CLOTHING.

Purposes : (1) Protection of body from extremes of heat and cold ; saving of food by preventing loss of heat essential in sedentary pursuits where digestion fails to produce sufficient heat ; more clothing less food ; (2) adornment ; (3) satisfaction of modesty.

Hygienic clothing : Even layer of air inclosed ; non-conductor ; per cent. of air space in wool, silk, linen ; kind of weave ; per cent. of moisture contained by each. Looseness of clothing permits evaporation and better circulation.

Style of dress dependent on climate and occupation ; wide sleeves and loose trousers for warm countries, close-fitting for cold. Work calls for looser dress than leisure ; ideal housework dress for women ; business dress.

Æsthetic qualities : Becomingness ; artistic outlines ; softening of crude forms ; toning down of colour. Fashion cruel to all but a certain type. Dress may enhance beauty and render agreeable otherwise ugly forms and features.

Nothing more individual than dress ; part of oneself ; indicative of character. Historical development ; ideals expressed in costume.

Textiles : Study of as to fibre, weaving, colouring, dyeing, washing, cleansing, durability.

The function of clothing from the hygienic standpoint is to regulate heat. In its lowest terms clothing is a net to catch air, which is the best known non-conductor of heat. Even in a temperature greater than that of the body the air space prevents the penetration of heat. Clothing should be loose in summer and close-fitting in winter. The skin needs to breathe, as it were, hence air and moisture should have free but slow passage through all clothing. The products of excretion should not be retained. Rational clothing has the greatest useful effect with the least material ; it does not interfere with free movement of any part, acts as a dietetic measure, lessening the quantity of food required and promoting evaporation from the skin.

Loosely woven wool is rich in air (87 per cent. air, 13 per cent. solid substance), is elastic and soft, has little contact with the skin so that in addition to the contained air there is an isolating layer between the garment and the skin. It is also characteristic of wool not to be wet by moisture but to allow it to pass through and evaporate. Cotton over wool becomes saturated, and soon gives the odour of decay.

Fine, smooth linen is dense, poor in air (42 per cent. air, 58 per cent. solid substance ; when starched, no air), has close contact with the skin and so feels cooler, conducts heat away more rapidly, has little or no air between it and the skin, becomes saturated with moisture and causes the concentration of the skin waste in the smallest space near the skin. It takes thirty times as long for a given quantity of air to pass through linen as through wool tricot, hence little circulation. That cotton and linen bear washing by unskilled labour is the greatest argument for their use. Some modes of weaving may inclose as much air in a cotton or linen mesh as in wool, but the fibres lack elasticity, and tend to become matted and saturated with moisture. Silk lies between wool and linen.

For protection in different temperatures it has been estimated that :

1·7mm. suffices for high summer (if of loosely woven wool) ;

3·3mm. for ordinary summer weather ;

5·9mm. for spring and fall ;

12·6mm. for winter ;

26mm. for very cold days.

In a strong, cold wind an impervious layer-like skin of a fur garment prevents too rapid change of air.

To foot gear the same principles apply : Skin breathing is very important, as also circulation of air, free evaporation, and protection from too rapid loss of heat.   Air from next the skin in stocking feet gave only one tenth the amount of carbon-dioxid found when a narrow close-fitting boot was worn.   Stockings of cotton conduct heat one-third faster than those of wool, the thinner, less elastic layer preventing circulation of air and holding moisture.   Leather, if loose and soft, approaches wool in the property of not conducting heat.   As it is more dense and "filled" with water or enamel it becomes like linen, a good conductor.   Loss of heat by contact with cold surface depends on intimacy and area of contact.

Habit has much to do with clothing certain portions of the body, head, hands, etc.   The skin becomes non-breathing to a certain extent, but knees and wrists, where the arteries approach the surface, should be protected from sudden changes.

Costume—outer dress—may be quite independent of clothing, but it should not interfere by tightness, weight, or impervious material with the true office of clothing.

Beauty without health is incomplete.   Health can never be perfect for you so long as your eye is troubled with ugliness. . . . To dress well you must possess the gift of colour and be a master of form.   But this is not enough; with these accomplishments you might clothe a dummy or a corpse satisfactorily, but not a living human being; for there comes into the problem, with this word *living*, the element of motion.   I do not mean the mere action of moving the limbs, but the action of breathing, of growth and of decay, and it is here that the laws of hygiene must be faced. . We may obey them or disobey, but the measure of our obedience or disobedience will be the measure of our health or no health.—*Godwin.*

The pursuit of things fashionable, for the sole reason that they *are* fashionable, is, I think, not an exalted occupation, and is indeed, I think, a somewhat sheep-like attribute.—*Treves.*

REFERENCES.

Archiv für Hygiene.
Ballin.—Science of Dress in Theory and Practice.
Blanc.—Art in Ornament and Dress.
Bowman.—The Structure of the Wool Fibre.
Brooks.---Cotton.
Ecob.—The Well Dressed Woman.
Godwin.—Dress and its Relation to Health and Climate.
Haweis.—Art of Dress.
Robida.—" Yester-year " : Ten Centuries of Toilet.
Steele and Adams.—Beauty of Form and Grace of Vesture.
Treves.—The Dress of the Period in its Relation to Health.
Wilkinson.—Story of the Cotton Plant.
Williams.—Philosophy of Clothing.
Wykoff.—The Silk Goods of America.
U.S. Experiment Stations.   Cotton Plant (Bulletin 33).

TOPICS FOR PAPERS.

1. The ideal working dress.
2. Street costume.
3. Children's clothing.
4. Summer clothing.
5. Economic clothing.
6. Economic costume.
7. The choice of fabrics.
8. A study of textiles.
9. A history of " dress goods."
10. The development of costume.

LECTURE 7.

FOOD IN RELATION TO HEALTH.

The balanced ration. Object of the farmer to secure the highest efficiency of muscle or product. He has found that knowledge of the principle of feeding pays ; that while his animals may *live* on what they can pick up or what is by chance given them, they attain their best development only when he understands and supplies their needs.

Balanced ration for the human race. In man there is not only the animal or muscular efficiency to consider, but the intellectual output and the enjoyment of the higher nature ; hence additional need of knowledge and care.

Food the source of human energy. Metabolism in the body. Classes, costs, quantities ; variation for different ages, seasons, kinds of work.

Food material often spoiled in cooking. Food material often wasted in the body as well as in the kitchen.

Food a source of pleasure, but this is not its only or chief use. The art of cooking the right combination of æsthetic and nutritive qualities.

REFERENCES.

Atwater.—Methods and Results of Investigations on the Chemistry and Economy of Food.
——— *and Bryant.—Dietary Studies in Chicago.*
——— *and Woods.—Chemical Composition of American Food Materials*
Bevier.—Nutrition Investigations in Pittsburg.
Goss.—Nutrition Investigations in New Mexico.
Hart.—Diet in Sickness and in Health.
Hogan.—How to feed Children.
Knight.—Food and its Functions.
Richards, ed.—Rumford Kitchen Leaflets.
——— *and Woodman.--Air, Water, and Food. Ch. 8. 9.*
Thompson.—Food and Feeding.
Townsend.—Relation of Foods to Health.
Wait.—Nutrition Investigations at University of Tennessee.
Yeo.—Food in Health and Disease.

TOPICS FOR PAPERS.

1. How to feed the baby.
2. How to feed the school girl.
3. How to feed the business man.
4. How to feed the farmer.
5. How to feed the grandmother.
6. The summer dietary ; how it should differ from that of winter.
7. Why should I know anything about food ?
8. How to secure good food habits in children.
9. How to preserve the right attitude of mind toward food.
10. A dietary : What it is and how it is made.

LECTURE 8.

SCIENCE AND ART OF COOKERY.

INTRODUCTION :
    1. Cooking defined :
        Socrates's estimate of the art. Ruskin's interpretation.
        Scientific definition : Application of heat to food materials.
    2. Object of cooking :
        To make food safer, more digestible, palatable. The last formerly most important. Modern methods emphasise the first two.

CLASSIFICATION OF FOODS :
Goodfellow's chart :

Inorganic { 1. Water. 2. Salts. } Organic { 1. Nitrogenous.
    (*a*) Proteids.
    (*b*) Gelatinoids.
2. Non-nitrogenous.
    (*a*) Fats and oils.
    (*b*) Carbohydrates. }

EFFECT OF COOKING ON DIFFERENT FOOD PRINCIPLES :
1. Water : Cooked chiefly as a medium for conveying heat ; some times to render it safe.
2. Salts or mineral matter : Unchanged by heat, but may be dissolved out of food by water and lost. Effect of hard and soft water on food.
3. Proteids : As a rule changed from soluble to insoluble and less digestible forms.
4. Fats : Decomposed by high temperature and made less digestible.
5. Starch : Digestibility increased by cooking. Changed partially to soluble starch and often to dextrine and sugar.

TWO TYPICAL FOODS :
1. Meat :
    Contains albumen and allied proteids, extractives, gelatin, fat. Effect of different degrees of heat on each must be considered to find right cooking temperature for the whole. Different methods of applying heat : Boiling, baking, soup-making, etc.
2. Bread :
    Two classes of changes : By fermentation, by heat.
    ('*a*) Fermentation : Effect of yeast on gluten, the proteid of flour, not well understood. Starch changed into sugar ; sugar broken up into alcohol and carbon dioxide.
    (*b*) Heat : Gluten changed ; part of the starch changed into dextrine, and some sugar into caramel ; carbon dioxide and alcohol driven off and the ferments killed.

COOKING FOR SAFETY OR PRESERVATION OF FOOD :
    Dangers of uncooked food. Principle of canning and preserving. High temperature or long continued heat.

REFERENCES.

Abel.—Practical, Sanitary, and Economic Cooking.
Child.—Delicate Feasting.
Corson.—Practical American Cookery and Household Management.
De Salis.—Art of Cookery.
Dodds.—Health in the Household.
Goodfellow.—Dietetic Value of Bread.
Jago.—Textbook of the Science and Art of Breadmaking.
Richards and Elliott.—Chemistry of Cooking and Cleaning.
Thudichum.—Spirit of Cookery.
Williams.—Chemistry of Cooking.

TOPICS FOR PAPERS. |

1. Yeast fermentation in relation to breadmaking.
2. Effect on bread of different manipulations of the dough ; pulling, kneading, beating, etc.
3. Cookery of vegetables.
4. Canning industry and its methods.
5. Cost of cooking : Relative economy of gas, coal, etc.
6. Cookery of milk : Pasteurisation and sterilisation.

LECTURE 9.

DIVISION OF THE ANNUAL INCOME.

Money is spent for existence, comfort, luxury, philanthropy.

Aim should be that degree of comfort which enhances the capacity for work and enjoyment without weakening moral or physical characteristics.

Present restraint for purpose of attaining a future good an attribute of the higher nature of man.

REFERENCES.

Bosanquet.—Standard of Life.
Damon.—Wealth of Households.
Dawson.—Wealth of Households.
Devine.—Economic Function of Woman.
Dewson.—The 20th Century Expense Book.
Grant.—Art of Living.
Herrick.—Liberal Living upon Narrow Means.
Nitsch.—Ten Dollars Enough.
Richards.—Cost of Living.
Smart.—Distribution of the Income.
Stackpole.—Handbook of Housekeeping for Small Incomes.

TOPICS FOR PAPERS.

1. What sections of your city offer houses or apartments for $25 a month suitable for the young family of a student or literary or scientific man ? What improvements in housing up to $50 a month might be made ?
2. How to clothe a family of five on $300, $400, $500 a year.
3. A study of the markets of your city ; which are the best conducted ? Does it pay for the housewife to go to market herself ?
4. Household accounts : How to make them interesting. How to buy for two.
5. Make out a table of fruits, vegetables, and fish showing the season at which they are best in flavour and least expensive. Compare these prices with those that are highest.
6. How may running expenses be regulated ?
7. The little leaks in the household purse : How to stop them.
8. What relation should wages bear to rent ?
9. Does modern philanthropy take the place of the tithe for the church ?
10. How far is it wise to sacrifice present comfort for the possible " rainy day " ?

LECTURE 10.

MUNICIPAL HOUSEKEEPING.

The City of Hygiea : How nearly it can be approached. " Applied hygiene the condition *sine quâ non* of the farther development of mankind."

Clean soil : Requires removal, not burial, of all refuse ; cleanly collection and effectual disposal of garbage and street sweepings ; efficient subsoil drainage ; suitably paved streets, dustless and impervious, wide for circulation of air and admission of sunlight ; no dirty back alleys.

Pure air : Depends largely on clean soil ; free from dust and noxious vapours ; parks and promenades well supplied with vegetation. A crowd in an enclosed space, palace or hovel, defiles the air. Churches, schools, railroad waiting rooms, lecture halls, parlours used for social functions, all demand special attention.

Safe and abundant water supply : Intelligent use of appliances ; quick removal of used water ; complete sewerage system before the introduction of public supplies ; polluted soil means unsafe water.

Safe buildings : Construction, plumbing, air space. City regulations ; are they enforced ?

Urban hygiene : Inspection of markets, factories, sweat shops ; density of population. Before all other social reforms stands that of healthy living,

REFERENCES.

American Public Health Association.—Annual Reports.
Barré.—La Ville Salubre.
Burrage and Bailey.—School Sanitation and Decoration.
Engineering Record (files).
Municipal Affairs.—Vols. 1-3.
Parkes.—Hygiene and Public Health.
Poore.—Essays on Rural Hygiene.
Richardson.—The City of Hygiea.
——— *Health of Nations.*
Sykes.—Public Health Problems.
Tracy.—Handbook of Sanitary Information.
Waring.—Report on Final Disposition of the Wastes of New York, 1896.
——— *Street Cleaning.*
Weber.—Growth of Cities. Columbia University Studies in History, Economics, and Public Law. Vol. 11.

TOPICS FOR PAPERS.

1. Water supply of your city ; source, method of storage, distribution material of pipes, house pipes, certified quality of water.
2. Sewerage system ; how far extended ; disposal of sewage ; location of cesspools still used.
3. Ventilation of schoolhouses, churches, and public halls.
4. Sanitary condition of schoolhouses.
5. Afternoon teas and evening receptions ; how to make them endurable.
6. City dust : how can it be prevented ?
7. Cremation the sanitary ideal.

LIST OF AUTHORITIES REFERRED TO.

Volume and page numbers are separated by a colon ; e.g., 10:141 *means Vol.* 10, *p.* 141.

ABBOTT, A. C.—Principles of Bacteriology. Ed. 5. 590 p. O. Phil., 1899. Lea, $2.50.
ABEL, MRS. M. H.—Practical, Sanitary, and Economic Cooking. 188 p. D. Rochester, 1890. American Public Health Association, 40 cents.
AMERICAN JOURNAL OF SOCIOLOGY.—Vol. 1-date, O. Chic., 1894-date.
AMERICAN KITCHEN MAGAZINE.—Vol. 1-date. il. O. Bost., 1895-date.
AMERICAN PUBLIC HEALTH ASSOCIATION.—Public Health, Reports and Papers, 1873-date. Vol. 1-date, il. O. Concord, 1875-date. $5. (Earlier volumes published in New York and Boston.)
ARCHIV FÜR HYGIENE.—Vol. 1-date, il. O. Mün. 1871-date.
ATKINSON, EDWARD.—Science of Nutrition. 254 p. sq. O. Bost., 1896. Damrell, 1.25$.
ATWATER, W. O.—Foods : Nutritive Value and Cost. 32 p. O. Wash., 1894. (U.S.—Agriculture, Department of. Farmer's Bulletin. No. 23.)
——— Methods and Results of Investigations on the Chemistry and Economy of Food. 222 p. O. Wash., 1895. (U.S.—Experiment Stations, Office of. Bulletin. No. 21.)
——— AND BENEDICT, F. G. Report of Preliminary Investigations on the Metabolism of Nitrogen and Carbon in the Human Organism. 645 p. O. Wash., 1897. (U.S.—Experiment Stations, Office of Bulletin. No. 44.)
——— AND BRYANT, A. P.—Dietary Studies in Chicago. 76 p. O. Wash., 1898. (U.S.—Experiment Stations, Office of Bulletin. No. 55.)
——— AND WOODS, C. D.—Chemical Composition of American Food Materials. 45 p. O. Wash., 1896. (U.S.—Experiment Stations, Office of Bulletin. No. 28.)

BALLIN, MRS. A. S.—Science of Dress in Theory and Practice. 288 p.,
il. O. Lond., 1886. Low, 6s.
BARRÉ, L. A. AND PAUL.—Manuel de Génie Sanitarie. 2 Vol., il. D.
Par., 1897. Baillière, 4 fr. each. (Vol. 1. La Ville Salubre. Vol. 2.
La Maison Salubre.)
BEAUTY IN THE HOME.—Bost., 1898. (20th Century Club leaflets.)
BEVIER, ISABEL.—Nutrition Investigations in Pittsburg, Pa. 48 p. O.
Wash., 1898. (U.S.—Experiment Stations, Office of. Bulletin.
No. 52.)
BILLINGS, J. S.—Ventilation and Heating. 500 p. O. N. Y., 1893.
Engineering Record, $6.
BLANC, CHARLES.—Art in Ornament and Dress. 267 p. O. Lond., 1881.
Warne.
BOSANQUET, MRS. BERNARD.—Standard of Life. 219 p. D. N. Y., 1898.
Macmillan, $1.50.
BOWMAN, F. H.—The Structure of the Wool Fibre. 366 p., il. O. Phil.,
1885. Baird, $5.
BROOKS, C. P.—Cotton. 362 p., il. O. N. Y., 1898. Spon, $3.
BROWN, GLENN.—Healthy Foundations for Houses. P. 5-143, il. T.
N. Y., 1885. Van Nostrand, 50 cents. (Science Series. No. 80.)
(Reprinted from the *Sanitary Engineer.*)
BURRAGE, SEVERANCE AND BAILEY, H. T.—School Sanitation and Decora-
tion. 191 p., il. D. Bost., 1900. Heath, $1.50.
CAMPBELL, MRS. HELEN (STUART).—Household Economics. 286 p. O.
N. Y., 1897. Putnam, $1.50.
CHILD, THEODORE.—Delicate Feasting. 214 p. D. N. Y., 1890. Harper,
$1.25.
CHURCH, MRS. E. R. (MCILVANE).—How to Furnish a Home. 128 p.
O. N. Y., 1881. Appleton, 60 cents. (Appleton's Home Books.)
CLARK, T. M.—Building Superintendence. Ed. 14. 336 p. O. N. Y.,
1896. Macmillan, $3.
CONN, H. W.—Story of Germ Life. 199 p. S. N. Y., 1897. Appleton,
40 cents. (Library of Useful Stories.)
COOK, C. C.—The House Beautiful. New ed. 336 p., il. O. N. Y.,
1895. Scribner, $2.50. (Originally published 1878, $7.50; new
ed. 1881, $4; new cheaper ed, 1895, $2.50.)
CORFIELD, W. H.—Dwelling Houses: Their Sanitary Construction and
Arrangements. 156 p. S. N. Y., 1880. Van Nostrand, 50 cents.
(Science Series.)
CORSON, JULIET.—Practical American Cookery and Household Manage-
ment. 591 p., il. D. N. Y., 1887. Dodd, $1.50.
CURRIER, C. G.—Outlines of Practical Hygiene. Ed. 3. 482 p. O.
N. Y., 1898. Treat, $2.
DAMON, J. T.—Wealth of Households. N. Y., 1886. Macmillan, $1.25.
DAWSON, J. T.—Wealth of Households: Political Economy of Daily
Life. 366 p. O. Lond., 1886. Frowde, 5s.
DEMOLINS, EDMUND.—Anglo-Saxon Superiority. 427 p. O. N. Y., 1896.
Scribner, $1.
DE SALIS, MRS. H. A.—Art of Cookery, Past and Present; with anec-
dotes of noted cooks and gourmets. 198 p. O. Lond., 1898. Hutchin-
son, 2s.
DEVINE, E. T.—Economic Function of Woman. Ed. 2, p. 45-60. O.
Phil., 1894. American Academy of Political and Social Science,
15 cents. (Publications. No. 133.)
DEWING, MRS. M. R. (OAKEY).—Beauty in the Household. 183 p.,
il. S. N. Y., 1882. Harper, $1.
DEWSON, M. P.—Twentieth Century Expense Book. Bost., 1899.
Women's Educational and Industrial Union.
DODDS, S. W.—Health in the Household, or Hygienic Cookery. Ed. 2.
608 p, D. N. Y., 1899. Fowler, $2.

EARLE, MRS. ALICE (MORSE).—Customs and Fashions in old New England. 387 p. D. N. Y., 1893. Scribner, $1.25.

———— Home Life in Colonial Days. 470 p. D. N. Y., 1899. Macmillan, $2.50.

ECOB, MRS. HELEN (GILBERT).—The Well Dressed Woman. 253 p., il. D. N. Y., 1892. Fowler, $1.

EGBERT, SENECA.—Manual of Hygiene and Sanitation. 368 p., il. O. Phil., 1899. Lea, $2.25.

ENGINEERING RECORD, BUILDING RECORD, AND SANITARY ENGINEER.— Vol. 16–date, il. F. N. Y., 1887–date. Being Vol. 16–date of *Sanitary Engineer.*

FRANKLAND, P. F.—Our Secret Friends and Foes. Ed. 3. 238 p. S. Lond., 1897. Young, 90 cents. (Romance of Science Series.)

GARDNER, E. C.—Homes and all About Them. 710 p., il, D. Bost., 1885. Osgood, $2.50.

———— The House that Jill Built. 268 p. D. Springfield, Mass., 1896. Adams, $1.

GARRETT, RHODA AND AGNES.—Suggestions for House Decoration, in Painting, Woodwork, and Furniture. il. D. Phil., 1877. Porter, $1.

GERHARD, W. P.—House Drainage and Sanitary Plumbing. Ed. 7. 231 p. S. N. Y., 1898. Van Nostrand, 50 cents. (Science Series.)

GODWIN, E. W.—Dress, and its Relation to Health and Climate. 80 p., il. O. Lond., 1884. Clowes. (International Health Exhibition. Lond., 1884. Health Exhibition Literature. 1884. Vol. 10.)

GOODFELLOW, JOHN.—Dietetic Value of Bread. 328 p. D. Lond., 1892. Macmillan, $1.50.

GOSS, ARTHUR.—Nutrition Investigations in New Mexico. 20 p. O. Wash., 1898. (U.S.—Experiment Stations, Office of Bulletin. No. 54.)

GRANT, ROBERT.—Art of Living. 353 p., il. D. N. Y., 1895. Scribner, $2.50.

GRIGGS, E. H.—The New Humanism.

GRIMSHAW, ROBERT.—Hints on House Building. Ed. 2 enl. 77 p. T. N. Y., 1889. Practical Publishing Company, 50 cents.

HART, MRS. A. M.—Diet in Sickness and in Health. 219 p. O. Phil., 1897. Putnam, $1.50.

HAWEIS, MRS. M. E.—Art of Dress. Il. O. Lond., 1879. Chatto, 6s.

HERRICK, MRS. CHRISTINE (TERHUNE).—Liberal Living upon Narrow Means. 275 p. D. Bost., 1890. Houghton, $1.

HOGAN, L. E.—How to Feed Children. Ed. 2. 236 p. D. Phil., 1898. Lippincott, $1. (Practical Lessons in Nursing.)

HÜPPE, FERDINAND.—Principles of Bacteriology. 467 p. D. Chic., Open Court Publishing Company.

JAGO, WILLIAM.—Textbook of the Science and Art of Breadmaking. 648 p. O. Lond., 1895. Simpkin, 15s.

KNIGHT, JAMES.—Food and its Functions. 282 p. D. Lond., 1895. Blackie, 2s. 6d.

LASSAR-COHN.—Chemistry in Daily Life. Translated by M. M. P. Muir. 324 p. D. Phil., 1898. Lippincott, $1.75.

LOFTIE, W. J.—A Plea for Art in the House. Phil., 1876. Coats, $1 (Art at Home Series.)

LYON, I. W.—Colonial Furniture of New England ; A Study of the Domestic Furniture in use in the 17th and 18th Centuries. Ed. 2. 285 p., pl. sq. Q. Bost., 1892. Houghton, $10.

MASON, O. T.—Woman's Share in Primitive Culture. 295 p. D. N. Y., 1894. Appleton, $1.75. (Anthropological Series.)

MASS. LABOUR STATISTICS, BUREAU OF.—Hours of Labour in Domestic Service. Bost., 1898. Women's Education and Industrial Union.

MUNICIPAL AFFAIRS.—Vol. 1–date, O. N. Y., 1897–date.

NITSCH, MRS. H. A.—Ten Dollars Enough ; Keeping House well on 10 Dollars a Week, by C. O. Ed. 11. 279 p. D. Bost., 1893. Houghton, $1.

ORMSBEE, MRS. AGNES (BAILEY).—The House Comfortable. 232 p. S. N. Y., 1892. Harper, $1.

OSBORNE, C. FRANCIS.—Notes on the Art of House Planning. N. Y., 1889. Comstock, 5s.

PARKES, L. C.—Hygiene and Public Health. Il. O. Lond., 1889. Lewis, 9s.

PARSONS, SAMUEL, JR.—How to Plan the Home Grounds. 249 p., il. D. N. Y., 1899. Doubleday, $1 net.

PATTEN, S. N.—Development of English Thought. 415 p. O. N. Y., 1899. Macmillan, $3.

PLUNKETT, MRS. H. M. (HODGE).—Women, Plumbers and Doctors. 248 p. D. N. Y., 1893. Appleton, $1.25.

POORE, G. V.—Essays on Rural Hygiene. Ed. 2. 372 p., il. D. N. Y.. 1894. Longmans, $2.

PRUDDEN, T. M.—Dust and its Dangers. 111 p. D. N. Y., 1894. Putnam, 75 cents.

—— Story of the Bacteria. 143 p. D. N. Y., 1889. Putnam, 75 cents.

PUTNAM, J. P.—Lectures on the Principles of House Drainage.—125 p. D. Bost., 1886. Ticknor, 75 cents.

RICHARDS, MRS. E. H. (SWALLOW).—Cost of Living. Ed. 1. 121 p. D N. Y., 1899. Wiley, $1.

—— ed. Plain Words about Food. 176 p. D. Bost., 1899. Home Science Publishing Company, $1. (Rumford Kitchen Leaflets.)

—— AND ELLIOTT, L. M.—Chemistry of Cooking and Cleaning. Ed. 2.. 158 p. D. Bost., 1897. Home Science Publishing Company. 50 cents.

—— AND TALBOT, MARION.—Home Sanitation. 85 p. S. Bost., 1898. Home Science Publishing Company 25 cents.

—— AND WOODMAN.—Air, Water, and Food. 225 p. N. Y., Wiley, $2.

RICHARDSON, B. W.—Hygiea, a City of Health. 47 p. D. Lond., 1876. Macmillan, *paper*, 25 cents.

—— The Health of Nations. Review of Works of Edwin Chadwick. 2 Vol. O. Lond., 1887. Longmans, 28s.

ROBIDA, ALBERT.—" Yester-year " : Ten Centuries of Toilet ; from the French by Mrs. Cashel Hoey. 264 p., il. O. N. Y., 1872. Scribner, $2.50. (Also published in London.)

SALISBURY ——.—Principles of Domestic Taste.

SALMON, L. M.—Domestic Service. 307 p. O. N. Y., 1897. Macmillan, $2.

SMALL, A. B. AND VINCENT, G. E.—Introduction to the Study of Society. 384 p. D. N. Y., 1894. American Book Company, $1.80.

SMART, WILLIAM.—Distribution of Income. 341 p. O. N. Y., 1899. Macmillan, $1.60 net.

SNYDER, H., FRISBY, A. J. AND BRYANT, A. P. Losses in Boiling Vegetables and the Composition of Potatoes and Eggs. 31 p. O. Wash., 1897. (U. S.—Experiment Stations, Office of. Bulletin. No. 43.)

—— AND VOORHEES, L. A.—Studies on Bread and Bread-making. 51 p. O. Wash., 1899. (U. S.—Experiment Stations, Office of. Bulletin. No. 67.)

STACKPOLE, FLORENCE.—Handbook of Housekeeping for Small Incomes. 439 p. O. Lond., 1898. W. Scott, 2s. 6d.

STEELE, F. M., AND ADAMS, MRS. E. L. (STEELE).—Beauty of Form and Grace of Vesture. 231 p., il. D. N. Y., 1894. Dodd, $1.75.

STETSON, C. P.—Women and Economics. 340 p. D. Bost., 1898. Small, $1.50.

SYKES, J. F.—Public Health Problems. 370 p., il., maps, D. N. Y., 1892. Scribner, $1.25. (Contemporary Science Series.)

THOMPSON, SIR HENRY.—Food and Feeding. Ed. 10. 312 p. D. N. Y., 1899. Warne, $1.75.

THUDICHUM, J. L. W.—Spirit of Cookery. 701 p. D. Lond., 1895. Warne, $2.25.

TOWNSEND, G. H.—Relation of Foods to Health. 427 p. D. St. Louis, 1898. Witt Publishing Company.

TRACY, R. S.—Handbook of Sanitary Information. 114 p. S. N. Y., 1895. Appleton, 50 cents.

TREVES, FREDERICK.—The Dress of the Period in its Relation to Health. 32 p. Lond. National Health Society.

TYNDALL, JOHN.—Essays on Floating Matter in the Air. 338 p. D. N Y., 1882. Appleton, $1.50.

U.S.—EXPERIMENT STATIONS, OFFICE OF.—Cotton Plant. 422 p. O. Wash., 1896. (Bulletin. No. 33.) Supplemental Bibliography of Cotton, p. 423-33.

VOORHEES, E. B.—Food and Nutrition Investigation in New Jersey. 40 p. O. Wash., 1896. (U. S.—Experiment Stations, Office of. Bulletin. No. 35.)

WAIT, C. F.—Nutrition Investigations at University of Tennessee. 46 p. O. Wash., 1898. (U. S.—Experiment Stations, Office of. Bulletin. No. 53.)

WARING, G. E.—Report on the Final Disposition of the Wastes of New York, 1896. 155 p., il. N. Y. Brown.

—— How to Drain a House. Ed. 2. 223 p. S. N. Y., 1895. Va Nostrand, $1.25.

—— Principles and Practice of House Drainage. 1884. Century Magazine, 7:45, 253.

—— Sanitary Condition of City and Country Dwelling Houses. Ed. 2. 130 p. S. N. Y., 1898. Van Nostrand, 50 cents. (Science Series.)

—— Sanitary Drainage of Houses and Towns. Ed. 11. 366 p. D. Bost., 1876. Houghton, $2.

—— Street Cleaning. 230 p., il. D. N. Y., 1898. Doubleday, $1.25 net.

WATSON, MRS. R. M.—Art of the House. 185 p. il. O. N. Y., 1897. Macmillan, $2 net.

WEBER, A. F.—Growth of Cities in the 19th Century. 495 p. O. N. Y., 1899. Macmillan, $4. (Columbia University Studies in History, Economics, and Public Law. Vol. 11.)

WHARTON, EDITH AND CODMAN, OGDEN, JR.—Decoration of Houses. 240 p., il. O. N. Y., 1897. Scribner, boards, $4.

WHEELER, MRS. CANDACE.—Household Art. 204 p., nar. S. N. Y., 1893. Harper, $1. (Distaff Series.)

WILKINSON, FREDERICK.—Story of the Cotton Plant. 191 p., il. S. N Y., 1899. Appleton, 40 cents.

WILLIAMS, W. M.—Chemistry of Cooking. 328 p. O. N.Y., 1897. Appleton, $1.50.

WILLIAMS, W. M.—Philosophy of Clothing.—O. Lond., 1890. Laurie, 4s.

WOODS, C. D.—Meats: Composition and Cooking. 29 p. O. Wash. 1896. (U. S.—Agriculture, Department of. Farmer's Bulletin. No. 34.)

WRIGHT, C. D.—Industrial Evolution of the United States. 362 p. D. Meadville, Pa., 1897. Flood, $1.

WYKOFF, W. C.—The Silk Goods of America. Ed. 2. 158 p. O N. Y., 1880. Van Nostrand, $1.

YEO. I. B.—Food in Health and Disease. 592 p. D. Phil., 1896. Lea. $2.50.

INDEX.

6490.

Z

Volume 1 of Special Reports (Education in England, Wales, and Ireland, France, Germany, Denmark, Belgium, &c.) (1896–7) contains the following Papers:—

This volume (Cd. 8447) can be obtained, either directly or through any Bookseller, from Messrs. WYMAN AND SONS, LTD., FETTER LANE, E.C., and 32, ABINGDON STREET, WESTMINSTER, S.W. ; or OLIVER AND BOYD, EDINBURGH ; or E. PONSONBY, 116, GRAFTON STREET, DUBLIN.

Price 3s. 4d. ; post free 3s. 10d.

[At present out of print.]

Volume 2 of Special Reports (Education in England and
Wales, Physical Education, the Heuristic Method of
Teaching, University Education in France, &c.) (1898)
contains the following Papers :—

This volume (Cd. 8943) can be obtained, either directly or through any Book-
seller, from MESSRS. WYMAN AND SONS, LTD., FETTER LANE, E.C. ; and 32,
ABINGDON STREET, WESTMINSTER, S.W. ; or OLIVER AND BOYD, EDIN-
BURGH ; or E. PONSONBY, 116, GRAFTON STREET, DUBLIN.
       Price 6s. 2d. ; post free 6s. 7d.

Volume 3 of Special Reports (National Organisation of Education in Switzerland, Secondary Education in Prussia, Baden, and Sweden, Teaching of Modern Languages, Higher Commercial Education in France, Germany, and Belgium) (1898) contains the following Papers :—

This volume (Cd. 8988) can be obtained, either directly or through any Book-seller, from MESSRS. WYMAN & SONS, LTD., FETTER LANE, E.C., AND 32, ABINGDON STREET, WESTMINSTER, S.W. ; or OLIVER & BOYD, EDINBURGH ; or E. PONSONBY, 116, GRAFTON STREET, DUBLIN.

Price 3s. 3d. ; post free 3s. 8d.

The Board of Education issued in 1900 :—

Report on Technical and Commercial Education in East Prussia, Poland, Galicia, Silesia, and Bohemia.
    By Mr. James Baker.

This volume' (Cd. 419) can be obtained, either directly or through any Book-seller, from MESSRS. WYMAN AND SONS, LTD., FETTER LANE, E.C., and 32, ABINGDON STREET, WESTMINSTER, S.W. ; or OLIVER AND BOYD, EDINBURGH ; or E. PONSONBY, 116, GRAFTON STREET, DUBLIN.

Price 6d. ; post free 8d.

Volume 4 of Special Reports (Educational Systems of the Chief Colonies of the British Empire—Dominion of Canada, Newfoundland, West Indies) (1901) contains the following Papers :—

    This volume (Cd. 416) can be obtained, either directly or through any Bookseller, from MESSRS. WYMAN AND SONS, LTD., FETTER LANE, E.C., and 32, ABINGDON STREET, WESTMINSTER, S.W. ; or OLIVER AND BOYD, EDINBURGH ; or E. PONSONBY, 116, GRAFTON STREET, DUBLIN.

Price 4s. 8d. ; post free 5s. 2d.

Volume 5 of Special Reports (Educational Systems of the Chief Colonies of the British Empire—Cape Colony, Natal, Commonwealth of Australia, New Zealand, Ceylon, Malta) (1901) contains the following Papers :—

A. AFRICA—

    1. Cape Colony, The History and Present State of Education in.
        Part I., Sections 1–74.
            By Mr. G. B. Muir, B.A., of the Department of Public Education, Cape Town.
        Part I., Sections 75 to end, Part II. and Part III.
            Prepared from official documents by Mr. M. E. Sadler.

    2. Natal, The System of Education in.
            By Mr. R. Russell, Superintendent of Education, Natal.

B. COMMONWEALTH OF AUSTRALIA—

    1. New South Wales, The System of Education in.
            Prepared from official documents supplied by the Department of Public Instruction for New South Wales.

    2. Victoria, The System of Education in.
            By the Hon. A. J. Peacock, late Minister of Public Instruction, Victoria.

    3. Queensland, The System of Education in.
            By Mr. J. G. Anderson, Under Secretary for Public Instruction, Queensland.

    4. Tasmania, The System of Education in.
            Prepared from official documents by Mr. A. E. Twentyman.

    5. South Australia, The System of Education in.
            By Mr. C. L. Whitham, Member of the Board of Inspectors of Schools, South Australia.

    6. Western Australia, The System of Education in.
            By Mr. Cyril Jackson, Inspector-General of Schools, Western Australia.

C. NEW ZEALAND—

    New Zealand, The System of Education in.
            Prepared by Mr. M. E. Sadler, from official documents supplied by the Department of Education for New Zealand.

D. CEYLON—

    Ceylon, The System of Education in.
            By Mr. J. B. Cull, late Director of Public Instruction, and Mr. A. Van Cuylenburg, Inspector of Schools, Ceylon.

E. MALTA—

    Malta, The System of Education in.
            By Mr. N. Tagliaferro, Director of Education, Malta.

This volume (Cd. 417) can be obtained, either directly or through any Bookseller, from MESSRS. WYMAN AND SONS, LTD., FETTER LANE, E.C., and 32, ABINGDON STREET, WESTMINSTER, S.W.; or OLIVER AND BOYD, EDINBURGH; or E. PONSONBY, 116, GRAFTON STREET, DUBLIN.

Price 4s. 0d. ; post free 4s. 6d.

Volume 6 of Special Reports (Preparatory Schools for Boys.
Their place in English Secondary Education) (1900)
contains the following Papers :—

23. Games in Preparatory Schools.
    By Mr. A. J. C. Dowding.
24. The Employment of Leisure Hours in Boys' Boarding Schools.
    By Mr. Arthur Rowntree.
25. Preparatory School Libraries.
    By Mr. W. Douglas.
26. A Day in a Boy's Life at a Preparatory School.
    By Mr. P. S. Dealtry.
27. School Management in Preparatory Schools.
    By the Rev. J. H. Wilkinson, with an Appendix by Mr. A. J. C.
    Dowding.
28. Economics of Preparatory Schools
    By the Rev. C. Black.
29. Preparation for the Preparatory School.
    By Mr. E. D. Mansfield.
30. Preparatory Boys' Schools under Lady Principals.
    By Mr. C. D. Olive.
31. The Preparatory Department at Public Schools.
    By Mr. A. T. Martin.
32. The Preparatory Department at a Public School.
    By Mr. T. H. Mason.
33. The Relations between Public and Preparatory Schools.
    By the Rev. Herbert Bull.
34. The Preparatory School Product.
    By the Rev. H. A. James, D.D
35. The Preparatory School Product.
    By the Rev. the Honourable Canon E. Lyttelton.
36. The Preparatory School Product.
    By Dr. Hely Hutchinson Almond.
37. The Preparatory School Product.
    By Mr. Arthur C. Benson.
38. The Home Training of Children.
    By Mrs. Franklin.
39. The Possibility of Co-education in English Preparatory and other Secondary
    Schools.
    By Mr. J. H. Badley
40. Notes on a Preparatory School for Girls.
41. Appendix.

This volume (Cd. 418) can be obtained, e ther directly or through any
Bookseller, from MESSRS. WYMAN AND SONS, LTD., FETTER LANE, E.C.,
AND 32, ABINGDON STREET, WESTMINSTER, S.W. ; or OLIVER AND BOYD,
EDINBURGH ; or E. PONSONBY, 116, GRAFTON STREET, DUBLIN.

Price 2s. 3½d. ; post free 2s. 7½d.

Volume 7 of Special Reports (Rural Education in France) (1902) contains the following Papers :—

1. The Rural Schools of North-West France.
   By Mr. Cloudesley Brereton.

2. Rural Education in France.
   By Mr. John C. Medd.

This volume (Cd. 834) can be obtained, either directly or through any
Bookseller, from MESSRS. WYMAN AND SONS, LTD., FETTER LANE, E.C.,
AND 32, ABINGDON STREET, WESTMINSTER, S.W. ; or OLIVER AND BOYD,
EDINBURGH ; or E. PONSONBY, 116, GRAFTON STREET, DUBLIN.

Price 1s. 4d.; post free 1s. 8d.

Volume 8 of Special Reports (Education in Scandinavia, Switzerland, Holland, Hungary, &c.) (1902) contains the following Papers:—

I.

1. The New Law for the Secondary Schools in Norway.
   By Dr. Kand. Mag. Otto Anderssen.
2. Education in Norway in the year 1900.
   A short summary reprinted from " Norway." (Official Publication for the Paris Exhibition, 1900.)
3. Education in Sweden.
   Summarised translation of " Enseignement et Culture Intellectuelle en Suède," issued in connection with the Paris Exhibition, 1900, by the Swedish Government.
4. Note on Children's Workshops in Sweden.
   By Mr. J. G. Legge and Mr. M. E. Sadler.
5. The Nobel Foundation and the Nobel Prizes.
   By Mr. P. J. Hartog.
6. The Training and Status of Primary and Secondary Teachers in Switzerland.
   By Dr. Alexander Morgan.
7. The Main Features of the School System of Zürich.
   By Dr. H. J. Spenser and Mr. A. J. Pressland.
8. The Écoles Maternelles of Paris.
   By Miss Mary S. Beard.
9. The Simplification of French Syntax. Decree of the French Minister for Public Instruction, February 26, 1901.
   Translation prepared by Mr. W. G. Lipscomb.
10. Primary Education in the Netherlands.
    By Mr. R. Balfour.
11. Primary and Secondary Instruction in Portugal.
    Translated and abridged from publications issued in connection with the Paris Exhibition of 1900 by the Portuguese Government.
12. Technical Instruction in Portugal.
    Translated and abridged from publications issued in connection with the Paris Exhibition of 1900 by the Portuguese Government.
13. Hungarian Education.
    By Miss C. I. Dodd.
14. Public Instruction in Servia.
    Summarised translation of " Notice sur l'instruction publique en Serbie," published on the occasion of the Paris Exhibition, 1900, by the Ministry of Public Instruction in the Kingdom of Servia.
15. Commercial Education in Japan.
    By Mr. Zensaku Sano.

II.

16. The Study of Arithmetic in Elementary Schools
    By Mr. A. Sonnenschein.
17. A suggestion as regards Languages in Secondary Day Schools
    By Mr. S. R. Hart.
18. Newer Methods in the Teaching of Latin.
    By Dr. E. A. Sonnenschein.
19. Three School Journeys in Yorkshire.
20. The School Journey (London to Caterham, etc.) made by the Students at the Westminster Training College, 1879-1900.
    By Mr. Joseph M. Cowham.
21. A plea for a great Agricultural School.
    By Mr. James Mortimer.
22. The Education, Earnings and Social Condition of Boys engaged in Street-Trading in Manchester.
    By Mr. E. T. Campagnac and Mr. C. E. B. Russell.

III.

23. Sketch of the History of Educational Work in the late South African Republic.
    By Mr. John Robinson.
24. The Education of Asiatics
    By Mr. R. J. Wilkinson.

This volume (Cd. 835) can be obtained, either directly or through any Bookseller, from MESSRS. WYMAN AND SONS, LTD., FETTER LANE, E.C., and 32, ABINGDON STREET, WESTMINSTER, S.W. ; or OLIVER AND BOYD, EDINBURGH ; or E. PONSONBY, 116, GRAFTON STREET, DUBLIN.

Price 3s. 2d. ; post free 3s. 7d.

Supplements to Volume 8 of Special Reports (1902 and 1903) contain the following Papers :—

A short account of Education in the Netherlands.
By Mr. John C. Medd.

Report on the School Training and Early Employment of Lancashire Children
By Mr. E. T. Campagnac and Mr. C. E. B. Russell.

These Reports (Cd. 1157 and 1867) can be obtained either directly o through any Bookseller, from MESSRS. WYMAN AND SONS, LTD., FETTER LANE, E.C., and 32, ABINGDON STREET, WESTMINSTER, S.W.; or OLIVER AND BOYD, EDINBURGH; or E. PONSONBY, 116, GRAFTON STREET, DUBLIN.

Price 5d. ; post free 8d.   Price 3d. ; post free 4d.

Volume 9 of Special Reports (Education in Germany) (1902) contains the following Papers :—

1. The Unrest in Secondary Education in Germany and elsewhere.
   By Mr. M. E. Sadler.
2. Note on Revised Curricula and Programmes of Work for Higher Schools for Boys in Prussia, 1901.
   By Mr. A. E. Twentyman.
3. Higher Schools for Girls in Germany: An Introductory Sketch.
   By Miss Mary A. Lyster.
4. The Smaller Public Elementary Schools of Prussia and Saxony, with Notes on the Training and Position of Teachers.
   By Mr. E. M. Field.
5. Note on impending Changes in the Professional Training of Elementary School Teachers in Prussia.
   By Mr. A. E. Twentyman.
6. School Gardens in Germany.
   By Mr. T. G. Rooper.
7. Impressions of some Aspects of the work in Primary and other Schools in Rhineland, etc.
   By Mr. R. E. Hughes and Mr. W. A. Beanland.
8. The Continuation Schools in Berlin.
   By Geheimregierungsrat Professor Dr. Bertram. (Translated by Mr. A. E. Twentyman.)
9. Note on the Earlier History of the Technical High Schools in Germany.
   By Mr. A. E. Twentyman.
10. Recent Developments in Higher Commercial Education in Germany.
    By Mr. M. E. Sadler.
11. On the Measurement of Mental Fatigue in Germany.
    By Mr. C. C. Th. Parez.
12. Report of the Congress on the Education of Feeble-minded Children, held at Augsburg, April 10–12, 1901.
    By Dr. A. Eichholz.
13. On the Education of Neglected Children in Germany.
    By Dr. Fritz Rathenau.

This volume (Cd. 836) can be obtained, either directly or through any Bookseller, from MESSRS. WYMAN AND SONS, LTD., FETTER LANE, E.C., and 32, ABINGDON STREET, WESTMINSTER, S.W.; or OLIVER AND BOYD, EDINBURGH; or E. PONSONBY, 116, GRAFTON STREET, DUBLIN.

Price 2s. 7d. ; post free 3s. 0d.

Volume 10 of Special Reports (Education in the United States of America, Part I.) (1902) contains the following Papers :—

This volume (Cd. 837) can be obtained, either directly or through any Book-seller, from MESSRS. WYMAN AND SONS, LTD., FETTER LANE, E.C. : and 32, ABINGDON STREET, WESTMINSTER, S.W. ; or OLIVER AND BOYD, EDINBURGH ; or E. PONSONBY, 116, GRAFTON STREET, DUBLIN.

Price 2s. 3d. ; post free 2s. 8d.

Volume 11 of Special Reports (Education in the United States of America, Part II.) (1902) contains the following Papers :—

This volume (Cd. 1156) can be obtained, either directly or through any Bookseller, from MESSRS. WYMAN AND SONS, LTD., FETTER LANE, E.C., and 32, ABINGDON STREET, WESTMINSTER, S.W. ; or OLIVER AND BOYD, EDINBURGH ; or E. PONSONBY, 116, GRAFTON STREET, DUBLIN.

Price 2s. 6d. ; post free 2s. 11d.

(xi)

Volume 12 of Special Reports (Educational Systems of the Chief Crown Colonies and Possessions of the British Empire, including Reports on the Training of Native Races : Part I.—West Indies and Central America, St. Helena, Cyprus and Gibraltar) (1905) (published simultaneously with Volumes 13 and 14) contains the following Papers :—

A. WEST INDIES AND CENTRAL AMERICA—
  1. The System of Education in the Bahamas.
       By Mr. G. Cole, Inspector and General Superintendent of Schools, Bahamas.

  2. The System of Education in Barbados.
       By the Rev. J. E. Reece, Inspector of Schools, Mr. J. A. Carrington, Assistant Inspector of Schools, and the Rev. J. R. Nichols, Secretary to the Education Board, Barbados.

  3. The System of Education in Bermuda.
       By Mr. George Simpson, Inspector of Schools, Bermuda.

  4. The System of Education in British Honduras.
       By Mr. A. Barrow Dillon, Inspector of Schools, British Honduras.

  5. The System of Education in Trinidad and Tobago.
       By Mr. R. Gervase Bushe, late Inspector of Schools, Trinidad and Tobago.

  6. The System of Education in the Windward Islands.
       (a) Grenada.
              By Mr. John Harbin, Inspector of Schools, Grenada.
       (b) St. Lucia.
              By Mr. Fred. E. Bundy, Inspector of Schools, St. Lucia.
       (c) St. Vincent.
              By Mr. Frank W. Griffith, Secretary of the Board of Education, formerly Inspector of Schools, St. Vincent.

B. ST. HELENA—

  The System of Education in St. Helena.
       By the Rev. Canon Alfred Porter, Inspector of Government Schools, St. Helena.

C. EUROPE—

  1. The System of Education in Cyprus.
       By the Rev. F. D. Newham, Inspector of Schools, Cyprus.

  2. The System of Education in Gibraltar.
       By Mr. G. F. Cornwall, K.C., Colonial Inspector of Schools, Gibraltar.

APPENDIX—

  A. WEST INDIES AND CENTRAL AMERICA—

       Education in Jamaica in its relation to Skilled Handicraft and Agricultural Work.
              By the Most Rev. the Archbishop of the West Indies.

This volume (Cd. 2377) can be obtained, either directly or through any Bookseller, from MESSRS. WYMAN AND SONS, LTD., FETTER LANE, E.C., and 32, ABINGDON STREET, WESTMINSTER, S.W. ; or OLIVER AND BOYD, EDINBURGH ; or E. PONSONBY, 116, GRAFTON STREET, DUBLIN.

Price, 2s. 0d. ; post free, 2s. 4d.

Volume 13 of Special Reports (Educational Systems of the Chief Crown Colonies and Possessions of the British Empire, including Reports on the Training of Native Races: Part II.—West Africa, Basutoland, Southern Rhodesia, East Africa Protectorate, Uganda, Mauritius, Seychelles) (1905) (published simultaneously with Volumes 12 and 14) contains the following Papers:—

This volume (Cd. 2378) can be obtained, either directly or through any Bookseller, from Messrs WYMAN AND SONS, Ltd., Fetter Lane, E.C., and 32, Abingdon Street, Westminster, S.W.; or OLIVER AND BOYD, Edinburgh; or E. PONSONBY, 116, Grafton Street, Dublin.

Volume 14 of Special Reports (Educational Systems of the
Chief Crown Colonies and Possessions of the British
Empire, including Reports on the Training of Native
Races: Part III.—Federated Malay States, Hong Kong,
Straits Settlements, Fiji and Falkland Islands) (1905)
(published simultaneously with Volumes 12 and 13) con-
tains the following Papers :—

A. ASIA—
    1. The System of Education in the Federated Malay States.
        Report supplied by the Federal Education Office, Federated Malay
        States.
    2. The System of Education in Hong Kong.
        By Mr. Edward A. Irving, Inspector of Schools, Hong Kong.
    3. The System of Education in the Straits Settlements.
        By Mr. J. B. Elcum, Director of Public Instruction, Straits Settle-
        ments.

B. FIJI—
    The System of Education in Fiji.
        By the Hon. W. L. Allardyce, C.M.G., Colonial Secretary and Re-
        ceiver General, Fiji.

C. FALKLAND ISLANDS—
    The System of Education in the Falkland Islands.
        . By the Very Rev. Lowther E. Brandon, Dean, Colonial Chaplain
        and Government School Inspector, Falkland Islands.

APPENDICES—
    1. Note on the Work of the Industrial Missions Aid Society.
        Prepared from materials supplied by the Industrial Missions Aid
        Society.

    2. On the Education of Native Races (C.M.S.).
        By Mr. R. Machonachie.

    3. Industrial Education in Catholic Missions.
        By the Right Rev. the Bishop of Salford.

    4. Education in British New Guinea.
        By the Right Rev. the Bishop of New Guinea.

    5. Work of the American Board of Commissioners for Foreign Missions
        in regard to Industrial and Agricultural Education in India.
        Prepared from materials supplied by the American Board of Com-
        missioners for Foreign Missions.

    6. Memorandum on Technical Education in Southern India.
        By the Rev. Canon A. Margöschis (Fellow of Madras University),
        Nazareth, Southern India.

    7. Industrial Schools and School Gardens in Ceylon.
        By Mr. S. M. Burrows, late Director of Public Instruction in Ceylon.

    8. The Education of the Indians of Canada.
        By Mr. Harry Moody, of the Canadian and Pacific Railway
        Company.

    This volume (Cd. 2379) can be obtained, either directly or through any
Bookseller, from MESSRS. WYMAN AND SONS, LTD., FETTER LANE, E.C.,.
AND 32, ABINGDON STREET, WESTMINSTER, S.W. ; or OLIVER AND BOYD,.
EDINBURGH ; or E. PONSONBY, 116, GRAFTON STREET, DUBLIN.

Price 1s. 8d. ; post free 2s. 0d.

The following Reports from Volumes 2, 3, 4, 5, and 9 of Special Reports on Educational Subjects have been issued as Reprints :—

Special Reports on Intermediate Education in Wales and the Organisation of Education in Switzerland.
(Nos. 1 in Vols. 2 and 3 respectively.)   Price 1s. 1d. ; post free 1s. 3½d.

Special Reports on Modern Language Teaching.
(No. 26 in Vol. 2 and Nos. 7, 8, 9, 10 in Vol. 3.)   Price 6½d. ; post free 8½d.

Special Reports on Secondary Education in Prussia.
(Nos. 2 and 3 in Vol. 3.)   Price 1s. ; post free 1s. 3½d.

Special Report on Secondary Schools in Baden.
(No. 4 in Vol. 3.)   Price 5½d. ; post free 7d.

Special Reports on Education in France.
(Nos. 22, 23, 24, 25 in Vol. 2.)   Price 4d. ; post free 5½d.

Special Report on the Heuristic Method of Teaching.
(No. 19 in Vol. 2.)   Price 3d. ; post free 4d.

Special Report on the Connection between the Public Library and the Public Elementary School.
(No. 13 in Vol. 2.)   Price 2½d. ; post free 3½d.

Special Report on the System of Education in Ontario.
(No. A 1 in Vol. 4.)   Price 8d. ; post free 10½d.

Special Report on the System of Education in the Province of Quebec.
(No. A 2 in Vol. 4.)   Price 8d. ; post free 10d.

Special Reports on the Systems of Education in Nova Scotia, New Brunswick, Prince Edward Island, and Newfoundland.
(Nos. A 3, 4, 8 and No. B in Vol. 4.)   Price 8d. ; post free 10½d.

Special Reports on the Systems of Education in Manitoba, North-West Territories and British Columbia.
(Nos. A 5, 6, 7, in Vol. 4.)   Price 8d. ; post free 11d.

Special Reports on the Systems of Education in the West Indies, and in British Guiana.
(Nos. C 1, 2, 3, in Vol. 4.)   Price 8d. ; post free 11d.

Special Reports on the Systems of Education in Cape Colony and Natal.
(Nos. A 1, 2 in Vol. 5.)   Price 8d. ; post free 11½d.

Special Report on the System of Education in New South Wales.
(No. B 1 in Vol. 5.)   Price 8d. ; post free 9½d.

Special Report on the System of Education in Victoria.
(No. B 2 in Vol. 5.)   Price 8d. ; post free 10d.

Special Report on the System of Education in Queensland.
(No. B 3 in Vol. 5.)   Price 8d. ; post free 9d.

Special Report on the System of Education in Tasmania.
(No. B 4 in Vol. 5.)   Price 8d. ; post free 9d.

Special Report on the System of Education in South Australia.
(No. B 5 in Vol. 5.)   Price 8d. ; post free 9½d.

Special Report on the System of Education in Western Australia.
(No. B 6 in Vol. 5.)   Price 8d. ; post free 9½d.

Special Report on the System of Education in New Zealand.
(No. C in Vol. 5.)   Price 8d. ; post free 10½d.

Special Report on the System of Education in Ceylon.
(No. D in Vol. 5.)   Price 8d. ; post free 9d.

Special Report on the System of Education in Malta.
(No. E in Vol. 5.)   Price 8d. ; post free 9d.

Special Report on School Gardens in Germany.
(No. 6 in Vol. 9.)   Price 3d. ; post free 4d.

These can be obtained, either directly or through any Bookseller, from MESSRS. WYMAN AND SONS, LTD., FETTER LANE, E.C., AND 32, ABINGDON STREET, WESTMINSTER, S.W. ; or OLIVER AND BOYD, EDINBURGH ; or E. PONSONBY, 116, GRAFTON STREET, DUBLIN.

| [Cd. 2192.] | STATISTICAL ABSTRACT OF THE UNITED KINGDOM. | 1889–1903. Price 1s. 3d. |

[Cd. 2192.] STATISTICAL ABSTRACT OF THE UNITED KINGDOM. 1889–1903.
Price 1s. 3d.
[Cd. 1912.] Ditto ditto COLONIES. 1889–1903. Price 1s. 10d.
[Cd. 2202.] Ditto ditto FOREIGN COUNTRIES. Years 1892-1901-02.
Price 1s. 6d.
[Cd. 2299.] Ditto ditto BRITISH INDIA. 1893-1894 to 1902-1903.
Price 1s. 2d.
[Cd. 2043, 2081.] TRADE OF THE UNITED KINGDOM, 1903. Vols. I. and II. Price 12s. 1d.
[Cd. 2340.] FOREIGN IMPORT DUTIES, 1904· Price 2s. 0d.
[Cd. 2185.] COLONIAL IMPORT DUTIES, 1904. Price 2s. 1d.
[Cd. 2199.] LABOUR STATISTICS—UNITED KINGDOM. Changes of Wages and Hours
of Labour. 1903. Price 7d.
H.C. 321.—WHOLESALE AND RETAIL PRICES—UNITED KINGDOM, 1902. Report on.
Price 2s. 1d.
[Cd. 2122.] NAVIGATION AND SHIPPING STATEMENT. 1903. Price 3s. 2d.
[Cd. 1672.] AUSTRO-HUNGARY. Proposed New General Customs Tariff. Price 9d.
[Cd. 1756.] FOOD STUFFS. Foreign Legislation respecting Gambling in "Options" and
"Futures." Price 5½d.
[Cd. 1761.] BRITISH AND FOREIGN TRADE AND INDUSTRIAL CONDITIONS. Memoranda,
Tables and Charts. Prepared by the Board of Trade. Price 3s. 6d.
[Cd. 2337.] BRITISH AND FOREIGN TRADE AND INDUSTRIAL CONDITIONS. (Second
Series.) Price 3s. 6d.
[Cd. 2286.] EAST INDIA. Review of the Trade of. Year 1903-1904. Price 5d.
[Cd. 1807.] TREATIES OF COMMERCE AND NAVIGATION WITH FOREIGN COUNTRIES.
Most Favoured Nations Clauses in force 1st July 1903. Price 10½d.
[Cd. 1931.] EAST INDIA. Views of the Government of India on the Question of
Preferential Tariffs. Price 5½d.
[Cd. 1938.] TARIFF WARS BETWEEN CERTAIN EUROPEAN STATES. Price 8½d.
H.C. No. 344. CONTINENTAL FREE PORTS. Price 2½d.
[Cd. 2184.] STATISTICAL TABLES RELATING TO BRITISH COLONIES, POSSESSIONS, AND
PROTECTORATES. Part XXVII. 1902. Price 7s.
H.L. No. 190.—PREFERENTIAL AND RETALIATORY DUTIES. DIFFERENTIAL DUTIES.
Years 1823 to 1860. Price 1s. 6d.
[Cd. 2326.] COLONIES. PREFERENTIAL TRADE. Resolutions passed since 1890 in favour.
Price 3d.
[Cd. 2395.] STATISTICAL ABSTRACT OF THE BRITISH EMPIRE, YEARS 1889–1903. Price 6d.
[Cd. 2414.] NEW GERMAN TARIFF, AS MODIFIED BY TREATIES; come into force
1st January 1906. Price 1s. 10d.

Military :—
COMMISSION IN HIS MAJESTY'S REGULAR FORCES. Short Guide to obtaining a. Price 4d.
FIELD SERVICE REGULATIONS. Part I. Combined Training. Price 1s.
INFANTRY TRAINING. 1905. Price 1s.
KING'S REGULATIONS AND ORDERS FOR THE ARMY. (Provisional edition.) 1904.
Price 1s. 6d.
MUSKETRY EXERCISES. (Provisional.) 1904. Price 3d.
YEOMANRY, IMPERIAL. TRAINING. Price 1d.

Hydrographical :—
MEDITERRANEAN PILOT. Vol. I. Fourth Edition. 1904. Price 4s.
EASTERN ARCHIPELAGO, Part II. (Western Part). Second Edition, 1904. Price 3s.
RED SEA AND GULF OF ADEN PILOT. 1900. Supplement to, 9th December 1904. Price 6d.

Local Government Board :—
SMALL POX AND SMALL POX HOSPITALS IN LIVERPOOL. Report on. Price 2s. 6d.
SANITARY CIRCUMSTANCES OF THE HAVERFORDWEST RURAL DISTRICT. Report on.
Price 1s.

Emigrants' Information Office, 31, Broadway, Westminster, viz. :—
COLONIES, HANDBOOKS FOR. April, 1905. 8vo. Wrapper.
No. 1. Canada. 2. New South Wales. 3. Victoria. 4. South Australia. 5. Queensland. 6. Western Australia. 7. Tasmania. 8. New Zealand. 9. Cape Colony.
10. Natal. 11. Transvaal. 12. Orange River Colony. Price 1d. each.
No. 13. Professional Handbook. 14. Emigration Statutes and General Handbook.
Price 3d. each.
No. 15 (viz., Nos. 1 to 14 in cloth). Price 2s.
INTENDING EMIGRANTS, INFORMATION FOR :—Argentine Republic, price 2d. British
East Africa Protectorate, 1904, price 6d. Ceylon, Oct. 1900, price 1d. Federated
Malay States, Jan. 1904, price 6d. Newfoundland, Jan. 1904, price 1d. British
Central Africa Protectorate, price 6d. Uganda Protectorate, price 6d. Uganda,
1904, price 6d. West African Colonies, Dec. 1904, price 6d. West Indies, 1904,
price 6d.

Foreign Office :—
AFRICA BY TREATY. The Map of. By Sir E. Hertslet, K.C.B. 3 Vols. Price 31s. 6d.
COMMERCIAL TREATIES. (Hertslet's.) A complete collection of Treaties, &c., between
Great Britain and Foreign Powers so far as they relate to Commerce and Navigation,
&c. By Sir E. Hertslet, K.C.B., &c., Vols. I. to XXI. and XXIII. Price 15s. each.
STATE PAPERS. British and Foreign. Vol. 93. (Index vol.) and Vol. 94. 1900-1901.
Price 10s. each.

Board of Trade Journal, of Tariff and Trade Notices and Miscellaneous Commercial
Information. Published weekly. Price 1d.
Index to Vols. 1 to 14. Price 2s. And to Vols. XV. to XX. July 1893 to June 1896.
Price 1s. 6d.

BOARD OF EDUCATION.

SPECIAL REPORTS

ON

EDUCATIONAL SUBJECTS.

VOLUME 15.

SCHOOL TRAINING FOR THE HOME DUTIES OF WOMEN.

PART I.

THE TEACHING OF "DOMESTIC SCIENCE" IN THE UNITED STATES
OF AMERICA.

Presented to both Houses of Parliament by Command of His Majesty.

LONDON:
PRINTED FOR HIS MAJESTY'S STATIONERY OFFICE,
BY WYMAN & SONS, LIMITED, FETTER LANE, E.C.

And to be purchased, either directly or through any Bookseller, from
WYMAN AND SONS, LTD., FETTER LANE, E.C.; and
32, ABINGDON STREET, WESTMINSTER, S.W.; or
OLIVER AND BOYD, EDINBURGH; or
E. PONSONBY, 116, GRAFTON STREET, DUBLIN.

1905.

[Cd. 2498.]   *Price* 1*s.* 9*d.*

Lightning Source UK Ltd.
Milton Keynes UK
UKHW020802301218
334665UK00007B/611/P